25 June 2002

Dearest Matthew,

We honor your
commitment to fighting
social injustice.
We are so proud of you.
Happy Birthday,
Love,
Mom & Lou

D1598851

Fighting Injustice

SECTION OF LITIGATION
American Bar Association

Michael E. Tigar

Cover design by Andrew O. Alcala, ABA Publishing
Cover photograph by Wyatt McSpadden

06 05 04 03 02 5 4 3 2 1

Tigar, Michael E., 1941 –
Fighting Injustice / Michael Tigar
    p. cm.
    Includes index
    ISBN 1-59031-015-2
    1.Tigar, Michael E., 1941 – 2. Lawyers—United States—Biography
3. Defense (Criminal Procedure)—United States—History. I. Title.
KF373.T58 A3 2002   2002003505
340'.092—dc21

Go to www.ababooks.org to order books, or
Call 1 (800) 285-2221 and ask for product code 5310309.
Bulk order discounts are available.

CONTENTS

DEDICATION

This book is dedicated to the person who steers me into safe harbors.
You know who you are.

INTRODUCTION

This is a memoir of sorts. So I had best make one thing clear. I am going to recount events differently than you may remember them. I will reach into the stream of memory and pull out this or that pebble that has been cast there by my fate. The pebbles when cast may have had jagged edges, now worn away by the stream. So I tell it as memory permits, and maybe not entirely as it was. This could be called lying, but more charitably it is simply what life gives to each of us as our memories of events are shaped in ways that make us smile and help us to go on.

I do not have transcripts of all the cases in the book, so I recall them as well as I can. I have changed some names to protect privacy and to fulfill my obligation as a counselor. Sometimes I have simply omitted the last names of those who were public figures at a certain time but who may not wish to be so now. Some people who shared these events will remember them differently. That is, to repeat, the nature of memory. It is, for lawyers in the common law tradition, the nature of what we do. We re-create events from the varying and fallible recollections of witnesses. This book contains what I saw, or at least remember having seen.

I have argued seven Supreme Court cases, and briefed more. I have argued more than 100 federal appeals in almost every circuit, and have been in countless federal and state trial courts, as well as before tribunals in other countries. To talk about the theme of justice requires that I choose from these experiences.

Those who have known me will find details scarce about some personal relationships. In telling this story, I am not entitled to usurp the stories of others, which they may prefer to keep to themselves.

My friend John Mage said that it is too soon to be writing anything like a memoir, because it can lead only to embarrassment. If I go ahead and do more things than are recounted here, I will have to put out sequels, and then I will become like one of those aging musicians who keep doing farewell tours. There is merit to that view. Somebody said: "When is your life work finished? Are you alive? Then, not yet." Racehorse Haynes was questioning a prospective juror in Tyler, Texas, and asked her, "Have you lived in Tyler all your life?" She said, "Not yet." Same idea.

So this is not a complete work. I want to tell some stories for their own sake, and hope to entertain, instruct, and maybe point a direction.

I will in this retelling be unjust to hundreds of people with whom I have worked, for I will not mention all of their names and all they did. Brecht, writing of Cortez, asked, "Were there no cooks in his army?" More than cooks, I tell you. Comrades, colleagues, clients, friends, and lovers were all along on these journeys. I salute them all, and apologize if their recollections and mine diverge. Mary Kay Rockwell had the idea for this book, and Priscilla Anne Schwab edited it with customary patience and flair. Caeb Colravy and Rachel Gader were my diligent research assistants.

St. Francis, it is said, prayed to understand and not to be understood. It would be entire vanity for me to suppose that this book has no element of self-justification in it. But I have tried, as with the other things I have written, to keep all that to a minimum.

The first three chapters of this book are chronological, charting my path into the legal profession. The later ones are thematic, grouping cases and other struggles that focused on particular issues. In deciding to become involved in a case, or in looking back in self-evaluation, I have tried to see how the case jarred awake my sense of injustice. The thematic organization seems to make that analysis clearer. To be sure, many of these cases overlap, and the arrangement is necessarily somewhat arbitrary. When a predominantly black university fires a professor for expressing his views on the Vietnam war, is that a civil rights, free speech, or anti-war case? It is, of course, all three, but you will find it in the chapter on free speech and academic freedom.

Where possible, I have put in citations to cases, court records, and historical accounts. You will find these in the notes at the end of each chapter. I have not broken up the text by putting in footnote or endnote numbers. In several places, I have borrowed from articles and books that I wrote, and those attributions are in the Chapter Notes as well.

Finally, as times change, our way of speaking about people and events may change as well. I have tried to keep references consistent. One issue deserves mention: In times past, African-Americans have been referred to by other terms. I have generally used the current, preferred term throughout, except where there seemed to be a good reason not to.

PROLOGUE

All rise! The Supreme Court of the United States, November 20, 1969. I sat at counsel table, ready for my first Supreme Court argument. Chief Justice Warren Burger, Associate Justices William O. Douglas, Hugo Black, John M. Harlan, William J. Brennan, Jr., Potter Stewart, Byron R. White, and Thurgood Marshall. Their chairs were not all alike. Each had his own.

The chamber is massive, with imposing columns and bas-relief. You can tell that William Howard Taft had a hand in designing it. Yet the space between counsel and the Justices is relatively small, the setting more intimate than many federal courts of appeals and even some district courtrooms of the older, ceremonial variety.

It can't, I thought, be better than this. Now, after hundreds more cases, hearings and trials, I am moved to deconstruct that thought. "It can't be better than this."

What was "this?" I had been a member of the bar for little more than two years. Mel Wulf of the American Civil Liberties Union asked me to brief and argue this case. Because I had not been admitted to the bar for three whole years, Mel had to file a motion to admit me *pro hac vice*, for this time only.

This was an oral argument. Thirty minutes on a side, down from the hour on a side that the court used to provide. I had been to the court. I had helped Edward Bennett Williams prepare to argue. But "this" was my argument, or as much mine as it could be after weeks of working on it with co-counsel and days of intensive review of every possible question the justices might ask.

In retrospect, it is arrogant to think of "this" as my argument. On October 16, 1967, as part of a nationwide demonstration, David Earl Gutknecht had tossed his draft card on the ground in a gesture of protest against the Vietnam war. His local draft board punished him for this act

1

by calling him for immediate induction. He refused to submit, and was tried, convicted, and sentenced to four years in prison. If I lost, he would join some 3,000 other young men in federal prison who had done similar things with similar consequences.

So "this" was David Gutknecht's argument, just as one of my later cases was Gary Graham's argument, and one was Dorsie Johnson's argument. The state of Texas killed those two young African-Americans, even though the jury was never told in so many words that their youthful age could mitigate against a sentence of death. "This" is a search for at least five votes out of nine, and if you get only four you lose.

It is so easy for lawyers to forget that it is not about them, but about the client. Emile Zola is reputed to have said of Dreyfus: "He is the one who has not understood it at all. He is completely unworthy of the Dreyfus affair."

"This" argument was unique in Supreme Court history. At the government's counsel table sat William Ruckelshaus, an assistant attorney general. The Solicitor General of the United States, Erwin Griswold, sat in the spectator seats with his arms folded. Griswold, who had been dean of Harvard Law School, looked pleased to be there, and especially pleased to be sitting a couple rows back from Ruckelshaus.

The Solicitor General is the government's lawyer in the Supreme Court, and supervises most government appellate litigation. Supreme Court law clerks seek jobs in his office. In Gutknecht's case, Dean Griswold thought that the government's position was wrong. He told Attorney General John Mitchell that he would not sign the government's brief. This was 1969, of course, well before Attorney General Mitchell and his cohorts were convicted of obstruction of justice and other crimes they committed along with President Nixon.

In any given year, the Solicitor General refuses to uphold the government's position in, at most, a handful of cases. That is usually the end of it. Only rarely will the Attorney General or the President overrule such a decision. The last time it had happened was 1954, when Solicitor General Simon Sobeloff refused to argue a "Red Scare" case. Then-Vice President Richard Nixon found an assistant attorney general named Warren Burger to do the job. The government lost.

Dean Griswold was a man of such integrity that his sitting there silently was more eloquent than I could hope to be. Griswold's legendary rectitude extended to abstinence from alcohol. Thinking of his famously bibulous predecessor, Judge Landis, people said that on average the deans of Harvard Law School drank the right amount.

The brief from which Ruckelshaus was soon to argue was remarkable in another way. Attorney General Mitchell had his name on the cover. But even Mitchell would not go as far as Selective Service Director Lewis Hershey wanted. So there was a whole section of the brief signed by Hershey's lawyers as well. As the mocking song goes: "General Custer split his men. Well, he won't do that again." Mitchell's forces were not all marching in the same direction.

"This" had quill pens. Every morning, deputy clerks put quill pens on the counsel tables. If your argument is first of the day, you are supposed to take a pen as a souvenir. I hope this is right, because my children all have pens. If it is not, the Court's current clerk will, no doubt, call me up and we will work it out.

"Compared to what?" as the old joke goes. It is better to win than to lose. But you cannot make that comparison at the time of arguing, unless you are in a court that rules right away. The Supreme Court takes its time. The Justices have a conference and issue an opinion. It is also better to make a good argument than a lousy one. But I was having this thought without having opened my mouth.

"Better" was a way of anticipating something exciting, a challenge that I was about to meet. In the Terry Lynn Nichols trial, every day just before court, my friend and co-counsel, Ron Woods, would say jokingly, "Well, time to go throw up." I laughed, because I can remember throwing up every morning before court during the first major trial when I was lead counsel. Even if I can hold on to my breakfast, every time I go to court, any court, I have that same sense of anticipation. In a trial court, it may come as the jurors file in. In an appellate court, it is that time when the judges take the bench.

What was "it?" What was I looking for? What did I expect to get? Advocacy is overrated and underrated these days.

It is verbally overrated by judges who hold that poor people get justice because they have access to lawyers under the Constitution. The right to counsel stops well short of the death-house door for capital defendants. Civil litigants have almost no constitutional entitlement to counsel. Some of the lawyers appointed for the poor sleep through the trial and when awake do more harm than good. Even qualified and motivated lawyers do not have equal resources. The courts that uphold such inequality do so by treating advocacy as essentially a fungible good. Any lawyer will do.

The same judges who praise an abstract idea of advocacy often show they don't really believe in it. The Supreme Court now limits argument to thirty minutes on a side. And if the Court has invited the Solicitor

General to participate, it cuts some time from one or both of the lawyers for the parties. Some of the Justices don't ask questions to help clarify things, but rather to speechify. And some Justices don't ask any questions at all. In the appellate courts, oral argument is more severely rationed every year.

Some trial judges won't hear arguments on legal motions, and when trial approaches they put strict limits on the lawyers, lest a vagrant persuasive thought burst out and sway the jurors.

Even the pundits of the profession, whose official canons of ethics once firmly required the advocate to exercise "warm zeal" on behalf of the client, are backing away. In the latest version of Model Rule of Professional Responsibility 3.1, the words "warm zeal" are dropped. The commentary says that the rule really does permit warm zeal, but is phrased in terms of professionalism and competence and so on, because the bar leaders are afraid that if we say warm zeal, people will think that means you need to be a zealot on behalf of your client, and nobody likes zealots. So, in the name of softening up the image of our profession, the warm zeals are a threatened species. They are clubbing the warm zeals to death to make coats for rich people. I think that's what is happening, and I don't approve. In litigation as in love, I once wrote, technical proficiency without passion is not wholly satisfying.

As advocates, we are condemned to signify. That is, we are communicators. We are trying to convince this or that decider to rule for our clients. That is a limited though vital meaning of signifying. We also signify in a broader sense. The kind of work we do, the cases we take, the way in which we accept or defy injustice: the entire body of our work speaks to the world about our values. It tells the world whether and how much we believe we can get justice in the present state of things. Our advocacy to deciders is better if we continue to see the links between theory and practice, and understand the narrow and broad senses in which we signify.

Whatever "it" was, that magic morning, it would include warm zeal. Advocacy is an exercise in skill, craft, and daring. But would zeal be enough? When the Court decided, we would find out if it were enough for David Earl Gutknecht. But would it be enough for me? That is really two questions. First, zeal is not enough unless I am being zealous about justice as I see it. The form of the answer may change with years and shifting perspective, but the question is always there for me. Looking back, there are some clients, causes, and actions that I took in the firm belief I was serving justice, and now I am not so sure. There are times when I declined a case, and now feel some regret. It has never been enough for me to say that the adversary system is its own justification. If advocacy is to be about more than self, it must be about the service of something. I have striven for a view of justice, and I want to share it with you. The great Irish advocate Daniel O'Connell was put on trial for conspiracy against English rule, and he said to his jury:

> I am ready to reassert in court all that I have said, not taking upon myself the clumsy mistakes of reporters—not abiding by the fallibility that necessarily attends the reporting of speeches, and, in particular, where those speeches are squeezed up together, as it were, for the purposes of the newspapers. I do not hesitate to say that there are many severe and harsh things of individuals, and clumsy jokes, that I would rather not have said, but the substance of what I have said I avow, and I am here respectfully to vindicate it; and as to all my actions I am ready, not only to avow them, but to justify them. I have struggled for human freedom. Others have succeeded in their endeavors, and some have failed; but succeed or fail, it is a glorious struggle.

O'Connell did his work in an Ireland under English rule, seeking open spaces in a repressive state apparatus, taking advantage of the contradictions between formal guarantees of fairness and the reality of colonial oppression. That was exciting work. That was a part of "it." O'Connell not only represented the cause of Irish independence, but also led a movement to abolish the slave trade in England and America.

But invoking justice and struggle evades the second problem of what is enough. I often say that the litigating lawyer is a massive blob of ego suspended over a chasm of insecurity. Our striving is perhaps no more compulsive or intense than that of our brothers and sisters in other parts of the profession. I don't know.

In this book, every time I tell of a meeting, a trial, or an appeal, I am speaking of a period of time when I was not home with my children. I am speaking of a time when I was so intensely focused on my task that I was running on adrenaline and nervous energy. For what? I remind myself of Dryden's lines:

> A daring pilot in extremity;
> Pleased with the danger, when the waves went high
> He sought the storms; but for a calm unfit.

I paraphrase the moral philosopher and country singer Kinky Friedman. There is a fine line between needs and desires, and many in my generation snorted it sometime in the 1970s. I never did cocaine, only watched what it did to a lot of people like me. No, in my wake were quite a few empty bottles and failed relationships. This is not a tell-all book, so I provide no details. This is not self-immolation, so I spare you the apologies. I have tried to make all the right amends. If you are reading this book and think you are owed one you didn't get, write to me. Maybe yours got lost in the mail. My friend Fernando Fajardo, a great lawyer, said once, "Do you remember that night in East Tucson?" "No," I said. "I didn't think so," he replied. "It is just as well."

My father died of a heart attack at the age of 49. I thought that I would not live much longer than he did. If I were going to get anything done about justice, I would have to do it in a hurry. Indeed, if I were going to get anything done about anything, to have any experience that might be out there, I would have to do it in a hurry. A very wise therapist named Anya Rylander said to me, "You are an intensity junkie." The sheer magical sensations of trial and appellate argument, of the search for justice, fed not only my ego but also a craving so real it was almost physical. My doctor daughter points out that it *is* physical. Intensity, fight-or-flight, puts adrenaline in the system. So when the fight is over, I have the inevitable letdown.

We lawyers do not stand at the center of all the events by which the world is moved. We did not really invent, and we surely do not own, the law. We play our role because somebody is at risk, or took a risk, and needs counsel or defense. That person, who courted or encountered that risk, is at the center. And the collective struggle of all those people is the forward march of human history. We are, when we do it right, simply interpreters of visions about justice.

I know, too, that I have been very lucky. Folk singer Pete Seeger tells the story of two maggots sitting on a shovel handle. A worker picked up the shovel and as he walked along the sidewalk, the maggots fell off. One fell into a crack in the sidewalk and the other bounced into the gutter and a pile of horse manure. This latter fellow ate and ate for three days, and then thought, "I better go see about my brother." So he crawled up on to the sidewalk and eventually came to the crack. His friend looked up and said, "My brother, I have been down here for three days without a drop to drink or a bite to eat. But look at you. You look so sleek and fat. To what do you attribute your success? "Brains and personality, brother. Brains and personality," the other replied.

There is a character in mystery stories who inquires about somebody he doesn't know by saying, "Who is he when he's at home?" It is a good question to ask of oneself. I have inveighed against the law firms that require young lawyers to bill 2,500 or 3,000 hours a year to have a chance of making partner. These firms create a culture that encourages bad lawyering while pushing young people to work such long hours and under such conditions that their personal lives suffer.

As I look back more than 30 years, and think of "it doesn't get any better than this," I am humbled. "It" was an intensity that could not be sustained. "It" was seductive. But after "it" was done, I needed to understand and even relish the quiet that inevitably overtook me. We are warriors for justice, but must also be scholars of the law. In the afterlight of combat, the warrior needs to take counsel from the scholar. The warrior needs the scholar's patient understanding.

I tell you, though: It has been a hell of a ride. Let me share it with you.

Notes

1. The case of which I speak is *Gutknecht v. United States*, 396 U.S. 295 (1971). The case Warren Burger argued is *Peters v. Hobby*, 349 U.S. 331 (1955).

2. Because I am still out there litigating, I decline to give a list of cases. On Westlaw or LEXIS, you can put my name in the federal and state databases and retrieve the cases where I entered an appearance or where my work was cited.

3. On the right to counsel in civil cases, see *Legal Services Corp. v. Velasquez*, 121 S. Ct. 1043 (2001); *Mallard v. United States District Court*, 490 U.S. 296 (1989).

4. On oral argument in the courts of appeals, *see* MICHAEL E. TIGAR & JANE B. TIGAR, FEDERAL APPEALS: JURISDICTION & PRACTICE § 10.02 (3d ed. 1999).

5. Many of my ideas about advocacy are contained in two books, EXAMINING WITNESSES (1993) and PERSUASION: THE LITIGATOR'S ART (1999), both available from ABA Press. *See also* LAW & THE RISE OF CAPITALISM (new edition 2000)[M.R. Levy assisted in preparation of the original 1977 edition, which was translated into Spanish, Portuguese, Greek, and Chinese]. Other ideas discussed in this book can be found in some of my essays and articles; e.g., *What Would Thomas More Think?*, 2 J. INST. FOR THE STUDY OF LEGAL ETHICS 187 (1999); *Defending, an essay*, 74 TEX. L. REV. 101 (1995); *Paul Touvier and the Crime Against Humanity*, 30 TEX. INT'L L. J. 286 (1995)[with Casey, Giordani & Mardemootoo]; *Discovering Your Litigator's*

Voice, 16 LITIGATION 1 (Summer 1990); *Query: Judges or Lawyers—Who Are the Keepers of the Flame?*, 74 JUDICATURE 125 (Oct.-Nov. 1990); *2020 Vision: A Bifocal View*, 74 JUDICATURE 89 (Aug.-Sept. 1990); *Voices Heard in Jury Argument: Litigation and the Law School Curriculum*, 9 REVIEW OF LITIGATION 177 (1990); Book Review, *Whose Rights? What Danger?* 94 YALE L.J. 970 (1985); *The Right of Property and the Law of Theft*, 62 TEX. L. REV. 1443 (1984); Book Review, *Law and Revolution: The Formation of the Western Legal Tradition*, 17 U.C. DAVIS L. REV. 1035 (1984); *The Foreign Sovereign Immunities Act and the Pursued Refugee: Lessons From Letelier v. Chile*, 1982 MICHIGAN YEARBOOK OF INTERNATIONAL LEGAL STUDIES 421; Book Review, *The Great Fear*, 15 HARVARD CIVIL LIBERTIES - CIVIL RIGHTS REVIEW (1980); *Can We Be Equal and Free?*, in THE UNFINISHED REVOLUTION (C. Snow ed. 1976); *Judicial Power, the Political Question Doctrine, and Foreign Relations*, 17 U.C.L.A. L. REV. 1135 (1970), reprinted in THE VIETNAM WAR AND INTERNATIONAL LAW, Vol. 3 (R. Falk ed. 1972); Book Review, *Freedom & Order in the University*, 56 CALIF. L. REV. 236 (1968); Book Review, *Anti-Politics in America*, 77 YALE L.J. 597 (1968). I have also written three plays on legal history, dealing with the Zenger trial, the Haymarket trial, and Irish advocates (this last one co-authored with Kevin McCarthy).

Chapter 1
THE SENSE OF INJUSTICE

"Were there no injustice, men would never have known the name of justice." The Greek poet and philosopher Heraclitus wrote this some 2,500 years ago. Edmond Cahn captured this idea in his provocative book, *The Sense of Injustice*. I have never been able to parse all the theories of what is right—natural law, positivism, utilitarianism. I have tried to pay attention to what is going on around me, and to look at what needs correcting. This approach is necessarily based on conflict, on a sense of the dialectical way in which history moves through the struggle and resolution of opposites.

In self-improvement meetings, this sort of thinking is known as doing "the next right thing." More elegantly, C.S. Lewis reassured someone who complained of lacking a grand vision, saying that on a dark mountain path at night, he would rather see a few yards ahead than have a view of some far horizon. Derrida captured the thought with his aphorism, "*Je voudrais apprendre à vivre enfin.*" Finally, I want to learn to live, and to teach what I know about living.

I begin, however, by answering a question: "What kind of a name is Tigar?" Different people ask this, sometimes to figure out which ethnic niche to put me in, and sometimes just from friendly curiosity. My father was born Charles Henry Locke in 1906, in Ionia, Michigan, one of five children. His father was a sheriff or constable, and the local history says the Lockes are descended from Benjamin Rush, who signed the Declaration of Independence. I don't know. My father's older sister went into vaudeville, and she changed her name to Zyska Tigar, apparently because it was an exotic gypsy name. In her declining days, alone in a Hollywood apartment, she would take out an old trunk and show me her dancing clothes. My father's older brother, Gene, changed his name to Gene Tigar and became a barnstorming pilot, the kind who entertained at county fairs. Later, Gene moved to Los Angeles and did some stunt flying for Warner Brothers.

When my dad was 14, his father committed suicide one Sunday morning. My father left home soon thereafter and joined the army by lying about his age. He had only eight grades of school. After the army found him out and discharged him, he went on to hold a lot of different jobs, including working on ranches in Wyoming, Montana, and Alberta. In the 1930s, he moved to California, and about that time changed his name to Charles Tigar. I think Uncle Gene helped him get a job breaking horses for movies. He rode as an extra in a couple of films, but the movie work didn't last, so he drove a truck for a time, and then went to work at Lockheed Aircraft.

My dad continued his love of horses and riding. There were some stables down by the Los Angeles River in Burbank, and he would give riding lessons evenings and weekends. It was there that he met Elizabeth Lang, my mother. That brings the story up to about the time I arrived.

To understand injustice, one must see the human condition. Growing up, I had a fairly narrow view of that condition. I was born on January 18, 1941, in Glendale, California. By that time, my father was executive secretary of the International Association of Machinists, Local 727. He had been instrumental in organizing the union, which was the machinists' first foray into industrial unionism. His name, Charles Tigar, was a great help in the organizing drive. My mother had been a secretary at Lockheed.

My earliest real memories date from about four years of age, when I started kindergarten. By that time, my father and mother were divorced, and we lived with my grandmother in a small house in Glendale. I walked five blocks to elementary school, passing the Lake Street Baptist Church where my grandmother played the violin every Sunday and my sister and I went to Sunday school.

I remember the Glendale municipal swimming pool, where I learned to swim. There was a sign on it, "No colored allowed." I was told that Glendale had a municipal ordinance that forbade any African-American from remaining overnight in the city. Whether that was true or not, I never saw any African-Americans in my school, in the stores, or on the streets of Glendale. Nearby, though, were the barrio and the ghetto, and I saw those. My mother spoke Spanish; she had learned it in college and used it while working at Lockheed when foreign buyers would tour the factory. Sometimes we would go shopping in the barrio one city over from Glendale, in Burbank.

We mostly lived in that Glendale house until I was in the seventh grade. My grandmother had twin boys who were a lot younger than my mother, and only about 12 years older than I.

That Baptist church introduced me to the literature of the Old and New Testaments, and Bible verses still spring to mind from the days when I won competitions for remembering more of them than other kids. In later years, I have come to a different attitude toward houses of worship. Then, the church was the place where you learned what to believe, and you heard it and believed it. This was called faith. I was baptized in that faith, by total immersion in a big tub under a velvet painting of Jesus praying at Gethsemane.

I still go to places of worship, and find myself doing devotional exercises from time to time. I do not hold a firm belief that God exists, but I have taken in moral and spiritual teachings from that time and along the way. They are my moral compass. On the path, I have sat in Catholic cathedrals, admiring the sense of peace and the idea of consecrating one's life to a set of values, even as I remembered vividly the horrors committed in the church's name. I have sat in Quaker meetings, in the meditation places of Buddhists, and in reform Jewish synagogues, where the social justice message seems right.

Perhaps God exists. If so, I doubt she minds that I don't really believe in her. If she is the ultimate author of the moral and ethical precepts I have adopted, then she believes in me and in everybody else. And that is what matters.

No such thoughts entered my mind when, in elementary school, I went to services at the Baptist church, went to the summer school, and even attended released-time services on school days. Yes, this was before the Supreme Court had begun to consider the constitutionality of this interweaving of church and state.

Even then, I did have doubts. I remember one revival meeting at the church. The speaker was announced as a "missionary among the Jews of New York." I was about 10, but I always went to the Sunday night adult services. I had no clear idea about New York, except that my mother's older sister, Patricia, lived there. I knew that Patricia was something of a family scandal, for she had gone off to Yale Music School on a scholarship in the 1930s, when most of Yale was closed to women. There she had become quite radical. My maternal grandfather had stopped speaking to her, and she to him. "My dear," she said archly, explaining this break in relations, "he ordered me not to go to a Paul Robeson concert, and not because Robeson is Red, but because he is Black."

My idea about Jews was based entirely on the Old Testament. Only later, when I was about 13, did my mother begin working for a medical group staffed largely by Jewish doctors who were battling the county medical society prohibition on group practice. When I was 10, I knew that Jews were still waiting for the Messiah, but I had no sense of Jewish ritual, culture, or life.

Looking back, I think this revivalist-missionary was probably innocent of most of this learning as well. He described his street-corner preaching in the New York garment district, which he identified as a veritable center of Jewishness. He spoke of the crowd's indifference and sometimes hostility to his message. And then his voice rose, as he intoned what must have been one of his open-air messages:

My friends, did you ever walk past a graveyard in the middle of the night? And you are afraid of what is in there? And you start to hear noises? So you begin to whistle, to keep your courage up. My friends, the Jews are whistling in the dark!

This prediction of damnation for those of another faith seemed wrong. My friend Leon had taken me to Catholic services, and I even sat in on Catholic summer school one day. I had never seen or been to a Jewish service, but I knew that different people looked at religion differently. I also saw a few examples of backsliding by folks in our own congregation.

Because my mother and grandmother worked all day, I was on my own after school. A neighbor was officially assigned to baby-sit my younger sister and me, but from the fifth grade on I had my paper route, went to Cub or Boy Scout meetings, or found other things to do.

There was a branch library on the way from home to school, halfway along the six-block walk. You could take out 10 books at a time. Some days, if I didn't want to be outside, I would get 10 books, take them home, and read them. There was, and may still be, a series of orange-bound biographies of historical figures. I read them all, though I cannot remember that any of the heroes was a person of color, and only a few of them were women. A bus ride to the main library in downtown Glendale cost 10 cents, and I often took the bus down there for a better selection. Sometimes I would see a book that looked interesting, and the librarian wouldn't let me have it until my mother had called to say it was all right.

By the time I was 10, I was riding my bicycle all over. From Glendale, I would ride to the Verdugo foothills and on into Burbank. I rode into Hollywood and almost to downtown Los Angeles. I rode up to Griffith Park and the observatory. My travels took me to some project housing down by the Los Angeles River, called Rodger Young Village, over the border from Glendale into Los Angeles itself. The project was named after a legendary World War II infantryman, about whom a song was written. The village consisted of Quonset huts left in place from the war. The families there were black and white and brown. I had never seen a community with such diversity of people or such living conditions.

Our own home was not luxurious. We did not have one of those automatic washers. My mother and grandmother drove 15-year-old cars to work, and so on. But we had a yard to play in, and six people in a three-bedroom house with one bathroom did not seem really crowded. The project living conditions surprised me because they were so much more straitened than those at home. I stopped off at a community center and talked to the people there. There was a signup sheet for volunteers to do political canvassing in the neighborhood. I thought that was a fine idea, but they said that a 10-year-old was too young for it. So I signed up my mother.

When they called a few days later to set up times for mom to do this work, she was at first not pleased. She worked long days. But she saw that it was important to me, and so she volunteered, and brought back more stories of that community.

When I was in the seventh grade, we moved to Burbank for a few months and then into Hollywood. I went to Bancroft Junior High School in Hollywood for the eighth and ninth grades. It was not a very diverse school, although there were many Jewish kids, and I finally got to see what Jewish life—and cuisine—were about. One summer I went on a Boy Scout camping adventure up into Canada, and some of the boys on the trip were from Chicano communities in East Los Angeles and the San Fernando Valley.

By this time, Aunt Patricia had moved out to California with her two children, Leslie and Johnny, both younger than my sister and I. Pat brought with her some of those radical ideas, and she went to work for a labor union in Los Angeles. My mother had begun working for the Kaiser Health Plan, which was serving a lot of labor union members. My view of the world was getting wider.

At my mother's urging, I did a book report on Rachel Carson's *The Sea Around Us*. The conservationist values that were later to shape Carson's influential *Silent Spring* were already in that earlier book. In English, we had to memorize poetry and prose, much like the rote work of Bible study. In this way, bits of Emily Dickinson, William Shakespeare, and Ogden Nash came to live side-by-side in my head. Of course, with the hormonal angst of early adolescence, I was taken by such writers as Robert Service and William Ernest Henley, and would sonorously intone *Invictus* or *The Ballad of Sam McGee* at the slightest provocation. This sense of drama helped in some ways. School plays and shows let me write and act. I was elected student body president of the junior high school.

When I was about 11, my dad moved back to the Los Angeles area. He had moved down to Blythe, California, a desert town on the lower Colorado River. I never knew exactly why he went there. For a time, he had a restaurant called Tigar's Pantry. My dad loved to cook, and he taught me a lot about that. The more adventurous cooking I later learned from my Aunt Patricia, who had, after all, lived in New York. My sister and I had visited my dad and stepmother one Christmas in Blythe. By that time, he had closed the restaurant because it wasn't working out. I think I was 10.

But I remember that visit because we were all having dinner in a local restaurant in Blythe when Roy Rogers walked in with some other people. Now, I revered Roy Rogers and Gene Autry, along with the other iconic figures from the big Zenith radio in the front room of our house. Bobby Benson of the B-bar-B, Straight Arrow, the Green Hornet, Superman. I wondered how those voices got into that radio, a mystery that I never worked out even when my uncles built a crystal set and tried to teach me about radio waves. Roy Rogers was also the hero of the movies I would see some Saturdays in downtown Glendale, using my paper route money for entry and popcorn.

I had—and still have—autographed pictures of Roy and Gene that my dad had gotten, probably in his union days when he was moving in some pretty hot company. That night in Blythe, my dad got up from our table and went over to tell Roy Rogers that his son wanted to meet him. I shook hands with Roy, and then he and my dad got into conversation. Roy was down there to hunt duck and doves. My dad was a great hunter. I never went with him because you had to be 14 to take the rifle training, and he died before we ever got to do it. I never picked up his fascination with guns. He kept a loaded .38 in his bedside table. When he was off in Washington during World War II, he left my mom a rifle and taught her how to use it. She, too, was an ace shot. But Roy Rogers actually asked my dad's advice on hunting, and they sat there for an hour talking. I was awestruck by the whole situation.

In Los Angeles, my dad and my stepmother eventually found a house not too far from where I was living. I used to visit him, and we would watch television or work on projects or cook together. By that time, he worked for a small trucking company as its safety director. A couple of times, we went to breakfasts where he would have to make a speech about safety. He would betray his sense of unease. Hardly anybody in the room would have a college degree, but he had only eight grades of school.

I can remember one day, when I was about 11 or 12, telling him that I wanted to be a lawyer. He went into his bedroom and brought out a copy of Irving Stone's book, *Clarence Darrow for the Defense.* "You need to be a lawyer like Darrow," he said. "He was for the people."

I think my dad kept reaching for goals and then suffering because he felt he had come up short. Because he was funny, sometimes stern, and always with that edge of insecurity, it seems looking back that there were things he wanted to tell me and show me that somehow never came out. I think a lot of people feel that way about their parents. Your sense of what you missed doesn't ripen until they are gone, and then it's too late. Dad's job in California came to an end. I think the trucking company wasn't doing too well. So he packed up and moved to Phoenix to take another job in June 1956, when I was 15. He had a mild heart attack just before he moved, but kept on going. The last time I saw him, he was smoking a cigarette and drinking a martini from a crockery cup, joking that if he could have only one drink a day it would be a good one. He spoke to me earnestly, questioning me about what I was doing and critically analyzing my answers. Maybe he was trying to fill up all the gaps in our relationship.

Two weeks later, he was working in his yard in Phoenix. He came in and sat down on the couch and died of a massive heart attack. He was 49.

By this time, my mom had married again and we were living in the San Fernando Valley. Reseda High School had just opened, and I went there. This meant getting a new group of friends, and learning the ways of a new community. Without dwelling on it too much, I did not like my stepfather much. My mother wanted this relationship, and I respected that. But his presence in the house meant that I stayed away a lot.

As my stepfather's business faltered, he drank more. Mom and I would hold his head as he vomited into the toilet, having by some miracle managed to drive home. He lost our house because he couldn't make the payments, and fortunately mom's salary was enough that she could find us another house in the same school district. Through it all, mom was always there for my sister and me, even though she worked long hours herself.

The summer after my dad died, my stepfather decided to lease a restaurant in the resort community of Big Bear, about 100 miles from Los

Angeles. The place was open mainly on weekends. He thought he could make a success of it. So I worked from 9 to 3 as a day camp counselor, then from 3 to 6 for a printer, running the presses as I had been taught in the print shop classes in junior high and high school. Then at 6 P.M. on Friday, I would buy bags of charcoal and drive up to Big Bear. Mom would have driven up after her job and would work as a waitress. I was second cook and kitchen helper. Then on Sunday nights we would all drive back home to face our Monday jobs.

In every spare moment, often at night, I would read. Mr. Lewis, at the local bookstore, helped me find more books on Clarence Darrow and I read them all. I still have them.

I was lucky in so many ways. The print shop where I worked taught me a lot about how the printed word is fashioned. The day camp where I worked in the summer gave me insights into the lives and dreams of children—and their parents. Reseda High School, being a new facility, attracted teachers from all over the Los Angeles system who relished the challenge of building programs at a new facility.

I leapt into this new experience. I even tried out for the football team, which only showed the gap between my lofty dreams and my limited ability. I made "B" football, not varsity, and played five minutes in one game. I was better in print shop, drama, literature, math, and student government. I wound up representing the school in youth in government programs, in drama and speech competitions, and in scholarship meetings. I was Petrucchio in *Taming of the Shrew*, Mr. Hale in Susan Glaspell's *Trifles*, and Danny in *Night Must Fall*. I was elected student body president on the strength of borrowed jokes that I thought funny and could work into my campaign speech. Sample: "I call my car Calvin Coolidge because it does not choose to run."

The school had paid a lot for band uniforms, and I was one of the few who fit into the drum major's outfit—being tall and gangly. The band teacher asked me to be drum major, then regretted it when it turned out I had neither musical talent nor the coordination required to look good while marching. I never got the musical talent, but I could wave my stick in 4/4 time. And a teacher named Osborn showed me how to do a kind of strutting walk that was odd enough to look like I was being gangly on purpose.

In these years, 1955 through 1958, Dwight Eisenhower was President, Senator Joe McCarthy had his flight of fame and then fell in disgrace, and the civil rights movement was given new energy by the Supreme Court's decision in *Brown v. Board of Education*. Amidst all my comings and goings, these events shaped my perceptions. From the skein of memory, these strands and colors stand out.

My mother had worked some for the Adlai Stevenson presidential campaign in 1952 and 1956. In 1954, when I was in the eighth grade, the Army-McCarthy hearings were on the radio. My Aunt Pat and her children lived with us. She and my mom subscribed to *Harper's* magazine, which carried articles on McCarthyism, foreign policy and other political issues. I read some of this. The Army-McCarthy issues captivated me. I became adept at mimicking the voices of Joseph N. Welch, Senator McCarthy, and the other characters. Being played out here was, albeit in a limited sense, a trial of the entire loyalty-security system. I did not have a detailed understanding, but I saw that attacks on good people because of their supposed political views were harming the social fabric. People were afraid for no good reason; that much I could see. I remember speaking up in my eighth grade social studies class, based on the hearings and on a *Harper's* article by (as I remember it) Richard Rovere. After class, my teacher, Mrs. Yarrow, nervously took me aside and said that while she agreed with what I was saying, would I please not bring up these issues in class because somebody might tell and she would get fired. I was startled by her fear, and then angry that she would be afraid to discuss things that we talked about at home.

There were no African-Americans at my junior high or high school, but the issue of civil rights caught our attention. I can remember the fall of 1957, when President Eisenhower sent troops to Little Rock, Arkansas, to enforce federal court desegregation orders. The papers carried those dramatic pictures, and I can remember opening a school assembly, where I was presiding as a student body officer, by saying, "Folks, we were scheduled to have a performance by a drill team from the 101st Airborne Division, but they are performing at another school this morning."

Of course, these were also the years of nuclear deterrence, atomic and hydrogen bomb controversies, the Rosenberg spy trial and their execution, and the Central Intelligence Agency's repeated invasions and interventions in the politics of other countries. I don't remember having much of this in my consciousness at the time. Certainly, the threat of nuclear warfare was an issue. In junior high and high school, we had "drop drills" as well as fire drills. The teacher would say, "drop!" and we would crouch under our desks, assuming the position that would protect us if there were a nuclear attack. We must have known that this was nonsense, and that the only reason to crouch would be to kiss our little asses goodbye.

I do not remember what spurred my interest in the death penalty. California had its gas chamber, and the fate of convicted kidnapper/murderer Caryl Chessman was being debated. Chessman's alleged crimes were robbery, sexual assault, and kidnaping. The prosecution obtained a death sentence under a California statute that would be held unconstitutional today, because the Eighth Amendment permits a death sentence only for homicide. The Chessman case dragged on until May 1960 when he was executed, still protesting his innocence and his lawyers still pointing out all the holes in the evidence and all the errors of procedure. I had read and reread Darrow's autobiography, and books on Darrow arguing against death in the Leopold and Loeb case. Whether it was Chessman's case, or Darrow's powerful arguments, or some other influence, I reacted to a review of Arthur Koestler's book *Reflections on Hanging*. The American edition was published in 1958, my last year in high school, with introductions by philosopher Edmond Cahn and British Member of Parliament Sidney Silverman. Silverman, whom I met some years later when we spoke on the same platform in London, in Conway Hall, Red Lion Square, had led the movement to abolish capital punishment in the United Kingdom.

Koestler's prose captured me from its opening sentence:

England is that peculiar country in Europe where people drive on the left side of the road, measure in inches and yards, and hang people by the neck until dead.

I read the book in the library and then went to Mr. Lewis's bookstore to order my own copy. Even now, I pick up the book often. Britain, along with all other members of the European Community, has abolished the death penalty. Abolition was the first order of judicial business by South Africa's Constitutional Court. Most other nations in the world have done the same.

Edmond Cahn's introduction to the book still rings true. Of course, nobody seriously argues any more that the death penalty deters crime more effectively than any other sanction. Cahn noted the racial disparity in charging, convicting, and sentencing in death cases. This disparity contributed to the debate that led the Supreme Court in 1972 to declare the death penalty unconstitutional in every state that enacted it. The disparity still exists, quite dramatically, but later Supreme Court cases first disparaged its significance, then put great hurdles in the path of defendants who challenged their sentences on that ground.

Cahn also made the point that has come to dominate my thinking about the death penalty, after being trial and appellate counsel in a few of these cases. In capital cases, he wrote, there is a disturbing amount of police haste, sloppiness, and outright falsification of evidence.

Over the past 20 years, four score defendants have been liberated from death rows because of definitive proof that they were innocent. A crime that would lead the prosecutor to call for the death penalty is likely to have shocked the community. The media echo the public's need to have the case solved so that everybody can breathe easier. The police are encouraged to indulge their early suspicions and prejudices and make an arrest. Then the machinery goes into operation. Other leads are ignored. Exculpatory evidence is overlooked. And in a distressing number of cases, lies, false reports, and fake forensics enter the fray. I have tried those cases, seen this done, and tried to deconstruct it for juries and appellate courts. Because the system for appointing counsel in capital cases is painfully inadequate, defense lawyers often lack the skill, commitment, and resources to challenge the falsehoods.

In reflecting on the choices I made during my last year in high school, I think I would have chosen differently if I had studied foreign policy issues more closely. I did not have a world view as much as a bunch of ideas about justice and injustice. Of course, I shared with almost everybody my age the arrogant sense that I had it all together. This sense was reinforced by my self-developed independence, having worked several jobs from the age of 14, not to mention those paper routes and other efforts before then.

Both my twin uncles had passed all the rigorous tests for enrollment in the regular Naval Reserve Officers' Training Corps (NROTC). This meant that the Navy paid tuition, books, and living expenses at the colleges of their choice, and that they became commissioned officers on graduation, Ensign USN and not USNR, regular Navy just like Annapolis graduates. Bud and Chuck followed an engineering curriculum at the University of Southern California, and their stories of summer training cruises filled my head with wonder. Bud went off to work for Admiral Rickover in nuclear engineering, and Chuck got a good assignment on other engineering duties. My mother had known Nancy Nimitz, daughter of the famous admiral, growing up in San Diego.

For me the Navy offered a chance to go to sea, the best-looking uniforms, a free education at the school of my choice, and some externally imposed order in my life. It simply did not occur to me that there was little room, even for people studying to be officers, to debate the serious issues of war, peace, life, death, and destruction. I was not very well informed about the nuclear test ban debates, the discussions of disarmament, and the brewing troubles in Southeast Asia. There was hardly any military draft at that time, so I was free to decline military service and just go on to college. But when I competed for and was awarded an NROTC scholarship, I embraced it. This meant I could still have my National Merit Scholarship, but that I would get only $125 a year from that source.

Later on, the Navy and I parted ways. That lesson propelled me into my later defense of war resisters and military dissidents, as I recount in Chapter 6. But having my books paid for, and $50 a month, was a big item for me. I could have gone to a private college where the tuition was expensive, but the University of California at Berkeley seemed ideal. It was away from home, but only a Greyhound bus ride away. These days, air travel has become so commonplace that college recruiters visit cities and schools. High school students tour colleges, as my own kids did. I had never been east of Montana. All those eastern schools seemed foreign and far away.

So I chose Berkeley. That was 1958. For the four years of my undergraduate education, then three years of law school (with a year off between the two to work and figure out if law school was really what I wanted to do), Berkeley and the Bay Area offered up a set of intellectual and emotional challenges. I arrived with a set of values and an image of self. Even today, if I walk along the Berkeley streets, or hike along the hills of San Francisco, or stroll the waterfront, memories flood in, of all the rich and varied experiences that a boy from the 'burbs of Los Angeles suddenly found.

These days, people write and ask what kind of college experience they should have to prepare for law school. I think college is the most luxurious opportunity you will ever have to meet and wrestle with ideas. I kept looking around and wondering if my classmates had a better high school education than I did. They seemed calmer, with less of a sense of wonder than I. Of course, we are always comparing our insides to other people's outsides, so I can't really say what they were thinking and feeling. For me, it was a glorious adventure.

The adventure began two weeks before classes formally got under way. I asked my mom and stepfather to drop me off in Berkeley, and I moved into temporary dorm quarters at the cooperative housing. The co-op dorms required you to work five hours a week to keep the place going, but your room and three meals a day cost just $50 a month. That was the amount of the Navy stipend. I also had $12.50 a month from my

National Merit Scholarship. My father's widow, Virginia Vaughn Tigar, wrote to say that he had set aside $1,500 for my college education, and I could have it at the rate of $375 a year. I thought that she was probably contributing the money herself, because when I visited her in Phoenix it did not seem that my dad had left any kind of estate. So for a 10-month school year, I had that extra $37.50 a month plus what I had saved from working in high school.

I had read in *Sunset* magazine of walking tours in San Francisco. After I unpacked my stuff, I found the bus stop and went into the city. Each day for a week, I repeated the ritual. I rode the bus to San Francisco's East Bay terminal, and walked or took a cable car. I covered dozens of little neighborhoods, snapping pictures and visiting stores, museums, and bookshops. A lot of those places are paved over, or redeveloped, but every time I have a few hours in San Francisco I retrace some of those old steps. Some of the stores are still there, and the steep steps up Telegraph Hill, and some traces of what Fishermen's Wharf was like. I had never seen so rich and diverse a place. I had been to San Francisco just once before that, when I was about six and my dad flew me up on a non-scheduled airplane flight run by a company of which he was part owner.

My temporary roommate for three weeks in Berkeley had an FM radio, usually tuned to a non-profit radio station called KPFA. He said he would sometimes volunteer as an announcer at the station, and if you wrote away for an FCC license, they would even let you run the station control board. You mean, I thought, a person could be on the radio? Radio news had been important in our house. Edward R. Murrow covered Senator McCarthy. Our high school social studies teacher asked us to listen to Edward P. Morgan's ABC radio news broadcast, which was sponsored by the AFL-CIO: "Fifteen million Americans bring you Edward P. Morgan and the news." Morgan and Murrow had the radio voice.

I went to KPFA's studio above an ice cream store on Shattuck Avenue in Berkeley, and said I wanted to be a volunteer. A person named Bill Butler, who was the literature and drama director, greeted me with an air of detached boredom.

"Well, we would have to see if you can speak properly," he said. He gave me a book and sat me in a studio. Those KPFA studios were sound-proofed with old acoustical tiles and worn carpet. The microphone was the venerable RCA 44BX. I learned only later of the amazing qualities of this instrument. It was ideal for interviews, for it was bi-directional—it picked up from two sides. But if you started by speaking into it, and then swung your head, it sounded to the listener like you were moving across the room away from him or her. We used this to great effect in drama shows. For those old Pacifica radio fans who listened to my Thurber dramatizations, the sound of jewels being counted one by one on a hard surface in *The Thirteen Clocks* was created by Dave Elster tossing thumbtacks at a 44BX.

Anyway, Butler told me to read aloud Maeterlink's *Massacre of the Innocents*. I had never read it. "All of it?" I asked.

"Please," he said. He adjusted the volume level from the control room, started a tape and left the engineer's booth. There were two such booths at the station, so the broadcast must have been running from the other one. I read the story, put the book down and left the studio with the tape running. Butler never reappeared. I said to the receptionist that I had finished, and I left.

Once the semester started, I moved from my erstwhile room into another dorm. A few weeks later, I was walking across campus. My temporary roommate hailed me and said, "I heard you reading that story on the radio. Sounded great."

I biked down to KFPA and saw Bill Butler. "Oh, yes," he said. "I liked the reading, so I broadcast it. I had lost your phone number. Would you like to volunteer for us?"

I learned how to operate the control board, and became an announcer on Saturday mornings at the station. At first, I simply announced programs and musical selections, and recorded interviews and other events. I worked my way into drama, news, and public affairs broadcasting. My senior year in college, 1961-62, I was a half-time paid employee doing mostly news and interviews. When I graduated from college in June 1962, I worked for six months as Pacifica's European correspondent, based in London, and then was Public Affairs Director for KPFK-FM, the Los Angeles station.

Pacifica had been founded in the late 1940s as a listener-supported station in Berkeley. This was before the days of National Public Radio and federal funding. KPFA, and later its sister stations in Los Angeles, New York, and elsewhere, subsisted on listener donations and some foundation grants.

KPFA in the late 1950s and early 1960s was a training ground for talents who would later make their names in more mainstream journalism. It was where people who had mastered the craft of communication came to spend the latter part of their careers. Elsa Knight Thompson, who had worked at the BBC during World War II, knew interview techniques that we all struggled to learn. Gene Marine had made a career in print journalism. Among the younger ones, John Leonard went on to become cultural editor of the *New York Times*, and Chris Koch became a producer with National Public Radio. The music director was Alan Rich, who went on to write for the *New York Herald Tribune*, and is today one of the wittiest music critics around. I worked alongside Fred Haines, who wrote the screenplay for *Ulysses*.

Radio news at that time consisted mostly of five minutes at the top of the hour, where announcers read copy torn off the Associated Press teletype. At KPFA, an AP teletype chattered away in a closet, but was only one source of our news. Gene Marine decreed that we would do one half-hour of news every weekday night at 6:00 P.M. Two newscasters would be on the air. Gene was usually one of them, along with Bill Plosser. The rest of the work was done by volunteers, or by part-timers like me. We sat at our manual typewriters and typed out the stories. Sometimes we would use a paragraph from the AP wire, but most of this news was written by us for delivery over the radio. A radio lead is different from a print journalism lead—it has to convey more key information, and the simple declarative sentence is even more essential.

We might call up people in the news and record brief interviews, which we would edit for broadcast. From about 2:00 P.M. until 6:00 P.M., there was the deadline pressure to produce about 6,000 words of copy. During this time, we were deciding which would be the main stories of the day. In addition to the AP, we had news from the BBC, from the local media, and from alternative sources. We might do a news feature on political developments in a foreign country, based on sources that were several days old. The world of Internet-based instant communication did not yet exist. Learning to write clear communicative prose in the form of stories was perhaps the most important single part of my preparation to be a lawyer. Radio journalism also gives practice in asking questions, one after another, to avoid dead air and keep the discussion moving. I think my entire style of courtroom examination began in those radio studios.

At 6:00 P.M., the announcer would say, "And now the news, read this evening by Gene Marine and Michael Tigar." I might then say, "Good evening, this is Michael Tigar. In Havana today, Cuban President Fidel Castro. . . . " That was our type of lead. Tell them where, tell them who, and then tell them what.

Just being at Pacifica was perhaps the most important educational experience of my life. I read and listened and learned from an array of people who in turn brought talented folks into the station to record programs on almost every subject and from all points of view. During an evening on the control board, and between announcements, I might be called on to record a discussion of opera, a one-act radio play, or a commentary by Caspar Weinberger.

For several months, I was even director of children's programs, which meant mostly finding recorded items for broadcast. But I did dramatic readings of a couple of James Thurber's books, and read all of *Treasure Island* aloud, doing all the voices of the different characters.

You have probably heard it said, carelessly I think, that a good trial lawyer is theatrical. People assume that the qualities of a good actor are the same as those of a good litigator. I think not. Acting is a profession and involves skills all its own. Actors speak lines written by others, seeking to communicate the thoughts and feelings of characters that somebody else has created. At a purely technical level—understanding the importance of movement, speaking clearly, conveying emotion with one's voice—there are superficial similarities between the discipline of acting and that of lawyering. The resemblance, however, ends there.

I had done feature journalism before, in print and on the radio. A 15-minute radio commentary is from 2,500 to 3,000 words. There must be a story, with clearly drawn characters. You are trying to persuade the listener to hear you out, and to take seriously what you are saying. Evocative prose, written sparely and in declarative sentences. This, too, is part of the lawyer's preparation.

I was so wrapped up in learning journalism that I almost jumped off the lawyer path. After all, a journalist might have as much effect on social change as a lawyer. There was a course at Berkeley in the journalism department called The Literature of the Press. It sounded wonderful— the chance to read works from Daniel Defoe's *Journal of the Plague Years*, the "muckraking" work of Upton Sinclair and Lincoln Steffens, and the masterful and haunting reportage of John Hersey. The professor was Pete Steffens, and not until the first day of class did I realize that he was Lincoln Steffens's son. In addition to teaching an exciting course, he introduced me to people in his father's generation who had been influential in California radical politics.

By the time I was a college junior, I was writing something every day— an article to sell to a local magazine, a news story for KPFA, or a paper for a class. My senior year, I earned money typing up my class notes in one course and marketing them. To improve my ability to write narrative, I took another journalism class on magazine article writing. I was making a few dollars here and there selling freelance pieces, but this course gave me a chance to learn from Allan Temko, architectural critic for the *San Francisco Chronicle* and a prose craftsman whose work I admired. At an outdoor rally at Berkeley, Temko referred to Dwinelle Hall, a blocky, ugly campus building, as "a symbol of man's eternal search for a lavatory." Temko's course on article writing forced me to tackle projects that were about the length of a good appeals brief.

In Temko's course, we could write critical articles under the direction of a critic. In Steffens's class, we read and analyzed social criticism. As C.S. Lewis says, we learned how good writers make every word work, and how to do that ourselves. More to the point, in summing up to a jury or arguing to a court, I always try to put the issue into a pungent phrase. Aphorism is often a powerful rhetorical device—though laden with danger. A pithy phrase may overstate, and make the advocate seem too crafty. It may invoke an overbroad analogy, so that the opponent can destroy the argument by knocking down the analogy.

Arguing the case of John Demjanjuk in the U.S. Court of Appeals for the Sixth Circuit, I was confronted by a broad statement in a Justice Oliver Wendell Holmes opinion. I responded that "Justice Holmes' gift for aphorism often outran his power to state the law clearly." This is true of Holmes. For example, he dismissed a policeman's challenge to restrictions on his free speech with, "The petitioner may have the constitutional right to speak, but he has no constitutional right to be a policeman." Today, we understand that the opportunity—one cannot quite call it a right—to hold public employment may not be conditioned on complete deprivation of the right of free speech. Because overstatement is dangerous, I always ask one or more members of our litigation team to act as metaphor police, restraining my more exuberant figures of speech.

The most compelling images invoke iconic images in the popular culture. This culture has changed over time. People's receptivity to images has changed as well.

Ralph Waldo Emerson is said to have asked Henry David Thoreau, "What branches of learning did you find at Harvard, Henry?" To which the latter is said to have replied, "All of the branches, and none of the roots." Berkeley in 1958 had roots and branches, but they did not all grow in the confines of the classroom or even the campus. KPFA had, if the metaphor holds, leafy branches and long roots.

My first morning of classes that September 1958 was a Monday. English 1A or Speech 1A was required of all freshmen. I chose Speech, and enrolled in the section that was listed as prelegal. I did not suspect from the course catalog what the speech department had become. It was not simply a place where one learned oral expression, although there were courses of that nature. It had been converted into a department of what used to be called rhetoric and would today be termed semiotics. Courses dealt with all aspects of persuasive communication, and they even included offerings on freedom of speech. Sheer good fortune brought me that Monday into the classroom of Jacobus ten Broek.

Ten Broek was blind. He held a law degree and a doctorate. He was founder and leader of a militant organization for the blind. He had been head of the California Department of Social Welfare. He was co-author of a leading article on equal protection and a book on the World War II Japanese relocation. He had written a book on the history of the Civil War amendments. He was tall and slender and bore a fierce mien that could dissolve into gentle mockery or laughter. Our assignment sheet for the semester had us reading John Milton and John Stuart Mill on free speech, some dialogues of Plato, and other works on free expression.

At the appointed time, ten minutes past eight, he strode into the classroom where about 50 of us waited. He put his white cane in the chalk tray and called the roll from Braille cards. That way, he learned the sound of our voice and where we sat. He asked us to keep those seats throughout the semester, and he would thereafter recognize us when we spoke up, or turn toward one of us to require us to speak.

This was Socratic instruction in the way that Socrates did it, and not the imitation variety one sees in so much law school teaching. Ten Broek would take a passage from the reading and ask about it. One of us would venture an interpretation. "Oh, yes," he might say, "but have you considered what he says just one paragraph farther on." Or even, "You are forgetting how the punctuation might change the meaning." From his flawless memory of the text, he would challenge us to move deeper and deeper into what we were studying.

That semester, I copied out whole passages of Milton, Mills, and Plato. All of it was new to me, but it opened up my eyes to the theory and value of free expression. I rejoiced at John Milton's words:

> I cannot praise a fugitive and cloistered virtue, unexercised and unbreathed, that never sallies out to see her adversary. . . . [T]hat which purifies us is trial, and trial is by what is contrary.

Here was an idea not only about free expression, but also about the very dialectical process by which the world advances and great causes are disputed. And we were being led, or perhaps propelled, through it by mastering both its content and its technique.

Speech 1B turned us to equal protection of the laws, to see the tension between freedom and equality. Years later, I was asked to contribute an essay to a collection entitled *Can We Be Equal and Free?* I wrote what I learned in those two magical semesters, that one is useless without the other. Free speech is valueless without equality of access to the forum.

There were 25,000 students at Berkeley in 1958. In that great impersonal place, many lower division courses were given in cavernous lecture halls by professors who seemed to be using notes from long ago. True, these were giants in their respective fields, and we were at least getting to hear from them personally, albeit in a hall that held 600 students. Some of these professors were, however, inspirational, even in the lecture hall. Professor Louis Simpson brought English poetry alive. Bertrand de Jouvenel illuminated modern European history and politics. For the most part, however, getting a good undergraduate education depended on your luck in having a graduate teaching assistant who cared about teaching.

I was lucky. One example tells the story. I took the basic economics course, taught by a middle-of-the-road Keynesian and based on the classic textbook by Paul Samuelson, with some economic history added via Robert Heilbroner's book, *The Worldly Philosophers*. By this time, my sophomore year, the KPFA experience and the political climate of Berkeley had attuned me to radical politics. I had shown up at Berkeley with an interest in the labor movement. My teaching assistant for this economics course was an older student named Clinton Jencks. Now, where had I heard that name before?

Clinton Jencks had been leader of the International Mine, Mill & Smelter Workers in Silver City, New Mexico. A motion picture of the miners' struggle, *Salt of the Earth*, had achieved notoriety. Clint was back in school to earn his Ph.D. in economics, and would go on to write his thesis on the life and work of miners, titled *Men Underground*. As a teacher, he was anxious to share with us his insights on the way economic theory interacted with real life.

I began to read the writings of Paul Sweezy, Leo Huberman, Paul Baran, C. Wright Mills, and Christopher Caudwell. Caudwell's inflammatory 1930s criticism, in *Studies in a Dying Culture*, led to John Berger's 1950s and 1960s work, collected in his book of essays on art, *Permanent*

Red. Some of this material was assigned in classes, most of it not. It was the stuff of discussions at KPFA or among friends.

In April 2000, my daughter Elizabeth and I spent a day at UC Berkeley on her tour of colleges she might attend. The large-scale anonymity of this state university bore in upon us. But she saw there, and expressed to me, what I had found. You could find small classes. You could make the place respond to your need and wish to be educated. And the campus is set in a rich and diverse urban area that also has the intellectual and social ferment of a university town.

Berkeley has a reputation for student activism, but stories of the Free Speech Movement (FSM) of 1964-65 overshadow the longer and truer tale of student concern. Beginning in the late 1950s, some Berkeley students began to organize in support of farm workers' rights, disarmament, and free expression. The influence of McCarthyism was waning on the campus. At first, the university administrators could ignore these protests, but the students' ideas began to catch on.

A group that had organized around issues, rather than ideology, called itself TASC: Toward an Active Student Community. It changed its name to Slate in 1958, to run candidates for student body office. Among its goals was to orient student government more toward concern with social issues. When Slate's candidate, David Armor, was elected student body president, the administrators stepped in. Clark Kerr, a labor economist, was president of the UC System. He issued directives that forbade student government from taking positions on outside or off-campus issues. Because graduate students voted in greater numbers for Slate candidates than undergraduates, he kicked the graduate students out of the Associated Students, thus depriving them of any say over how their mandatory dues were spent, and helping to ensure that no Slate candidate would get a majority in a campus-wide election. In this effort, Kerr was not entirely successful. Another Slate candidate and I won student body office, and I was narrowly defeated for student body president. When the student newspaper, the *Daily Californian*, endorsed my candidacy, the Kerr administration fired all the student editors and imposed a regime of censorship on the newspaper.

The Kerr directives of 1959-60 were the direct antecedent of the protests that became the Free Speech Movement. Ordering student organizations not to be concerned with the world outside was like, to take Milton's phrase, trying to pound up the crows by shutting your park gate. For Clark Kerr, however, it all made perfect sense. He wrote a book called *Industrialism and Industrial Man* to justify his views. Kerr foresaw a new stage in social development called industrialism, in which society would be divided into two classes, managers and managed. The managed need to be trained to follow orders, and the managers would be agents of technological change. As for intellectuals, Dr. Kerr had both fear and contempt. "They are by nature irresponsible," he wrote. "Consequently, it is important who best attracts or captures the intellectuals and who uses them most effectively, for they may be a tool as well as a source of danger." In industrial society, Kerr wrote, "there will not be any revolt . . . , except little bureaucratic revolts that can be handled piecemeal."

With that world view, it is no wonder that the students under Kerr's care rose up in ways that he found both frightening and mystifying. His understanding of his own time proved as lamentably poor as the predictive power of his hypothesis. The domestic drive for civil rights, the anti-war protests that carried on into the 1970s, and then the worldwide upsurge of liberation movements confounded him and his theory at every turn. In my 1961 essay about his ideology and his book, I predicted that his vision of quiet on the campus and in society as a whole would not be borne out by events. I was grateful for the chance to think and write about these issues in the context of the youthful upsurge of protest that we were seeing and in which I was learning to play a part.

In everything I did, I wanted to unravel the reasons for things. Four sets of events helped, and perhaps required, me to define who I was and where I stood. The first was the sit-in movement in the American South. The second was the debate over free speech and free association in those waning days of McCarthyite influence. Third was capital punishment. Fourth was American military policy. I was trying to see, in Paul Sweezy's memorable phrase, the present as history. That is, history was not something that once happened, and that we study for its own sake. We are in history now, and the events and institutions around us came from someplace, are changing as we experience them, and will be altered or abolished by human and natural forces in our lifetimes and beyond. In the study of history, and particularly the injustices we can see so clearly in hindsight, we can gain a sense of what needs to be done today. We can also try to see the mechanism of change, so that our actions are more likely to have an effect.

The sit-in movement began at a lunch counter on February 1, 1960, in Greensboro, North Carolina. From there, direct action to break the color barrier spread across the South. In Berkeley, we organized sympathy pickets and boycotts of the chain stores that had refused service to African-Americans in the South, principally Woolworth's and Kresge's. To the tune of *Hallelujah, I'm a Bum*, the depression ditty, we sang

Hallelujah, picketing Woolworth's
And I like it just fine
Hallelujah, I'm carrying
That big freedom sign

In this civil rights struggle, the two basic ideas we had studied in ten
Broek's class—free expression and equal protection—were interwoven.
Direct action was a form of expression that courts, including the Supreme Court, had held could be regulated more stringently than pure
speech. And yet the isolation of African-Americans from access to the
mass media, coupled with the intransigence of the southern power structure, made such tactics not only inevitable but also, it seemed to me,
defensible. Over and over again in the decades to follow I was drawn into
study and later litigation about the line between regulated conduct and
protected speech.

The loyalty-security issue came to us at first gradually, then dramatically. Politics in the San Francisco Bay Area, including Berkeley, were
eclectic. The California university system had experienced its own loyalty oath crisis in the early 1950s, and memories of those events were still
fresh in the minds of some faculty members. In Slate, for which I was a
candidate in both my junior and senior years, there were unaffiliated
folks, those who labeled themselves liberal Democrats, and socialists of
various organizational tendencies. As a group, we took positions and
action on issues, not ideologies. But this issue orientation was not to the
taste of powerful professors and some administrators. Some professors
denounced Slate, and called on it to make a public declaration that communist sympathizers were not welcome in its ranks. We refused. We had
seen the damage wrought by the loyalty-security witch-hunts of the 1940s
and 1950s.

I studied this issue. I read the history of loyalty oath fights, and of state
and federal investigating committees. I read Supreme Court cases. Then
in the spring of 1960, we all had the chance to see the issue up close. The
House Committee on Un-American Activities (HCUA) came to San
Francisco to hold hearings on alleged communist infiltration into the
labor movement and education. These hearings followed a familiar pattern. The visiting subcommittee would be presided over by an ascetic
midwestern or jowly southern congressman. In this case, it was Louisiana Congressman Richard Willis who showed up. Committee Counsel
Richard Arens would by turns exude sanctimony and disgust. The hearings would begin with the public testimony of witnesses who claimed to

have been members of the Communist Party, and to be revealing insidi-
ous Communist plots as well as giving out the names of their friends and
neighbors who, so they said, had been in there with them. This pattern
was unbroken since at least the late 1940s, and indeed some of the witnesses had been recycled so often they were running out of names to
name.

I had absorbed some of this history by reading the story of Clinton
Jencks himself. In his trial for allegedly being a Communist while holding a union office—which was a violation of the Taft-Hartley Act—the
witness against him was Harvey Matusow. Matusow later confessed that
he was a liar who had been induced to parrot his lies in criminal cases and
before congressional committees, and wrote a book on that experience,
titled *False Witness*.

The San Francisco hearings took their predictable course. One witness
intoned the evils of communist infiltration, and counsel Arens encouraged her by asking:

Q: Now, Mrs. Hartle, can you tell us all please whether in the ideology of communism, with its goal of world domination, is there
any room for the basic ideas of God and patriotism as we are taught
them at our mother's knee?

That particular question led to a spate of tasteless remarks in our group
about "my mother's knee and other low joints."

Following the professional tale-bearers, the committee had subpoenaed
several prominent left-wing figures from the Bay Area as hostile witnesses,
asking each under oath if they were members of the communist party, or
had ever been, and receiving from each a constitutionally based refusal to
answer. None of this so-called investigating would lead to any legislation.
The Supreme Court had questioned its bona fides. Congressman James
Roosevelt had begun a drive to abolish the committee.

In May 1960, however, the committee hearings were different from
those that had been held in other places. Thousands of students, union
members, and others formed a peaceful picket line around the San Francisco City Hall, where the hearings were being held. The main theme of
their signs and chants was Abolish the Committee. On May 12, 1960,
two California legislators addressed a large crowd in Union Square, attacking the committee and its work. One of the speakers was Phil Bur-
ton, who later served in Congress. The committee, not wanting a hostile
audience, arranged that its supporters would take up all the hearing room

seats. Students lined up for places at the hearing, but were disappointed to see that their long wait in line was fruitless. Holders of committee-issued white cards showed up and trooped in to fill the seats.

The tension grew inside and outside the hearing room. Hostile witnesses upbraided the committee for stacking the audience. Among the witnesses was the redoubtable Archie Brown, an elected leader of the International Longshoremen's and Warehouseman's Union (ILWU), who publicly proclaimed his communist party membership. Archie later ran for San Francisco County Board of Supervisors and got 33 percent of the vote. On Friday, May 13, the waiting students began to show their impatience by chanting, "Mr. Willis, we're still here." San Francisco police in riot gear moved into position and turned on the powerful fire hoses. The students were on the city hall's second floor rotunda, just outside the hearing room door. The police simply washed them down the long marble stairs, and then followed them down, clubbing at them randomly as they slipped and slid to the ground floor. Police on the ground floor scooped up about 100 demonstrators and carted them off to jail.

Upstairs, the hearings continued. The next hostile witness, William Mandel, began his first answer to a committee question with, "Honorable beaters of children, uniformed and in plain clothes, distinguished Dixiecrat wearing the clothing of a gentleman. . . . " Eventually the protesters were all acquitted. Pete Seeger sang at a benefit concert to raise defense money. I was the master of ceremonies, fascinated by the interplay of political action and legal theory. As some of us met with the lawyers who volunteered to represent the arrested students, we learned some constitutional lore about direct action and the First Amendment.

HCUA, anxious to rebut the attacks on its handling of the San Francisco protest and to preserve itself if possible, sponsored a movie about the protests, entitled *Operation Abolition*. This film was widely shown to community groups and on college campuses, and was the set piece for many debates. At some of these, I was the invited speaker, confronting Fulton Lewis III, son of the conservative columnist. In Berkeley, we thought there should be an answer to the film, so Fred Haines, Ken Kitch, and I (along with some others whose names I forget) wrote and produced a 12-inch long-playing (LP) record entitled *Sounds of Protest*. Slate raised money for the project. We wove together a montage of sound clips from news coverage of the hearings and protests. Beyond that, however, we constructed a constitutional argument for abolishing the committee, stressing its chilling effect on protected expression and its lack of legitimate legislative purpose.

The third issue that spring of 1960 was the death penalty. Caryl Chessman had been on death row for many years, for kidnaping, robbery, and sexual assault, ever since his 1948 trial. The details of this are foggy in my memory, but elements of it stand out. He had written a book about his case and death row. He had taken appeal after appeal, proclaiming his innocence. California's kidnaping law had changed, so that had his case been retried he would probably not have received the death penalty. He and his case came to symbolize the debate over capital punishment, and his lawyers, who included George Davis of San Francisco, were in the news. I went one day to San Quentin prison with another KPFA reporter who was to interview Chessman, but they let only him in, so the closest I got to him was the waiting room. Chessman's case embodied one of Edmond Cahn's criticisms of capital punishment—that the horror of a crime could often lead to hasty judgments about the alleged criminal.

On May 2, 1960, the day Chessman was executed, Governor Edmund G. Brown refused the final clemency request. Students and others demonstrated at the prison, including members of Slate. Their direct action tactics, which got some of them arrested, were echoes of the civil rights struggles of the South.

In the academic year 1959-60 I was a sophomore. These political currents were pushing me this way and that, and yet I was still a midshipman in the NROTC, faithfully attending classes and drills. By the fall of 1960, the Navy and I had parted company, although we were working out the details until January 1961. (That story, the fourth issue of that year, belongs in Chapter 5.)

Pamet Ayer Jones and I were married in September 1961, a marriage that lasted until 1972. My son Jon and daughter Kate were born in that marriage. My senior year I worked two jobs, a total of 40 hours, half time at KPFA and half time at a professional lecture notes service.

I graduated from Berkeley in June 1962, with a B.A. in political science. I found that the political science department was dominated by professors who loved to count things, to the detriment of political and social theory. So I arranged to get four political science credits for a thesis project under the direction of a history professor, Richard Drinnon. I had been fascinated by the story of J. Robert Oppenheimer, the brilliant Berkeley physicist who had led the scientific team at Los Alamos in the wartime years. Oppenheimer is still known as the "father of the atom bomb."

In the 1950s, Oppenheimer was subjected to a loyalty hearing by the Atomic Energy Commission, which revoked his security clearance. The hearing was largely a charade, a study in systematic character assassination of a principled and dedicated scientist. It was directed not entirely at Oppenheimer, but as a warning to the entire community of atomic scientists. Under Professor Drinnon's direction, I read the entire 1,000-page transcript. I also studied the decision to drop the atomic bombs on Hiroshima and Nagasaki. In this study, I encountered a book by P.M.S. Blackett, *The Military and Political Consequences of Atomic Energy*, which persuasively argued that we had dropped the bombs on Japan unnecessarily. The Japanese had been ready to surrender, Blackett concluded, and our dropping the bombs was designed to keep the Soviets out of the Asian theater post-war peace process. I also found a great deal of evidence that the atomic scientists at Los Alamos were told that the atomic bomb needed to be ready for possible use against the Nazis, even though by 1943 the German ability to make a nuclear weapon had been neutralized by destruction of the German heavy-water facilities.

Studying this material led me to question even more the loyalty-security apparatus that continued to have influence in government and academic circles. The Supreme Court's series of 1961 decisions, mostly 5-4, rejecting First Amendment challenges to that apparatus, caught my attention. Going to law school seemed an even better idea than before. Then, too, the civil rights movement had progressed from litigation-based challenges such as the school desegregation suits to the direct action movement. Here were more challenges for lawyers, defending demonstrators on various theories. We needed a firm First Amendment foundation for protest marches, rallies, and leafleting. We needed theories—and lawyers to put them into practice—to combat the excesses of southern police and the arbitrary operation of southern justice.

To be a lawyer in those times was, it seemed, to have the right, the power, and the duty to influence events. In the early days of civil rights litigation, the lawyers were in a real sense leaders of the movement. Litigation was to be the means to obtain court orders to end Jim Crow. The direct action movement called for lawyers with a different, deeper understanding. The movement—people in motion—made demands and confronted its opponents. The lawyers were helpers, followers. They did not have so much sway in inventing the story to be told in court. They had to listen to their clients and develop the story from their clients' experiences.

Years later, I tried to put this tension into a play. I imagined conversations between Clarence Darrow and labor/anarchist leader Lucy Parsons. Some of their imagined exchanges went like this:

Lucy Parsons: Your lawyers' victories, Clarence, are like fireflies. You catch them and put them in a jar. By morning, their light has gone out. And your bugs are dead. Your lawyer's ego wants you to think you stand at the center of every event by which the world is changed. Your right to stand there is only because some brave soul has risked death or prison in the people's cause and you are called to defend him—or her. When you put law and lawyers at the center of things, you are only getting in the people's way, and doing proxy for the image of the law the state wants us to have. The law is a mask that the state puts on when it wants to commit some indecency upon the oppressed.

Darrow: (Angry) If I believed that, I would still be lawyer for the railroad, and not making do with the fees the union can pay. Lucy, the law is a fence built around the people and their rights.

Lucy Parsons: (Kindly) What an image! And you, Clarence, are a fierce old dog, set to bark and warn off intruders. Maybe so. I wish it so. We are all on trial in this life we have chosen, Clarence. All we can know is that none of us will live to see the verdict.

In 1962, when I got my B.A., I wanted to be relevant in some way to important changes that were taking place, not only in America but also elsewhere in the world. So instead of plowing right into law school, I decided to work as a journalist for a time. Pacifica Foundation had expanded, and KPFA was joined by KPFK in Los Angeles and WBAI in New York. I asked if I could be their European correspondent for six months, for a modest salary, based in London. They agreed.

The great thing about being a journalist is that people who otherwise would not talk to you will take your telephone calls and actually make appointments to see you. My time in London, with trips to Scotland, Wales, France, and Switzerland, was exciting. I interviewed Labour Party leaders about whether Britain should enter the Common Market. I covered the efforts of right-wing paramilitary groups in France to bring down the French government, in the wake of Algeria's independence, by bombings and assassinations.

I was even arrested, though briefly. When I arrived in London, the BBC people agreed to help me by lending tape-recording equipment, and even providing a little income through freelance appearances on BBC programs. One of these people was Bill Ash, an American expatriate who had enlisted in the Canadian Air Force in 1939 to fight the Nazis. He was a decorated hero of the war, and his hatred of Nazism was unabated by the passage of time. He invited me to join him at a British Nazi Party rally in Trafalgar Square, promising that if I wanted to "join me and my friends in the action," I would be welcome. It turned out that his friends were young people who would try to break up the rally. When the British Nazi leader, Colin Jordan, embarked on some of his more odious anti-Semitic stuff, some people rushed the platform. I joined in and wrestled one of the storm troopers off the Nelson Monument plinth. A British bobby pulled me off and said sternly, "All right, young man. That's it. You're under arrest. Now you wait right here until I come back." I was impressed by his courtesy, but I took the opportunity to leave Trafalgar Square and catch the tube train home to Maida Vale. I suppose I am still a fugitive from British law, but nobody has made an issue of it.

Konni Zilliacus, a Labour member of Parliament, and his wife Janet took Pam and me in and helped us meet people in London. Zilliacus was an amazing man, and our evening discussions still come back in memory. He had been born in Finland, was educated at Yale, and was a naturalized British subject. Between World Wars I and II he worked at the League of Nations. He spoke 13 languages, including Russian and most Eastern European languages. He had written several influential books on foreign affairs, and was a formidable figure in House of Commons debates. He shared my love of cooking.

Our son Jon was born at home in our London flat on October 8, 1962, due to the shortage of hospital beds, but with a doctor and midwives in attendance. I interspersed my Pacifica duties with an occasional freelance journalism piece for the BBC, which paid £5, about $14, for a three-minute radio talk. To put that in context, a bus ride was 10 cents at that time.

Radio journalism was exciting, but did I want to do it as a career? I had written what I thought was a persuasive thesis on atomic energy and social policy. Did I want to get a Ph.D. and keep on writing about American history? I corresponded with historians like William Appleman Williams to inquire about graduate programs. Law school continued to beckon. I took the Law School Aptitude Test in London—without going to any prep sessions—and scored high. I was accepted at Boalt Hall, the University of California law school, where tuition was still virtually free for California residents. By the way, I do not regard my LSAT score as signifying anything other than that I could take the test. I have taught and lectured at many law schools, and have found that LSAT scores do not correlate with legal ability.

Having come back from London in the spring of 1963, I was working at KPFK, the Pacifica Radio station in Los Angeles, producing public affairs and news programs and editing the program guide. That had its own excitement, which went beyond broadcasting. KPFK had its studios near one of the movie studio's back lots, which was a big open space. Two devoted KPFK supporters, Ron and Phyllis Patterson, suggested that the station raise money by holding a Renaissance Faire, re-creating a medieval market for a long weekend. This seemed a good idea, and in fact the fairs have since become a California institution much imitated elsewhere. But I was there at the start. We needed somebody to open the fair by galloping on horseback dressed as a knight down busy Cahuenga Avenue, while brandishing a sword and giving "the call of the faire." I was the only male staff member who knew how to sit a horse, so I did it. Twenty-five years later I reprised the role along with my daughter Kate, who was working for the outfit that produced the Renaissance fairs.

But as the summer of 1963 continued, I had to make this decision. I went to see Al Bendich, who had been staff counsel of the Northern California American Civil Liberties Union. He convinced me that I had convinced myself—long before—that law school was in my future. But he had a warning. "It will be hard for people to take you seriously, with your history of being a dissenter, a radical. You will have to convince them. And you know how to do that? By being first in your class." This was not a dialogue. When Al was on a roll, he reminded you of a guy who said about him: "There was a time I didn't talk to Al for three months. But that was only because I didn't want to interrupt him."

Al continued, "And the way to be first is to study more than the next person. You see him studying 12 hours a day, you do 14. That's all there is to it." So I entered law school in September 1963. I did study hard, typing up my notes every night. Boalt computed grade-point averages to three places past the decimal. I agonized so hard over my first semester exams that I wound up in the hospital. I tied for third place in a class of 315. I was chagrined. I worked harder. At the end of the first year, I was first and managed to keep that rank for the rest of my time there.

Notes

1. The Heraclitus quote is from Felix S. Cohen, 63 HARV. L. REV. 1481 (June 1950) (reviewing Edmond Cohen, *The Sense of Injustice*).

2. The cases dealing with the death penalty as a punishment for homicide, and not for other crimes, are *Coker v. Georgia*, 433 U.S. 584 (1977), and *Tison v. Arizona*, 481 U.S. 137 (1987).

3. The South African case declaring the death penalty unconstitutional is *State v. Makwanyane & Mchunu* (Const. Ct. Republic S. Afr. 1995).

4. On racial disparity in sentencing, *see, e.g., McCleskey v. Kemp*, 481 U.S. 279 (1987).

5. The idea about the community response to shocking crimes was captured in part by Judge Richard Matsch's grant of change of venue in the McVeigh/Nichols case, *United States v. McVeigh*, 918 F. Supp. 1467 (W.D. Okla. 1996).

6. On the quality of death penalty counsel, see, e.g., Stephen Bright, *Counsel for the Poor: The Death Sentence Not for the Worst Crime, But for the Worst Lawyer*, 103 YALE L.J. 1835 (1994); *Martinez-Macias v. Collins*, 979 F.2d 1067 (5th Cir. 1992)("Macias was denied his constitutional right to adequate counsel in a capital case in which actual innocence was a close question. The state paid defense counsel $11.84 an hour. Unfortunately, the justice system got only what it paid for.")

7. The Holmes quote is from *McAuliffe v. Mayor, Etc., of City of New Bedford,* 29 N.E. 517 (1892).

8. For more information about Clinton Jencks, see *Jencks v. United States*, 353 U.S. 657 (1957); Harvey Matusow, *False Witness;* and *The Cold War Against Labor*, Ann Fagan Ginger and David Christiano eds.

9. My critical essay, *The Brave New University of Clark Kerr*, appeared in the November 1961 issue of THE LIBERAL DEMOCRAT, published in Berkeley, Calif. For a fuller account, see the CALIFORNIA LAW REVIEW symposium cited in the Chapter Notes to the Prologue.

10. The Supreme Court case questioning the good faith of investigative committees was *Watkins v. United States*, 354 U.S. 178 (1957). The promise that *Watkins* seemed to contain was dashed by the 1961 decisions in *Braden v. United States*, 365 U.S. 431 (1961) and *Wilkinson v. United States*, 365 U.S. 399 (1961). Volume 367 of the U.S. reports contains two scandalously illiberal cases on the Subversive Activities Control Act and the Smith Act.

11. Of course, the ILWU had long been under attack for leftist leadership. *See* Bridges v. United States, 346 U.S. 209 (1953), *and* Bridges v. Wixon, 326 U.S. 135 (1945). On Archie Brown, *see* United States v. Brown, 381 U.S. 437 (1965).

12. Richard Drinnon is author of several leading works on American history, including REBEL IN PARADISE, a biography of Emma Goldman. On the Oppenheimer case, *see* Philip M. Stern's book, THE OPPENHEIMER CASE: SECURITY ON TRIAL (Harper & Row, 1969).

Chapter 2
WHAT LAW SCHOOL WAS ALL ABOUT

I followed Al Bendich's advice, and established my study routine. I typed out a brief summary of every case we were to study. I took careful notes in class, and then each night I typed up my notes and integrated them into the case briefs. This was well before the days of word processors, so my product was cut, pasted, and stapled.

I could not, however, drown out what was going on in the wider world. The power of those events over our lives came home to us when President Kennedy was assassinated on November 22, 1963. In every one of our classes, we took time to talk about what the assassination meant.

Beyond, before, and after those events, however, the constitutional crisis in the country at large bore in on us. The Supreme Court had begun to decide cases arising from the sit-in movement. The Court's majority reaffirmed some important principles about the right to demonstrate, and held that the state could not use its criminal justice apparatus to enforce racial segregation.

These Supreme Court decisions seemed far removed from the basic first-year curriculum—property, contracts, torts, and civil procedure. Make no mistake: I thought then and think now that the first-year curriculum can be understood as giving insight into the basic structure of legal ideology. I could see how civil procedure helped lawyers to litigate civil rights cases. But the point of the private law courses was sometimes hard to see.

Some of that changed when we began to study offer and acceptance in contracts. If a storekeeper puts up a sign, "Refrigerators $100," is that an offer, such that if I walk in and say "I'll take one," there is a binding contract? Or is it simply an invitation to make an offer? What difference does it make? In our contracts book, there was a case, *Rex v. Crawley*, decided in the Transvaal in 1909. Crawley went into a tobacconist shop, but was told that he would not be served. He persisted in demanding to make a purchase and was arrested for trespass. He was convicted on the theory that the shopkeeper's sign was only an invitation to make an offer.

I read the short reference to the case, in the casebook note material. Who was Crawley? What was going on in the Transvaal? What and where was the Transvaal anyway? In the library, I read the entire case. Transvaal was part of South Africa. Rex was in the name because South Africa was under British rule. That was all I could learn. I kept digging. There had been protests in South Africa about the refusal of merchants to serve "colored" and "African" customers. Indeed, the young Mohandas Gandhi had lived and practiced law in South Africa, and had joined those protests. Gandhi had begun to preach Satyagraha—non-violent resistance—in 1906 in Natal Province. Was the holding in *Crawley* in some way related to racial discrimination? I never found that answer, but the case spurred me to more research.

Here, it seemed, was a theory. If Woolworth or Kress stores opened their doors to the public, why should courts not hold that they had offered to sell their merchandise and dispense the food at their lunch counters to anybody who showed up? Why not hold, in first-year, law-student terms, that they had made an offer that was "accepted" by the customer sitting at the lunch counter? As a matter of contract law, this seemed at least arguable. I was therefore pleased to find that Justice Douglas, concurring in the reversal of sit-in demonstrators' convictions for criminal mischief in *Lombard v. Louisiana,* had expressed a related thought. He, of course, was able to carry the idea into the realm of constitutional law.

Contract law is generally the business of state courts and legislatures. Contracts between private parties do not usually involve any constitutional command because those parties are not acting as agents of the state. The state and its agents are the only ones subject to constitutional commands. I found *Lombard* because in the searches that began with *Crawley v. Rex,* I was reading all the sit-in cases I could find. Those were the days before Westlaw and LEXIS. So I began by reading all the sit-in cases in the current Supreme Court reports, then followed the trail in the indices.

Justice Douglas had said that lunch counters are not unlike innkeepers and common carriers. In the old common law, those merchants had a duty to serve everyone. That is, their signage was to be regarded as an offer, which any traveler or customer would accept by demanding service. The Justice carried the analysis further, stating that the extensive public regulation of lunch counters and other places of public accommodation gave the state an obligation to see that all were served regardless of race. He wrote:

There is no constitutional way, as I see it, in which a State can license and supervise a business serving the public and endow it with the authority to manage that business on the basis of apartheid, which is foreign to our Constitution.

This expansive view of state action and the Constitution never gained a Supreme Court majority, although it certainly reflected the reality of property and contract rights. The institution of private property means nothing unless it is backed up with the state's power. In our property course, we were reading case after case defining English land law—the foundation of our present system. The device most often used to establish a land law precedent was the writ of trespass, in which someone claiming that "his" or "her" property had been invaded demanded that the royal court bring the trespasser into court and enter a binding order. Without that exercise of royal—that is, state—power, there would be no property rights worth talking about.

Having gone this far in a big hurry—I did not want the class discussion of offer and acceptance to pass by without having reached some conclusions—I tried to find other cases dealing with civil rights but based on contract principles. Even if there were not a constitutional issue here, perhaps state courts would interpret broadly the right to serve all comers. I could find only one helpful case, perhaps because I was limited to legal digests and indices. And I was, after all, less than a month in law school.

The case I found was *Johnson v. Sparrow*. The holder of a theatre ticket showed up and was denied admission to the performance because he was black. The court held that the theatre was obliged to serve everyone with a ticket, as a matter of contract law. You can quibble about the case because maybe the ticket is a contract, and thus not like simply putting up a sign advertising the performance. But I was proud of my find.

At the next contracts class, I was ready. In alphabetical order, Tigar sat next to Thompson, about five rows back from the front, and in the middle. The room held 100 or so law students. I raised my hand at the right moment and told Professor Jackson that there was authority for the view that advertising your goods or services was an offer. He demurred. I began to read from *Johnson*. The case was from Quebec and was in French. Jackson was impatient so I blurted out, "I am sorry to be going slowly. This case is in French and I am translating as I go along." The class burst into laughter. The story has dogged me, and in some versions has the case in Latin or Greek.

The point of it all—for me, anyway—is that this is how we are supposed to think about things to make the law serve people's needs—if we can. As Karl Renner pointed out, the categories of private law have proven capable of holding quite different content at different historical periods. Despite major changes in social systems, these categories have themselves remained fairly constant, if we consider them simply as forms of words. A contract requires an offer, an acceptance, and (in the common law system) some consideration for the bargain. However, the interpretation of these concepts may change radically with changes in social conditions. At different times, the permissible scope of contract law and the definitions of these elements have been quite different. So basic is this idea that the codifiers and compilers in the common law and civil law systems became quite adept at remaking old ideology to serve new purposes; there are traces of this technique from the tenth century onwards.

The law of property also fascinated me, as I followed the movement from customary rights to modern ideas of dominion over things. The expansion of categories of property—into the field of intangible rights such as intellectual property—engaged my attention. Later, in books and articles, I would pick up these themes. My interest owes a great deal to Professor Stefan Riesenfeld. He taught international and comparative law as well as property. He was fluent in several languages, and held degrees from German and American universities. His fluency, however, did not extend to English, in which language his accent remained, to the end of his life, nearly impenetrable. He had arrived in the United States at the outbreak of World War II, so I think his spoken English was a kind of mask he donned.

I had met Riesenfeld when I was an undergraduate, for he offered a political science department course in international law. We met in a cavernous lecture hall, and I struggled to hear and understand him. One key concept in international, as in municipal, law is estoppel. A sovereign state may be precluded from asserting a position by its own prior conduct that is inconsistent with what it now claims. It was a week's worth of lectures, however, before I understood the word estoppel as pronounced by Professor Riesenfeld. What I heard was "Gestapo," and I wondered how the hell the Gestapo had such influence over modern international law.

In law school, Riesenfeld began the property course by diagramming the forms of property on the blackboard. Over in the corner where intangible property rights were diagrammed, he used the classic common law term, incorporeal hereditaments. I copied the diagram faithfully. Years later, it came in handy. While arguing *United States v. London, Wallach and Chinn*, I was dealing with the intangible rights doctrine in the law of federal mail fraud. In mock surprise, Judge Altimari interjected, "What? Have you never heard of incorporeal hereditaments?"

My mind flashed back to Professor Riesenfeld's chart, but instead of giving him credit, I began by saying, "Judge Altimari, in the little town in Texas where I come from, people talk of little else." Then I answered what I considered the question must have been.

During that first year in law school, workers at the San Francisco hotels and automobile dealers were demanding better wages and working conditions, and an end to racially discriminatory hiring practices. My wife, Pam, was very active in the organizational work that led to large-scale protests. Sit-in demonstrations at the offending hotels and dealers led to arrests, and to larger picket lines in sympathy. Pam walked the lines one weekend, carrying a protest sign and joining in the chants and songs. She brought our year-old son Jon along with her. At day's end, she returned to our small apartment. Jon was in his high chair, fussing and carrying on despite our efforts to placate him with food, smiles, and little games. Finally, Pam, in desperation, snapped, "Jon, what do you *want?*" Jon smiled and called out, "Freedom!"

Pam's involvement in political action meant that I participated only vicariously, bound as I was to my books, classes, and typewriter. One first-year event did, however, call for action. Every first-year law student in California had to fill out a form stating his or her intention to practice law. (I say her, recognizing that there were just six women in our entering class of about 315.) The form contained many questions about one's background, and included a question something like this: "Are you now or have you ever been a member of, affiliated with, or supported any group or organization that advocates the overthrow of the government by force and violence?" In short, a loyalty oath, for one had to swear to the truth of one's answers.

When I saw this question, I had a sense of foreboding. I thought back to the Supreme Court's series of decisions rejecting First Amendment claims in the spring of 1961. Among those cases were two dealing with loyalty/security inquiries as a basis for denying membership in the bar. I knew that loyalty qualifications for bar membership were widespread, and that I would have to answer some questions about adherence to the Constitution to become a member of the bar. In *Konigsberg v. State Bar of California*, the Supreme Court held 5-4 that California was justified in refusing the petitioner bar membership because he refused to answer questions concerning membership in the Communist Party. Konigsberg had said that he did not belong to any organization that to his knowledge advocated violent overthrow of the government, and did not himself believe in violent overthrow. The same 5-4 majority upheld denial of bar membership in an Illinois case, *In re Anastaplo*.

Was there a difference between the questions that Konigsberg and Anastaplo declined to answer and the one posed by the California bar? If not, did I want to become a test case to try to reverse the results in those cases? I quickly answered the second question "no." I did not want to stand alone or virtually alone in this fight, and I would surely have done so by attacking two Supreme Court decisions head-on.

To the first question, I could answer "yes." The California bar question swept considerably more broadly than those upheld in *Konigsberg* and *Anastaplo*. If I could convince some of my classmates that this was so, then we might stage a fairly effective protest against the question and actually make the bar change the form. So I did some research.

I began with the nature of this question. One answered it under oath. I remembered Governor Goodwin Knight of California telling an audience why he supported loyalty oaths. "You can't prosecute people for being Communists—at least the Supreme Court has made it very hard to do that. But you can ask people if they are Communists, and make them swear they are not. And if they lie, you can send 'em to jail for perjury." In thinking about that comment, I deconstructed it.

I went to the library and found that despite Supreme Court decisions upholding some loyalty questions, there was a countercurrent of relevant law upon which I could argue that this particular question was improper. The case, *Cramp v. Board of Public Instruction*, was from that same year, 1961, that had seen the Supreme Court split 5 to 4 on a number of civil liberties issues—sometimes in one direction and sometimes in another. *Cramp* was, however, from December 1961, and was unanimous. A Florida statute required every teacher to swear under penalty of perjury that he or she had never given "aid, support, advice, counsel or influence to the Communist Party." The Court held that these terms were too vague to have any settled meaning and that the oath-taker was denied due process because he or she could not determine whether or not particular conduct fell within the oath's terms.

Armed with this case, I wrote a memo to the first-year students saying that I would not sign the bar form with this question on it, and inviting them to join me. Before I sent the memo, I made an appointment to see Professor Geoffrey Hazard, who taught civil procedure and seemed to be quite active in the California bar. I took volume 368 of the *U.S. Reports*, where *Cramp* was reported, with me. I put the bar form and the case before Professor Hazard. He read both of them, looked up, and to my surprise said: "You are absolutely right. What do you want me to do?" I said, "Help me."

Hazard was then and is now witty, articulate, and given to grand gestures. He picked up the telephone and dialed the general counsel of the California bar, whose name I no longer remember. Let's call him Bill.

"Bill, this is Geoff Hazard. I am sitting here with one of my students and we have been looking at this form you make all first-year law students sign." Hazard read the question aloud. "I also have a Supreme Court case right in front of me—unanimous, by the way—that holds that question cannot be asked. Denies due process, because it's too vague. Now, Bill, the question is, are you going to delete the question, or are we going to have a dispute about it? I have to support these students, because they are right about this one."

I was amazed at the alacrity and commitment of Hazard's response. One-third of the first-year students signed on to support deleting the question, and in due course the bar relented without more of a fight. This vignette showed why I came to law school. If you read the cases, worked hard to understand the issues, and either had courage or found a client who had it, you might find wonder-working power in all of this doctrine. My vision of law's power has been tempered in struggle over these past four decades, but I have not fallen utterly into cynicism.

I was not uniformly successful in my first-year courses. In the second semester, the criminal law professor was Rex Collings. I got a 72 in the course, a C, but still managed to average high enough to be first in the class. Given my later career in practice and teaching, it is sometimes hard to figure out why I resisted Professor Collings's message so strongly. I disliked him from the first day. He appeared unkempt. His stomach peered through the stretched-out front of his dress shirt. We began the course with cases on constitutional criminal procedure. In 1961, the Supreme Court had followed the lead of the California Supreme Court and held that if the police obtained evidence by an illegal search and seizure, that evidence could not be used by the prosecution at trial. The Supreme Court thus took a long step along the road to incorporating all the criminal procedure guarantees of the Bill of Rights into the due process clause of the Fourteenth Amendment. The older idea, that state courts had to provide only those basic rights essential to "ordered liberty," was being abandoned.

This change from ordered liberty to incorporation was to continue through the 1960s. There was another aspect to it. In March 1963, the Supreme Court had decided *Fay v. Noia*. The majority opinion, by Justice Brennan, expanded the rights of state prisoners to attack their convictions by seeking habeas corpus in federal court. A longer list of federally guaranteed rights meant more possible bases on which to challenge state convictions.

Professor Collings detested these developments. In his first lectures, he did not so much analyze as deprecate. He referred to the Supreme Court's current trend as "the spreading buttocks of due process." Rising (or descending) to this level of intellectual analysis, I wrote and posted on the bulletin board (anonymously, until now), a bit of doggerel:

Under the spreading buttocks see
The state policeman stand
His blunted anti-crime implement
Shriveled in his hand

And see the happy criminals
Frolic wild and free
Secure that incorporation
Has replaced ordered liberty

And see the law professor
He has buttocks too
"O bring us back the hose and rack
The sandbag and the screw!"

But look out, Rex, stand back, beware!
Due process' buttocks spread
And with eloquent judicial groaning
Shit, constitutionally, on your head

My criminal law experience was the only disappointment of law school. For sure, I was too often impatient, arrogant, or just plain wrong. But Boalt Hall had assembled professors who cared deeply about their respective fields. I tell students these days to take courses that deal with the basic elements of the legal system—business associations to learn about capital pooling, taxation to learn about this aspect of government policy, evidence, criminal procedure. And I believe also that in every law school there are professors whose courses are essential because of who they are and not for what they happen to be teaching. This search for teachers, today sometimes called mentors, helps explain the need for diversity in law school hiring, as the crop of entering law students becomes more diverse.

In law practice, I have gone back over and over to these basic course concepts, to see what the old rules can yield in terms of new results. And so I learned corporations from Professor Jennings, criminal procedure from Professor Caleb Foote, and tax from Adrian Kragen. Friedrich Kessler had come from Yale to visit, and afternoons at his home or in his jurisprudence class yielded insight. Kessler also taught contracts, and I used to go sit in on his first-year classes as a third-year student, just to listen to his views. Albert Ehrenzweig taught us conflict of laws and international law and, in the Austrian tradition, hosted his seminar at sherry hour in his home.

In those days, one made law review by being in the top 10 percent of the class. As a second-year law review member, in addition to hours spent checking cites, I had to write something that could be published. I wanted to do something that stretched my consciousness, but was acceptable to the editorial board. My eye fell upon California Code of Civil Procedure section 440, which provided:

> When cross-demands have existed between persons under such circumstances that, if one had brought an action against the other, a counterclaim could have been set up, the two demands shall be deemed compensated, so far as they equal each other, and neither can be deprived of the benefit thereof by the assignment or death of the other.

Our law school casebook said simply that this section appeared to derive from the French *compensation* or Roman law *compensatio*. A California case held that this extinction of demands operated to prevent the statute of limitations from extinguishing a claim. That is, if your creditor sued you, and there had at some past time existed an offsetting claim, you could plead the offset even if your claim would otherwise be time-barred.

I am not sure why this topic interested me, but it led me on a journey that has continued to this day. The very idea of counterclaims and cross-claims, as they are now called, or setoffs, which is the older word, is relatively recent in Anglo-American law. Permitting a defendant, or a co-defendant, to assert claims against other or opposite parties is regarded as one of the great innovations that took root in the mid-19th century with code pleading and continued with the 1937 adoption of the Federal Rules of Civil Procedure. This is, you might say, hardly the stuff of drama. It might look good on one's résumé, but was good for little else.

My journey began by looking at basic Roman law sources, then moving deeper into that material. I could not bear to read only those bits having to do with bilateral agreements and offsetting claims, so my gaze wandered farther. I devoured material on the origins and structure of Roman legal ideology, and glanced back at Greek procedure.

Then, I encountered a challenge. The French Civil Code, known as the Code Napoleon, did indeed have a section identical to California section 440. But how had the Roman law ideas been transmitted into French law, and how in turn had that very language found its way into a California code adopted in 1872?

There was no narrow answer to those questions. Rather, I had first to see how Roman law was generally received and refashioned in pre-revolutionary France and then reworked into the Code Napoleon. Then, taking a leap forward, I had to see how a new state, California, had decided on a thoroughgoing codification of its basic laws, and reached out rather eclectically to find relevant provisions. Only then, after the general questions were answered, could I look at this specific rule.

I won't retell the story in detail, for it is there in the *California Law Review*, but these researches accomplished something for me. Of course, as I plowed through medieval French and Latin sources in the rare book rooms, my research techniques sharpened. I visited the Bancroft Library at UC Berkeley to read letters and memoranda from California's early leaders. I found the only extant copy of one source at the San Francisco City Hall library. I had help, of course. David Daube, the Regius Professor visiting from Oxford, was there to guide me through the old books.

More deeply, this voyage confirmed for me that law is not news from nowhere. Rules are elements of legal ideology, but can be considered only as objects captured at a moment in time. The process by which rules come into being and change is far more important than content at any given time. I would spend three years in law school, from 1963 to 1966, and learn rules. I would pass the bar examination and perhaps impress, even astound, prospective employers. But now, with decades of distance, the rules have changed. I am no good to my clients, to the profession, or to the search for justice, unless I seek to see the process by which that change happened and is happening.

Having managed to keep my grades up, I was elected editor-in-chief of the *Law Review* at the end of my second year. That position generally went to the person who was first in the class. The appointment ought, therefore, to have been unremarkable. The *San Francisco Chronicle* nonetheless reported it on June 5, 1965, under the headline, "UC Honor for Former Firebrand." I was only 24, and already I was "former."

My second year in law school was 1964-65. That summer and fall, the Free Speech Movement (FSM) burst upon the Berkeley scene, leading in December 1964 to a sit-in demonstration in the university's administration building. FSM began during the summer of 1964, when young Republicans supporting William Scranton for the Republican presidential nomination were prevented from handing out their materials at the entrance to the UC Berkeley campus. I talk about the movement itself in more detail in Chapter 11. My law school studies kept me away from much of the FSM activity, but I kept up a lively discussion with student activists and with faculty members about the constitutional free speech issues.

By June 1965, the criminal cases arising from the FSM sit-in were still in the local courts, but the entire series of events called for the kind of analysis that the *Law Review* could provide. So we planned an issue devoted to free speech and due process on the campus, inviting law professors with widely differing views to contribute. A student, David Frohnmayer, who would later be attorney general of Oregon, contributed a thoughtful comment analyzing free speech rights on the university's premises. I wrote a long introduction, trying to put the Free Speech Movement into the historical perspective of student political action at Berkeley.

We were among the first to address the due process rights of university students who were subjected to school discipline. The Supreme Court's landmark decision on procedural fairness, *Goldberg v. Kelly*, was still five years away. A state university was, of course, bound to respect the Fourteenth Amendment due process clause. But that observation did not answer the question of what process would be due a student who had allegedly committed some infraction for which the university thought suspension or expulsion was appropriate.

One principal issue was factual reliability, which raised a number of specific questions. By what means could the student challenge the evidence against him or her? Cross-examination? The right to call witnesses? The right to compel attendance of witnesses subject to the university's control? The right to testify? If the student refused to testify, might an adverse inference be drawn from the refusal?

A second issue was the relationship between the potential harm to the student from an adverse decision and the amount of process required. That is, as the cases that came along in the 1970s explored in more detail, the process that will be due increases with the potential sanction. This tension between reliability and efficiency is key to due process analysis.

These issues were, in the 1960s debates, overshadowed by the university's institutional arguments concerning its relationship with students and its autonomy from official regulation. All universities in that era claimed to act in loco parentis, in the place of a student's parents. They claimed an obligation not only to provide an education but also to regulate a broad range of student conduct without any outside interference. The university was arguing, in essence, that it fulfilled a role somewhat like that of a tutor in Roman law.

The students, however, saw it differently. They argued that the university was a place where they should learn self-reliance, with the right to make their own choices and the obligation to accept corresponding consequences. They spoke of *lehrnfreiheit*—the freedom to learn—as a basic student right. Students have a vital role to play in shaping the university's mission.

Then there was the issue of fairness in student discipline. From the student point of view, the discipline mechanism should be conducted at arm's length, rather than by the university asserting that informal procedures best suited some relationship of tutelage. The students pointed out that the disagreements between students and the administration increased the risk that charges would be brought for the wrong reasons, or on flimsy evidence, and that the informality the university craved would therefore be a cover for suspect decision-making.

As a related matter, the university stressed its institutional independence. Here it was on solid historical ground. One core meaning of academic freedom is immunity from outside interference in internal governance. Detailed due process standards for university discipline would inevitably entail judicial review of discipline decisions and hence overt state control of the discipline process. Citing the example of South African universities in the time of apartheid, the university rejected adoption of any system that would permit that sort of control.

The students countered with their own theory of academic freedom, again using the concept of *lehrnfreiheit*—the freedom to learn. On this theory, the Berkeley students found faculty allies, in a pattern that was to be repeated on other campuses throughout the 1960s and 1970s. In the European universities where models of academic freedom were developed, the faculty governed and the students learned, or at least that was the model. At the University of California in 1964, as with all large universities, the faculty had some power by virtue of its academic senate. But the Cold War and the loyalty-security fights of the 1950s had firmly established political control of the university's major activities and mission. Government contracts were endemic in all departments; remember that the Berkeley physics department was a major resource for developing both the atomic and hydrogen bombs.

Professors as well as students felt constrained by political pressures originating from the legislature and governor's office, and transmitted through the chancellor of the Berkeley campus and the president of the UC system. The Free Speech Movement began, as I have noted, because a powerful California Republican politician, William Knowland, pressured the Berkeley chancellor to shut off speech by campus young Republicans.

The university had espoused a contradiction. To preserve the university's independence, students should not speak on "outside" issues. Independence from what? From the political pressures that would result if students spoke out on such issues. In fact, the administration was bowing to the conservative forces that had held sway from time to time in California politics. Thus, the university's claim to independence from outside control was ironic at best. That outside control already existed in overtly political form, and the question was whether it would be mediated by the intervention of judges applying constitutional principles.

In 1965, the landscape of this debate was not so thickly planted with argument as it was to become. The other editors and I felt that we were staking out new territory. In other articles and comments that academic year of 1965-66, authors explored direct action and the law, economic contracts in China, and other issues that we thought were on the edge.

That year also gave us all a chance to work with Jacobus ten Broek, my professor from undergraduate days. Professor ten Broek had founded the National Federation for the Blind, and was a leader of movements to protect the dignity of welfare recipients and the disabled. He proposed that the *Law Review* should host a conference on "the law of the poor," and publish the conference papers. Charles Reich of Yale had published his path-breaking 1964 essay, *The New Property*, arguing that welfare benefits and other social services were not government largesse but a form of entitlement that should be protected under the due process clause just like other property. Writers had noted the similarity between shabby treatment of welfare recipients and the vagrancy laws of Elizabethan England. We had come a long way from the Supreme Court's 1837 denunciation of the "moral pestilence of paupers." Hans Linde, then a professor and later a justice of the Oregon Supreme Court, had written of "freedom in the welfare state." President Lyndon Johnson had proposed his war on poverty.

In the end, this one *Law Review* issue totaled 690 pages and included more than two dozen articles. Of course, we had to raise money for the extra pages from foundations and by selling republication rights. The entire issue was then printed as a book, with the *Law Review* getting its share of the credit. For the two conference days, and throughout the painstaking editorial process, I felt I had a front-row seat at a new and energetic debate. The old image of a *laissez-faire* Constitution was giving way, and a new idea of people's rights was coming into being.

At Boalt Hall, constitutional law professor Robert O'Neill had clerked for Justice Brennan. Professor Robert Cole had clerked for Justice Minton, during Brennan's first year on the Court. Brennan apparently asked O'Neill for recommendations of students to be his law clerk. Being a Supreme Court law clerk is an honor. These days, most Justices choose their clerks from people already clerking on the federal courts of appeals. In 1965, this practice had not begun. Today, each Justice has four law clerks. In 1965, each Justice was allotted two clerks, although Justice William O. Douglas used one clerk position to hire an extra secretary, so he had only one clerk.

During my second year in law school, Cole and O'Neill asked me if I would be interested in clerking for Justice Brennan. Of course I said yes. Up to that time, only Justice Douglas would search for clerks among Boalt students, using the help of an Oakland lawyer who had clerked for him.

So in June 1965, just after the spring semester was over, Justice Brennan wrote me a letter: He said he "had just been talking with Professors Cole and O'Neill" and that they had said I would like to be his clerk. Would I accept that position?

The night I received the letter, I went home and celebrated. Jon was two and a half. Pam was six months pregnant with Katie. We had a cheap record player and had just bought an album of Clancy Brothers songs. My friend Al Katz came over, and we put on *Brennan on the Moor*, a fine Irish song about "a brave young highwayman, Willie Brennan was his name." We played it over and over, and drank cheap rum. I can remember a dreadful hangover the next day, which passed in time for Pam and me to go to San Francisco and spend more money for dinner at the Mark

Hopkins Hotel, with a view of the bay, than we would normally spend on food in two weeks.

The summer of 1965 had a magical quality. I was editor-in-chief of the *California Law Review*, I worked at the American Civil Liberties Union in San Francisco, and I attended a summer symposium on law and economics. In September, my daughter Kate was born. In the fall, when word of the clerkship got out, things heated up.

A local right-wing rag called *Tocsin*—the pronunciation says it all—attacked the clerkship appointment because of my leftist leanings and activities. As the school year went on, this attack was picked up and echoed. Fulton Lewis, Jr., a reactionary columnist, fulminated. Congressman Tuck, of the House Committee on Un-American Activities, put something in the *Congressional Record*. The redoubtable James J. Kilpatrick wrote an editorial, *The Lady and the Tigar*, for the Richmond, Virginia, *News-Leader*.

I was somewhat accustomed to this sort of thing. Yes, I had attended the Helsinki Youth Festival in the summer of 1962, and was a leader of the American contingent there. The Soviet Union participated in that event to a great extent. I was proud that, as a condition of American participation, all points of view were welcomed and there was no effort (as there had been at prior festivals) to suppress anti-Soviet speech. Indeed, I had opposed the House Committee on Un-American Activities. I had supported the Free Speech Movement—although being in law school precluded any active role because of the hours of study I was putting in.

Apparently, the Supreme Court was not accustomed to this sort of controversy, particularly when abetted by the FBI. During the spring of 1966, as my law school graduation approached, people in Washington were busy. The FBI was providing information to Justice Brennan about my real—and alleged—political activities. Justice Fortas was a conduit for some of this material.

One day in the late spring, as I was later told by a Brennan clerk for the 1965 term, Brennan walked into the office where his clerks were sitting and said, "The chief told me to fire Tigar." The chief was Chief Justice Earl Warren, who had been governor of California before President Eisenhower appointed him to the Court. Warren had no doubt been talking with Justice Fortas. According to Brennan, Warren was worried that the clerkship furor would influence the 1966 California gubernatorial election, perhaps helping the campaign of Ronald Reagan. Reagan won anyway by a large margin, of course.

With all of these pressures on him, Brennan called Professor O'Neill and said he needed to meet with me. By this time, it was early June. I had graduated from law school and had leased a house in Washington, D.C., on Capitol Hill. The house had been occupied by another Boalt graduate, Jerry Falk, who was clerking for Justice Douglas in the 1965 term.

Professor O'Neill told me to go to Washington that night, and arranged for an air ticket. I took the American Airlines "red-eye" from Los Angeles to Dulles Airport. I was afraid and alone. I can remember getting on that 707 jet plane at Los Angeles International Airport. My mother-in-law had given me a sleeping pill just in case I wanted to get some sleep on the six- or seven-hour flight. I don't think I took the pill. I do remember going into the airplane lavatory, in a cold sweat, sometime in the night, and throwing up.

I got to Dulles Airport about 6:00 A.M. The people-mover took the passengers to the Saarinen-designed terminal. In the men's room, I washed my face, brushed my teeth and shaved. I am sure I looked a mess. Then I took the shuttle bus to downtown Washington, 12th and K Streets. There I got a taxicab to the temporary home of Sanford Kadish, a Boalt criminal law professor who was on leave in Washington working on some project or other. We ate breakfast and waited until it was time to go to the Supreme Court for the 9:00 A.M. appointment with Justice Brennan. I am not sure, looking back, why Kadish went along. I don't think I asked him to. Maybe Professor O'Neill thought it was a good idea.

This was my first visit to the Supreme Court. It has more marble in and on it than any other public building in Washington. Justice Holmes had a major role in designing it. From any perspective, it is a dominant building. I walked up the broad front steps, and under the marble lintel that said "Equal Justice Under Law." Inside, the building was quiet. Kadish and I were taken back to Justice Brennan's chambers. As one entered, there sat Mary Fowler, the Justice's secretary for many years. Brennan's first wife, Marjorie, died in 1982, after a long battle with cancer. Justice Brennan and Mary Fowler were married in 1983 and the joy she brought to him added years to his life.

As we waited, Mary Fowler was handling telephone calls. Attorney General Ramsey Clark was on the line for the Justice. Ms. Fowler put the call through. In a few minutes, Justice Brennan came out and greeted us. That greeting, looking into your eyes as he shook your hand, was not only a trademark—it was emblematic. It seemed to symbolize his power on the Court—the Justice who strove relentlessly to put together five-person majorities to advance a humane and decent vision of the law.

I had read many Brennan opinions. Professor Hans Linde, visiting at Boalt Hall from Oregon, had sat in my *Law Review* office during the 1965-66 school year conducting a one-person seminar on the work of Justice Brennan.

Memory serves me ill, but I think on that morning we also ran into someone who was just finishing up clerking for Chief Justice Warren. This man was to become a Boalt professor, and he arrogantly criticized Brennan's search for good majorities as dishonorable, as though constitutional judging can take place without a context. Of course, English judges to this day deliver their opinions individually, one by one, and then one counts the votes for a result. Our Supreme Court started out working that way, but when John Marshall became Chief Justice in 1801, he began the practice of having an opinion "of the Court" authored by a Justice in the majority. This device was one mechanism by which Marshall imposed his own personality on the Court, but it also favored the development of consistent constitutional doctrine. In any case, I was privately contemptuous of this fellow's arrogance—he was a little too young to be putting on those airs.

Brennan asked us into his chambers. He sat behind his big desk and began to show me letters he had received, and communications about the congressional responses to news of my clerkship. I remember one card. The envelope was addressed in a spidery scrawl to Justice Brennan, The Supreme Court, Washington, D.C. Inside was a greeting card like you can buy at the drug store, with an embossed lacy pattern and the words "To Hope You'll Soon Be Well." Inside the card, the same spidery penmanship proclaimed, "You must be sick, you senile fool. You coddle the criminals and let the Reds take over America." I thought Brennan's bemusement at the card, and even his showing it to me, boded well for our interview.

But then things got serious. He reviewed the press stories and the rumblings in Congress. He reminded me that ever since the school desegregation decision, reactionaries in Congress pushed legislation every year to strip away the Court's power in civil rights cases. Such legislation would be of doubtful constitutionality, and perhaps that had helped to ensure that these efforts never succeeded. But the threat had been and remained real.

Then, the Justice turned to the alleged "facts." He went briefly over some of the public reports of my political activities. He then asked, "Weren't you at a Communist Party training camp in Paterson, New

Jersey?" The question startled me. It startled Professor Kadish, who was sitting beside me. Why did I think that I felt Kadish easing his chair away from mine, like the lawyer who begins to see his client in a new way?

I peered across the desk at the Justice. I tried to organize the thoughts that tumbled around in my head.

"First," I said, "I have never been in Paterson, New Jersey, and I have never been to a Communist Party training camp at any time or any place." Then, thinking that the call from Ramsey Clark might have had to do with me, I added, "This sounds like some of that FBI gossip that the Court addressed in the loyalty-security cases, such as *Greene v. McElroy.*"

"Second, your question raises a very serious issue for me. I have regarded my political views and associations as my private business, and I applauded the Court's decisions that agreed with this view. You probably know that when I was a first-year law student I led a campaign to take the unconstitutional loyalty oath off the California bar student application." I paused, trying to see where this was going.

"I don't mean any disrespect," I went on, "but I really admired what you did in your own Senate confirmation hearing, refusing to answer Senator McCarthy's questions."

I had gone too far. Kadish looked apoplectic. The Justice looked nettled, and he said: "It is important for you to remember that I am the Justice and you are the clerk. These issues are for me to decide."

"Well, sir," I began, "I think that the relationship of clerk and Justice is as confidential as could be imagined. If you lack confidence in me for any reason, you shouldn't hire me. I am willing to answer all of your questions, on any subject. I am just unwilling to make a public exhibition of my private views." I struggled to be calm, in visible control of all that was going on inside me. I needed to grab hold of my own moral compass, to forget how badly I wanted this job and how much losing it would mean to me and my career. And I needed to be very clear about what I was doing and why.

That seemed to mollify the Justice, but not Kadish. "All right," the Justice said, "I want you to write out your complete political history—everything you have done, every organization you have joined. I want you to call me Sunday morning—two days from now—and read it to me. Then, I'll decide what to do." He gave me a copy of AO Form 79, which all Court employees were to fill out. This included an oath to support the Constitution and other affirmations that I read and found consistent with the constitutional law principles I had been taught.

The interview was over. Kadish and I walked outside. He grumbled that I had not shown the Justice proper respect. I was hardly listening. I had work to do. I got to a phone and called Professor O'Neill. He told me to fly to San Francisco and come to the home of Professor Mike Heyman, another Boalt faculty member. Heyman had been a good friend; he was later to serve as chancellor of the University of California at Berkeley and then secretary of the Smithsonian Institution.

I flew to San Francisco. I was worn out, and I slept. Saturday morning, at Heyman's house, Professors Cole and O'Neill joined us. They began to echo some of Kadish's concerns that I had been less than respectful toward the Justice. I had a duty, they said, to the law school to make this thing work.

Of course I wanted the clerkship. It is as big an honor as a law student can get. Sure, there were several hundred other law students who could serve equally well—this clerkship business is a little like winning the lottery. My ego didn't let me dwell too long on this thought. But I was worried. I had told so many people I had the clerkship. I had rented a house in Washington, D.C. Our stuff was in boxes, ready to go into the VW bus. I felt pressured. I called my friend Al Bendich and asked him to join us. When he walked into the living room of the Heymans' Berkeley Hills home, he already radiated energy. Al listened to my story of events. He made a right fist and slammed into his left hand. "Well," he said, "let's get to first principles. We can't compromise the First Amendment right of private political belief. Right?" Cole, O'Neill and Heyman looked blank. Bendich continued. "Nothing in this situation asks Mike to change his beliefs, nor should it. Can't we agree on that?"

The others seemed to agree, drawn along by Al's infectious energy. I sat down at the typewriter and banged out a long letter, giving the information the Justice requested. At the end, I wrote that this was for his eyes only. I would, if asked by any public body—such as a congressional committee—for a political autobiography, decline on First Amendment grounds to provide it. I called my wife, told her what was going on, and read the letter to her.

Bendich and the professors read over the letter. I did not sleep well that Saturday night. Justice Brennan had given me his home number in Washington, D.C. I waited until it was 11:00 A.M. in Washington and called. Slowly, in cadences learned from my years as a radio announcer, I read the letter.

"That's it, sir," I concluded.

There was a silence. It seemed longer than it no doubt was. Then Brennan's voice, chipper and strong, "You're my clerk!"

"Thank you, sir," I said, and hung up the phone. I don't remember if I wept then with relief, or later and alone.

Back at my in-laws' house in Sherman Oaks, we packed up our VW bus for the trip to Washington. I bought the bus in September 1965, when Katie was born and our old Mercury died. It was as basic as you could get—the Kombi model, without insulation or floor mats—a metal box. I bought carpet and made a floor liner. I installed an insulated headliner. Inside went Jon, who was three and a half, and Katie, who was nine months old, and most of our stuff. We sent some boxes on to the Supreme Court in Washington.

Heading east, I remember stopping at public campgrounds every night, until we reached Lawrence, Kansas. Former neighbors from Berkeley were living there while studying physics at the University of Kansas. Phone messages awaited us. Justice Brennan's office had called. He was in California visiting friends but would return to Washington within days. Hurry up and get to Washington. Something has come up.

We had planned to take more time on the trip, so that we would arrive in Washington just as our lease began on the house we had rented at 120 7th St., S.E. But we hurried, arriving in Washington with about $10 in our pockets and one credit card—a Wilshire Oil Company card that would be accepted at Holiday Inn and Gulf Oil stations. We checked into the Holiday Inn on North Capitol Street. That first morning at breakfast, a woman was mugged in the parking lot and staggered into the dining room, blood streaming from cuts on her forehead.

I went to the Court. Justice Brennan was grave. "I have been thinking this over. I want your permission to give out your personal political history to anybody I choose. That will be a condition of your employment. Take a day or so to think about this."

I didn't know quite what to say or do. Some of the 1965 term clerks were anxious to help. Jerry Falk was clerking for Justice Douglas, who was in Goose Prairie, Washington, where he spent the summers. Justice Douglas told Jerry that he could use the Douglas chambers as a meeting place on this issue. "I heard about this," Douglas had said. "People sent me letters about it. Obviously cranks. I ignored them." From the other clerks, I learned of the pressures under which Brennan was operating.

Brennan was under pressure from Warren because of California politics. But the main pressure seemed to come from the FBI, encouraged by Justice Fortas, who maintained close ties to the Johnson White House while he was on the Court. The FBI reports were overblown, largely inaccurate, the results of the bureau's efforts to discredit the American left. I was a small player in this drama, but the FBI was busy creating files on many civil rights leaders and anti-war activists. Also, I think Brennan feared that if he expended political capital to keep me as his clerk, he might be less able to forge majorities for cases before the Court.

The next morning, about 10:00 A.M., I answered the phone in our motel room. "One moment, please, Justice Brennan calling." I assume it was Mary Fowler, putting the call through. "Mike, this is Justice Brennan. I have been thinking this thing over. I am sorry, but no matter what you decide about your statement, we can't go through with this. I am withdrawing the clerkship."

"Yes, sir. Thank you for calling." I hung up the phone. OK, there it was. One off-brand credit card, ten bucks, a VW bus not yet paid for. Married, two kids. A lease on a house, with the rent soon due. I could borrow some from my parents and my in-laws, but the immediate future did not look too good.

I spent the next two weeks looking for work. My friend John Griffiths, who was clerking for Justice Fortas, arranged interviews at Yale Law School. I could teach there on a one-year contract. As word trickled out, I got letters from law firms in California, renewing job offers that I had declined because of the clerkship.

My friend Dick Prosten, whom I had met in connection with the youth festival, offered a place to stay. Dick worked at the AFL-CIO headquarters in downtown Washington, and had a one-bedroom apartment on Vermont Avenue. He and his wife opened their doors to the four of us for the 10 days until our house was ready. For this loving support, I have never properly thanked them.

Professor Kadish called. He wanted to help me find work, so he arranged an interview at Shea & Gardner, then, as now, a top law firm in Washington. I decided instead to seek a job with Edward Bennett Williams; that story is in Chapter 3.

While this was going on, the story of my clerkship hit the front page of the *Washington Post*. Jack McKenzie, the *Post*'s Supreme Court reporter, is a great reporter and today a good friend. I had decided that I would not say a word to the press about any of these events. Indeed, I kept silent for years about it all. But McKenzie happened upon the story. He was in the Supreme Court cafeteria and saw Abe Sofaer, a recent law school graduate. Sofaer said he would be clerking for Justice Brennan. McKenzie asked what happened to Sofaer's clerkship with Judge J. Skelly

Wright of the U.S. Court of Appeals for the District of Columbia. "Well, Brennan had a sudden vacancy so he asked Wright if I could work for him," Sofaer reported.

McKenzie then went around the building and put the story together. His *Washington Post* article led to several phone calls. One morning, I answered the phone and a voice said, "Michael Tigar, this is Ralph Nader."

"Sure," I said, "and how is your Chevy Corvair? Really, who is this?"

"I am Ralph Nader. I want to say I think you have been treated shabbily. And I want to meet you."

I agreed to meet this person the next morning at the Dupont Plaza hotel for coffee. He was late, and I began to think that I had been hoodwinked. But Nader eventually arrived, and we talked about politics and Washington and my admiration for his work.

The Brennan affair was not really closed. Andrew Kopkind wrote a *New Republic* article about it. When Bob Woodward and Scott Armstrong were writing their book on the Court, they came to see me. My FBI file, which I got in much-edited form under the Freedom of Information Act, contains several snide and self-congratulatory passages about my losing the clerkship. From a FOIA request to military intelligence, I got a report that was not declassified until 1978. It reported on my pending appointment, in 1969, to the UCLA law faculty, and looked back at the Brennan episode. The intelligence report, from the Sixth Army HQ, was titled, "Oliver!"

> Oliver Twist won the awed admiration of his fellow orphans when he had the supreme audacity to take his empty porridge bowl back to ask for more. Oliver, apparently, has his counterpart among our young radicals. In 1966, Michael TIGAR was a candidate for the post of law clerk to U.S. Supreme Court Justice William J. Brennan, Jr. The appointment fell through when Brennan was apprised of TIGAR's left-wing background.

The report then cites an earlier dispatch, which I never received, titled, "Tigar in the Courts—Almost" and dated July 1966. The 1969 report concluded:

> TIGAR may still be as radical as he ever was, but even if his political position has changed, he may find that his widely publicized left-wing activities as a young man will plague him far into the future. This is a bitter lesson many of today's young radicals may have to learn.

After I lost the Brennan job, friends and acquaintances, and people I did not even know, wrote to me. I rejected calls to make some sort of public stink about it. I had a new job and was moving into work I wanted to do. I wrote a letter on July 28, 1966, and sent copies to everyone who had written or called. I tried to make three points.

First, I said, please don't mount a campaign. I did not want my political views to become an issue. "I would like to retain my personal satisfaction at having kept the political faith in the sense of not having disclosures of [my political views and associations]." Second, I said, "Justice Brennan is not an evil man." After all, he had in his own career stood up to personal and political attacks, and had championed great constitutional causes. The episode was more about the political climate than about Justice Brennan. "The oaths, disclosures under pressure, security apparatus, and suspicion and hatred of the McCarthy heyday are still with us. The lesson of this affair is that we must be cognizant of forces which great men find they must bow to, and not that we must think men small who bow to these forces." Finally, I said that I continued to feel an obligation to the Justice. "He has not," I wrote, "by word or deed intimated that my conduct is other than honorable."

The next year, after I had begun work at the Williams firm, I got a letter from Justice Douglas's chambers, inviting me to submit a résumé for consideration as Douglas's law clerk. I called his secretary, Nan Aull, whom I had met during the Brennan episode. She told me that Justice Douglas wanted to make things right for me. I thought deeply about this, and talked it over with Ed Williams. I decided that my legal career was well under way, and that I did not want to relive any of what had happened.

Nine years later, in 1976, the Court decided a very bad First Amendment case, *Greer v. Spock*, restricting freedom of expression in and near military bases. Justice Brennan dissented. I had already argued three cases before the Court and had won them all. But Brennan's dissent had an edge of disappointment to it. I felt that I should not write to Brennan about my feelings because I had a case up there that term. Maybe I hesitated because I did not know what to expect in reply. In June 1977, however, I summoned my courage and wrote him a letter. I said I thought his opinions were compelling and wondered if he was discouraged by the conservative turn the Court had taken in several cases.

I was surprised to get a two-page handwritten reply two weeks later:

Dear Mike

Your most generous note of July 7 has just reached me here at Nantucket. I'm deeply touched that you wrote me—far more than I can say. I confess to periods of discouragement at times but they quickly pass—particularly when views of those I respect express their support.

When the next Term is underway, won't you telephone me and come in for lunch in Chambers. I've followed your progress with keen interest and would like to hear much more.

With warmest personal regards & again my grateful thanks.
    Sincerely,
    (signed) Wm. J. Brennan, Jr.

I took him up on the invitation and visited in early 1978. I had just started my own firm with Sam Buffone, and we had taken on the case of a young Vietnamese accused of espionage. Fourth Amendment issues were already evident, and the Justice commented that the case seemed headed for the Supreme Court. So we dropped the subject. We sat in chambers, ate lunch, and talked. Brennan was affable and outgoing, seeking news of my doings and commenting on some of the certiorari petitions before the Court. Speaking of *Gelbard v. United States*, which I had argued in 1972, he joked: "You don't know what trouble I had getting five votes in that case. I thought Byron [White] would never see it." Cordial as it was, the conversation seemed a little artificial, for we never broached the subject of the clerkship.

I saw the Justice again in the mid-1980s at a judicial conference, and then several times more in the late 1980s. We would talk over issues before the Court, and he would inquire about what I was doing and about my family. When he was preparing his speech for the dedication of the Edward Bennett Williams Library at Georgetown Law School, he wrote and asked me to come see him. He had Ed's Court argument transcripts spread out on his desk, and we shared our vision of Ed's power and intellect as an advocate. I was honored to have a role in shaping the Justice's remarks. But again, no talk of the clerkship.

At one of those visits, I took a mild initiative. I asked him for an autographed picture of himself. He discovered there were no photos in chambers, so he promised to send one. The letter with it read:

February 2, 1989

Dear Mike:

I'm much flattered that you should want the enclosed. It goes with my best wishes for your continued magnificent success. Please drop in again very soon, even at the cost of that delightful cuisine.

All the best.
Sincerely,
(Signed) WJB, Jr.

The picture was inscribed "To Michael Tigar, whose tireless striving for justice stretches his arms towards perfection." The cuisine was the soup and sandwiches served in chambers by the Supreme Court cafeteria.

Finally, I decided on a somewhat more direct approach. I knew that Justice Brennan had selected Steven Wermeil to write his biography, and had given Steve unprecedented access to his papers, as well as spending many hours in conversation with him. Steve, at the Justice's suggestion, contacted me to ask what I remembered. I gathered that the entire 1966 episode was still in Brennan's mind, an impression I had first gained several years before as people told me of things he had said.

So in the fall of 1990, after Brennan had retired from the Court, I wrote a letter. I said simply that my respect for him and his work had grown throughout the years, and I admired his contribution to the cause of human dignity and freedom. I hoped that nothing I had done or said during that 1966 period had seemed to him improper. He wrote back:

November 19, 1990

Dear Mike:

That morning in June 1966 is a date I shall never forget. I've often wondered whether I overreacted. I must say in all candor that, given the circumstances, I probably did. It's been you who have made it possible for me to justify myself. I hope we shall always remain the friends we have become.

All the best.
Sincerely,
(signed) Bill

I saw him again shortly before he died, at a conference on the death penalty, clear of vision and speech though in a wheelchair, and passionate for justice to the end.

Notes

1. My law review comment is *Automatic Extinction of Cross-Demands: Compensation From Rome To California,* 53 CAL. L. REV. 224 (1965).

2. The case where Judge Altimari interrupted is *United States v. Wallach,* 935 F.2d 445 (2d Cir. 1991).

3. The loyalty-security issues are chronicled in*, e.g., Cramp v. Board of Public Instruction of Orange County, Florida,* 368 U.S. 278 (1961), *Greene v. McElroy,* 360 U.S. 474 (1959), *In re George Anastaplo,* 366 U.S. 82 (1961), *Konigsberg v. State Bar of California,* 366 U.S. 36 (1961). *See also* Schware v. Board of Bar Examiners, 353 U.S. 232 (1957). For a review of the cases and other literature, *see generally* Thomas I. Emerson, *The System of Freedom of Expression* 176-91 (New York: Random House, 1970).

4. In later years, my interest in the law of property is reflected in *Law and the Rise of Capitalism* (New York: Monthly Review Press (new ed. 2000), and in the TEXAS LAW REVIEW property article cited in the Notes to the Prologue.

5. *Rex v. Crawley,* [1909] Transvaal 1105, is discussed in my contracts casebook, Friedrich Kessler & Malcolm Sharp, *Contracts: Cases & Materials* 101 (1st ed. 1953).

6. Fay v. Noia, 372 U.S. 391 (1963).

7. Lombard v. Louisiana, 373 U.S. 267 (1963). *See* Douglas, J., concurring, 373 U.S. at 274-83. A recent state action case, *Brentwood Academy v. Tennessee Secondary School Athletic Association,* 531 U.S. 288 (Feb. 20, 2001), contains some analysis that Justice Douglas would find congenial, as the Court uses the idea of "entwinement" between state and private actors.

8. I wrote on academic freedom in THE OXFORD COMPANION TO THE SUPREME COURT OF THE UNITED STATES 7-8 (New York: Oxford Univ. Press, 1992).

9. Charles A. Reich, *The New Property,* 73 YALE L.J. 733 (1964). *See also* Charles A. Reich, *Individual Rights and Social Welfare: The Emerging Legal Issues,* 74 YALE L.J. 1245 (1965). Hans A. Linde, *Justice Douglas on Freedom in the Welfare State: Constitutional Rights in the Public Sector,* 39 WASH. L. REV. 4 (1964).

10. *The Law of the Poor* (ten Broek and editors of CALIFORNIA LAW REVIEW, eds.) (San Francisco: Chandler Publishing Co., 1966). More on the

Brennan story appears in Alexander Charns, CLOAK & GAVEL 63-64 (1992). *See also* Kim Eisler, A JUSTICE FOR ALL 198-203, 247 (1993); Robert Woodward & Scott Armstrong, THE BRETHREN 77 (New York: Simon and Shuster, 1979). The entire episode was also written up in the WASHINGTON POST and in an article by Andrew Kopkind in the NEW REPUBLIC, Aug. 27, 1966, p. 21, under the title *Brennan v. Tigar.*

11.   Greer v. Spock, 424 U.S. 828 (1976). My case that year was *Lefkowitz v. Cunningham*, 431 U.S. 801 (1977).

12.   The Supreme Court case referring to the "moral pestilence of paupers" is *The Mayor, Aldermen and Commonalty of the City of New York v. George Miln*, 36 U.S. 102 (1837).

Chapter 3
WASHINGTON— UNEMPLOYMENT COMPENSATION

So there I was in the summer of 1966 without a job. I wanted to practice law, to try cases, to do work that made a difference. I was seeing the Supreme Court set out a sharper understanding of the Bill of Rights— free speech, free press, rights of the accused, the right of privacy. Being a lawyer gave you a ticket to that arena—as participant and not spectator. How could I gain entry, and still support my family?

I had already missed the deadline for the summer 1966 bar examination—I had thought there would be time for that after my clerkship. So I was not worth quite what a lawyer who had taken the bar exam was worth.

In my third year of law school, I had written a letter to Edward Bennett Williams, saying that I was clerking for Justice Brennan and would like to meet him and perhaps interview with his law firm when I was in Washington. I don't think he replied. Williams was a distant but persuasive ideal. He had represented Frank Costello, Senator Joe McCarthy, James Hoffa (in the first trial, when Hoffa was acquitted), Congressman Adam Clayton Powell, and other famous figures. More important, he had written widely and wisely about the lawyer's obligation to represent clients, and the clients' right to competent and aggressive representation. He had argued leading constitutional cases before the Supreme Court.

I confessed my interest in Williams to Professor Kadish—who had made his reputation writing and teaching about criminal law. We were sitting one summer day at an outdoor restaurant eating Italian food. His answer surprised me, and put a crimp in our relationship for the ensuing years. "You don't want to work for Williams," he said. "He represents criminals. You want to be in a law firm like Shea & Gardner where all the lawyers are law review editors just like you." I did not mention that Williams had graduated at the top of his class, and had taught criminal law at Georgetown. I simply said that I thought that the Williams firm offered a chance to do what I found most important.

Funny, isn't it, in how many different ways you can define yourself. The definition, and its perspective, can lead to quite different approaches to life. Yes, I had been first in the class and editor-in-chief. But I did not define myself by these things—I strove for them to have a better chance at doing what I really wanted to do. They were means to achieve a self-definition. The work I did to get these honors, and what I learned along the way, better equipped me to serve in the way I wanted to. I did not want to be co-opted into a world of law practice that did not represent the values and priorities I had struggled so hard to define.

One of my Boalt professors had been a law clerk at Williams's firm, and he called to set up an appointment for me. The firm was then Williams & Wadden, with 10 lawyers on one and one-half floors of the old Hill Building. I came into this huge office, where Williams sat behind the desk. He was over six feet tall, with brown hair that hung loosely over one side of his forehead. He had one of the most expressive and mobile faces I have ever seen. He stood and extended his hand. We sat.

"What can I do for you?" he asked.

"Well, sir, I sent you a letter and a résumé last year, and I find myself looking for a job sooner than I thought."

"A letter?" He shouted to his secretary, "Mrs. Keats, did we get a letter from Mr. Tigar?" She found the letter. Williams glanced at it.

"What happened?"

I told him the story of my clerkship—winning it and losing it. He looked at me with an expression that I imagined he used on witnesses.

"Bill Brennan is one of my best friends. He wouldn't do something like that."

"His telephone number is EXecutive 3-1640. You could call him and ask him what happened."

"Maybe I will." Another pause, while Ed looked out the window; later I would know this as a trademark gesture. "I wasn't thinking of hiring anybody."

The interview was not going well, it seemed to me. "Well then, sir, if you are not hiring then I guess you shouldn't hire anybody. I am not seeking charity. I am not the United Way." A voice inside told me I was getting defensive and a little arrogant. OK, more than a little.

I continued. "I want to work for you. My résumé is there. I think I am qualified. I respect what you do and have for a long time. That's why I'm here."

Williams nodded. "Let me think about it. Does Mrs. Keats have your number? No? Leave it with her on the way out." He came around the desk and we shook hands.

I walked back to the Prostens' apartment, about six blocks. I was talking to Pam about the interview when the telephone rang. "Mr. Tigar, this is Lillian Keats. One moment, please, for Mr. Williams."

"Mike, OK. If you want a job, you've got it. Show up Monday morning at 9 o'clock. Mrs. Keats will have an office for you. I don't know what we'll pay you, but I'll call over to Covington & Burling and whatever they pay is probably about right. Is that OK with you?"

"Yes, sir."

"See you Monday."

I no longer remember what day of the week this was. It was not Friday, I think. Somehow, the vigilant Jack McKenzie found out that Williams had hired me. Maybe Brennan told him, off the record. Since Williams was best friends with *Post* reporters, maybe the story got out that way. Whatever day it was, Jack McKenzie's *Post* article about the clerkship appeared before I showed up for work. The *Post* had a story, complete with an old picture, titled "Law Firm Hires Rejected Clerk." An old man in Pennsylvania with a legal problem read the story and called Williams over the weekend. When I came in on Monday, I had a case to work on.

The case was an administrative proceeding, as I recall it, and it had come to Williams because the client had read about my hiring and admired Williams for it. I remember taking my family along to the Pennsylvania horse country to do the initial client interviews. Ed's secretary had made sure we had a nice motel room in which I could spend the spare time with my wife and children.

In this first "real" case, I had to learn how trotting horses are bred. Horse semen cannot be, or is not (I forget), frozen like bull semen. Artificial insemination of horses requires that a trained person palpate the mare's ovaries to check ovulation. This is done anally, wearing a long latex gauntlet. If the mare is ready, then stallion semen is collected in a large condom. And so on.

I returned from out of town, and Mrs. Keats had furnished my office and hired a secretary from the local Catholic secretarial school. I dictated my notes. My secretary sat at her desk with earphones on, becoming more and more agitated as she listened to my description of the marvels of horse conception. About halfway through the tape, she rose from her desk, collected her belongings, and went upstairs to Mrs. Keats's office to resign. I never knew if it was horse sex or the idea of condoms that horrified her.

Ed Williams was my mentor and friend. The other lawyers in that office shared their time and talent. Once I returned from working on the horse case, I found case files and research requests on my desk that took me from arcane evidence points to Fourth Amendment theory, to the basics of criminal procedure.

The term mentor has taken on many shades of meaning. One of Ed's biographers called some of us who came through the law firm his surrogate sons, and surely he treated a handful of us young male lawyers with all the love and protective instinct of a good father. But the image does not quite capture the relationship, except perhaps in one way. Ed had these special ties to young male lawyers. He never dealt with female lawyers as fully his equals—with one notable exception, Agnes Ann Neill. Agnes worked with Ed in the years before I came to the firm. When Ed's first wife, Dorothy Guider Williams, died, Ed married Agnes. She stopped practicing law, and I never saw her participate in the firm's work. Their relationship was no doubt troubled in many ways that we never saw, but it was for him an anchor and comfort and defining experience of which we could only glimpse and in which we were permitted to share only at its edges.

When I came to the firm, I was the 10th lawyer. Two of those already there were Judith Coleman Richards, later to marry Bob Hope's son Tony, and Barbara A. Babcock. I spent a lot of time with Judy and Barbara. They shared their knowledge of law and of Ed's way of practice. Not too long after I arrived, Barbara left to join and then to lead the Public Defender Service, and today she teaches at Stanford Law School. Judy moved to Los Angeles when she married. Ed could not see either of these good lawyers in the same way that he did the males. They were not part of the same inner circle.

Ed's own idea of our relationship is captured in a series of pictures and letters. On my wall are two reproductions of courtroom sketches—one of the Bobby Baker trial in 1967, and the other from the John Connally trial of 1975. Ed inscribed the first one "The Baptism of Michael E. Tigar, from his Godfather Edward Bennett Williams," and the second "The Graduation of Michael E. Tigar, from his Godfather Edward Bennett Williams." In all the years from 1966 to Ed's death in 1988, I have the occasional note from him, sometimes signed "Goombah," invoking the Italian godfather image.

What was it to be in Ed's circle in that way? First was the law. It was all about doing the law, about living its challenges and its stories—for both were important. It is not simply some Irish Catholic eccentricity that Ed had a story for every case, for every situation in every case. He was trained in classical rhetoric and knew the importance of story. He had tried case after case as a young lawyer, focusing on the story in every one. He was a raconteur and he hung out with great storytellers like Ben Bradlee of *The Washington Post* and humorist Art Buchwald. The law's challenge was and is to put the story into a mold, the form of which was dictated by legal rules—either ones that now existed or that you would argue must be recognized.

The case of Bobby Baker was full of stories and challenges. Robert G. Baker had been secretary to Senate Majority Leader Lyndon Johnson during the 1950s and 1960s, when Johnson was among the most powerful men in America. Baker helped Johnson manage the political deals that kept Democrats in the majority and Johnson's legislative program on track. Johnson did not invite Baker to share in his vice-presidential duties; nor did Baker join the White House staff when LBJ became President. I have often wondered what mental reservation LBJ had that led him to trust others to help him put his key programs through Congress in those later days.

There was no question, though, that Johnson trusted Baker and that Baker in turn exercised great power, albeit mostly vicariously. So when in 1965 Baker's financial dealings became a major Washington scandal, the Baker story was front-page news for months. An ambitious set of federal prosecutors, whom neither LBJ nor Attorney General Nicholas Katzenbach restrained, pored over Baker's financial records and finally came up with a nine-count indictment. The principal charges were two. First, that Baker had collected more than $100,000 in political contributions from California savings and loan executives, ostensibly for Democratic Senate candidates, and then kept the money while not paying taxes on it. Second, that Baker had used his political power to solicit monthly retainers from people seeking political favors, but had routed the money through a lawyer named Wayne Bromley and had therefore not properly reported it on his tax returns—even though he did pay tax on every dollar of it. The government did not allege that Baker had done anything improper in exchange for the money, or that the money was for the performance of any official duty. Its whole emphasis was on the means by which he had reported it. Then, there were unrelated charges that for two successive years Baker had underpaid his federal income tax by a few thousand dollars. The variety of charges stretching over years was a central, though ultimately unsuccessful, focus of the defense attack, for it seemed to us that a severance of the case into its constituent parts would have been fairer.

By the time I arrived at the firm, the pretrial motions had been filed. One significant issue was electronic surveillance. There was no federal statute authorizing bugging and tapping until 1968, but that had not deterred the FBI and Internal Revenue Service from listening to people's private conversations. Baker had wandered into three listening zones. He was picked up on an embassy tap because of some Latin American business dealings, but nothing of significance had been heard. Then, he had visited Las Vegas. The FBI, with authorization from Attorney General Robert Kennedy, had targeted alleged Mob figures in the casino industry, and installed taps on their telephones and bugs in their living and working quarters. A tap intercepted phone calls. A bug was a microphone that picked up conversations in a particular room. Indeed, the firm was already litigating civil suits based on the Vegas surveillance.

Baker was also a friend of a powerful Washington lobbyist named Fred Black, who had a suite at the Sheraton-Carlton hotel near the White House. The FBI rented the adjacent suite and drilled a hole in the baseboard. It put a spike mike through the hole and picked up all the noises in the Black suite. Agents worked shifts and recorded everything, then FBI clerks transcribed the tapes.

Baker did not figure greatly on the Las Vegas tapes, but had often used the Fred Black suite. Because he was so often a guest, he unquestionably had legal standing to challenge the unlawful surveillance, which was done without a warrant. The Black tapes contained not only political discussions, but also an assortment of other sounds including coition and post-coital conversation.

Williams called me to his office one morning and explained what I was to do about the Baker case. "Counts three through seven of the indictment are in the alternative," he began, telling me what I already knew. "They charge larceny and larceny after trust for the same two sets of funds that Baker got from the savings and loan executives.

"Larceny," he continued, "consists of a trespassory taking and carrying away with the intent permanently to deprive the owner of possession; that is, caption, asportation, and animus furandi." This description of the elements was not showing off; it was Ed's methodology for every claim or defense in litigation. As I learned, it was his style for every element of every case. When we talked about a cross-examination he was outlining, he would rehearse aloud the points at which leading questions were important. He would divide the examination into its parts: "I start by clearing away the underbrush. Short, focused questions to make sure we have the basic facts, such as when he came to Washington, where he stayed, whom he met. Keep the documents in front of him. Put a leash on him. Get him under control. Then, in the second part, I can swing a little wider, give him a little room." Or, discussing a Supreme Court argument, he would set out the main points in the order he was to make them by way of introduction, then go on to plot the structure of the argument as a whole.

Ed Williams was, in short, the most self-aware and disciplined advocate I have ever known. He talked to us with a double purpose. We were expected to contribute ideas and even to challenge his approach, leading to changes and refinements. Ed even remembered to note the ethical limits on what an advocate could do in given circumstances. And we, his acolytes, had the benefit of the best practical legal education that we could possibly have.

This method, which is the best use of the term mentoring, is too often missing in litigation offices and firms, public and private. Young lawyers have both too much and too little responsibility. They have too little because they are assigned only pieces of cases, such as a motion to write, discovery to draft, a memorandum to prepare for the litigating partner's attention. Young lawyers used in that way do not see the case as a whole, and therefore they may fail to see the relationship between their work and the overall goal.

By the same token, the lawyer doing piecework has too much responsibility, in the sense that memoranda or discovery or motions done without knowing the whole case are likely to be overdone, just to make sure one is not missing anything. The young lawyer wants to make sure it is all in there, and thus overbills the case, even to the point of arguable misconduct. In my observation, much of the discovery and motions practice excess in litigation is caused by litigation partners permitting young lawyers' work product to pass into the system unedited.

I can remember several years ago working with a major law firm on a case. I thought one of the associates did superb paper work but lacked litigation judgment, even though he had been practicing for several years. When I asked the firm's senior partner about this, he indignantly replied, "What do you mean, lacks judgment? Why, he billed 3,000 hours last year!" My only reply was that this seemed to prove my point. In every case for which I have ever been lead counsel, I have followed Ed's example and seen that all the lawyers, paralegals, and investigators on the case meet together so that everybody sees the whole picture.

For the Baker case, I had three main jobs. First, I was to help Peter Taft, who had been with the firm several years, research the law and facts about unlawful electronic surveillance. Second, Ed gave me primary responsibility for running down every fact concerning Baker's alleged underreporting of income on count one, income tax evasion. Third, I was to try and corroborate Baker's story about what he did with the money that the California savings and loan executives had given him.

The electronic surveillance issues began my introduction to an issue that cropped up again and again in later years, as I describe in Chapter 8. The first time I saw Ed at work was during Baker pretrial motions on electronic surveillance. The first witness was an FBI clerk who had been assigned to monitor the spike mike at the Sheraton-Carlton hotel. Ed stood near the end of the empty jury box and began to put questions. As he asked each question, he took a small step forward until he was looming over the witness. The prosecutor objected, "Mr. Williams is intimidating the witness." Judge Gasch asked the witness, "Is he too close?" In a surprised and strangled voice that revealed his nervousness, the witness replied, "Well, if he could move back a little. . . . "

Ed moved back by stepping backwards a bit at a time with each of his next questions. How did he know what was behind him, I asked myself. He had, in this as in all courtrooms, memorized the space so that his decisions to place himself within it were deliberate but seemingly natural.

The Baker case showed me the value of meticulous research, and gave me an introduction to the world of FBI illegal activity. From that introduction, I have become involved in dozens of cases involving unlawful electronic surveillance, each time returning to those lessons. Indeed, I continued to be involved in the Baker case even after I left the firm in 1969 to teach at UCLA. Ed called me in Los Angeles and asked me to argue Baker's second appeal, which dealt entirely with the fruits of FBI bugging and tapping.

There were other lessons in the case. Brilliant tax lawyer Boris Kostelanetz was Ed's co-counsel. Their styles were so different that I think Ed never again would let anyone share the limelight in that way. At one point in the trial, Boris put his partner, Jules Ritholz, on the stand for half a day to discuss the legal theory that Baker had used on his tax return. Ritholz's testimony was complicated and something less than riveting. The direct examination seemed like a conference in Boris's office rather than an effort to reach a middle-class District of Columbia jury. Some of the testimony dealt with capital gains versus ordinary income.

The next morning, the marshal in charge of the jury, which was sequestered, told us that on leaving court one juror had said to another, "Who is that Captain Gaines they're talking about?" And the other replied, "He's going to testify tomorrow."

The atmosphere in the Williams office consumed me. We worked a half day on Saturdays, followed by lunch at Duke Zeibert's restaurant if Ed was in town. The corner table in Duke's front dining room, or sometimes a big table in the back, were the gathering places of Williams's salon. He had the most eclectic coterie of drinking and dining friends of any person I ever knew. His ability to swap stories with all of them was one measure of his success with juries. Some weekends, Washington Redskins quarterback Sonny Jurgensen would be at lunch—one of the greatest passers in National Football League history. One Saturday, Jurgensen carried my son Jon, who was then five years old, on his shoulders all the way from the office to Duke's. He regaled Jon with a story: "Jon, I ate a dozen oysters last night. But only ten of them worked. Do you understand that?" Jon did not.

The Williams table attracted journalists, broadcasters, and social commentators. Gamblers that Ed had represented, like Julius Silverman and Joe Nesline, came by to talk. The firm had an apartment in New York, at 55th and Lexington Avenue. There, and in the back room of P.J. Clarke's saloon on the corner of 55th and Third Avenue, the New York characters showed up: actor Don Ameche, publisher Billy Hearst, alleged Mafioso Frank Costello.

The palpable excitement of those days and nights, coupled with the cases on which I was working, sent adrenaline through my veins. But though all of this work was exactly the introduction and education I had craved, something was missing. This world of Ed's was both mine and not mine. It was mine because of its intellectual challenges. It was mine because Ed Williams was like my father in that he had come from a family without wealth. He was like my father in his energy. The booze and cigarettes were part of an environment that held fascination. The café society side of Williams's life has transfixed more than one person. His biographer, Evan Thomas, was so taken with researching it that he wrote a foolish book that failed to capture Ed's brilliance as trial and appellate lawyer. I can remember upbraiding Thomas about this when the book was in galleys, and then finding that I was not alone in this view.

By running up a big bar bill, Thomas managed to interview people who had dined or drunk with Ed. Thomas's book was a pseudo-biography of Ed from the waist down. It repeated stories of Ed's penchant for drink, of which we all knew, for we shared it. Thomas deliberately ignored Ed's unparalleled brilliance as an advocate for constitutional principle, even after I and others responded to Thomas's requests for research that he then disregarded.

At that time, in the late 1960s, I worried that the litigation life as Ed lived it carried too many dangers for me. I had little in common with most of these folks I was meeting. The Vietnam war was heating up, and there were increased draft calls. The poor and black in Washington, D.C. were clearly ghettoized and marginalized. Unless I listened to those voices, and tried to put forward their demands for justice, I feared that I would become a well-to-do and skilled, but irrelevant, lawyer.

I am not saying that Ed lacked principle. He had stood for the right to counsel, and had argued the most important Fourth Amendment cases in recent years. But I needed to begin to make my own way. I began to search for cases I could do on my own, outside the office but with Williams's at least tacit blessing. Indeed, that showed another part of his character: Although the work I wound up doing was not what he would have chosen, he supported me all the way.

I thought my work at Williams & Wadden, later Williams & Connolly, was a perfect preparation for doing cases on my own. The criminal cases the firm handled paid well enough so that the young lawyers could research and write every potential motion, and run down every potential argument. When we went out to do our own cases, we carried that idea of preparation with us. I tell this because I have met so many young lawyers who feel trapped and under-used in the jobs they find on leaving law school. I am not talking about the lawyers who work in public defender or legal services offices. They get plenty of responsibility as soon as, or more quickly than, they can handle it. But in the medium to large firms, a young lawyer is likely to spend several years doing discovery work and writing motions before ever getting a chance to see how that plays out in court.

Bottling up young and talented lawyers in the library to handle litigation paper, and never letting them handle cases on their own, is bad for them and bad for the future of the firm. Thirty and more years ago, even the largest law firms had a docket of smaller cases that associates were given to try. That is the way the young Edward Bennett Williams learned trial work.

I had this idea in some workable form in 1967 and 1968. Indeed, in later chapters you will read of cases in which I became involved even before I passed the bar, helping pro bono lawyers but not entering an appearance. Like every lawyer, however, I remember my first solo trial. I have yet to meet a lawyer who does not have such a memory. For all of us, the recollection, though perhaps softened by time, still drives us in some important way. For me, my first case was also a response to my sense of injustice. I was choosing how to use my legal skills, rather than accepting a choice made by the law firm.

In our Capitol Hill neighborhood, a young African-American, James Wilson, was arrested for threatening a woman with a knife. The arresting officer, Burns, also African-American, was the one who walked the beat past our house, though I didn't know that until later. Ms. Jacobs, who ran the local community center, called me because this young man sometimes volunteered there. His court-appointed lawyer had not moved to get him out on bail, and he was in danger of losing his job if he continued to miss work.

I prepared a bail motion and ventured down to the general sessions court, where all relatively minor criminal cases were tried. Since 1970, there has been a District of Columbia Superior Court, which handles the bulk of District of Columbia civil and criminal litigation. In those days, the really serious cases were all heard in federal district court. The Court of General Sessions was a kind of colonial backwater, a typical urban court staffed mostly by politically connected judges. There were notable exceptions to this rule. Judge Howard, an African-American, tried to care about the cases before him. Judge Tim Murphy wrote scholarly opinions, including one holding that merely calling a police officer a "son of a bitch" was not disorderly conduct. Of course, the police continued to use their discretion to arrest suspicious characters for bad words, but the police reports began to swear that the defendant had called the officer something that would colloquially but accurately describe Oedipus—and that was a word that Judge Murphy had said would merit arrest.

But general sessions was where Ed Williams had started. It was a place to learn the craft of lawyering. Ed used to tell a story about his early days, before there was Xerox. He staggered into the courthouse one day with books under each arm to argue a legal motion. An old lawyer, a courthouse habitué, looked at him and drawled: "Get rid of those books, son. Get yourself a witness!" The story may have been apocryphal, but its lesson was not. The old lawyer and dozens like him lined the halls looking for business. Some of them had no offices, and simply printed the courthouse pay phone number on their cards.

I wound up in front of Judge McIntyre, lean and dyspeptic. "Why are you here?" he demanded.

"I have filed a bail motion," I said.

"I know that. I mean why are you here when this man has counsel appointed? You think you are better than what the court can provide?"

"I am not saying that," I said, biting back my feeling that I was being insulted. I wanted to win this motion. "The local community center has contacted me, and this is a case where bail would really help this young man. He has the kind of community ties that the bail legislation was designed to honor." I was referring to the recent bail reforms that have since been eroded by congressional and judicial hostility.

"Well," the judge said. "I am not appointing you. If you want to enter an appearance, you can come in as retained counsel."

That was fine with me. I would be retained, but would not get a fee. That was the only way to displace the appointed lawyer. Judge McIntyre groused a bit more but granted release on personal recognizance and set a trial date.

I interviewed the young man at some length. He said that he and his girlfriend had been arguing, and that he had indeed said some harsh words. He denied brandishing a knife, but admitted that the knife taken from him by the police officer was his and that he had it in his pocket. He was charged with CDW—carrying a dangerous weapon. The government had to prove that he had the knife and that he had used it in a threatening manner. The police officer would testify to seeing him wave the knife toward the young woman. The young woman refused to talk to me, probably because the prosecutor or police had told her not to. This was a routine tactic in those days.

Wilson would have to be ready to testify. I spent hours on the case. On trial day, I heeded the advice of others and got to court early. The assignment system was everything they said it would be—loud and seemingly disorganized, but underneath this exterior like a cattle or tobacco auction. The courthouse regulars knew the assignment clerks, and their pushing and shouting were designed to get their cases continued, shifted, or directed toward particular courtrooms.

Wilson and I had decided that if we could get before Judge Howard, we should waive a jury. With any other judge, we would not take that risk. So I shoved my way to the front of the pack and shouted my case name and number. "U.S. v. Wilson. We'll waive jury trial if Judge Howard has calendar room." This mantra worked, and was my first introduction to the assignment system that prevails in urban criminal courts. Lawyers who can make it work can make a good living playing the plea bargain game, like the one in New York who handles 1,600 cases a year. Prosecutors who work the game put their cases where they can win motions and get the results they want.

Outside the assignment court, I met the prosecutor who had the Wilson case. He was a young assistant United States attorney named Bob Bennett. Years later, he was President Clinton's counsel. That day, he was an overworked prosecutor who had barely read the file and planned no doubt to use the police report as his direct examination notes. This was not, for him, a big case. He would not, however, take a plea for time served and a disposition that would let Wilson clear his record if he successfully served a probationary sentence.

By this time in our short discussion, he had given me a copy of the police report—which he was not required by law to do until after the officer and the alleged victim testified. I sat down and looked at it. Even the Xerox copy showed me what the officer had done. I wondered if Bennett had caught it. Officer Burns, whom I now remembered as the young cop in our neighborhood, had initially charged Wilson with PPW—possession of a prohibited weapon. He began to write his police report on this theory. Only then did he measure the knife blade and find it too short to qualify as prohibited. So Burns erased PPW and added a sentence or two claiming that he had seen Wilson brandish the knife—thus making the case CDW.

We waited our turn in Judge Howard's court. The alleged victim could not be sure that Wilson even had his knife out of his pocket, but she was sure their argument had been very loud and that harsh words were traded. As often happens in domestic violence cases, the alleged victim had by the time of trial become a reluctant witness. This is one of the difficulties in getting justice in cases where the victim has really been harmed.

I cross-examined Officer Burns as I had learned from Ed Williams. Take him through his booking procedure. Get him to explain how important that police report could be. It would be the basis on which the case would be charged and tried. Then confront him with the erasures, the change of theory.

Judge Howard sat back and let all this happen, and I moved for judgment of acquittal at the close of the prosecution's evidence. I was entitled to that, I thought. But Judge Howard had another lesson to teach me.

Maybe I should have an acquittal. And if I did not get it, maybe I could take an appeal and hope the court of appeals would see it that way. But there was no jury here, for we had waived one. And Judge Howard was in charge, just as were all those judges in their own courtrooms. He administered his own law, mostly untouched by anything the court of appeals would ever say, for most of the cases in his court never made it there.

"Mr. Tigar, I am denying your motion. Maybe this girl changed her mind, and maybe the officer changed things around. But I am not going to grant your motion. Not right now."

"Yes, Your Honor."

"The way I see it, you have only one witness you can put on if you have to go forward. You can rest now and keep Wilson off the stand, or you can put him on. I'm giving you that choice. But I sure would like to hear from him."

We all understand the right not to testify. But I was facing down a judge with an agenda of his own, not sure what that was. I took the risk. Wilson took the stand and denied any threatening conduct. Not guilty, said Judge Howard, even before Bennett had risen to cross-examine.

By this time I had been at the firm more than a year. Baker was convicted in February 1967, and I wrote the motions for a new trial, in arrest of judgment, and for acquittal. The new trial motion was based on the jury foreman's failure to disclose that he was a reserve police officer. As often happened in later years, I had high hopes for this motion and not enough appreciation of the legal system's inertia. This was the first motion I argued in a Williams & Connolly case. As I sat down after arguing, Ed whispered: "Good job. You made chicken salad out of chicken shit."

What had I learned in that year? What would I do with it? This profession presents us with choices, and we can truly reinvent ourselves by tracking different parts of it, and using our training in different ways. Some choices, as I have said, have to do with following the sense of injustice, and wanting to make things right. Other choices have to do with what part of the law we want to explore. I had learned the anatomy of a criminal case, how to take apart its substantive elements and how to analyze procedural issues, from search and seizure to electronic surveillance, to evidence, to criminal pleading, to jury selection, to getting a fair hearing. I had learned to do research and to write motions.

I had worked alongside older lawyers in writing appellate briefs. When Ed agreed to take on the appeals for the African-Americans convicted of killing Malcolm X, he assigned me to write the brief—after I had gone to a Harlem office to pick up the fee. The appeal was probably hopeless to start with, although the legal issues seemed compelling. When Ed argued the case in the appellate department, one of the judges interrupted his first sentence and kept hammering him with rude and rather abusive questions. After a few minutes of this, Ed smiled and said: "Judge, we have another hour here together. May I suggest that we think of this time as though we were trapped together in an airport waiting room waiting for a delayed flight, and needed to make the time pass as pleasantly as possible." I have never had the chutzpah to address a judge in that vein, but Ed did get to make the rest of his argument.

I had watched Ed try complex factual motions, and a jury trial. I had seen him argue legal points, and I had made arguments myself. I felt more prepared and experienced than I was, but that first trial whetted my appetite to follow my sense of injustice. So I worked on cases involving racism, on wiretap cases, and on anti-war issues. I was publicly and often identified with this or that cause. Some of this publicity caused discomfort at the firm, but Ed quieted it down.

Ed even had a sense of humor when I went a bit too far in my enthusiasm. During my first stint at the Williams firm, from 1966 to 1969, I had become friends with leaders of the local Students for a Democratic Society (SDS) in Washington, D.C. They inhabited rented space in a building near Dupont Circle. The realtor wanted to kick them out, disliking their avowed politics and their alleged lack of personal hygiene. He wrote a letter stating that the zoning for the building was limited to nonprofit corporations. I drafted and filed papers establishing the Washington chapter of the SDS as a nonprofit corporation in the District of Columbia.

I did not notice that the incorporation papers were on Williams & Connolly paper. Columnist Drew Pearson picked up the story and attacked the firm for giving aid and comfort to radicals. The firm at that point had about 12 lawyers in it, with eight partners. The vote to fire me was 7 to 1, but Ed was the 1. He thought the whole episode funny. From that representation, I met other SDS figures who were clients and comrades in later years.

When in early 1968 I wanted to edit the *Selective Service Law Reporter* (SSLR), as I discuss in Chapter 5, Ed insisted that I keep an office at the firm and said he would pay me a reduced amount just to be available to consult on firm cases. The reduced amount, when added to my SSLR salary, put me in a league with my peers in private practice. As I began to do draft law and represent protesters, there were times that Ed was professedly grateful for my work. Sons of his friends and clients faced draft problems and I could help. Sons and daughters would from time to time be arrested in demonstrations for this or that cause, and Ed would ask me to represent them.

When Columbia University students demonstrated in 1968, part of the worldwide student protests that year, the daughter of one of Ed's good friends was arrested. I was dispatched to the New York Criminal Courts at 100 Centre Street. I had thought that D.C. General Sessions was dreary, but the dirty wood-paneled courtroom of Judge Weiss was a step beyond. There was never any doubt about the outcome of these Columbia cases as far as I was concerned. The police had arrested people without much regard to the elements of any offense such as trespass or disorderly conduct. The sheer number of cases made it unlikely that the DA's office could try everybody if they all insisted on a trial. And the police would no doubt be confounded at any trial by failure to remember and record what each defendant had done.

On arraignment day, the judge began by clearing the docket of nighttime arrests—prostitutes, drunks, and the other business of a morning calendar. I sat next to my client and my eye traveled around the room. The American flag was behind the judge's chair and off to one side. In a forlorn attempt to save it from harm, a plastic bag was draped over it. The bag itself had yellowed and was streaked with grime. On the wall behind the judge an incomplete set of metal letters proclaimed

IN GOD WE RUST.

When Martin Luther King was killed on April 4, 1968, the District of Columbia, like many American cities, witnessed a great deal of violence. I was appointed to represent people charged with uprising-related offenses. By the time I left Washington in June 1969 to become a law teacher at UCLA, my legal experience was more varied than that of any other lawyer who had been out of law school for only three years. I had been lead lawyer or co-counsel in cases ranging from sit-ins to murder. I had worked on complex civil cases involving civil rights and anti-war protests. I had written a book on draft law, and several law review essays. I was preparing for my first Supreme Court argument. My ego had become, as one of my law students wrote on an evaluation form years later, "as big as the Asian continent." I thought that I would go to Los Angeles, teach law and write about it, and find some sort of peace. I was wrong. Before leaving Washington, I had signed on to pro bono cases and even one that promised to help pave the transition from practice. When I got to California, my restless urge continued.

Was I sensing injustices that needed to be righted, indulging some passion to stand at the center of things, or simply living out that same changing, striving pattern that my father had lived? From here on out, this book departs from chronology and deals with issues. Is this editorial decision itself a way of arguing that injustice moved me more than ego or insecurity? I hope not, and in a way I don't care. I would like this work to be judged on its merits, on its fidelity to some idea of human rights that can be validated by people's experience. I wrote on this theme in 1995:

> When I speak of a prosaic and down-to-earth idea of justice, I mean simply that one can deduce principles of right from human needs in the present time. That is, I reject the cynical, or Stoic, or no-ought-from-an-is idea that one set of rules is just as good as another. I reject the notion, as Professor Martha Nussbaum has characterized it, "that to every argument some argument to a contradictory conclusion can be opposed; that arguments are in any case merely tools of influence, without any better sort of claim to our allegiance." Rather, again borrowing from Professor Nussbaum, my notions of justice "include a commitment, open-ended and revisable because grounded upon dialectical arguments that have their roots in experience, to a definite view of human flourishing and good human functioning." One element of such views is that "human beings have needs for things in the world: for political rights, for money and food and shelter, for respect and self-respect," and so on.

Notes

1. The Murphy opinion is unreported. I first discussed it, and my New York "debut," in *Foreword: Waiver of Constitutional Rights: Disquiet in the Citadel,* 84 HARV. L. REV. 1 (1970).

2. On prosecutors advising witnesses not to talk, *see Gregory v. United States,* 369 F.2d 185 (1966).

3. The Baker case is the subject of *Baker v. United States,* 430 F.2d 499 (D.C. Cir. 1970); *Baker v. United States,* 401 F.2d 958 (D.C. Cir. 1968); *United States v. Baker,* 301 F. Supp. 977 (D.D.C.); *United States v. Baker,* 301 F. Supp. 973 (D.D.C. 1969); *United States v. Baker,* 266 F. Supp. 461 (D.D.C.); *United States v. Baker,* 266 F. Supp. 456 (D.D.C. 1967); *United States v. Baker,* 262 F. Supp. 657 (D.D.C. 1966). Larry King and

Bobby Baker wrote a good book about Baker's career and the case, WHEEL-ING & DEALING: CONFESSIONS OF A CAPITOL HILL OPERATOR (New York: W.W. Norton & Co., 1978).

4. On Edward Bennett Williams's style of oral argument, see PERSUA-SION: THE LITIGATOR'S ART (Chicago: ABA Press, 1999).

5. The quotation on justice is from *Defending, an Essay*, 74 TEX. L. REV. 101, 106 (1995), reprinted in PERSUASION: THE LITIGATOR'S ART (Chicago: ABA Press, 1999).

Chapter 4
CIVIL WRONGS

To put this chapter, and my own sense of injustice, into perspective, I want to contrast two approaches as they have evolved in the civil rights debate: First, the historical approach, as illustrated by Professor ten Broek's masterful book, *The Anti-Slavery Origins of the Fourteenth Amendment*, and second, an analytical approach, as illustrated by the ten Broek and Tussman article, "The Equal Protection of the Laws," in the *California Law Review* more than 50 years ago. When one says civil rights, that is only the beginning of discussion.

Analytically, one can approach equal protection cases as simply involving categories or classifications chosen by the state. One then asks whether the classification is rational in light of its avowed or intended purpose, and whether it is under-inclusive or over-inclusive with respect to that purpose. By using this kind of analysis, we can tell whether a law treats like things alike. The Supreme Court has superimposed on this framework a set of categories of governmental activity. These were designed at first to respect state power to regulate economic activity, while restraining actions that seemed likely to result in or be motivated by invidious discrimination. The Supreme Court's decisions of the late nineteenth and early twentieth centuries had been hostile to economic regulation and quite generous in permitting state and federal action that discriminated against African-Americans and Asian-Americans.

These superimposed categories are phrased as levels of scrutiny of classifications. Economic regulation gets very limited and deferential scrutiny. Racial classifications receive strict scrutiny, while gender may receive intermediate scrutiny. This sort of classification may be helpful as a shorthand way of seeing classification problems, but in the hands of reactionary judges it has become an instrument for holding back progress toward true racial justice.

In the days when segregation was written into the law of many states, race-based classifications served no legitimate purpose and were properly struck down. When states and the federal government sought to promote fair housing, access to public accommodation, and equal educational and economic opportunity, it was easy to use classification systems that forbade decision making, by public or private actors, based on race. From there, it is deceptively easy to conclude that any classification system that uses race is illegitimate.

Not so, I have argued. The classification system arose in a discrete historical framework, to reflect the historic reality of Jim Crow legislation and patterns of overt discrimination. It is risky to disengage that system from its historical basis and manipulate its categories as independent of their origins.

Ten Broek's historical analysis of the Civil War amendments sets one on the right track. The fact is that American society has been permeated with racial bigotry in ways that have disadvantaged many groups. It is commonplace knowledge that the Constitution expressly recognized slavery. When the Civil War ended, systematic discrimination against the former slaves continued, resulting in creation of a ghettoized underclass. In 1831, the Supreme Court decided *Cherokee Nation v. Georgia*, holding that Native Americans were incapable of forming social organizations that were entitled to recognition by the conquering European powers, and hence incapable of claiming political or property rights except as those might be recognized by the United States. Indian land rights and political rights hardly existed. In the latter half of the nineteenth century, the Supreme Court upheld federal and state legislation that discriminated against Oriental people from China and Japan. One can view these historic events in different ways, but if you believe that these decisions and actions were wrong, there should be a correlative duty to provide a remedy.

The people originally displaced are dead, as are those who took immediate advantage of them. The traces of wrong remain, however. We can see them, as we note that people of color are underrepresented in the upper reaches of our own legal profession, as well as in the higher-paid positions in many other areas of endeavor. We might add that until fairly recently, law school admission patterns were skewed against women and people of color. One cannot begin to fashion a remedy unless one understands the historical roots of the problem, and tries to envision what the disadvantaged class has lost as a group. Any remedy at that point would necessarily take race into account, to redress the inequality produced by race having been a factor in the old, discredited decisions.

In short, I believe that race-conscious remedies, including quotas, are necessary to redress historic imbalances. Widespread and overt racial and ethnic discrimination is not some relic of a distant historic past, but lies within the memory of all of us. For example, when I arrived at the University of Texas in 1984 to teach, the law school had begun to ensure that its student population reflected the ethnic and racial diversity of Texas itself. Inevitably, this meant that some students gained admission despite their lower scores on allegedly objective tests that are, in fact, culturally biased. In my first class, there was a Hispanic student from the Rio Grande Valley. He was the product of an educational system that was systematically underfunded to an extent that many students did not even have books for their classes. He was the first person in his family to go to college, let alone to law school. His test scores were not really high, but he showed great ability in law school in courses dealing with advocacy.

He returned to his community to put his legal skills to work. He came to see me from time to time and I still hear from him. I think that a public law school served its proper purpose by offering education to all sectors of society, and helping to see that underserved communities had better access to legal services.

The dry, analytical method rejects this reasoning. Under that view, race cannot be a factor, without some overwhelming justification that will almost never be present. Thus, equality as a concept for redressing past wrongs is pushed aside in favor of a mechanical analysis that precludes any such redress.

When I speak of analysis based on history, I am not retreating into some imagined original intent of the Constitution's framers or the authors of the Civil War amendments. It is very difficult to get inside the minds of those who wrote those documents at the moment they were writing them. A more accurate view of their desires may be gathered from examining the entire historical context of their work.

I think there is one abiding certainty about the views of those who assembled at Philadelphia in 1787. They were not so arrogant or foolish as to think they knew everything there was to know about government, science, or the human condition. They believed it was a constitution they were drafting and not a set of fetters they were forging. They stood on the shoulders of those who had gone before them, so that they could see farther. They understood that we would go beyond where they had gone.

When, in litigation or simply in formulating arguments about justice, I have thought about history or precedent, I have tried to do so in this way. I set out these views, which you are free to call my prejudices, as an introduction to what follows. This chapter deals mainly with racial justice and injustice. It comes first among the topical chapters because such issues have pervaded almost every aspect of my work. As I think back on the issues of free expression, protests against an illegal war, or illegal wiretapping, I am reminded again of how government policy that curtailed basic rights struck more harshly at people of color in all of these areas. That thought, too, underlies my views about the need to press on until all vestiges of racism are gone and we have achieved a nonracial society.

I have already talked about how civil rights issues surfaced in my law school classes. Outside of classes, and in my first year in law school, I got a job with Ann Fagan Ginger helping her edit the *Civil Liberties Docket*. This unique publication, which Ann produced from her Berkeley home, summarized civil rights and civil liberties cases. It covered not only reported decisions but also unreported opinions. We summarized briefs and pleadings, which Ann had me and my compatriot, law student Dennis Roberts, collect from the lawyers involved. Then, Ann began to archive these materials in what became the Meiklejohn Civil Liberties Library. She edited a practice guide for civil rights cases that became the model of our *Selective Service Law Reporter* some years later.

These days, students seem to seek out jobs in law firms from the moment they enter law school. At that time, this was much rarer. The *Docket* was a dream job. I sat at a typewriter and read litigation materials. If I read of a significant case in the newspapers, I would write the lawyers to get their pleadings. I felt like a medical student doing dissection, learning the anatomy of litigation. Except, of course, these were not cadavers but living cases. Voting rights, attacks on free expression by civil rights organizations, desegregation battles—all the racial justice issues that had led to the 1963 march on Washington where Martin Luther King had spoken. This was the continuation of the reportage I had done at Pacifica Radio, where during the summer of 1963 I had covered Dr. King's visit to Los Angeles.

The summer of 1964, after my first law school year, was Freedom Summer. The Mississippi Freedom Democratic Party challenged the official segregationist Mississippi delegates at the Democratic convention in Atlantic City. My friend Dennis, a year ahead of me in law school, went to Albany, Georgia, to work with the great civil rights lawyer C.B. King. Thousands of students went south to work on civil rights. The record of violence visited on these young people, and on those whose struggle they had come to help, is still cause to wonder. This was, you may remember, the summer when students Goodman, Schwerner, and Chaney were murdered in Mississippi as they worked for civil rights.

I did not go south. I earned money for my second year in law school, and I did a weekly KPFA/Pacifica Radio program called "Mississippi Report." Our memories of that time have somehow faded, and perhaps our sensitivity along with them. I remember when the 1990s film *Mississippi Burning* retold the story of those killings. A court of appeals judge who is at least my age—and therefore in a position to remember—remarked that he found the film overdone and exaggerated. I pulled out my old scripts from "Mississippi Report" and sent him the statistics showing hundreds of black churches burned, thousands of illegal arrests, and a pattern of terror and intimidation.

The official Democratic parties of Mississippi and other southern states proclaimed their continuing faith in segregation and what they called states' rights. I attacked them on the air, recognizing that they might demand equal, but separate, time. President Johnson temporized but sought congressional and political support for some compromise that would seat some black delegates from the South at the Democratic convention.

The pace of political change seemed so slow, despite the imminent passage of the Civil Rights Act of 1964. The Democratic Party seemed unwilling to welcome the African-American voters who were being registered in the South, and the Republican Party was not doing any better.

At this time, civil rights lawyers had to consider how they could bring about more and faster change. Arthur Kinoy and William Kunstler were developing broad-scale injunctive strategies against efforts to shut down civil rights organizations. I wondered how the Johnson administration could be prodded into more decisive action. The investigations into Ku Klux Klan violence dragged on, and local FBI agents in southern field offices were too often allied with local law enforcement. The administration did prosecute in egregious civil rights violation cases, but more was needed.

I was talking to one of my professors about this, and he suggested that I look at President Eisenhower's response to the 1958 Little Rock school desegregation. I did so, and found a trove of information about presidential power to enforce civil rights. What I found is important to this day, for it supports a view for federal power and against states' rights that a slim Supreme Court majority in the late twentieth and early twenty-first centuries has ignored.

First, I read or reread the reconstruction legislation that made civil rights a federal matter, conferred jurisdiction on federal courts to enforce them, and directed the executive branch to enforce these laws. True, the courts had rejected suits that relied on the mandatory language of this post–Civil War legislation. The courts ruled that despite a congressional command that civil rights violations be prosecuted, the Attorney General still retained discretion not to act. Despite such limiting constructions, the reconstruction legislation and the environment in which it passed supported my view that the Civil War had resulted in a promise of liberation and equality for African-Americans, without the keeping of which the government became illegitimate.

There was, however, an earlier chapter in the conflict between sectional hostility and national power. In September 1957, when Arkansas authorities, led by Governor Orval Faubus, defied desegregation orders, President Eisenhower's Attorney General, Herbert Brownell, looked back at legislation that had been passed to assist President George Washington in putting down the Whiskey Rebellions. President Eisenhower, based on that advice, announced that a governor has no power to resist the authority of a federal court order, and that he as commander in chief had the power and duty to federalize the state militia and send federal troops to see that federal court orders were carried out.

In 1963, President Kennedy refused to use troops when Mississippi Governor Ross Barnett factitiously defied a federal court order to admit James Meredith to the University of Mississippi. President Lyndon Johnson also refused in the summer of 1964, despite the dozens of beatings, burnings, and shootings carried out by the Ku Klux Klan, aided in many cases by local law enforcement agencies.

In this storm, brave judges of the United States Court of Appeals for the Fifth Circuit did their part. When racist district judges, many appointed by Democratic administrations, refused to enforce federal law, the Fifth Circuit stepped in. President Eisenhower had appointed four judges who, being Republican, had no ties to the segregationist Democratic establishment. They were John Minor Wisdom, Elbert Parr Tuttle, Richard Rives, and John R. Brown. Their opinions, particularly those of Judge Wisdom, were eloquent testaments to the constitutional command of racial justice. When Presidents Kennedy and Johnson refused to send the massive federal force necessary to enforce desegregation, the Fifth Circuit did the best it could. It even cited Mississippi Governor Ross Barnett for contempt, though it later withdrew the citation over Judge Wisdom's dissent. From

Judge Wisdom's perspective, Barnett was a lawyer who knew perfectly well that his segregationist constitutionalism was factitious.

Twenty-five years later, the Fifth Circuit held its judicial conference in Mississippi. Governor Mabus invited us all to dinner at the governor's mansion. I fell into step beside Judge Wisdom as we walked up the front steps.

"Judge," I asked, "did you ever think you would be invited in the front door of this mansion?"

He laughed and said no.

In those law school years, from where I sat, writing, studying, and broadcasting, my views on this struggle took shape. You cannot count on the government to do its job when that job involves acting on behalf of people's rights. The initiative must come from a popular movement, which should not permit itself to be co-opted. Litigation strategies on behalf of the people's movement may welcome official support but cannot count on it. Finally, the movement for change is the primary motor of change, because in the final analysis only the movement's coherent demands stand any chance to convince a court.

Living in the District of Columbia gave me a new perspective on racism. We rented a house on Capitol Hill, seven blocks from the Supreme Court building. The gentrification of this neighborhood had already begun. After a year, we bought a house a little farther from the Capitol, and in a neighborhood where more African-Americans lived.

At that time, the District of Columbia was governed by commissioners appointed by the President. It was a feudal enclave, without meaningful self-government and, of course, without any voting voice in Congress. Nothing more clearly showed the district's political situation than the condition of its schools. Our son Jon was born in 1962 and would be entering kindergarten in 1967. He was already in a neighborhood day care center.

The district's revered civil rights leader, Julius Hobson, had filed a lawsuit challenging the way D.C. schools were run. Because the board of education was appointed by the U.S. district judges, Hobson made the judges defendants. This disqualified them all from sitting. As a result, appeals court Judge J. Skelly Wright heard the case. There could not have been a better choice. Wright had been a district judge in New Orleans, where his path-breaking civil rights decisions quickly earned him the enmity of the Louisiana establishment. President Johnson could not appoint him to the Court of Appeals for the Fifth Circuit, for the nomination would have been blocked by Louisiana's senators. So he named him to the D.C. circuit.

Judge Wright was temperamental, often quick to anger. His opinions were concise and powerful. He was decisive. He had courage. He wrote and spoke in support of pro bono lawyering on behalf of civil rights and anti-war groups. His opinions in the Hobson litigation are indictments of the racial bias that dominated D.C. politics.

Judge Wright found that schools in black areas of the district, which was most of it, were run-down, underfunded, and understaffed. Schools in the white neighborhoods were actually places where you would willingly send your children. Per-pupil expenditures in white and black neighborhoods varied dramatically.

The Hobson litigation was being conducted by some lawyers who lived near us, and William Kunstler himself was nominally lead counsel for Hobson. This was my introductory education about Washington's racial politics. One of the remedies being discussed was a judicial decree mandating expenditure of money for better schools in black neighborhoods. Could a judge order such a thing? I set to work and mined the old cases. In the nineteenth century, municipalities issued revenue bonds and then sometimes defaulted. There were old cases requiring assessment and levy of taxes to pay the bondholders. And a California case, as I recall it, had ordered a community to buy a school bus. So I wrote my brief and handed it in. It was a very small part of the entire litigation, but writing it and talking to people in the neighborhood gave me a chance to know the district's racial tension firsthand.

The next year, I worked with ACLU lawyers in the defense of students and teachers disciplined for their part in civil rights and anti-war demonstrations at Howard University. Howard was founded after the Civil War to serve predominantly the African-American community. It was the premier African-American educational institution in the country, and many civil rights leaders—including Thurgood Marshall—had been students or professors there. Our key argument was that the interaction between Howard and the federal government meant that its action was state action. Therefore, we argued, Howard was obliged to respect the First Amendment and to afford students and teachers due process hearings before acting against them. The Supreme Court's decisions of the 1960s, and quite a few lower federal court and state court decisions, supported our argument. But we lost. As a junior member of the litigation team, I learned a lot about civil rights pleading and practice, supplementing the criminal law and criminal procedure work I was doing at the law firm. Drafting a complaint, researching motions, filing papers, presenting arguments, choosing among potential forums—serving on litigation teams with lawyers of different views and backgrounds—provided the best possible supplement to the legal education I got in law school.

So in 1968, I was ready when the state action issue came around again. The Maryland suburbs of Washington, D.C. boast a necklace of first-rate golf courses. Most of these are private, and some are famous locales for political and business meetings. I don't know much about that, as I never learned to play golf. One such course was at Kenwood Country Club. This was not, strictly speaking, a membership club. The Kenwood subdivision developer built the course and its associated facilities and offered memberships to those who bought houses. The membership entitled you to use the facilities, but did not give you any property interest in the club facilities or land. In the Kenwood subdivision lived several prominent Washingtonians, including American Friends leader Blake Tartt, Michigan Senator Robert Griffin, Idaho Senator Frank Church, and CBS reporter Robert Pierpoint. Church was a leading Democrat and Griffin a Republican. If these folks ever knew that the developer had mandated that the club have a no-Jews-or-blacks policy, this fact had not impressed itself upon them.

Until, that is, two celebrated events rent the Kenwood calm. One lovely day, Senator Barry Goldwater was playing golf as the guest of Senator Griffin. The club owner learned of this and hurried out to the tenth tee. He ordered Goldwater off the premises. This made the papers, and Goldwater remarked that he was only half-Jewish and had only played nine holes. Not too long afterwards, columnist Carl Rowan, an African-American, showed up at the club as an invited dinner guest. He, too, was turned away, and he made sure the world knew about it.

The leading citizens of Kenwood called and asked me to a meeting. Maryland law professor Sandy Rosen and I took on the case. The key issue was whether this was truly a private club. Our research showed that all the local golf clubs received substantial tax benefits, supposedly as recompense for keeping their property green and not building houses on it. I am not sure that this tax policy is wise, for golf courses are notorious emitters of runoff that damages waterways. The clubs, however, slurped up the property tax largesse quite willingly. The state regarded them as having built a green belt around the District of Columbia. That was, we argued, a public function supported by public funds. The federal court in Baltimore agreed, and ordered the club desegregated. It even awarded modest attorney fees.

The racial issues in the District of Columbia obviously cut much deeper than people's right to play golf or have dinner at a country club. Every day, living where we did at the fringe of Washington's ghetto, I saw these issues. My wife was active in community organizations. My kids went to integrated schools and day care.

On April 4, 1968, at about 6:00 P.M., a sniper killed Martin Luther King, Jr. News of the killing spread quickly. We were home making dinner. Decca Truehaft, who wrote under the name Jessica Mitford, was visiting. As it turned out, she spent the night because the streets were quickly filled with rioting citizens protesting King's death.

In the aftermath of that night, I represented people charged with crimes related to looting. Reverend King was, particularly to African-Americans in the District of Columbia, a symbol of their aspirations. He had said that change would come by nonviolent direct action. He had stood in opposition to leaders who advocated or predicted violence. When he was killed, in the midst of a campaign against racism and in a southern city, the forces that held the community in some kind of equipoise simply dissolved. All the anger, focused and unfocused, burst out.

There was also, to be sure, plenty of opportunism on the streets that night. As police sirens mingled with the noise of people running and shouting on our street, our neighbor knocked at our front door. He was an African-American man of about 50. We opened the door and he came in to our living room.

"I can't keep my nephews from looting," he said. "I've told them that they are going to be arrested and maybe killed, but they don't listen."

"I guess I could explain what happens if they get caught," I said, "but I don't know it would do any good."

"Oh," he said, "I don't want you to do that. I just thought that since they were going down there, do you need a new TV or anything like that?"

The April 1968 uprisings, which took place in cities all over America, seemed to be part of a worldwide movement. I am not preaching any kind of conspiracy theory here. However, students in colleges acted out their frustration at the Vietnam war and the limits on academic freedom. Students and elements of the French left took to the streets and nearly brought down the French government. That summer, as I relate in Chapter 8, young people demonstrated in Chicago against the machine-dominated Democratic Party Convention and against the Vietnam war.

There were these deep divides in American society, which had been papered over in the McCarthy era and were now appearing. The divisions were not simply of age, class, race, gender, or politics, although each of these things was involved. As I was working through my own position, I met a judge who seemed to embody the entire set of problems.

In 1968, a student at a local university came to me with his parents. He had been driving in Prince George's County, which adjoins the District of Columbia and is where the University of Maryland is located. He was with some friends, one of whom was smoking marijuana in the car. The police officer noted the odor and arrested everybody in the car. In those days, penalties for first-time marijuana possession were not as heavy as now, and the young man might have been technically guilty of possession but had an argument to make on that point. There was also a search-and-seizure issue about the vehicle stop.

I took a ride out to the county to talk to the prosecutor. The county seat is in Upper Marlboro. In those days, and now, law enforcement and judicial administration in Prince George's County are dominated by archetypal white southern attitudes toward race. The county police are notorious for ignoring the constitutional rights of suspects. In short, this is not the place to litigate a Fourth Amendment claim, or the place to be tried for a narcotics offense.

The prosecutor, Ben, agreed that my client was a good candidate for something called probation without verdict. That is, he would plead guilty to possessing a small amount of marijuana. The judge would award probation. If my client completed the probation without incident, the case would be dismissed without a judgment being entered on his plea. He would not have a conviction on his record. It seemed to be a good deal. But, Ben explained, the judge would have to approve it.

So we went to see Sam, the judge. Sam seemed to be in his 50s, with a military-style brush cut. He cordially invited us into his chambers, and began immediately to share a story of his trip to San Francisco, from which he had just returned.

"You know, Ben," he began, hardly noticing me, "I got selected to attend this program on sensitivity, out in San Francisco. Now, you know San Francisco is not my kind of place anyway, but you should have seen what they had there. This program was in a big auditorium, and they had state judges, federal judges, and then a whole bunch of ex-convicts. I mean, Ben, they had everything from cop-killers to queens.

"Well, right off, they asked me to be part of a psychodrama." He pronounced the word one syllable at a time, with evident distaste. "I knew something was up. They had me up on this platform, and they had three chairs. They called one chair ego, the next one superego and the third one was your unconscious self, maybe like your id. So I stood up there and this black ex-con is up there and he puts his face right up in my face and says, 'You white judge, how come you don't treat black people with respect in your courtroom?'" Sam's voice, while repeating what the ex-con said, imitated his version of African-American street talk.

Sam continued his story. "So I sat in the chair marked ego and I said, 'Hah, hah hah!' Then I sat in the chair marked superego, and I said, 'I am a judge and I decide every case on the law and the facts.' Then I sat in that id chair and I looked right at that ex-con and I said, 'You goddam nigger, who put you up to this?'"

Ben laughed obediently. I did my best to stay in my seat. Who was this judge? Why had Ben brought me here? And how would I avoid saying or doing something that would harm my client, who fortunately was not present? This was 1968, and we were only a few miles from the District of Columbia. But I felt I had taken a wrong turn and wandered into a past time.

His Honor switched from his recollection to the case we had brought. "Ben, Mike," Sam began, acknowledging me at last, "I know what you want. I won't do it. I am not going to cut these dope-smoking kids any slack." I thought about pointing out that this was a good deal for the prosecution, but a glance at Ben convinced me that this would not have been a good idea.

Outside, I reminded Ben that we had agreed this was not a case that should give this young man a criminal record. Ben agreed to uphold his part of the bargain. In Maryland, a prosecutor can stet a case—that is, take it off calendar. Ben agreed to do this for a year, and if my client stayed out of trouble Ben would dismiss the charges. So that's what we did. But my trip to Prince George's County sticks in my mind as a warning that racism and racist attitudes linger on.

Later on, race was an issue in so many cases—the wiretaps on the Black Panther Party and on H. Rap Brown, the prosecution of Angela Davis, and the discriminatory administration of the Vietnam war draft. I became so immersed in these issues that when, as I tell in Chapter 14, I moved into the arena of international human rights, I was prepared to see the worldwide racial and class divides.

Notes

1. JACOBUS TEN BROEK, THE ANTI-SLAVERY ORIGINS OF THE FOURTEENTH AMENDMENT (Berkeley: Univ. of California Press, 1951, revised and republished in 1965 as EQUAL UNDER LAW); Jacobus ten Broek & Joseph Tussman, *The Equal Protection of the Laws*, 37 CALIF. L. REV. 341 (1949).

2. For a discussion of Supreme Court classification lore, see *United States v. Virginia*, 518 U.S. 515 (1996). I have worked through the equal protection/equality issues, including a reference to the Native American cases, in LAW AND THE RISE OF CAPITALISM (New York: Monthly Review Press, 2000).

3. Cherokee Nation v. Georgia, 30 U.S. 1 (1831). The Hobson litigation is reported at *Hobson v. Hansen*, 327 F. Supp. 844 (D.D.C., May 25, 1971); *Hobson v. Hansen*, 320 F. Supp. 720 (D.D.C., Dec. 22, 1970); *Hobson v. Hansen*, 320 F. Supp. 409 (D.D.C., Dec. 14, 1970); *Hobson v. Hansen*, 44 F.R.D. 18, 5 A.L.R. Fed. 497 (D.D.C., Feb. 19, 1968); *Hobson v. Hansen*, 269 F. Supp. 401 (D.D.C., June 19, 1967); *Hobson v. Hansen*, 265 F. Supp. 902 (D.D.C., Feb. 9, 1967); *Hobson v. Hansen*, 252 F. Supp. 4 (D.D.C., Mar. 25, 1966).

4. On the courageous judges of the Fifth Circuit, see FRANK R. KEMERER, WILLIAMS WAYNE JUSTICE: A JUDICIAL BIOGRAPHY (1991); JACK BASS, TAMING THE STORM: THE LIFE AND TIMES OF JUDGE FRANK M. JOHNSON (1993). I received in later years the John Minor Wisdom award, and the judge presented it to me personally.

5. The Kinoy-Kunstler initiative led to *Dombrowski v. Pfister*, 380 U.S. 479 (1965), the later erosion of which is chronicled in, *e.g.*, Owen M. Fiss, *Dombrowski*, 86 YALE L.J. 1103 (1977).

6. Prosecutorial discretion was upheld in *Moses v. Kennedy*, 219 F. Supp. 762 (D.D.C. 1963), *aff'd sub nom. Moses v. Katzenbach*, 342 F.2d 931 (D.C. Cir. 1965).

7. Attorney General Brownell's opinion is included in *President's Power to Use Federal Troops to Suppress Resistance to Enforcement of Federal Court Orders*—Little Rock, Ark., 41 U.S. Op. Atty. Gen. 313 (1957).

Chapter 5
DIVISIVE WAR

United States involvement in Vietnam—from 1954 until the North Vietnamese victory in 1975—featured errors, lies, and violations of international and domestic law. Tens of thousands of soldiers were killed in Vietnam. Tens of thousands of Americans were drafted to serve in the military during the Vietnam war. The draft cut across all sectors of American society. It radicalized countless young men and their friends and families.

Protests against the draft were accentuated by escalating sanctions against draft resisters and those counseling resistance. The government lost sight of a basic truth—you cannot crush protest by repression. You only kindle more resentment.

My views on American foreign policy came together when I was an undergraduate at Berkeley. I had come to UC Berkeley as a midshipman. The Navy's $50 a month was my basic college money, plus another $125 a year as a National Merit Scholar and $375 a year that my stepmother told me that my father had left for me when he died.

I arrived in Berkeley in August 1958, ready to don a Navy uniform, get a degree and become a naval officer. By June 1962, when I graduated, I had received my honorable discharge from the Navy as a conscientious objector and had rejected war as an instrument of national policy. My path involved risk, anguish, and deep thought. But after treading this path, I would always listen carefully when a young person came to me facing difficult life choices and legal consequences that might flow from those choices. I was particularly attuned to the decisions that America's involvement in Vietnam—which began in earnest in the 1960s—forced upon young men and women.

In high school and as I began at Berkeley, a foreign policy based on nuclear confrontation began to seem suspect to me. I can remember visiting my mother's old friend, Mary Duffield, down the coast in Santa Cruz, on some weekends. I was sitting in her kitchen talking about the NROTC. Mary had gently wondered if I had thought about my role as naval officer in carrying out American foreign policy. "Well," I said, "I can wear the uniform. I get high marks as a midshipman. I feel it is right to serve. And, I could kill if that was necessary."

As I said this, I felt a hesitation. It was as though I was hearing a part of myself say something that gave the rest of me pause. I filed away this sense of unease, because it signaled the need to reflect on who I was and what I was doing. I have read William James's book, *The Varieties of Religious Experience*. I have heard and read of epiphanies that were sudden and dramatic. One minute someone holds a certain belief system, and in the next moment it is shattered and replaced by something else.

Maybe those happen, but not to me, or not usually. I suspect that sudden and qualitative leaps come only after a series of quantitative changes, which may be unobserved by the person to whom and in whom they are happening. That is, life changes occur like other changes in nature.

I have lashed out in anger and despair, with effects that lasted a long time. But every major shift in my life has been the product of thought and feeling that seemed at times to go on endlessly. A decision might be called for by an external event, but I wanted to feel that I was making the right choice.

I kept my uncertainties to myself. I studied hard, trying to get my mind around the political philosophy and rhetoric that I was there to learn. I devoured books on social issues. I listened to all the political views that were being expressed, on campus, at KPFA, and in the wider world. In the summer of 1959, as midshipman third class, I went on my summer cruise, serving aboard the destroyer *USS Maddox*—later to be involved in the Gulf of Tonkin incident that provoked a wider Vietnam war.

My second year at Berkeley, our NROTC instructor was Lieutenant Commander Steed. We got a new commanding officer, Captain Meyer. Steed was not your image of a naval officer. His khaki uniform was usually a little rumpled, and his manner diffident. A part of his job was to teach us something about foreign and military policy, from the Navy's perspective. There was a midshipman in our class, Pete, who stood out because he was outspoken, and because we all knew he was the nephew of some high-ranking Navy officer. One day in class we were talking about the atomic bombs dropped on Hiroshima and Nagasaki. Pete raised his hand and said, "Commander, I have read that we did not need to drop those bombs, that the Japanese were ready to surrender."

Steed paused a very long time. Finally, his voice soft, he said, "Mr. X, if I believed that, I would have to turn in my uniform." I am not giving his last name because for all I know he is still a naval officer somewhere.

Pete's concerns paralleled some of mine. As part of thinking things through, I decided to clarify my views by writing them out. For my NROTC term paper, I wrote on disarmament. We are now, I wrote, like villagers living on the slopes of Vesuvius, never knowing from one day to the next whether a lava flow will wipe out our community. Why are we living in this way, I asked? And I quoted John Donne, who prayed God to deliver man from needing danger. These are the parts I remember, and I am sure that I included in the paper research and analysis in addition to rhetorical flourish.

A week after I turned the paper in, Commander Steed called me. "Can you come to my house?" he asked. Somewhat fearfully, I went. We sat in his living room. At home, he looked more disheveled than on duty. I wondered where in the arc of his naval career he now was, and thought that he must be on the downward slope. He had my paper. "I have read this. It is very well done," he began. "You have a career in the Navy ahead of you, if you want it. You are bright. You present a good image. Your marks are high. You don't want something like this in your file. It would follow you. So I am going to give you a grade, and I am giving you back this paper."

I thought the concerns I raised in my paper were realistic, and that my approach to them was at least debatable. Did Steed mean that the Navy was intolerant of all but the narrowest official view of policy and history? I thought tolerance of dissent to be an important American value. I thought that those destined for leadership, even in the military, should develop the habit of independent thought.

During my second year at Berkeley, 1959-60, I went to meetings of campus political organizations. I spoke against the death penalty. I spoke out against the House Committee on Un-American Activities. I became active in Slate, a student organization that worked on issues of student rights, freedom of expression, farm worker rights, and disarmament. I met one of the KPFA commentators who was a member of a Quaker meeting, and I attended Sunday services there a couple of times.

The spring of 1960, as I recounted in Chapter 2, focused my attention on social change. The Cold War was at the center of my concerns that year, because it seemed a cover for stifling dissent and a way of diverting attention from the issues of racism and poverty. Things came to a head in the summer of 1960. I went on my second-class midshipman cruise. For half the summer, we were in Texas, where I was commander of one company of midshipmen. The Navy was recruiting us to be aviators, so each midshipman received eight hours of flight training. The second half of the summer, we were in San Diego, where our own Captain Meyer was in charge. Our job there was to learn amphibious assault tactics, including a full-scale landing on a California beach. We waded ashore from landing craft with packs and rifles, to the amazement and amusement of tourists parked along Highway 101 to watch. We then penetrated into imagined enemy territory, firing blank ammunition and scaring the hell out of rabbits and chipmunks.

In San Diego, Captain Meyer made us all watch a filmstrip called *Communism on the Map*, produced by Harding College of Searcy, Arkansas. In later years, commanding officers were disciplined for showing this stuff to the troops. The story line was that the Communists were poised to take over America, as shown, for example, by the number of legislators in Hawaii who had received electoral support from the International Longshoreman's and Warehouseman's Union. The film regarded every progressive political movement in America as part of a Soviet-dominated movement to destroy America.

As we marched back to our barracks from the showing, Captain Meyer fell into step beside me. "Well, Mr. Tigar, what did you think of the film?"

"I thought it was mostly half-truths, sir."

"Well, what about the rest of it?"

"The rest of it was lies, sir."

"Report to my office."

"Yes, sir."

In the office, Captain Meyer and another officer questioned me at length on my role as film critic. When classes resumed in the fall, Captain Meyer resumed his position as commanding officer of the UC Berkeley NROTC unit at the University of California. This was my junior year and I was rooming with Ken Kitch and Aryay Lenske, who were active in student political organizations.

In October, Meyer called me into his office and handed me a report prepared by the Office of Naval Intelligence. "These are the kind of people you are associating with," he said. The office had investigated me and my roommates. Its report was full of the clichés that dominated right-wing political discourse. An example, "Aryay Lenske is, among his other activities, chairman of the Students for Civil Liberties. This organization is affiliated with the American Civil Liberties Union, which claims to support the Constitution but which in fact is an apologist for Communist and Communist-front activity."

I was, first of all, angry at the invasion of my political privacy and that of my friends. What the hell was naval intelligence doing investigating students? I was angry at the nonsense in this report, authored by an agency responsible for national security. When I reported my concerns to the university's dean of students, he laughed them off. I thought that the university would be upset about the military spying on its students, but it turned out that the administration knew about it and welcomed it.

I was also scared. I was 19 years old. My Navy scholarship money was my main support in college. I had my part-time job at KPFA, but that didn't pay much.

It is hard to remember how many more times I sat in Captain Meyer's office. I know it was a few. I spoke to helpful friends. I had been a good midshipman, with high ratings, even company commander at the summer training program in Corpus Christi. I could drill a company with the best of them. I could not talk to my family. My mother would have understood, I am sure, but my stepfather was rabid on the subject of my politics, and it was all my mother could do to keep him from calling the FBI during his drunken rages to report his disloyal stepson.

In the end, I could not reconcile the things I believed in with what the Navy was doing and demanding. The Navy and I parted company. It was a difficult divorce. The NROTC terminated my status as a midshipman. This part did not bother me. I then received a notice in the mail saying that because I had been a midshipman for more than two years, I was hereby enlisted as a seaman in the United States Navy, and that I would soon be told where to report for duty. I had thought that maybe they would send me a bill for the several hundred dollars the Navy had spent on my state university fees and my books. I didn't think they would draft me.

I wrote a letter to Francis Heisler, a lawyer in Carmel, California, whose name someone had given me. In these days before the massive Vietnam draft calls, there were not many lawyers who knew anything about military and draft law. In my letter, I told my story. Heisler called a few days later. I tagged his accent as Viennese. I had never met him, but I conjured the image of a Freudian analyst with a three-piece suit and beard. I never saw him in person and have no idea if my image was right. Right or wrong, it comforted me.

"It sounds from your letter," he began, "like you have not made up your mind. Could you participate in warfare, or not? Are your objections to particular foreign policies or to all policies that include war?"

I do not remember all my words. I struggled to explain. I could see the possibility of armed forces in a true multinational force keeping the peace. I could understand how an oppressed people could take up arms. I thought that these instances were different from the use of warfare as an instrument of national policy, which was what I was being asked to do.

This was, Heisler said, a close case. Later, when I wrote a book on selective service law during the Vietnam war, I would understand just how close. If I rejected participation in war as I understood that term, and if my objection were based on religious or ethical principles, and if my definitions were reasonable, then I would be a conscientious objector as the draft law defined that term.

The trouble was that I was already in the military. Draft law did not apply to me. In later years, the military would codify conscientious objector standards almost identical to those used by the Selective Service System. This had not happened yet, nor were there regulations on processing people who claimed this status. This was 1960, before the law on conscientious objection had received the thorough judicial consideration that it was later to receive.

Heisler urged me to write a letter describing my beliefs and send it to the Navy. "Show on the letter that you have sent a copy to me," he said. "That might do some good." I sent my letter. Months went by. John F. Kennedy was elected President. In January, shortly after the inauguration, I received an envelope from the Navy. Inside was an honorable discharge from military service. Since there were no conscientious objector regulations as such, I don't know if I was discharged honorably as a pain in the ass or as a pacifist. Whatever the paper meant, it did not get me off the hook, because I had not served enough time to become ineligible for the draft.

But of all the personal decisions that I faced, this had been the most difficult. Thinking through my views on warfare as policy, I came to certain tentative views about the need for transnational rules to halt slaughter while legitimately using force to protect human rights. In the more than 40 years since then, I have returned to these themes again and again, usually without the compulsion of personal consequences. In later years, I changed my views about violence and armed struggle. I had not considered the issue outside the context of nuclear war. I had leapt from the nonviolent struggle of the civil rights movement to the possibility of nuclear annihilation. Later, I had to take into account such things as the South African struggle against apartheid, which included armed conflict. Such conflict was, I came to believe, necessary in the people's defense against an enemy with superior forces. One might call this defensive struggle and not war as such, thus preserving for me the label of conscientious objector. But a part of my journey has been to reject labels as being ways to falsify an underlying and changing reality. So I simply say where I was and where I am.

I rejected for myself and for those whom I represented the label "coward" for not wanting to put on an American military uniform. I have been shot at by white racists in Florida, beaten up by police, and held at gunpoint by South African security forces who made us lie on the ground while they debated what to do with us. I have had my share of conflict.

When I graduated from college in 1962, I went to London to work as European correspondent for Pacifica Radio. I wrote to Lord Bertrand Russell and asked him for an interview. He agreed, provided I would come to his castle home in Penhyrndreudrath, Wales. We set a date in October 1962. I lugged my heavy tape recorder to a small town in Wales and checked in at a pub that had rooms. That night in the bar, the television carried news of the Cuban missile crisis. American intelligence sources had detected missile installations in Cuba. President Kennedy demanded that the missiles be removed if already there, or not sent if they were on their way. Cuban President Fidel Castro defended his country's right to install whatever defenses it wished, particularly because in 1961 the United States had sponsored an armed invasion of Cuba in an effort to overthrow his government. Soviet Premier Khrushchev asserted that his government had the right to respect the Cuban wish to have the missiles deployed.

We now know more about President Kennedy's decision-making process than we knew then. Cuba was and is a sovereign state, and has the right to defend itself from armed attack. The United States is surely wrong in regarding the western hemisphere as its own backyard, and in thinking that it can intervene at will in the internal affairs of other states. Our repeated military and covert invasions of other countries have violated international law and gone a long way to create and maintain regimes that are either unstable or dictatorial.

The United States had placed and still maintains an illegal blockade on Cuba, preventing it from obtaining necessary goods by ordinary trade and from selling its products on the world market. To sell its principal export, sugar, the Cuban government had made long-term contracts with the Soviet Union. The Soviets had also negotiated a deal to maintain a military presence in Cuba and to sell military hardware to the Cubans.

While I respected the Cubans' right to self-determination, I never thought that the Soviet military presence was a good idea. When I later visited the island, I saw that many Cubans apparently agreed. The Russians were not popular. By contrast, most Cubans were eager to meet and talk to Americans. They made a sharp distinction between an American government whose policies they did not like and American people with whom they had long-developed friendships and business ties.

It was, I thought, crazy for the Soviets to install missiles in so provocative a way. Of course, United States missiles were trained on Soviet targets from several points in Europe, so it could hardly be said that the Soviets should not have missiles of their own. That was not the point. Their action was a dangerous escalation of the nuclear arms race. The American response was also absurd as a matter of logic, and became outright dangerous when President Kennedy announced an intention to stop Soviet ships on the open seas and to take other actions that might invade the territorial integrity of Cuba. That night, on the pub television, it seemed that the world was headed for a confrontation between the two great nuclear powers.

I can still remember the old taxi pulling up in front of Lord Russell's stone castle. The train trip through Wales had wound among hills still green in that early fall. Sheep, the animals best adapted to the terrain, grazed. They almost looked like devout parishioners, bowing to take communion. Is that image, I wondered, a reason for Bach's cantata that says "sheep may safely graze"?

Lord Russell was about 90 years old, frail but alert. He had seen the television reports and listened to the radio. My thoughts of an interview that ranged over his philosophical thoughts went out the window. Looking back, I wish I had been more prepared for the intellectual depth and fire that I was to meet. As it was, the interview was one of my most exciting mornings. Our talk turned to the Cuban missile crisis.

"I cannot tell you," Lord Russell said in that precise acerbic tone, "how wicked I think it." He had been a prominent figure in the Campaign for Nuclear Disarmament, and had even committed civil disobedience at one of its marches. Some dismissed him as a senile crank, well past any ability to think things through. Some said his private secretary, Ralph Schoenman, dominated his activities. That day, his words and actions laid all that to rest. Whether it was putting forward his views on nuclear arms or recalling his philosophical disputes of 40 years before, his vision and diction were clear.

I returned to London with the tape recording and followed the ongoing dispute. The Soviets pulled back their missile-carrying ships. The risk of nuclear war seemed to recede. The conflict had, however, raised serious questions about the western military alliance. As I continued to do interviews and report on those issues, I formed my views on the law of nations that have been the basis for my work ever since.

Throughout the fall of 1962, the French and English governments continued to discuss the missile crisis and its meaning. Harold Macmillan was Prime Minister, with a Conservative parliamentary majority. Hugh Gaitskell led the Labour opposition until his death in early 1963, to be succeeded by Harold Wilson. Charles de Gaulle was President of France. Macmillan was being challenged over the issue of Britain's relationship with Europe, and whether the United Kingdom should enter the Common Market. He was also under pressure from the left for making nuclear arms deals with the United States. De Gaulle was vulnerable because Algeria had become independent early in 1962 and the white settlers there were returning to mainland France. Some of those settlers, former French army men, thought they had been betrayed. They formed the OAS—*Organisation de l'Armée Secrete*, and began a campaign of bombings in French cities. There were attempts on de Gaulle's life.

I recorded interviews and reported on the parliamentary debates in London. I went to Paris that winter to interview French politicians about the political crisis created by the Algerian aftermath. One morning, I went to interview Claude Bourdet of the *Parti Socialiste Unifié*, and found that his apartment had been bombed the night before. Every political figure I met had armed guards.

The political debates in both England and France revolved around the evident fact that American military power was the principal strength of the NATO alliance and that the Americans were likely to use that power when and where they thought best. If the European members of the alliance disagreed, that was too bad. This perceived American arrogance led to different responses in England and France.

President de Gaulle insisted that France have an independent voice in nuclear decision making, and had built a uniquely French nuclear capability, which he dubbed the strike force, or *force de frappe*. French nuclear testing went on heedless of international agreements, and at one point the French secret service even destroyed a protest vessel in the South Pacific. President de Gaulle was outraged that the United States had turned a local battle with a small island nation into a potential nuclear war.

The English response was more complex. England had decided in the 1950s to develop nuclear arms. Prime Minister Bevan's rationale was that one should not be "naked at the conference table." In the ensuing years, Britain's colonial power had eroded, and her nuclear force was inexorably tied to that of the Americans. The Macmillan government revealed that it had mobilized Britain's nuclear-armed bombers during the Cuban missile crisis. Macmillan defended this action as an exercise of British power and sovereignty. Of that sovereignty, and speaking of Macmillan's foreign secretary, a Labour member of Parliament derided such pretensions: "The government is composed of impenitent Municheers and foiled Suez aggressors. Lord Hume has the melancholy distinction of being both." The point was that Britain had not acted independently. Nor had it any realistic capacity to do so. It had, so Macmillan's critics argued, used NATO nuclear might in the service of a non-NATO cause.

As I listened to these European leaders, I was greatly helped by Konni Zilliacus, the Labour member of Parliament for Manchester, of whom I spoke earlier. Zilly had written several books on collective security. In 1945, he published a work provocatively titled *Can the Tories Win the Peace and How They Lost the Last One*.

With Zilly's help, I unbundled the issue of collective security. I say "unbundled," because deconstruction had not yet been invented, as far as I was aware. The United Nations at its inception was divided into two governing parts: the Security Council and the General Assembly. There is also a Secretariat, which has administrative functions. The UN Charter envisioned a postwar world governed by collective security. The five permanent members of the Security Council—the United States, USSR, Great Britain, France, and China—had to be in unanimous agreement on any important matter, including the use of force. To some extent, this meant that the great powers had opted out of any significant control over their actions, because they could always veto any Security Council resolution directed at them.

Interestingly, the United States took the first steps to break down the Security Council's sole power. When the Korean conflict began, the Soviets would clearly have vetoed any Security Council resolution to send UN military force. The United States sponsored and achieved passage in the General Assembly of what it called the Uniting for Peace resolution. This empowerment of the General Assembly has helped to change the face of international law. As the newly liberated colonies took their place in the General Assembly, their plurality passed more and more resolutions addressing even the conduct of the great powers.

The UN Charter also envisioned regional alliances, although there is some question whether military alliances such as NATO are within the terms of that article. Regardless of interpretation, NATO and the Warsaw Pact were quickly formed as the Cold War began in the 1940s. However, regarding a dispute between the United States and Cuba as a legitimate subject of NATO concern seemed questionable, to say the least. Invoking NATO was, I thought, a cover for interventionist policies in the western hemisphere.

As the United States took over military security concerns from the French in Indochina, it also formed the Southeast Asia Treaty Organization, or SEATO. This grouping was, it seemed to me, completely inconsistent with the UN Charter. The United States is not a part of the southeastern Asia region, as a buffalo does not become a giraffe by sticking its neck out. As a matter of international law, therefore, I concluded that the use of force in Vietnam and the threat of force in Cuba were wrong. These were disputes that the United States ought to have submitted to the United Nations and resolved within the framework of that organization.

During my law school years from 1963 to 1966, President Johnson escalated American military presence in Vietnam, and the war was a major issue in the 1964 presidential election. In addition to my concerns about international law, I studied the constitutional issues related to making war. Later, we would litigate these issues in draft cases. Under Article 1 of the Constitution, the President is commander in chief and can, of course, order action to repel sudden attacks. However, Congress is given budgetary control over military expenditures and has the power to declare war and to authorize lesser belligerent activity such as "letters of marque and reprisal." Justice Joseph Story, in his *Commentaries on the Constitution*, believed that making war posed such threats to a republican form of government that it should be done only with the collective consent of all branches of government. In Story's view, the President could not conduct war on his own decision. He had to not only consult but also obey the will of Congress. In such a view, the Supreme Court would stand ready to decide, in an appropriate case, that legislative and executive power was or was not being properly exercised.

My thoughts were not new or original. Senator Fulbright of Arkansas had expressed similar views, and a prominent committee of international lawyers had prepared a report containing a detailed analysis of American Vietnam policy as a matter of domestic and international law. But I was frustrated once again by my law school, for there was nothing in the course offerings that permitted a detailed examination of these issues.

I turned my thoughts into a speech, which I delivered as valedictorian at my law school graduation. I spoke of an issue that has continued to concern me. Presidential and, more broadly, executive branch decisions to make war, conduct unlawful searches, stifle dissent, and otherwise endanger rights ought in our system to be subjected to review by the other branches of government as well as being the subject of popular protest. Yet here was a war that had been approved by Congress only by the stratagem of false reports. I said:

> The course of this war imperils the American system of separation of powers. We witness the erosion of any congressional check upon executive war-making activity.
>
> Article 1, section 8, clause 11 of the United States Constitution vests in Congress the power to declare war. The Constitutional Convention of 1787 considered giving the power to the Executive, where it had always rested under the British monarchy. But the convention rejected this thought, and gave the President only the power to repel sudden attacks.
>
> A century and more ago, Joseph Story, distinguished lawyer and justice of the United States Supreme Court and the greatest legal scholar of the 19th century, wrote this of congressional power:
>
> "The power of declaring war is not only the highest sovereign prerogative; but it is in its own nature and effects so critical and calamitous that it requires the utmost deliberation, and the successive review of all the councils of the nation. War . . . never fails to impose upon the people the most burthensome taxes, and personal sufferings. It is always injurious, and sometimes subversive of the great commercial, manufacturing and agricultural interests. . . . It is sometimes fatal to public liberty itself. . . . It should therefore be difficult in a republic to declare war, but not to make peace."

I went on to urge graduates to take an interest in the developing law of the United Nations Charter and other domestic and international principles regulating armed conflict and its dangers. Half the audience stood and applauded and half sat on their hands. That was about the division of opinion that I would have expected.

Notes

1. On the themes in this chapter, *see generally Symposium, Selective Service* 1970, 17 U.C.L.A. L. Rev. 893 (1970). The leading cases are *Oestereich v. Selective Service Local Board No. 11*, 393 U.S. 233 (1968); *Gutknecht v.*

United States, 396 U.S. 295 (1970); *Breen v. Local Board No. 16*, 396 U.S. 460 (1970); *Clark v. Gabriel*, 393 U.S. 256 (1968); *Wolff v. Selective Service Local Board No. 16*, 372 F.2d 817 (2d Cir. 1967) (enjoining induction of registrants who had, because of a sit-in, lost their student deferments, and holding that when the First Amendment was at stake, there is no need to exhaust administrative remedies or to refuse induction as a precondition of judicial review); *United States v. Wingerter*, 423 F.2d 1015 (5th Cir. 1970). The *Spock* decision is 416 F.2d 165 (1st Cir. 1969).

2. On selective prosecution of those who refused to carry draft cards, *see United States v. Falk*, 479 F.2d 616 (7th Cir. 1973) (en banc). *See* my articles: *The Rights of the Selective Service Registrant*, in THE RIGHTS OF AMERICANS (1970); *Selective Service: Some Certain Problems and Some Tentative Answers*, 37 GEO. WASH. L. REV. 433 (1969) [with R. Zweben]. On the Cuban blockade issue, *see* Michael Krinsky & David Golove, *United States Economic Measures Against Cuba* (1933).

Chapter 6
DRAFT BOARD DAYS AND NIGHTS

When I went off to Washington and wound up practicing law, the war in Vietnam had become a topic not only of discussion but also of litigation. Draft calls increased, putting pressure on young men and their families. All of a sudden, parents concerned with their children's well-being were taking notice of the escalating American military presence in Vietnam. The war had become more controversial. A part of this controversy was reflected in a provision of the 1967 Military Selective Service Act that required a young man who claimed conscientious objection to military service to demonstrate that the objection was based on "religious training and belief." In addition, the act guaranteed a 2-S student deferment to any undergraduate but eliminated the largely discretionary practice by which students had been able to remain in college through their graduate years without serious threat of induction into the armed forces.

The 1967 act therefore guaranteed that a young person whose family could afford to send him to college would be able to get a bachelor's degree. But upon graduation, he would be a prime target for induction because draft calls were supposed to be oldest first.

The Selective Service System of rules was Byzantine to say the least. More than 4,000 local draft boards, each composed of citizens without legal training, decided whether a registered young man was to be classified 1-A and thus eligible for service, or 1-O and thus entitled to exemption as a conscientious objector, or 1-A-O and thus eligible only for noncombatant service. The other principal exemptions and deferments included the 2-S student deferment and the 4-A ministerial exemption. All of these were the focus of controversy.

The local draft boards followed not only the Selective Service regulations that were published in the Code of Federal Regulations, but also a series of Local Board Memorandums (LBM) authored by the Director of Selective Service, General Lewis Hershey. These explanations of local board practices and procedures were often more important than the regulations themselves.

Once the local board had made a classification decision, it communicated that to the registrant by letter and by issuing a card showing the classification. Thus, in theory, every young man between the ages of 18 and 35 was required to carry two documents. One was a registration certificate, showing the name and address of the local draft board where he happened to be registered. The second was the classification card. Failure to possess both of these, or destruction or mutilation of them, was a five-year felony.

Of course, conscription had been with us for a long time. Those familiar with American history will remember the draft riots that accompanied the imposition of conscription during the American Civil War. Then, it was fairly easy to avoid being drafted into the Union Army if you could pay someone to substitute for you. Also, investigation and pursuit of those who avoided service were lax.

The first truly organized system of conscription was established during the first World War. The World War I draft treated inductees in a rather summary fashion. The statute provided that all persons drafted into the service of the United States shall, from the date of said draft, be subject to the laws and regulations governing the regular army—that is, from the moment you received your draft notice, you were a soldier. If you did not report, the Army rounded you up and court martialed you as a deserter. Roundups of slackers occurred regularly. There is little formal record of the disposition of most cases resulting from such mass arrests. What we do have suggests that opposition to the war was centered in groups of political radicals and in some German communities. Thus, opposition to the war was reflected in the leaflets and demonstrations and other activities that formed the basis of some of the Supreme Court's early First Amendment decisions sharply restricting the rights of Americans to criticize the foreign policy of their government during war time.

As World War II approached, Congress passed the Selective Training and Service Act of 1940. This was a significant departure from the World War I experience. Enforcement was left to the civil courts, and we had a draft system pretty much like that which obtained during the Korean and Vietnam wars. A registrant who claimed to be exempt or deferred from service would file an application with the local draft board. If the local draft board sustained the claim, then the registrant was deferred or exempt. If the board refused it, the registrant had the right of appeal to a board that was also composed of volunteer citizens. If that right was exhausted unsuccessfully, the registrant was subject to induction in the order of oldest first.

There was, in most cases, no right of any pre-induction judicial review of these very important determinations. However, if a registrant showed up at the induction center when called and refused to take the symbolic step forward, signifying entrance into the armed forces, he would then be prosecuted for the five-year felony of refusing to submit to induction. The Supreme Court held, in the waning days of World War II, that such a person could obtain judicial review of the draft board's classification as a defense to such a prosecution. The local board's decision was regarded as final, unless it had no basis in fact or was wrong as a matter of law. Alternatively, if the local board had failed to give the registrant some procedural rights, such as declining to give him a form on which to claim conscientious objection or denying him an appeal to which he was entitled, the induction notice was also void.

One can see, therefore, that the administrative process of the draft board and the regulations by which the board purported to operate were all-important. I was largely ignorant of this law and lore, except for the limited personal experiences of which I've spoken. However, it became clear, as I've said, by the end of 1967, that mounting resistance to the draft was creating a challenge for lawyers and other concerned with fairness in the operation of the Selective Service System. A few lawyers in cities around the country were studying the Selective Service regulations and advising registrants about their options. Some universities had established counseling centers where students could go and get some advice about what faced them. The historic peace churches, such as the Quakers, advised those who wanted to claim conscientious objection for military service and use their time in some civilian capacity for a nonprofit organization instead of serving in the military. In addition, the Jehovah's Witnesses had reached a kind of standoff with the Selective Service System whereby members who devoted more than 100 hours a month to preaching could obtain exemption as ministers.

The Supreme Court also upheld the Jehovah's Witnesses' claim that adherents to their creed were objectors to war in any form, even though they did believe in the final conflict of Armageddon. This decision helped to establish the principle that a conscientious objector need not be a pacifist. One could believe in using violence under certain circumstances, but reject the idea of uniformed warfare as an instrument of national policy.

In the waning days of 1967 three friends of mine called and asked if I would be willing to edit a publication to be called the *Selective Service Law Reporter* (*SSLR*). They were Tom Alder, Charles Halpern, and Brian Paddock. Tom had been around Washington, working in a number of nonprofit organizations, for many years. Charlie Halpern was an associate at the law firm of Arnold and Porter, and Brian Paddock had longtime association with peace organizations in his capacity as a lawyer. I agreed to edit *SSLR* and we hired a staff. The *Selective Service Law Reporter* was a loose-leaf service. Our job was to inform lawyers, draft counselors, and even registrants about the options that they faced in the draft.

The publication consisted basically of three parts. First, we wanted the draft boards' regulations to be public so that anyone could read them. It was fairly easy to copy the regulations published in the Code of Federal Regulations, but we wanted to go further. We thought that the local board memoranda, authored by General Hershey for the guidance of local draft boards, should be available to everyone and not just to the board members. The Selective Service System took a different view, and only on threat of litigation did it release to us these local board memoranda so that everybody could know the regulatory basis on which these life-and-death decisions were being made. Brian Paddock, a lawyer with draft law experience, and Bud Schoefer, who had been a draft counselor, brought their expertise to assembling the regulations so that we could reprint them.

The second part was a publication of judicial decisions, both those destined for inclusion in official reporters and the unreported decisions that increasingly formed the basis of the growing body of draft law.

The third part of *SSLR*'s effort was the most challenging. It was the practice manual, a treatise on the administrative Selective Service process, the prosecution of those who refused to report and for other offenses, and on the use of federal habeas corpus to get out of the military, assuming that you were already in.

You can imagine the circumstances under which we began work. *Selective Service Law Reporter* began in earnest in the early months of 1968. Already the anti-war movement had become so strong and strident that it had threatened Lyndon Johnson's presidency. It was to lead to his refusal to seek a second full term. Robert Kennedy and Eugene McCarthy were poised to challenge Lyndon Johnson's nomination. The Democratic party, riven by the disputes that had marked the 1964 Democratic Convention, had reorganized itself in a way that would grant increased floor time to dissident factions. The 1968 Democratic Convention was to be held in Chicago, political base of powerful Democratic Mayor Richard J. Daley. Demonstrations by anti-war groups were already being planned. The Vietnam war had become a centerpiece of student protest, though by no means its only element.

Nobody had written a comprehensive treatise on draft law. Some lawyers were gaining experience in these cases and developing their own forms. Organizations such as the Central Committee for Conscientious Objectors and the Jehovah's Witnesses had their specialized publications for religion-based exemptions. The issues were also beclouded by the Military Selective Service Act of 1967, which recast significant portions of draft law.

In early 1968, I wrote the administrative section of the practice manual. LEXIS was in its infancy, and slow modem speeds made online research impossible. But I wanted a crash course in draft law. So I took out *United States Code Annotated* and turned to the Selective Service law sections in Title 50. I read every case in the annotations. I then copied out the West key numbers from those cases, and read every case decided under older versions of conscription law, dating back to the Civil War.

I wanted to see patterns of legal development, and to make sure that nothing escaped me. I am convinced that this method of research, tiresome though it is, is the only way to capture a complex subject. In these electronic days, law students are learning to rely too much on computer-assisted research. They think up a query and plug it in. The cases the machine spits out define the borders of their galaxy of thought. They have no idea that the boundaries might be different than they believe, or where their chosen galaxy lies in the universe of legal ideology. Simply put, computer research alone is incomplete. It confines thinking. It misses important citations. It is not very helpful in finding analogies, which are a key element of common law reasoning.

For me, learning conscription law was only the beginning. The local draft board's errors in construing draft law did indeed invalidate its actions. But if we were to help lawyers shape the law, we needed to overlay two more bodies of knowledge. These were administrative law and criminal procedure.

The Selective Service System had functioned for too long as a law unto itself, outside the mainstream of administrative due process. Yet several Supreme Court decisions had recognized the system's obligation to respect its own procedural rules. The system was exempt from the Administrative Procedure Act, but surely there were relevant notions of administrative due process.

The need to understand criminal procedure was obvious as well. To challenge an erroneous order to report for induction, the registrant usually had to show up, refuse induction, and then defend a criminal case. For years, draft advice was given mostly by lay counselors. The lawyers who were entering the field were in many cases innocent of any knowledge of federal criminal practice. I was lucky. Williams & Connolly had introduced me to complex federal criminal litigation.

By early summer I had the administrative section done. In that summer of 1968, I took a family vacation in California for a month. For three weeks of that month, I sat down at an electric typewriter every day and worked on the criminal practice section of the manual. I drafted at speed, marking the need for footnotes and authorities with cryptic notations. Once the text was finished, I went back and put in the footnotes, drawing on the conscription cases I had read and my knowledge of criminal law.

In those days before the word processor, the three-ring binder was the height of technology. I typed the draft with large margins on three-hole punched paper. This kept the pages in some kind of order. When it came time to do the footnotes, I typed them on separate pages and then cut and pasted them so they would be at the bottom of the correct page.

I look back at those sections of the practice manual on occasion. Sometimes lawyers of my generation will mention *SSLR* and its role in their professional lives. Sometimes younger lawyers will remember that their lawyer or draft counselor had a copy. And I look too at the reviews of our work, including one in the *Yale Law Journal* by Circuit Judge J. Skelly Wright.

In 1968, 1969 and 1970, I crisscrossed the country, talking to bar groups, law schools, and draft counselors about draft law. In the debate about the Vietnam war, our work was controversial for its own sake. Many people thought it disloyal to be telling young men how not to serve in the military. I got some of this sentiment from lawyers at Williams & Connolly, where Ed Williams was still paying me well to work part-time. Their criticism was muted when well-heeled clients called and asked if their sons could come in and consult with me.

We put into the field a cadre of trained lawyers and counselors, and with their work the conviction rate in draft cases plummeted, and even those convicted got lighter sentences. Although there were no statistics, these lawyers and counselors also achieved a creditable record of success before the local draft boards. The downside of these developments was that the burden of military service tended to fall more heavily on those

without access to counsel and information. That group was dispropor-
tionately young men of color. For that reason, I did not inveigh against
the institution of conscription, but rather against the pursuit of national
military policies that were used to justify it.

The most strident attacks on draft advising were mounted by seg-
ments of the organized bar. For years, non-lawyers had been the best
experts on the draft, generally working from church-related groups. With
the advent of *SSLR*, and the increased need for reliable information on
the draft, non-lawyer counselors began to work from civic organizations,
colleges, and political groups. Bar associations claimed that these folks,
most of whom were not charging for their services, were engaged in the
unauthorized practice of law. In some instances, bar associations sought
injunctions.

The theory of unauthorized practice is that non-lawyers are not competent to interpret the law, and the public must be protected from them.
Behind these noble words often lurks a desire to keep the profession's
monopoly intact, by requiring that only lawyers perform even services
that non-lawyers could do just as well or better, such as real estate clos-
ings. In this instance, there was no financial motive at work. Most lawyers did not know draft law, did not care to practice it, and would not
have taken on the job of counseling young men for free. Unauthorized
practice became a screen for political motivations, rather like the attacks
on lawyers in the South who were trying to encourage African-Americans to join civil rights cases.

I also helped young men who were having trouble with the draft. In
all of this work, I saw—and tried to get others to see—the unity of legal
theory and practice, in itself and in a social context. To do a good job as
a draft lawyer, you had to understand administrative law. You had to see
how concepts like free expression, religious tolerance, and due process
overlay the more technical aspects of advising draft registrants. And if the
draft board denied relief, and the administrative process did not work,
you had to defend the ensuing criminal case with both technical proficiency and a broad view of what your client stood for.

For example, in most of the conscientious objector cases, victory at
trial came because the draft board had denied the registrant some procedural right, or misapplied its own regulations. Yet it was necessary in
every case to stress the client's sincerity, and even to challenge the legality
of the war in which he had been summoned to fight. The Supreme
Court, over Justice Douglas's lone dissent, refused to consider these legal
challenges to the war itself, but their power and logic helped fuel oppo-

sition to American foreign policy. That opposition brought changes in draft law and eventually an end to the war. The activism spilled over into the Chicago conspiracy trial of 1969 and 1970.

I opened this book with my first Supreme Court argument, which was a draft case. I also represented many young men who were indicted for various crimes related to the draft and the war. The issues in draft litigation were an education in administrative law, constitutional law, and federal procedure. The draft was not only a means to raise an army for Vietnam. Selective Service Director Lewis Hershey had authorized local draft boards to help curb dissent against the war by issuing draft notices to dissentient registrants. Looking back, of course, there was finally amnesty for the draft offenders during the Carter administration, but that came only after the judicial tide had turned and conviction rates were down. A few stories will paint the picture.

Rick lived in suburban Maryland. I remember him as frail and bespectacled, with a wispy beard. He dressed in dark colors, neatly. You could envision him with a yarmulke, although he did not wear one. He looked like a yeshiva student. He had grown up as part of the Washington-area Jewish community, traditionally a strong center of social justice concern.

It came as no surprise, therefore, that when he reached 18 and registered for the draft, he applied for conscientious objector status. He was articulate. He was able to show that in the strands of religious doctrine was a basis for saying that he was conscientiously opposed to war in any form. Of course, the Supreme Court had helped by interpreting the selective service laws to avoid an overly God-based test that would have fallen afoul of the First Amendment by establishing religion. His local board classified him I-O, conscientious objector to all participation in war.

With his I-O classification in hand, Rick was ready for the mandatory alternative civilian service. He was not ready for the vindictive attitude of his local board and the Selective Service System. He was ordered to report for service to a Baptist social service center in Mississippi. During his first week on the job, the overt anti-Semitism of his supervisors was combined with hostility to his "draft-dodging." He quit the center and came home. When he was, in due course, indicted in Mississippi for refusing to do civilian work, he came to see me.

This was a case about objectives. Rick wanted to do civilian work. He was not particularly interested in risking, much less going to, federal prison. The federal court in Mississippi was a legendary harbor of reactionary sentiment. Appellate review in the United States Court of Appeals for the Fifth Circuit was much more likely to be unfavorable than in, for example, the Second Circuit (which covered New York and Vermont).

For Rick, therefore, the goal was to get him into some civilian work that would not be a punishment for his views, and to avoid the stain of a criminal conviction on his record. In those days, in the District of Columbia federal district court, you could plead your client guilty before any district judge who would agree to take the plea. So if your client were a gambler, you had a good idea which judge to choose, and if a white-collar criminal, a different judge. I approached Judge William Bryant and told him about the case. He agreed to take a guilty plea, but with no promise of what he would do about sentencing.

Next, I negotiated a transfer of Rick's case from Mississippi to the District of Columbia under Federal Rule of Criminal Procedure 20, which is designed to let a defendant who wishes to plead guilty do so in a district of his choice.

I thought, naively, that once the case was before Judge Bryant, all would be well. I could not imagine a judge with compassion and a background in criminal defense and community law sending Rick to prison. I reckoned without the pressure that other judges would put on a relatively new appointee to the bench, and without Rick's own misguided judgment.

On the day appointed for sentence, Judge Bryant's secretary called me and asked me to come to court immediately. I was not to wait for the afternoon calendar call. The judge was furious. Rick, in a gesture of love, had sent the judge a bouquet of flowers. He did not mean any harm, and he had not asked my advice. It was a nutty thing to do.

As Judge Bryant vented his anger at me, our conversation turned to what he was going to do about sentence. "I won't do it today," he said. "I am too angry. But let me ask you this: What am I supposed to do? Here is young man who gets everything the system has to offer. He gets his CO classification. He just can't stand the pressure down there in Mississippi with those Baptists. I don't necessarily buy that. I am a black American, and I have lived with hostility all my life one way and another. Why can't this kid grow up?"

I thought about this. "Well, Judge, the decision is yours. This is not an isolated case. Thirty-seven per cent of Harvard's graduating students say they would not serve in the Vietnam war. What do we tell those people? What do we do about the draft boards being hostile to conscientious objectors? These young people are not dropping out. Almost all of them recognize some obligation to serve their country in some way that does not involve killing. So why not figure out a way to tap into that desire?"

"Well," the judge said, "that's not all. The other judges around here are not happy about your client. There is no induction center in D.C., so we don't get the routine draft refusals, but I am getting some pressure to make an example of him."

"I can't answer for that," I said. "I know what you are saying, and I can only hope you will listen to our sentencing plan." The prosecutor was not there, and I did not want to descend into an argument for a particular result.

I left chambers and got a new sentencing date. Our proposal was that Rick be sentenced to probation on condition that he do alternative civilian service with a community group I had found. We asked that he be sentenced under the Young Adult Offender Act, so that when his probation was finished his conviction would be expunged. That would put him more or less back where he would have been if the local board had not sent him to Mississippi. I went to talk to the assistant United States attorney, who had children of his own. He agreed to stand mute at sentencing. Rick got his probation.

I don't remember how I met Louis. No doubt somebody told him about this young lawyer who had written a guide on trying draft cases. He was, I remember, from Louisiana. He had asked his local draft board to be classified as a conscientious objector, but the local board didn't do that sort of thing. In his hometown, there wasn't much war resistance going on, nothing to affiliate with. So he and his girlfriend drifted north. Louis was by no means a leader. He was just one of the tens of thousands of young men who were saying no to the Vietnam war and to the draft.

In Washington, he joined a group that was demonstrating in front of selective service headquarters. And there, in view of the television cameras, he took out his selective service registration and classification cards and tore them up—two five-year felonies right there.

The theory of this requirement was presumably that if a nuclear war erupted and wiped out the selective service records, the military could round up enough able-bodied young men to get the fighting done. Prosecutions under these sections were very few in the mid-1960s. However, once draft-age young men began to hand in, tear up, or refuse to carry their cards, prosecutors began bringing more cases. The Selective Service System even adopted a policy of immediately drafting anybody who tossed away, tore up, or failed to carry his card. This policy did not survive Supreme Court review—as we shall see—but thousands went to jail for refusing these punitive induction orders.

Louis's protest was on the cusp of these changes. A guard picked up the pieces of his card and sent them to the FBI. The United States attorney prosecuted. I had been admitted to the bar for about a year, and this case might be nicknamed "pathways of illusion." I had learned how to pick apart, and move to dismiss, an indictment that did not spell out the offense with enough detail and certainty. I had learned the value of a bill of particulars, to refine the indictment's allegations. Under the case law and Federal Rule of Criminal Procedure 7(f), a prosecutor was required to give the defense details of the charge. Variances between those details and the proof at trial might be seized upon to obtain dismissal or acquittal. Too, the prosecutor was required to give discovery.

Beyond these procedural issues, I wanted to address the meaning of this statute that authorized punishment of anyone who "alters, knowingly destroys, knowingly mutilates, or in any manner changes" a draft card. The Supreme Court had held that such action did not qualify as protected speech, but rather as unprotected though expressive conduct. Surely, however, one could argue that the First Amendment dictated a narrowing construction of the statute. Louis had torn up his card, but with a little Scotch tape it would be as good as new.

All of these were good theories. I was sure that, given my status as associate in Washington's premier criminal defense firm, headed by Edward Bennett Williams, I would receive the same respectful attention that Williams observably received in the local federal court. And I had trouble imagining the visceral hostility of older conservative judges— and some not so conservative ones—to the protests against the Vietnam war and to the often unruly and ill-dressed protesters.

I wrote my motions to dismiss, for particulars, and for discovery. The case was assigned to Chief Judge Edward Curran, an aging Irish Catholic with a reputation for dealing softly with gamblers and white-collar defendants. The prosecutor was Assistant U.S. Attorney Earl Silbert, later to have some difficulty figuring out what really happened in the Watergate burglary. Earl was, and is, bright and able, but with a very short fuse.

For this argument on legal motions, Louis did not need to be present. It was just as well. I began my argument on the indictment, and I thought I ably distinguished a case decided by the United States Court of Appeals for the Second Circuit.

"What's wrong with the Second Circuit?" Curran demanded.

"Well, Your Honor, it is clearly less concerned with defendants' rights than our own D.C. Circuit," I ventured. The frown on Curran's face showed that he had doubts about the D.C. Circuit's innovative criminal procedure holdings.

"Maybe that's not all bad," said Judge Curran. "How many motions have you filed?"

"There are five, Your Honor," I said, and began to name them.

Judge Curran cut me off and held up his hand with fingers outstretched. "OK," he said, counting on his fingers, "denied, denied, denied, denied, denied. Let's set a trial date." So much for my legal theories.

Before Louis's trial came up, a group of protesters was arrested for blocking the entrance of the National Selective Service Headquarters on G Street, two blocks from the White House. In 1968, this sort of thing would not have attracted much attention, except this demonstration was led by Lea Adams, daughter of General Adams, one of Selective Service Director Lewis Hershey's top assistants. Adams was the only African-American in a leadership role in the Selective Service System.

The demonstrators were hauled off to jail for blocking the sidewalk. At that time, the misdemeanor court—the Court of General Sessions, as it then was—held night court. The idea was to get bailable offenders out of jail, and to clear up minor cases with on-the-spot plea bargains. Our misfortune was that Judge Charles Halleck was sitting that night. He was the son of a prominent Republican congressman. In later years, he found love and tolerance and let his hair grow long. But that had not happened yet.

My friend Spencer Smith and I came down to represent the protesters, no doubt because of a phone call to one of us from their friends. We thought we should move for bail first. If we could get everybody out on their own recognizance, then we could ask for a long continuance and maybe things would calm down and the U.S. attorney would drop the case. If bail was too high to meet, we didn't want these young people in the old D.C. jail, so we might ask for trial within a couple of days.

Speedy trial in a case like that can work for the defense. The police haven't had time to compare notes. They may not have found some good photographs to study, and may be confused about who sat where and when. Cross-examination can raise that reasonable doubt.

These protesters were really making the same complaint that drove Louis. The Selective Service System was probably the most uncommunicative part of government, apart from agencies like the Central Intelligence Agency, which dwelt in a world of its own. The Selective Service

System tried to keep its regulations and procedures a mystery. At every stage, it sought to make its decisions unreviewable by never giving—and perhaps not even having—a reason for saying that this young man would go to war and this other one would not. General Hershey, the longtime director and symbol of the system, ran the agency like J. Edgar Hoover ran the FBI—in a highly personal way that tolerated no dissent or interference. So a jury might well decide that this sit-in on a sidewalk did not so incommode the passersby that the protesters' message should be punished.

These were our thoughts as we faced Judge Halleck. "If the court please, we would like to get the issue of bail settled for these young people and then get a trial date," I said.

Halleck grinned and stroked his crew cut. "Not so fast, Mr. Tigar. First a trial date, then I'll think about bail."

Time for Plan B. "In that case, Your Honor, we would request a trial as soon as possible. We are ready."

"OK, Tigar," the Judge said, dropping the honorific Mr., "October 31. How'd you like to try these creeps on Halloween?"

My mouth moved more quickly than my brain. "That depends on whether Your Honor was thinking of a trick or a treat."

Judge Halleck did not think this funny, but he set bail fairly reasonably. The defendants went to trial and were found not guilty.

Louis's case was much more serious. The median sentence in draft cases was around three years, but because D.C. did not have an induction center where men actually refused to enter the armed forces, we did not have sentencing figures for the district's federal judges. The case was assigned for trial to Howard Corcoran, who was appointed by President Lyndon Johnson. Judge Corcoran was brother to Tommy "the Cork" Corcoran, a premier Washington insider since the days of Franklin D. Roosevelt. Edward Bennett Williams called Tommy and people like him "rainmakers," by which he meant that they would confide, as inside information, that it would rain or that it would not. Since they had at least a 50 percent chance of being right, their reputations grew. Tommy claimed, whether he had or not, influence over Howard's appointment. Judge Corcoran's politics were surely not conservative, but Louis was, after all, protesting Lyndon Johnson's war.

Judge Corcoran was patient, though. I had not much trial experience. I made a lot of objections to admissibility of evidence. Some were thin, to say the least. But he treated me as though I knew what I was doing. All my objections meant a lot of conferences at the bench, so the jurors would not hear. I thought of "going to the bench" as part of what lawyers did. Louis and his girlfriend Mary thought differently.

Mary was a sketch artist. She produced a drawing of Louis in the foreground, pensive, sitting at counsel table. In the distance sat the judge, with the prosecutor and me huddled with him arguing some legal point. The jurors sat off to one side in shadows. That picture—which Mary and Louis kept—has stayed with me. Here is somebody on trial for his liberty, and the important issues are being thrashed out off in the distance, in conversations he does not hear. The sense of alienation that every defendant feels must be heightened by such doings, as though the law's studied unconcern can be crueler than deliberate vengeance.

The jurors, too, must resent being excluded from important decisions in so visible a way. If the conferences are frequent and long, the interruptions become part of jurors' overall resentment at the waste of their time. "It is the privilege of the rich," says the English poet Stevie Smith mockingly, "to waste the time of the poor."

I have tried to learn this lesson. I make fewer objections, and try to make them in a way that does not interrupt what is going on unless absolutely necessary. I propose to trial judges that "speaking objections" and bench conferences be limited, and that lawyers and the judge deal with such matters before the jury arrives or during recesses. I make a file for every item of possible evidence and legal issues that may arise, so that I can file a two- or three-page memorandum on short notice. I try to phrase objections so that the jurors and everybody else can understand what is going on. For example, "Objection"—not "I object"—"hearsay." Most people know that hearsay is not a good substitute for direct testimony.

And I object to excluding my client from conferences with the court. Sometimes these objections are not successful. A criminal defendant need be present only at critical stages of the case, and some legal conferences are not thought by judges to be critical. Defendants whose life and liberty are at stake understandably disagree.

But I had not learned that lesson then. Judge Corcoran would not accept that tearing up your draft card was not mutilating it. The evidence against Louis was straightforward. Several police officers saw him tear up the card. The local CBS affiliate obediently gave its film to the FBI, so that Louis's actions could be projected on a screen. A newspaper photographer had still pictures. This was one of those cases that a prosecutor could not possibly lose.

So why not fold our hand right then and plead guilty, perhaps reserving for appeal a legal issue about whether the card was really mutilated?

One practical answer was that we didn't think Judge Corcoran would give Louis more jail time if he went ahead and got a jury verdict.

But hidden in there is a profound debate about what Louis had done. Was it civil disobedience, such that he should acknowledge that he had broken the written law and accept his punishment? This is the view popularly ascribed to Socrates in his dialogue entitled *The Crito*. Socrates had been condemned to death by the Athenian equivalent of a jury, for corrupting the youth. He had a chance to escape but refused. He spoke instead of his continued obligation as a citizen to accept the judgment, having accepted the opportunity to live in Athens and enjoy its benefits.

I understand this view. I have never agreed with it. Now, some protesters want martyrdom, and they are entitled to try for it. The perceived injustice of jailing or executing someone who has acted on principle may indeed help to bring about change. And the imprecations heaped on someone who escapes punishment by a technicality are real, as though enforcing some constitutional claim to freedom or fairness, or obtaining a jury acquittal, was technical.

There are many good reasons to disobey a law that one believes is unjust. Sometimes disobedience is a purely personal statement, and being punished for a violation is a part of the process that the protester finds congenial to the statement he or she wants to make. Such cases are rare. The disobedient one more usually wants to make a statement—to speak truth to power as the Quakers have it. Sometimes these truths are spoken to a prosecutor who declines prosecution, sometimes to a judge who dismisses the charges or to a jury that acquits. An appellate court may reverse a conviction or moderate the jail time.

The protester is seeking to strike a responsive chord. The tide of protest against the Vietnam war moved prosecutors, judges, and juries to acquit more and more protesters, and to moderate sentences for those whose convictions were upheld. This phenomenon had historical forebears. Prohibition did not work because so many people paid no attention to it and the courts were notoriously lax in dealing with offenders. At a much earlier time, the English Quakers, led by William Penn, were acquitted by a jury in 1670, thus making a statement about the right to demonstrate for one's beliefs and the independence of the jury.

John Brown was convicted and sentenced to death, but he made of his trial a convincing story of slavery's evils. As the song has it, "his soul [went] marching on." Susan B. Anthony voted in 1873 to make a statement about what the Fourteenth Amendment ought to mean, and was prosecuted for it. Woman suffrage protesters, angered that President

Woodrow Wilson reneged on his promise to support a suffrage amendment to the Constitution, chained themselves to the White House fence, provoking political turmoil that helped get the amendment ratified. In each of these cases, I would not expect the defendant to accept the court's judgment blandly and go down to jail or death.

I have no problem with a defendant accepting a plea that results in no jail time—going free to engage in politics another day. But that was not the issue in Louis's case.

So what were we doing? Louis's act of tearing up his card was, in my opinion, justified by the way he had been treated. And the way he had been treated mirrored what was happening to tens of thousands of young men. So Louis had something to say, and maybe his saying it could make a difference. We had not convinced the prosecutors or Judge Corcoran, but the case was not over yet. As I look back on that time, the stand taken by people like Louis was part of a national movement against the Vietnam war that changed the face of American politics.

So Louis took the stand and faced the jury. We were going to do what my mentor, Edward Bennett Williams, thought was a very bad idea. Ed was a Roman Catholic, devout in his way. He had little patience for the Catholic movements that encouraged civil disobedience, or for most of the Vietnam war protests that were on the fringes of the law. When Dr. Benjamin Spock, Reverend William Sloane Coffin, Dr. Marcus Raskin, and others were indicted for encouraging young men to resist the draft and turn in their draft cards, the American Civil Liberties Union staff counsel asked me to approach Ed to see if he would represent the defendants pro bono.

I went to see him on a Saturday. He said, "Being out of the office would cause real financial problems here. Can they at least pay something?"

"I think so," I said, sensing that this was not really the issue.

"Well, will they take direction? I need client control. I wouldn't want them mouthing off about the case."

"Ed, their political lives are centered in being in the public arena. It is a little difficult to think that they would be muzzled." I was losing this battle, I could tell.

"And at the trial, I suppose they all want to get on the stand and make speeches about the war in Vietnam. Right?"

"I think they want to tell their story and the reason for their actions."

"Well then, fuck them," Ed replied, although with the trace of a smile, "they don't need a lawyer. They need a toastmaster." So Dr. Spock was tried and convicted, but his conviction was reversed on First Amendment grounds under the brilliant leadership of Leonard Boudin.

I did not think I was Louis Landry's toastmaster. It was important how his story came out. We were also treading close to the line. He was entitled to tell the jurors his story so they could judge his intent. He was not entitled to make a frontal challenge to the judge's legal opinion that tearing up a card was mutilating it.

The testimony of a criminal defendant who takes the stand—and by no means all of them will or should—is in three strophes. This respects the Greek rhetoricians' theory that "triplets" are the most persuasive form. The three are: "Who am I?" "What did I do?" "What should happen to me?" The defendant may always be introduced to the jury, and may introduce himself. Judges can limit these presentations in terms of time and content, but may not curtail them altogether. So the jury can know the defendant's upbringing, background, and basic attitude toward life. The more central that state of mind is to the result, the more latitude the defense will have.

"What did I do?" presents a counterpoint to the prosecution's version of events, or at least a more ample context. When I make an opening statement, I will begin with a discussion of what happened, rather than starting with a long introduction of the defendant. This is because the jury has just heard the prosecutor's opening, with a graphic statement of what the defendant allegedly did. The jury is ready to hear the defense counter to this, and not an explanation of who this defendant is and what he stands for. So in the opening statement, we usually start with only a brief introduction of the defendant, then go into the facts, and then return to look at the defendant's life in more detail.

"What should happen to me?" is the most difficult part. In most American non-capital cases, the jury does not sentence the defendant, so there is usually little occasion for him to discuss a mild versus harsh sentence. However, there are sometimes lesser charges on which a jury can compromise, and a defendant's statement of intention can lead a jury to acquit outright.

Louis took the stand. His quiet, gentle manner was very much in evidence. The jury wanted to meet this young man that it had seen only in the prosecution's version and on news film. Because we knew that Louis would be testifying, I had introduced him during opening statement, but this was the real thing and not some lawyer's version. Like all trial events prefigured in opening statement, this was the time when jurors could see if I had been telling them the truth.

Louis had grown up in a middle-class home. He was successful in school. The Vietnam war, with its escalating demand for soldiers, was a big topic of conversation at his high school and in his community. The jurors watched Louis carefully. Their median age was between 35 and 40. Most of them were African-Americans. In their communities also, these discussions had taken place.

Q: Did you make a decision about the war?
A: Yes. I thought that we had no business there, that we were fighting for an unjust regime. I did not want to be part of that.
Q: What did you do about that?
A: I was registered with my local draft board. I knew about people who left the country to avoid service. I did not want to do that. The guys in my high school, some of them were enlisting, others were being drafted.
Q: So what did you do?
A: I got a book about the draft and read about what it means to be a conscientious objector.
Q: What did that mean to you—to be a conscientious objector?
A: It meant that you would serve just like you had been drafted into the military. But you would serve the community in some other way—some way that did not involve killing or war.
Q: Did you think you were a conscientious objector?
A: I thought I was opposed to war, and that I wanted to serve. To be what the draft board calls a conscientious objector, you have to fill out a form showing that you are opposed to any form of war. You have to show some religious belief.
Q: Did you think you met that test?
A: As I read about it, I did.
Q: What did you do about that?
A: I filled out the form, and I went to the local draft board for an interview.
Q: What happened?
A: They treated me like I was a Communist, a disloyal person.

Louis continued by telling about the local draft board refusing to classify him as a conscientious objector, and then the draft appeal board upholding that decision. He was barely 20 years old. He had taken a stand in his community for what he thought was right. And, as happened to literally thousands who had taken similar stands during all the time we have had the system of conscription for military service, he was rebuffed by petty officials in the rudest possible way.

He had not started out to resist the law—he started out to obey it, to serve his country in the manner guaranteed by the laws and the Constitution. His local board members were the lawbreakers, and there was no way to take them to court for their lawbreaking except by risking a felony conviction. That is, he could wait and get a notice to report for induction, and refuse to submit. Then a judge would rule on whether his conscientious objector claim was valid. The local board would probably dwell in ignorance of how his case came out—and would keep on interpreting the law as it wished.

In this system of non-accountability, Louis chose from among the limited alternatives. He hit the road. He had no clear idea of where he would end up. He wanted to be nearer people who shared his ideals. As things turned out, he made the right choice. Had he stayed home and refused induction, he would have faced a trial court in the Fifth Circuit, which at that time was for draft resisters the most hostile federal court system in the nation. He would have had at best a slim chance of victory and a long prison term if he lost.

Louis continued his story, right up to the day he tore his card. We took the card, which was in evidence, and put it back together so that the jury could see it was basically all there.

A: I wanted—I want—people to know that the war is wrong. I want them to know that whatever you think about the war, the draft system is unfair.

The jurors listened carefully. Then came final arguments and the judge's instructions. We ran into a little luck here. Assistant U.S. Attorney Earl Silbert had, as I said, a short fuse. In his summation, he laid out the evidence. He knew that the judge would tell the jury that to tear up a draft card was to mutilate it. This was, he told the jury, an easy case.

In my summation, I mostly ignored the legal instructions the judge would be giving. They were not helpful, except for the ones on reasonable doubt and on the jury's role.

In the end, members of the jury, this case is not so much about events as about a human being. It is about Louis [and] his journey. To be young, and to face decisions about war and peace, life and death, taking life or preserving life—is almost too much to bear. To have answers to those most basic and personal questions dictated to you by people who refuse to listen—that is so humiliating. For the young, in the face of injustice and intolerance, all journeys are uncommonly long and all roads suddenly uncommonly straight. So they may act out their beliefs.

Louis expected that the draft board would obey the law; that it would listen to and read what he had to say; that it would not rush to judgment. We are, it is true, engaged in a war. Young men like Louis Landry are asking, "What are we fighting for?"

I was deliberately provocative in this summation. If there were a few jurors ready to send a message to the Selective Service System, I hoped to arouse their interest. I also thought that Earl Silbert would have trouble keeping his temper. I was partly right.

Silbert's rebuttal was, as one of his colleagues later said with understatement, "problematic." He attacked Louis for disloyalty. He invoked the specter of men dying on foreign battlefields. The judge overruled my objections to this line of argument, saying that I had "opened the door."

The jury was out for many hours, but finally came in with a guilty verdict. The judge, after a pre-sentence report, sentenced Louis to three years in prison. We got bail pending appeal, so Louis remained at liberty.

I arrived early on the morning of oral argument on the appeal. The U.S. Court of Appeals for the District of Columbia Circuit sits in the same building as the district courts. In those days, back in 1969, you did not know which judges would hear your case until the panel of three came on the bench. As we waited for court to begin, I spoke with Tom Green, the assistant U.S. attorney who would argue the appeal. He smilingly said that he had rebuked Earl for his rebuttal summation.

In the real world of appeals, a prosecutor's misconduct in summation will seldom produce a reversal. But if the court is troubled about the case for other reasons, this is a good basis for decision because such cases are so fact-intensive and therefore have little effect as precedent for the next case.

The judges took the bench. I began my argument with a brief statement of the facts. In most federal courts, the judges have read the briefs and don't want to hear a long factual recital. But the wise advocate will have a couple of sentences at the beginning to put the case and client in perspective.

I had not been talking for long when Judge Wright said, "Mr. Tigar, is it clear from this record that this young man is sincerely a conscientious objector?" I said I thought so. The judge continued, "So where this all starts is that he wanted to do civilian service and the local board said no?" I said yes. This case was being argued after we had begun publication of the *Selective Service Law Reporter*, which Judge Wright had reviewed in the Yale Law Journal. Most law clerks were young males, and they would all have been sensitive to the issues that underlay the case.

"Mr. Green," the judge continued, "does the government agree that this young man was sincere?"

Tom stuttered a bit. This oral argument was not like any he—or I— had witnessed. "I have no reason to doubt what Mr. Tigar is telling you," he finally said.

"Then," the judge said, "if he is willing to do civilian alternative service, shouldn't the district judge have considered sentencing him under the Young Adult Offenders Act? That way, he would do civilian service as a condition of probation, and his conviction would be expunged at the end of that time." We had asked Judge Corcoran for this, and our request was in the record. But Corcoran had refused.

It was clear the judges had talked about this issue before taking the bench. So Judge Wright continued: "There are several difficult issues presented by this record. However, it may well be that Mr. Tigar and his client would be satisfied with a young adult offender sentence. We will hold this case in abeyance and remand to the district judge to reconsider the sentence. If the defendant is not satisfied with the sentence on remand, he can bring the case back up and we will decide it."

A couple of days later, the court's formal order to that effect came in the mail. Silbert and I went to see Judge Corcoran in his chambers. He was furious. "They don't have the power to do this. Sentences within the term allowed by law are not reviewable on appeal. This is blackmail." I sat quietly for this speech. My goal was clear—get that sentence—and provoking Judge Corcoran would not get me there. A chastened Earl Silbert urged the judge to go along with what the court of appeals had suggested.

"Very well," Judge Corcoran finally said, "on the government's suggestion, which is a change of position from when you asked me to give him hard time, I will re-sentence."

So Louis Landry wound up where he had wanted to be. He did his alternative service as a teacher, had his conviction wiped away, and took up teaching and counseling as a career. He called me some 20 years later to tell me how he was doing. Of course, to get where he wanted to be he had to risk prison and live on the fringe. His solace was that in processing his case, the legal system was forced to stop and think about what it was doing to young men like him.

Larry was the son of a San Antonio businessman. He took his consci-entious objector stand only after reading deeply in religious texts. His draft board was not convinced. Before the Military Selective Service Act of 1967, the FBI investigated all conscientious objector claims and filed a report with the local draft board. Larry's claim arose at a time when that was the procedure. FBI reports that supported claims of conscien-tious objection were rare; I don't remember hearing of one.

By 1969, when I got into the case, Larry had refused induction, had been convicted, and had been sentenced to three years in prison. I took his appeal to the U.S. Court of Appeals for the Fifth Circuit. That was my first oral argument in that court, but the case came to me through some San Antonio lawyers who became friends and colleagues over the years: Maury Maverick, Jr., Bernard Ladon, Jesse Oppenheimer, and Herb Kelleher, who is an even better airline executive than he is a law-yer.

At oral argument at the courthouse in Houston, Larry and his family sat in the spectator section. The assistant U.S. attorney arguing for the government adopted a high-dudgeon style. At the height of his rhetoric, he said: "And you know, this young man is not a Christian pacifist at all. The evidence shows he believes in the Karl Marx theory of Commu-nism!" Pretty strong stuff, I thought, for the year 1969.

In rebuttal, I gestured toward Larry and his family, "You know, I said, I need to answer this Karl Marx business, here before Mr. Wingerter and his parents. That allegation shows up in an FBI report, from an anony-mous person that Mr. Wingerter never had a chance to confront or an-swer. Probably some hostile neighbor."

Judge Homer Thornberry looked down at me. "You mean to say that this is one of those FBI anonymous neighbor things, and never tested or verified?"

"That's right, Judge Thornberry."

The judge looked with disapproval at the prosecutor. "Oh, my good-ness!" he said. The lesson is there for every litigating lawyer. You can lose the judge or jury with a single burst of over-the-top rhetoric. If you want your decider to come to a conclusion, you can't push him or her there with imagery. The court of appeals reversed the conviction.

Rosalio Muñoz was a student at UCLA, where I taught at the law school. He was head of the Chicano Peace Movement, active in opposi-tion to the Vietnam war. Chicano youth had a particular complaint against the Selective Service System, as they were drafted, sent to Vietnam, and killed in a larger percentage than Anglo youth. There were many reasons for this disparity. Lack of educational opportunity meant that kids in the barrio did not go on to college and therefore did not benefit from the automatic four-year student deferment. Young Chicanos had less access to information and counseling about their options with the draft. And there was certainly a great deal of anecdotal evidence that conservative Anglo draft boards favored Anglo youth in making up their draft calls and deciding exemption and deferment issues.

To be opposed to the war did not mean, however, that one was a conscientious objector, opposed to "war in any form." Rosalio wrestled with this question, but did not file his conscientious objector application until he had received an induction order. Under the law, that was too late—unless the local board actually considered the application and rejected it "on the merits," as opposed to simply refusing to hear it. The courts had held that the local board could itself waive any objection to late filing by its own conduct. What constituted review on the merits was a difficult and sometimes technical issue. One might also challenge the local board's refusal to hear a conscientious objection claim if the board officials had misled the registrant about the law or procedure.

Rosalio came to see me in my law school office in the fall of 1970, after he had been indicted for refusing to submit to induction. He knew that I had written a book on draft law, spoken on the issue, and trained lawyers and draft counselors. He also knew that I was representing my colleague, Angela Davis. I agreed to represent him.

In Rosalio's case, and later for Fernando Chavez, I had support from the Mexican-American Legal Defense & Education Fund (MALDEF). In the late 1960s, there was only one-third as many Chicano lawyers as a percentage of the Chicano population as there were African-American lawyers as a percentage of the African-American population. The historically black law schools had played some role in getting African-Americans into the legal profession. There were not equivalent law schools for the Hispanic population. Partly for this reason, MALDEF did not have Hispanic draft lawyers to call upon. The Muñoz case and later the Chavez case were sponsored by MALDEF, and I received a fee of $375 for each one. MALDEF paid some expenses as well.

We showed up in the federal courthouse on Spring Street one morning for arraignment. Along with dozens of other defendants, Rosalio would say he was not guilty. Along with the lawyers for these defendants, I would file a paper saying I represented him. The clerk would spin a wheel and announce that the case was assigned to this or that judge.

We were not prepared for Judge Andrew Hauk. Bellicose, quixotic—and not a little taken with his power as a life-tenured federal judge, Hauk was an equal opportunity autocrat. He verbally savaged prosecutors and defense lawyers, and both sides in civil cases. That morning, Rosalio and I wandered in to a concatenation of hostilities that was to endure for nearly two years.

I was not a member of the California bar. I had been admitted to the bar in the District of Columbia. I did not think much of this, because this was a federal criminal case, I would be serving almost pro bono, and there was a local district court rule providing that lawyers licensed in other jurisdictions could practice in federal court. Judge Hauk saw it differently. When I announced my appearance, he demanded to know whether I was a member of the California bar. I said no.

He then read the local rule, which said that a non-California lawyer who maintained an office for the practice of law in California could not practice in federal court. This rule was designed to protect the fees of California lawyers from competition, and raised some serious constitutional issues that we would have to argue later. I simply said that I did not have an office for the practice of law. I was a law professor. The rules of anticompetitive animus did not cover my situation.

"Nonsense," said Judge Hauk, "I am not going to let you appear." He was to boast of this moment for years afterwards, despite the eventual outcome. Judge Hauk was, it turned out, filled with personal hostility to the kinds of cases I was doing and the political positions I was taking. "Mr. Muñoz, how do you plead?"

Rosalio looked at me imploringly. This was not going as expected, but he thought his rights were being violated and he wanted to make some protest. I whispered that he could say that because he was being deprived of his right to counsel, he would stand mute and not plead. He did this.

In eighteenth-century England, standing mute would have entrained serious consequences. A defendant called upon to plead was supposed to say, "Not guilty, my lord," and then when asked, "How will you be tried?" he was to say "By God and my country, my Lord," meaning that he would "put himself upon the country," which was another way of saying that he wanted a jury trial. If a defendant stood mute at this juncture, he would be taken away, stripped, and laid on a table. Boards would be placed on his body, and weights added to the boards until he either agreed to say the magic words or expired. This sort of thing went on as late as the 1770s, and was called *peine forte et dure*, which was Norman French for "hard and strong punishment," or colloquially, "gosh, that hurts."

In the daintier days of 1970, the Federal Rules of Criminal Procedure provided, as they still do, that if the defendant stood mute, a not guilty plea would be entered for him. That happened, and the clerk announced that the case was assigned to Judge Jesse Curtis. This seemed like good news to us, for we thought that surely Judge Curtis would show a little more reason. I had forgotten the solidarity of the judicial robe. By this time, the prosecutors as well were enjoying making our lives difficult.

A couple of days later, Rosalio and I appeared before Judge Curtis. I asked Carol Krauthamer to come with us. Carol was a trial lawyer of skill and distinction, with a lot of experience in selective service cases. Before Judge Curtis, we were going to apply to have me represent Rosalio. It was at best awkward, and perhaps even unseemly as a matter of ethics, for me to argue my own qualifications and character. Carol agreed that we could make a better record if I were under oath and she asked me a series of questions. That way, Judge Curtis and the prosecutors could put any questions they liked, and even present any contradictory evidence. We would have a record, and if they chose not to challenge us on the facts, so much the better.

Carol had me go through my biography, with emphasis on my draft case and federal court experience. Rosalio affirmed that he wanted me to represent him. We argued the law. There was precedent. In one case, a California lawyer had given federal antitrust advice in New York. The client refused to pay, saying that the lawyer had violated New York ethical law by practicing law in New York without a New York law license. The U.S. Court of Appeals, no doubt having considered giving the client a chutzpah award, held that a lawyer admitted in any jurisdiction has a right under the privileges-and-immunities clause to give federal law advice in any other jurisdiction.

In a more recent case, arising from the civil rights movement in 1964, northern lawyers had come to Mississippi to help represent young people who had been tossed in jail as the result of demonstrating for civil rights. The local Mississippi judges refused to let these out-of-state lawyers appear in state courts, even with a local lawyer present. Given that few Mississippi lawyers would dare to represent civil rights protesters, these decisions effectively denied defendants their right to counsel. So the U.S. Court of Appeals for the Fifth Circuit, in *Lefton v. City of Hattiesburg*, held that out-of-state lawyers had the right to appear and the demonstrators had the right to their services.

Judge Curtis listened to our presentation and without hesitation said that I could not appear in his court. He gave Rosalio a week to find another lawyer. We were ready for this. We quickly finished drafting a petition for writ of mandamus, and got an expedited copy of the transcript of proceedings. Ordinarily, if a defendant is wronged by the trial court, he or she must wait until the trial is over. If convicted, an appeal will then lie to the court of appeals and all the claimed errors will be reviewed at once.

But sometimes an early trial court error is so serious, so clear, and so easily remedied that the court of appeals will reach out and tell the trial judge what do. This may avoid a long trial that would simply have to be done over if the trial judge were only later held to be wrong.

We wanted immediate relief, so we presented our petition to a court of appeals judge with chambers in the same federal building where the district courts were sitting. In those days, things were done a bit more informally than is the norm today, and we made an appointment directly with the judge rather than going through the clerk's office.

Judge Walter Ely agreed to see us, and he invited the prosecutors to be present. Walter Ely was from Texas. He had been a good friend of Lyndon Johnson. His easy Texas manner did not disguise his deep concern for justice. He listened to us. He asked his law clerks to bring him the books containing the cases we cited.

"All right," he said at last, "I am not going to decide this myself. I will confer with at least one other judge and we will get you a decision soon." Two days later, Judge Ely and Judge Shirley Hufstedler issued an order. They cited the *Lefton* case, and quoted the local rule. To avoid a constitutional issue, they said, it would be best to construe the local rule to allow Rosalio the right to counsel of his choice.

At Rosalio's next appearance before Judge Curtis, we presented the order and expected all would be well. Not so.

Judge Curtis said: "I see this order. A copy has come to my chambers. But it has not been spread upon the record." I had a mental picture of an order coming packed in a jar, like peanut butter, perhaps with "NEW" and "MORE SPREADABLE" on the label.

"When will the order be spread?" I asked, not knowing just what this might entail or how it was done. To avoid contretemps like this, the present rules provide clearly that the district court is to obey the court of appeals order when that order is received.

"This will happen in due time. The court will be taking certain measures with respect to this issue. Until this is resolved, this case is off calendar."

I was beginning to understand. Judge Curtis was going to force a show-down to try and keep me out of his court. That morning, as I came into the courtroom, I had run into my old friend, Joe Ball. Joe had been president of the California bar, a courageous fighter for defendants' rights and a warm friend of Ed Williams. I asked Joe what he had going, and he said that he was there to represent Judge Curtis. I thought it was a joke, based on Ball's decades of experience in that courthouse.

No, it was serious. The county bar association had decided to provide lawyers to keep Rosalio Muñoz from having his lawyer and to protect its monopoly. As this battle wore on, another agenda surfaced as well.

I protested that Rosalio's speedy trial rights were being endangered, to which Judge Curtis replied that he could have a trial with another lawyer. So we left it at that. Joe Ball and two other stalwarts of the bar establishment filed a brief in the Ninth Circuit attacking the ruling that I should be admitted.

The panel issued a new ruling, saying that the earlier ruling had been precatory in tone but unchallengeable in content. Judge Curtis was to admit me. This put the district judges into a mode of full resistance, which manifested itself openly and secretly. Openly, all but two of the district judges in that courthouse—which at that time housed all the judges in the Central District of California—signed a statement supporting the action of Hauk and Curtis. The judges added gratuitous and insulting statements that I had a reputation for representing disruptive and radical defendants and that the combination of my representation and Rosalio's temperamental nature would endanger the chances of a fair and orderly trial. This personal attack was without any cited basis in any court record, and was nonsense. But it made a deep impression in several quarters, as I later found out.

Stalwarts of the organized bar continued to file briefs. The court of appeals stuck to its guns. The judges' lawyers petitioned the court of appeals for a rehearing by all of the judges—not just the panel of three that had said I should be admitted. Unfortunately, all this legal talent was unable to get the petition filed on time. In fact, it was six weeks late. The court of appeals denied it. They then went to the U.S. Supreme Court—with these volunteer lawyers paying the costs—seeking a writ of certiorari to keep me off the case. The Court denied certiorari. I heard later from a clerk that there was some sentiment among the justices to address this issue, but that the untimely rehearing application proved an insurmountable obstacle.

In the meantime, of course, Rosalio was simply awaiting his fate—still under the cloud of indictment. When the Supreme Court's denial of certiorari came down, I filed a motion to disqualify all the judges (except the two who had not supported Hauk and Curtis) from hearing the case. They had all expressed personal opinions about Rosalio and me, based on extrajudicial knowledge—that is, on information not contained in any court record. This at least presented the appearance of bias.

I later found out that Judge Curtis was planning to deny the motion and try the case anyway. But one of the two "dissenting" judges, Warren Ferguson, saw Judge Curtis at lunch and said: "Jesse, do you want to keep up this fight, or do you want to get this case tried? If you want it tried, just send it over to me. You don't have to grant the motion or admit you are biased, but reassign the case." Curtis did so, and we wound up in front of Judge Ferguson.

I had already appeared before Judge Ferguson in a case involving warrantless national security wiretapping. He had admitted me to practice in that case, even knowing the controversy that had arisen before Hauk and Curtis. Judge Ferguson's older son, Jack, who had enlisted in the Marine Corps, had been killed in Vietnam. Whether despite this experience or because of it, Judge Ferguson listened carefully to the defense in selective service cases. When the defendant was convicted, he was willing to impose some sentence other than jail time if the defendant would perform community service. On the district bench, and later on the court of appeals, Warren Ferguson has always been compassionate, intelligent, and articulate. He embodies all the qualities that a federal judge should have.

Rosalio waived a jury. The government consented to the waiver—because even though you might think that jury trial is the defendant's right, the Supreme Court has held differently for almost all cases, and government consent is required as well as that of the court. The reasons are wound up with the same history as the *peine forte et dure* that I mentioned earlier.

My reasoning on the waiver was this: If Judge Ferguson convicted Rosalio, we would have the same legal issues on appeal as if a jury had done so. If Judge Ferguson acquitted, the government could not appeal that acquittal. If we had a jury that convicted, and Judge Ferguson granted a post-verdict acquittal, the government could appeal. All in all, it seemed the best choice.

The government's case was, then, fairly simple. It presented the draft board records, including Rosalio's request for conscientious objector status. The case then boiled down to a legal argument on whether the board had actually considered the application and thus waived the alleged untimeliness. We also presented evidence of the induction patterns in the San Gabriel Valley where Rosalio lived, showing that Hispanics were being drafted out of proportion to their numbers in the population. This, we claimed, invalidated the ethnically biased orders to report for induction.

Judge Ferguson heard the evidence and then listened to our legal arguments. He then said: "G.K. Chesterton once said of the English judges, 'They're not cruel. They just get used to things.' Well, I feel like that. I have heard many of these draft cases, and I have entered judgments of conviction in cases rather like this one. But no lawyer has pointed out to me, until Mr. Tigar did so today, that the local board cannot rely on the lateness of one of these applications if it goes ahead and denies it on the merits. When it does that, it is not relying on its procedural rights, it is making a decision about some young man's sincerity. And the law says that when the board does that, it has to give the young man the right to an administrative appeal and cannot issue an induction order until that appeal is over. The defendant is acquitted."

The prosecutor stood up and said rather belligerently, "But Judge Ferguson, the court of appeals has clearly held that when the registrant files his claim. . . . "

Judge Ferguson interrupted, firmly but softly, "Mr. Fox, do you understand that in that case, there was no consideration of the merits?"

Undeterred, the prosecutor continued, "But, Your Honor, in that case. . . . "

A little more firmly, Judge Ferguson said, "If you don't understand that, Mr. Fox, you are not likely to understand anything else I might say. We are in recess." And he strode off the bench.

For Rosalio, the case was over. He could resume his life. The *Los Angeles Times* reported the acquittal on February 17, 1972, noting that Judge Ferguson took seriously the allegation that the Selective Service System had committed "a terrible injustice against Chicanos." I went back to my mother's house in the San Fernando Valley to gather up my things and return to my law practice, research and writing in France. I had been there only a couple of hours when the phone rang. "For you, dear," my mother said.

"Mike," said a voice that I recognized, "this is Judge Walter Ely. I just wanted to tell you on behalf of myself and Judge Hufstedler how proud we are of how you conducted that trial."

"Well, thank you, Your Honor. I appreciate the call."

I was left by this brief exchange to wonder what conversations, fears, and expectations had swirled around in the courthouse. The disruptions in trials during the 1960s and 1970s had led to what I thought were hysterical and largely one-sided views on lawyers representing dissident defendants. I surmise that some of this lawyer-bashing rhetoric had created a fear that Rosalio and I would try this case some way other than to try and win it. Or perhaps the fear was that we would speak uncomfortable truths to judges who would resent hearing them. At any rate, I really did appreciate the call.

Cesar Chavez was, until his death, leader of the United Farm Workers, the labor organization that sought to represent agricultural laborers mostly in the American Southwest. Founded in the Central Valley of California, the UFW had faced stiff and often violent opposition from growers' organizations and other unofficial and official minions of the valley's establishment.

As part of the farm workers' struggle, Cesar developed and practiced a philosophy of nonviolence. All these things I had known since my undergraduate days, when we supported the farm workers by petition drives, volunteer efforts, and some meager financial help. My law school classmate, Jerry Cohen, went to work for the union. In the summer of 1968, Jerry called to say that Cesar's son, Fernando, had a problem with the draft. Fernando wanted to apply for conscientious objector status. I advised Jerry on what Fernando should do to file for such status, and how to take the necessary administrative appeals.

The draft board—this "little group of neighbors"—did not have any members identified with the UFW, or notably sympathetic to its goals. They denied Fernando's application outright, and the appeals board predictably affirmed. Once Fernando's student deferment expired, he received an order to report for induction.

Fernando, to challenge the local board's order, refused to take the step forward at the induction center. Like almost all the others who did the same, he was indicted for his refusal. He could defend his criminal case on the basis that the local board had committed one or more of the three kinds of errors I discussed above: First, that the local board's classification of him was so wrong that it lacked any basis in fact; second, that the local board had made a demonstrable and serious error of law in classifying him; or third, that the local board had committed a significant procedural error. Under the Supreme Court's teaching, the decision on these three issues was for the trial judge to make. The jury, unless Fernando waived it, would decide only whether he had indeed refused to step forward.

Nonetheless, we refused to waive a jury. This decision was the subject of much debate in the draft defense community, but it seemed to me right. I have never waived a jury in a criminal case. "What! Never?" as the Gilbert and Sullivan refrain has it. Well, hardly ever.

Fernando's case was bound to excite media attention. Every juror would know who he was, or least who his father was. Jurors have the power to vote for acquittal for any reason that seems right to them. We would challenge the rule that limited the jury's function, if only to save the issue for appeal. We would seek to introduce evidence about the legality of American involvement in Vietnam, and request jury instructions on those issues. We would do as William Penn and so many others have done—challenge the jurors to vote their consciences, having aroused their concern by our evidence and argument. Or so we hoped, perhaps from ego or self-delusion.

Cynics would say—and did—that trying to explain these things to the average American is like trying to explain a sundial to a bat. I have never believed that, no matter who was on the jury. Reading Clarence Darrow's summations—those masterful webs woven of history, evidence and law—left me thinking that every jury presented a challenge that could be overcome if I cared enough, thought enough, and worked hard enough.

Fernando's trial was set in Fresno, in the heart of the Central Valley, in the summer. The trial judge was M.D. Crocker. It was 1969. Judge Crocker had been an FBI agent. He was taciturn and conservative. The prosecutor was William Allen, who had come to the U.S. attorney's office from a stint as assistant district attorney in Bakersfield, another Central Valley community about 100 miles south.

The prospective jurors were sort of a cross-section. A young man from the community showed us how to research the names on the jury list to find their voter registrations and any initiative or referendum petitions they had signed, all from the public record. We did not have law enforcement files on them—the FBI gives that sort of thing to prosecutors, and few judges will make them share it with the defense. We knew from their answers where they worked, and something about their families. There is usually not much lawyer voir dire in federal court.

Judge Crocker denied our motion to strike all employees of the major growers who had been openly hostile to the UFW, so we had four of those on the jury and four more identified with grower interests, though less directly. They all said they could be fair. I spent a week in Fresno before the trial, in a local motel in the mid-price range. I listened to the most popular local radio stations, watched local television, and read all the local papers. I wanted to know as much as I could about the community.

One afternoon before the trial began, Fernando came over and we sat out by the pool. I realized that I had not spent more than a few hours with him up to that time. I had worked on legal theories with Jerry Cohen and with some others on our small team, but I did not feel I knew Fernando's story. The root questions—who are you, and why have you taken this risk—had eluded me. It was as though he had dwelt in his father's shadow.

Don't get me wrong. I knew the story, as Fernando had sketched it and as Jerry Cohen had told it at some length. Fernando was away at college in San José, at the southern end of San Francisco Bay. He had shown little interest in his father's work. One day, his mother called him and asked him urgently to come home. His father, Cesar, had begun another fast to protest an injustice against the farm workers. Because of Cesar's frail health, Mrs. Chavez feared the fast would do permanent injury and perhaps be fatal. Fernando drove home to Delano, a small community near Bakersfield, determined to talk his father out of it.

Father and son took a long walk through the fields. When they returned home, Cesar was still on his fast, and Fernando had determined that he was a pacifist. We have read and heard of such epiphanies, usually the product of accumulated experience that suddenly comes together to produce a qualitative change. In every religious tradition, these stories teach powerful lessons. In the Vietnam war era, many young men faced with an imminent draft notice discovered their opposition to war. Local draft boards were suspicious of these belated changes of heart. I worked with many of these folks and found that they were mostly sincere. At 18 or 21 years old, they had not thought about these issues in any coherent way until confronted with them.

In case after decided case, we showed that the local board's hostility to a conscientious objector application was misplaced, and sprang from an institutional and system-wide bias. But my opinions would not decide any particular case, and surely not this case about Fernando Chavez. They would not matter much to this judge and this jury.

So Fernando and I sat outside my room at the Del Webb motel and talked. I asked him about that walk in the fields. Tears formed in his eyes as he told me what his mother had said. As he recalled what his father told him, he began to cry. He had grown up in that house, amid the daily dramas of farm worker organizing, and yet he had never really listened to his father's story. Like so many other young people, what his father did was in a sense alien to him. On that walk, he was drawn into his father's place in an important chapter of history.

His father did not preach or make himself the center of events. It was the sort of patient and moving account that was the hallmark of Cesar Chavez's eloquence. By the time Fernando's account was well under way, he could hardly continue. I stopped him.

"That's enough," I said.

"Enough? There is more."

"I know there is more. And I will ask you to tell the jury all of it. But I don't want to make that moment of telling any less effective by having heard it all now. I want you and me to be talking about this for the first time."

So we changed the subject and went over the kind of cross-examination that William Allen could be expected to do.

The government's case went in quickly. There was the local board representative who identified the induction notice, and the government witness who said Fernando had not taken the symbolic step forward. The judge denied a motion for acquittal at the end of the government's case. He sustained government motions seeking to keep out of evidence any of our attacks on the legality of the Vietnam war.

Of course, we were entitled to present evidence of Fernando's intent and actions through his own testimony. His intent may be formed by a sense of perceived injustice. The court may rule that the injustice, if any, is not the jury's business, but the defendant's reasons for acting are always the jury's business.

So Fernando took the stand. I walked over near the jury box. Judge Crocker did not put shackles on the lawyers, as do so many judges these days. Within reason, I could stand wherever I wanted to when examining a witness. This business of standing where you want to is more important than most lawyers think. When you stand, you occupy space. If you stand close to a prosecutor, you occupy some of her space. If you move close to the witness box, you and the witness are seen as in the same space, and this makes any conflict between you sharper and any cooperation more intimate.

I did not want to be in Fernando's space. He was going to tell his story. Yet, I wanted to have this conversation with him, in as natural a tone as possible. So I stood at the far end of the jury box. That way, the jurors could easily see one of us at a time, by turning their heads back and forth. I leaned forward slightly. I had just a few notes on a yellow pad—nothing to take away from the sense that we were talking about something that interested both of us. We went through the introductory material.

Q: Did you get a call from your mother while you were at the college?
A: Yes, I did.
Q: What did she say?
The Prosecutor: Objection, Your Honor. It's hearsay.
Me: He's telling us why he felt this way, Your Honor. Not offered for the truth.
Judge Crocker: Yes, overruled. Go ahead.
Q: Tell us what your mother said.
A: She said that my father was going on a fast, and that the doctor told him that. . .
The Prosecutor: I'll object to that.
Judge Crocker: Overruled. It's the same issue. Go ahead.
Q: You can tell us, Mr. Chavez.
A: The doctor said that the fast could hurt him. That he might die. (Fernando began to choke up.)
Q: Did you go home?
A: Right away.
Q: Did you see your father?
A: Yes, I did.
Q: Did you talk to him?
A: Yes.
Q: Tell us about that. What happened?
A: We took a walk together. I told him what my mother and the doctor had said. I told him that too many people needed him. (Fernando's words were punctuated by labored breathing. He was struggling for control. I was having trouble with my own voice. Four jurors dabbed at their eyes. His telling of the scene was more vivid than the words can convey.)
Q: What did he say?
A: He began to explain to me the farm workers' struggle. He talked to me, for the first time I can really remember, about his faith and his example. . . .

Fernando continued the account, tracing their walk and his eventual understanding. He spoke then of filling out and filing the conscientious objector form for the local draft board.

As he spoke, all the jurors watched him carefully, only taking their eyes away to glance at me as I asked a question. You know, direct examination is funny that way. The witness cannot use narrative, and the lawyer cannot use leading questions. Yet when we tell stories to each other, the teller often narrates and the listener often probes with leading questions. But somehow this artificial method of discourse in the courtroom can bring a sense of immediacy and drama that narrative lacks.

By the time Fernando finished, at least eight jurors were tearful. Prosecutor Allen's cross-examination was short, devoted to exploring just how recent Fernando's conversion had been.

We next called Cesar himself to the stand. Allen had attacked Fernando's assertions of belief as fabricated. We were entitled to rebut. Contrary to all the rules, including my own, I put Cesar on the stand with no more than a few minutes' conversation; he had not had time to meet, so Jerry Cohen had prepared him. In this farming metropolis, his name and face were known to every juror. His presence ensured media attention for the day of his appearance—although the case itself had generated quite a bit of publicity. It was always a surprise to me just how diminutive he was in real life.

Cesar told the story of his and Fernando's walk. He spoke calmly, slowly, as if reliving each part of the event so as to evaluate it in his mind. Cesar Chavez was, in a small room like a court, the most charismatic person I have ever met. Despite themselves, the jurors seemed drawn to him. He was, for many of them, an ogre, a troublemaker—but one that they had never seen in person. And he was telling a story about his son, whom he clearly loved very much.

William Allen did not like this turn of events. He reacted in—apparently—the only way he knew. He attacked. Of course, cross-examination is about attacking, but foolish lawyers assume this means high dudgeon (is there such a thing as medium dudgeon?) and an aggressive manner. Allen no doubt thought of Chavez as several kinds of evil—he was up there vouching falsely, like a mother giving her bank robber son an alibi. He was just what Allen's conservative friends said—yes, a troublemaker.

After a few warm-up sarcasms, Allen warmed to his task:

Q: You are telling us, Mr. Chavez, that you are a pacifist? (He deliberately pronounced it CHAH-vez, in the manner that Anglos do— either from ignorance or in an effort to be insulting.)
A: I am a pacifist.
Q: And does that go for your whole union?

A: I cannot speak for all of them. Our philosophy is to resist evil with nonviolence.

Q: Well, Mr. Chavez, what if a Russian soldier were raping your wife. What would you do about it?

This question was so off the wall that you could hear a collective intake of breath. The effect was magnified by Allen's tone of voice and his manner. It was as though he were back in misdemeanor court in Bakersfield, cross-examining some hapless wrongdoer caught in the act.

Now, we have all heard of questions like this being put to pacifists. There is the famous World War I draft hearing in England of Lytton Strachey, the gay author and critic.

Q: And what would you do, Mr. Strachey, if a German soldier were raping your sister?

A: Why, sir, I should interpose my own body.

Cesar was unfazed. He leaned forward in his chair and peered at the prosecutor. He looked at him silently for perhaps 30 seconds. That is a long silence. Long enough that the prosecutor became anxious and fiddled with his notes.

Then Cesar spoke:

A: I am sorry. I have forgotten your name.

Q: Allen. William Allen. . . .

A: (Cesar, interrupting whatever Allen was about to say.) You see, Mr. Allen, the farm workers' struggle puts poor people with only strength of numbers against powerful interests. . . .

Allen interrupted. "Your Honor, I object to this speech."

Judge Crocker smiled. "Counsel, come to the bench." We did.

"Your Honor," Allen protested, "this is just a political speech. It's the very thing you have already ruled inadmissible."

"You're right, Mr. Allen," the judge replied, "I did grant your motion. But then you had to go and ask that damn fool question. So now you and the jury and everybody else are going to hear the answer—however long that might take. Understand?" Judge Crocker turned to Cesar. "Mr. Chavez, you go ahead with your response."

Cesar traced the farm workers' history, and put his walk with Fernando in context. I do not think any of the jurors will forget that day, as Cesar sat and looked at them, taking them all in with his eyes. When he was done, Allen had no more questions. We rested, the government had no rebuttal, and we made the pro forma motion for directed verdict, which Judge Crocker took under advisement.

That night, we worked on more proposed jury instructions, focusing on expanding the jury's role beyond merely deciding if Fernando had failed to step forward. If the judge would not give such an instruction, I could in any event tell the jury of its power to acquit. We thought that the power of Fernando and Cesar lingered in the courtroom, at least enough so that two or three jurors would hold out for acquittal and hang up the jury. If that happened, the government might not retry the case. Given the government's unbroken record of success in Fresno draft cases, we thought this result might not only help Fernando but also send a message about other cases as well. The court reporter shared our hopes and he wore a shirt with a subtle Mickey Mouse pattern, to show the prosecutor (he said) what he thought.

Judge Crocker had other plans.

At 8 o'clock the next morning, we were in court, ready to get the jury instructions settled and to argue to the jury at 9 A.M. Judge Crocker took the bench.

"The court has reread the various brief and legal arguments, and is of the opinion that the local board committed a legal error in processing Mr. Chavez's claim for conscientious objector status. The motion for judgment of acquittal is therefore granted. The defendant is acquitted and he is free to go."

Outside the courthouse, picketing farm workers set up a cheer. Of course, my jury argument notes were now unimportant.

Twenty-five years later, I was at the Ninth Circuit judicial conference and I saw Judge Crocker. I asked him if he remembered the case. "Of course I do," he said, as though insulted that I would think that age had taken his memory. "That fellow Allen, he lost that case. You can think you won it, but he lost it every way a person could do." I did not take this comment with humility—that would be out of character for me in a case where the client won. I took it as confirmation of what we thought—that Fernando and Cesar, helped by Allen's bad manners, had made enough of an impression on the jury that Judge Crocker decided to short-circuit things.

And Fernando? He went on to law school and continues to care about human rights.

Beyond the constant effort to provide draft counseling to young men and to explain the deferments and exemptions to which the system entitled them, and beyond the prosecutions for refusing induction, there were two hot draft law issues as the 1960s drew to a close. The first was preinduction judicial review. If a young man claimed exemption or deferment from induction, why should he have to refuse to submit to induction and then face a criminal prosecution in which he could finally get judicial review of selective service error? The statute was unclear, and the U.S. Supreme Court had never squarely held that preinduction review was not available.

The other issue was Selective Service Director Hershey's determination to use local draft boards to punish those who protested against the Vietnam war. In 1967, a federal appeals court had enjoined a local draft board from revoking the deferments of students who had been kicked out of school for holding a peaceable sit-in demonstration. The court's theory was that the students had a statutory right to their deferments, and a constitutional right to express themselves. A local draft board could not ignore those rights without triggering an immediate right to judicial review.

Thus, these two issues intersected at the point of accountability. The draft system did not have impunity from due process and free speech rules. In our constitutional system, an invasion of rights opens the doors of federal courts to provide a remedy. This basic principle was sounded by Chief Justice Marshall in *Marbury v. Madison*, and upholding it has been the central battle of human rights lawyers ever since *Marbury* was decided in 1803. Federal judges, whose powers derive from Article 3 of the Constitution, have been most squeamish about exercising their powers when doing so confronts the executive branch in its war-making and foreign relations modes. Yet, it is precisely those executive activities that are most in need of judicial scrutiny, for war and national emergency become powerful excuses for invading or ignoring individual rights.

In 1968, the Supreme Court confronted the issue of judicial review. In *Oestereich v. Selective Service Local Board No. 11*, a slim majority of the Court held that when a local draft board improperly denies a ministerial exemption from service, that decision is subject to immediate judicial review. However, in *Clark v. Gabriel* that same year, the Court majority held that a decision to deny conscientious objector status was not immediately reviewable, because that decision involved the exercise of board discretion, and conscientious objector classifications did not occupy the same clear place in the law as ministerial exemptions. In short, there was no clear Supreme Court majority for reining in the draft boards.

For its October 1969 term, the Supreme Court agreed to hear two cases that would settle some of these issues. Chief Justice Warren Burger had replaced Earl Warren. *Oestereich* had drawn dissents from Brennan, Stewart and White—three Justices whom a civil liberties litigant might need to prevail. Justice Harlan, by a concurring opinion in *Oestereich*, had shown that he was on the fence. Justice Fortas had been a Lyndon Johnson advisor and had publicly denounced civil disobedience as an anti-war tactic.

One of the two cases was *Breen v. Selective Service Local Board No. 16*, which presented the questions that the Second Circuit had decided in *Wolff*—pre-induction review and student deferments. The other was *Gutknecht v. United States*, which I discussed in the Prologue. Some 3,000 other young men had been convicted under similar circumstances, so the Court's decision in *Gutknecht* would affect many families.

I had been following these cases from my two offices in Washington, at the *Selective Service Law Reporter* and at Williams & Connolly. Early in the summer, ACLU staff counsel Melvin Wulf called me. He had argued *Oestereich*. He said: "I have a deal for you. If you will write the briefs in both *Breen* and *Gutknecht*, you can argue *Gutknecht*."

I accepted. I had only been a lawyer for two years. I would have to make a special motion to be permitted to argue in the Supreme Court. To be kind, one would say this was a rare honor. To be candid, it was an enormous ego boost. I was to begin teaching at UCLA law school in the fall, and this was a perfect summer project.

The *Breen* brief was straightforward. The Supreme Court had traced the judicial review issues in other cases. I outlined the history of selective service judicial review and wrote a brief, to be argued by another lawyer, in what turned out to be a winner.

Gutknecht was more difficult. The fragile *Oestereich* majority had suggested that the Selective Service System should not behave lawlessly. The Solicitor General, Erwin Griswold, had refused to present the government's position, which sent a powerful signal to the Court. Nonetheless, there were danger signs for us. The Court had held that burning or defacing one's draft card was not a form of expression protected by the First Amendment.

There were obvious due process problems with summarily revoking a registrant's deferment and putting him at the head of the list for induction. However, Gutknecht had clearly done the prohibited conduct, so the due process issue might seem abstract. And in raising an army, one would not expect a Supreme Court majority to insist on all the due process that would accompany more routine kinds of administrative action. Too, this was 1969, and the Court had not yet decided *Goldberg v. Kelly*, the 1970 case that broadly extended due process concepts into the administrative process.

I argued that the delinquency declaration was a kind of punishment, imposed without formal charges, a trial, and proof beyond a reasonable doubt. There was support for this view in Warren Court cases dealing with revocation of citizenship.

It seemed to me, however, that the Court would not wish to confront the Selective Service System in a head-on constitutional collision. The constitutional issues of free expression, due process, and imposition of punishment lurked, but I wanted to chart a course that avoided them. I turned to the history of conscription in America. I noted that during World War I, a notice to report for induction meant that you were from that moment in the military. The idea of local civilian draft boards began in 1940 as America prepared for possible war, and the idea was modified somewhat in the Military Selective Service Act of 1967. In all of this history, Congress had never given local draft boards the power and duty to punish registrants for not having their draft cards. These boards were created to decide cases of deferment and exemption, and to provide a mechanism for fulfilling induction quotas if that was necessary. The entire delinquency system was an invention of General Hershey and his staff.

I began to think of other instances in which the Warren Court had confronted possibly unconstitutional administrative action and had held that the agency had exceeded its statutory powers. For example, in *Greene v. McElroy*, a civil servant was fired for alleged disloyalty. He had never been able to confront and cross-examine those whose allegations were the basis for his firing. In those days, it was difficult if not impossible to get five Justices to hold that the loyalty-security program violated due process of law. So Chief Justice Warren wrote an opinion showing how unreliable the evidence against Greene was, and how he would surely have been helped if he had been able to cross-examine his accusers. This right of cross-examination, Warren wrote, is so important that we will not presume that Congress intended to let the agency dispense with it. Unless the authorizing statute clearly says no procedural rights, the Court will hold that those rights must be afforded.

The Court used the same reasoning in *Kent v. Dulles*. The State Department denied a passport to Rockwell Kent, a dissident artist, based on his political views. The Court avoided the First Amendment and right-to-travel constitutional issues by holding that Congress had not authorized the Secretary of State to withhold passports on such grounds. So this became the keystone of my brief. I would chart the constitutional issues, and then show the Court a way to navigate around them to our result.

It worked. The Court's opinion, without dissent, traced the history of selective service law and held the delinquency regulations invalid. A later decision confirmed that the others who had been drafted under these regulations, and who had refused induction, would have to be released.

Many young men, faced with hostile draft boards, left the United States in the 1960s and early 1970s. Many of them went to Canada and Sweden. In their absence, many were ordered to report for induction and then indicted when they didn't show up. From 1974 until the Carter administration issued an amnesty that covered all nonviolent draft offenses, I worked on obtaining dismissals of pending indictments so that these young men could come home. I let it be known that I would represent anybody who was abroad and the subject of a draft indictment. I thought that if I could get some of these cases decided, then other lawyers would step in to do the work.

In some cases, the local U.S. attorney would agree that the draft board had behaved illegally and would dismiss the case. In other instances, the prosecutors and the draft board would team up to not only deny any relief but also refuse me the right to look at the young man's draft file to see if there were any errors.

My legal theory was this: The defendants in all of these cases had never appeared in court. They had, therefore, never been arraigned or asked to plead guilty or not guilty. That plea, in federal procedure as at common law, is known as pleading to the general issue. Before the federal rules of criminal procedure were adopted, and still in many states, the defendant must make all motions addressed to the face of the indictment before entering a plea to the general issue. Failure to make those motions might be considered a waiver of the right to make them. This technical waiver jurisprudence no longer exists, but I argued that a defendant still had the right to move for dismissal of his indictment before being arraigned and therefore without actually appearing in court. I then argued that draft board errors presented purely legal questions that could be raised and heard on motion rather than at a trial.

The authority for this mode of argument was, as you may gather, old and thin, although there was an in-chambers opinion by Justice Douglas that supported my position. Prosecutors invoked the fugitive disentitlement doctrine, by which someone who does not appear forfeits the right to be heard. This doctrine applies, however, to someone who appears and then runs away. My argument was that there needs to be some check on prosecutors simply obtaining invalid indictments against people who are not in the country, with no way for those people to challenge them without submitting themselves to arrest.

Some district judges agreed with this analysis, and the case law was building nicely when the overall amnesty mooted the issue. But this is an example, it seems to me, of looking beyond the text of legal rules to their background and context. Speaking of civil procedure reform, Maitland said, "The forms of action are dead, but they rule us from their graves." He meant that legal forms persist across generations, and even across historical divides such as social revolution. They are invested at different stages with different content, but understanding the historical continuity of forms gives you new and creative ways to think about the law.

Notes

1. The Susan B. Anthony trial is reported at 24 Fed. Cas. 829 (N.D.N.Y. 1873) (No.14,459). I discuss the William Penn case and other instances of jury independence in Michael E. Tigar, *Crime-Talk, Rights-Talk and Doubletalk*, 65 Tex. L. Rev. 101 (1986).

2. The story of the *Maddox* and *Turner Joy*, two destroyers involved in an incident that led to Vietnam escalation, is available at http://www.fair.org/media-beat/940727.html.

3. Justice Douglas's dissenting view that the Supreme Court should consider the legality of American action in Vietnam was in *Mora v. McNamara*, 389 U.S. 934 (1967).

4. Rosalio's and my battles with Judges Hauk and Curtis are reported at 439 F.2d 1176 (9th Cir.), *rehearing denied*, 446 F.2d 434 (9th Cir.), *cert. denied*, 404 U.S. 1059 (1972).

5. Federal judges often take the motion for acquittal at the end of all the evidence under advisement and wait until the jury returns with its verdict before they rule. If the jury acquits, the motion becomes moot. If the jury convicts, the judge can grant the motion but the government can appeal that decision. The government cannot appeal if the judge grants the motion before the jury reaches a verdict. *See* Michael E. Tigar & Jane B. Tigar, Federal Appeals: Jurisdiction & Practice § 2.11 (3d ed. 1999).

Chapter 7
MILITARY JUSTICE—
AN OXYMORON

Somebody wrote a book subtitled *Military Justice Is to Justice as Military Music Is to Music.* That was about it. I was mostly a spectator to the 1960s and 1970s military cases, except for a few habeas corpus cases to get people out of the service. The law of courts-martial, and of judicial review of military decisions, was only of academic interest. I was not trying these cases. I did handle some discharge matters, helping young men assert in-service conscientious objector claims like the one I had made so long ago. I did not try my first court-martial until 1996, and I rediscovered all the issues that had held my attention in the 1960s.

The Air Force major sat in my office with tears in her eyes. She was about to be charged with sodomy and conduct unbecoming an officer and a lady. Conviction would ruin the career she had spent 22 years building, might forfeit the pension she had earned, and even send her to prison. The felony of sodomy, under the Uniform Code of Military Justice, includes any oral-genital contact between people of the same or opposite sex, whether married or not.

The Air Force proposed to charge that the major had carried on a two-year affair with a civilian woman, Pamela Dillard, who lived in her home. When the affair cooled, so the allegations went, the major demanded that the woman move out. When the woman refused, and instead threatened legal action, the major allegedly brandished a pistol and threatened her life.

Two lawyers—one military and one civilian—had urged the major to plea bargain. They couldn't think of a story that might raise a reasonable doubt before the military officers who are the jury in a general court-

martial. Of course, we made the pretrial arguments about equal protection, privacy, and a Department of Defense policy that made private
consensual sexual conduct none of the Air Force's proper concern. We
made those arguments to protect the record in case an appeal was necessary. But at trial, those issues would not be our story, our moral drama.

The first lawyers on the case rightly saw that the testimony of the
alleged lover/victim was, if believed, conclusive. The lover/victim, Pamela,
had made consistent statements to civilian law enforcement officers about
the alleged assault, and after several sessions with Air Force investigators
had told of the alleged sexual liaison in great detail.

We first had to ask to whom we would tell this story. In a general
court-martial of an officer, the jury consists of up to nine officers who
outrank the accused. So we would see colonels and lieutenant colonels.
Each of these career officers would have a college degree and some post-
graduate work. Each would have served in the Air Force for at least 20
years. They would all have some interest in military history and customs.
They would look across the courtroom and see the major, with her medals, and see reflected a distinguished service record. And, the military base
being a fairly tight community, and the case having been covered by the
media, they would already have some idea of the issues.

In the usual case, you anticipate facing a jury whose demographic composition is in a general way predictable. If that prediction displeases you,
choose another forum to begin with, or seek to undo your adversary's
choice. In the major's case, we doubted that a gay rights approach would
avail us. We were confident that the jurors would agree that privacy in
sexual matters deserves respect, by the military itself and by individuals
keeping their sexual preferences to themselves.

The standard of proof was beyond a reasonable doubt. We might have
made the classic defense error of analyzing the weaknesses of the
prosecution's case, deciding how best to reveal and emphasize them, and
stopping there. That would have been a mistake, as it is always a mistake
for a defendant to rely solely on weaknesses in the plaintiff's case. The
jurors will, one must assume, apply the burden of proof. However, they
will want a context—a how and a why.

The heart of the prosecution's case would be testimony by Pamela, the
alleged victim, describing in the same detail as at the preliminary hearing
her sexual liaison with the major in Virginia, followed by Pamela's move
to San Antonio to share the major's house and bed. The prosecution
would produce letters and cards allegedly from the major to Pamela.
Some of the letters were affectionate. Others were suggestive ("I can't

wait to see you face to face. Or face to. . . . ") One card was rather graphic, and spoke of tongues. A handwriting analyst was scheduled to testify.

In addition, the Air Force investigators who took Pamela's statement would produce a prior consistent statement if necessary, and a San Antonio police officer would testify that Pamela had called and complained that the major had brandished a gun at her. A former (and perhaps current) lover of Pamela's would say that she saw the major and Pamela being affectionate and that the major said at a public gathering that she was going to marry Pamela.

If we could undermine Pamela's credibility, we could win. We would also have to deal with the corroborating evidence. It would not be enough merely to show that Pamela had some animus, bias, motive to falsify. It never is. All witnesses are biased, if only in favor of their own prior version. That prior version becomes their truth. We must show why the witness is not to be trusted on a point—we must develop a reason.

As we pondered, we received a gift. The prosecution produced Pamela's journal for the year in question. The journal corroborated the brandishing charge—for it contained an account consistent with Pamela's present story—but it proved the prosecution's undoing. Here, written in Pamela's hand, was nearly a year's worth of reflections—the year leading up to her leaving the major's house and a few weeks beyond. In the diary, Pamela confessed her hatred and resentment of the major. She described her dream as being able to live off someone else's earnings. She explained that she wanted to live in the major's house rent-free until she could get around to applying for medical school, and that by having a Texas residence she would avoid out-of-state tuition. She described filing a false insurance claim and forging a signature on a medical school recommendation letter. She wrote of threatening to ruin the major's career by exposing her as a lesbian. The diary was written in a hand that resembled in many ways the handwritten portions of the more salacious of the correspondence Pamela claimed that the major had authored and sent.

I said that we needed to undermine Pamela's credibility. Not quite. We needed to do that while maintaining the major's dignity as a military officer. We were not going to put the major on the witness stand. In criminal cases, that is an acceptable option—tactically and legally. The major sat throughout the trial in uniform with her medals on her chest. She faced the court members—the military jury. Her response to the testimony being offered was visible. She did not shake her head, laugh, or otherwise display emotion. She was attentive, respectful, and at times dourly and subtly dubious.

In opening statements, I told our story. The major, having served for more than 20 years, was being accused by Pamela Dillard. Pamela Dillard's story does not make sense, is contradicted by her own diary, and is motivated by a demonstrable desire to inflict hurt. Perhaps knowing that Pamela's story is not convincing, the prosecutors will bring other witnesses, who they claim will add to her version. Not so. Everything these witnesses say depends on Pamela's credibility. Her friend repeated what Pamela told her, using the excited utterance hearsay exception. A police officer summoned by Pamela days later could not repeat her story, but admitted that Pamela did not ask him to search the house for a gun. Nor did he do such a search. He did check and see that in fact the major did not have a gun registered in her name. Photographs of Pamela and the major do not show them in any compromising positions, and the only one slightly suggestive showed the major—fully dressed—with her arm around a man.

The handwriting expert from the Texas Department of Public Safety would not, I said, be able to add anything. I left that part vague, because the expert's report was riddled with errors and we did not want to reveal the defense theory about the letters and cards.

Pamela's direct was predictable—describing sexual encounters with the major, and purporting to tell the story of their living together. Cross-examination took longer than the direct. I took Pamela one by one over the relevant parts of her diary.

One of Pamela's friends took the stand to describe a party in Virginia at which the major supposedly told the guests that she was going to marry Pamela. There were some pictures of the party, which showed fully clothed people of both sexes smiling. The friend had not told this story to investigators the first few times she spoke with them.

The handwriting expert did not do well for the prosecutors. He had mixed up the handwriting samples, showing some as being both the major's handwriting and not identifiable. He had made elementary errors in evaluating the handwriting sample given by the major. He had to acknowledge that the most provocative writings—on greeting cards that Pamela claimed the major had sent—were done with a different pen and in a different style, hand-printing rather than handwriting, than the letters from the major to Pamela.

Eventually—in closing argument—I wanted to argue that Pamela and not the major had written the inscriptions on the cards, but I did not ask the expert about this. After all, handwriting comparison can be done by the lay fact-finder as well as by expert witnesses. A prosecution expert was not likely to agree with our assessment of the writing.

To find a theme, we cast our minds back to an oration of Cicero, *Pro Murena*. Cicero defended General Murena on charges of corruption. The themes were military versus civilian accusers, and the dignity of military service. Of course, any civilian accuser may destroy a military career with a true tale of wrongdoing. But Pamela had threatened the major's military career with extortionate demands for money and lodging long before she told a story of a lesbian affair. The parallel with Murena's case, where civilians jealous of the general's power had made their accusations, was therefore clear.

In any jury case, the trial lawyer wants to have a theme with which the jurors will identify. The lawyer casts the case as championing a set of agreed values against an adversary who threatens those values. Sometimes the values are simply those of fairness, burden of proof, and neutral application of accepted principles. In the major's case, the ill-motivated civilian accuser was one strong element. Another element was the threat to military careers from allegations so easy to make and so difficult to dispel. If statistical evidence was any guide, most of the officers on the panel would at some time have had sexual relations with other than their spouse. Similarly, it is likely that most of the officers—in or outside their marriages—had engaged in some form of oral sex. The Uniform Code of Military Justice provision criminalized as sodomy all oral-genital contact, consensual or not. A sexual partner would therefore have a powerful weapon—the threat to report that he or she had been kissed below the belt.

Relying on our theme, I cross-examined Pamela on her admitted hatred, her admitted threats, and her admitted wrongdoing. I examined the officers who had questioned her on her delay in making the central accusation, and from the police officers Pamela had called I brought out that she had not sought to have the major's house searched. From Pamela herself, I showed that after allegedly being threatened, she came back and lived in the house for a few more days.

Then in closing argument, we could weave these elements around our central theme. After all, one could not cite Cicero in the opening statement, lest one be thought too argumentative. One could not refer to principles of law about credibility, for the fact-finder had not yet been instructed.

The major's case illustrates all the decisions you must make in choosing the story. A basic decision must be based on the theory of minimal contradiction. This theory has different names: KISS (keep it simple, stupid), don't assume a burden of persuasion that you do not have, everybody on the other side is not a damn liar, and so on.

Remember that the jurors come into court with a set of intuitions, sensibilities, and points of view. Lawyers might call these prejudices, and if any juror possesses them to an unacceptable degree, the lawyer would challenge for cause or peremptorily. We are fortunate to have voir dire and challenges, for these tools give us far more control over who decides the case than a speaker before a public assembly in ancient Greece or Rome—or even a candidate for office or member of a deliberative assembly.

For the jurors who are selected and sworn, trial lawyers dignify their presuppositions by calling them common sense, or we work to identify them and show how they cannot properly be applied in our case. Thus, the first canon of minimal contradiction is that our story should be one that jurors are ready to accept. Ideally, you will not challenge their basic assumptions—or not all of them. In the major's case, we had to accept that the jurors assumed sodomy to be a crime, and that some of them thought it an abomination against God. The military judge would instruct on the first of these principles, and voir dire revealed the second. We might have put the issue directly, and asked for a nullifying verdict. This is an honorable tradition in criminal cases, but it takes a jury convinced that a certain stance is so morally right that one ought properly to defy the judge's interpretation of strict law. We decided not to pursue this strategy—it would have been foredoomed.

But the legal rules of conduct were not the only principles in play. There was also the idea of reasonable doubt—of the prosecution's burden. The principal witness was a civilian, accusing an officer with a distinguished career. So rather than confront the principles of the prosecution and jurors head on, we counterpoised them to another set of equally compelling ones. Jurors are mindful of their oath. And they understand that they do represent a particular community—in this case, a military one.

A second form of contradiction concerns the story being put forth by our adversary. Both sides are working with almost the same body of data—allowing for whatever secrets remain in these days of open civil discovery. Why and how must our story differ from the adversary's? Most of Edward Bennett Williams's opening statement in Chapter 3 relates to evidence that will not be contradicted. He has chosen to emphasize different items of evidence than the government did, and has put them in a different context, but he has narrowed the scope of dispute to what is really important, and that is the credibility of just one witness.

As we work toward a theme, we must first examine all of the adversary's evidence and all their witnesses for material favorable to us. "Even their witnesses tell us," "even their documents say"—these are refrains we begin to develop. Perhaps my desire to mine the other side's ore has its basis in criminal defense practice, where the reasonable doubt standard and conventional wisdom often make the defense presentation of its own witnesses truncated or absent. But I am convinced that it has more general application. You are looking for the minimum perceptual shift that brings the entire story in line with your viewpoint. In the major's case, I was asking the jurors to take a giant step across their own prejudices against gays, and against a certain view of military discipline and order. We do not usually expect juror epiphanies of the character of religious conversion. When the jurors say "aha," it is because they have been willing for a time to see reality from a certain perspective that is not so very different from the one they brought to court.

The closing argument ended something like this:

I know that many of you have studied military history, and therefore you probably know about the case of General Murena in ancient Rome. General Murena was accused of corruption by a bunch of civilian witnesses. For his lawyer, he chose Cicero, the most brilliant advocate and orator of his time. In speaking to the tribunal, Cicero contrasted the profession of lawyer with that of general. General Murena had brought riches to Rome, and helped to guarantee the liberty of its free citizens. By contrast, and in his address Cicero was quite mocking in word and gesture, lawyers are all tied up with their technicalities, their pettifogging. And by this means, Cicero pointed out the importance of honoring those who serve in uniform and make their career doing so, and protecting them against the baseless charges that ill-motivated civilians might bring.

Members of the court, I became a lawyer because I believe in human rights. But I'll tell you something. These days, there are a lot of times when we lawyers run out of words. And that's when we call you. The finest hours of your service today, when you best fulfill the oath you took, are in defense of human rights where they are endangered in so many places in the world.

You know, in *voir dire* we talked about religious beliefs and upbringing. I was raised a Baptist, and was therefore taught that the story of the loaves and the fishes is quite literally, historically true. But whether or not you believe that, there is a powerful image there, a powerful message. And that is that there are two things that do not diminish, but grow greater as they are given away, and those are God's love and human justice.

The court went out to deliberate. In a court-martial, the senior officer is the foreperson, and he or she directs deliberations, and calls for a vote only when satisfied it is time to do so. The court members vote once. If two-thirds vote for conviction, the verdict is guilty; otherwise it is not guilty. Every time the court members need a break, the court must reconvene. The senior officer announces that the members want to eat dinner or go to the toilet, or even that there is a verdict.

The major's court members deliberated for nearly six hours, with several short meal and rest breaks. At each such break, our nervous anticipation increased, as we tried to see body language signs of which way things were going.

I was confident that the senior officer, a colonel, understood that no good would come from convicting the major. But it was hard to read the rest of them. For those hours, the defense team sat in an office and told bad jokes to pass the time and keep our minds off our fears and hopes.

Finally, late that night we had a verdict: Not guilty. Shortly thereafter the major was offered promotion to lieutenant colonel, but chose instead to retire. She did not want to hang around for a few more years and risk having to go through another experience like the one she had just survived.

In an ironic twist of fate, the commanding officer who had instigated the prosecution was soon thereafter relieved of his command. It seems that in a speech to a local business group he made some unkind and intemperate remarks about the wife of his commander in chief. Somebody had a tape recorder running. So it is indeed true that in the military, you have to be careful what you do with your mouth.

Notes

1. I have discussed the *John Brown* case and the Air Force court-martial in PERSUASION, and some material is taken from the treatment in that book.

Chapter 8
CHICAGO BLUES

The presidential race of 1968 seems at times so far away. It is, for the law students I teach, history. "He's history," people say, meaning that somebody is no longer relevant. Such an expression could find currency only in a society that devalues the lessons of the past. In 1968, President Lyndon Johnson decided not to seek a second elected term. The debate over Vietnam and the civil rights movement had riven the Democratic Party and the country. In an emotional speech, on national television, Johnson announced his decision. But the party regulars continued to embrace the failed politics that led him to that speech. When Johnson defeated Barry Goldwater in the 1964 presidential election, the Vietnam war was a major issue. Johnson voters believed that LBJ would keep his promise to end the war and bring the boys home. Instead, and despite impressive actions in domestic policy, he repeatedly heeded military advice and continued to escalate American involvement.

The year 1968 had seen nationwide demonstrations against the Vietnam war, including a huge protest centered in Washington, D.C. Thousands of demonstrators ringed the Pentagon building just across the Potomac in Virginia. Predictably many were arrested for minor offenses such as trespass and disorderly conduct. A group of us lawyers had set up a legal command post to give advice on constitutional and other aspects of direct action law, and to coordinate representation of those who might be arrested.

There were two sidelights to this intense work. After the weekend of protests, a thin bearded young man came to see me in my office. The park police had stopped him in Lafayette Park, just across from the White House. He had been picking a chrysanthemum. The police officer gave him a ticket, on which he wrote, "picking flowers." There was no statute or rule prohibiting the picking of flowers in public parks. The ticket recited a statute that punished harming the flora.

I did not think one should pick the flowers in our parks. However, I suspended my moral judgment and agreed to help the young man. I did not have the benefit of Jacques Brel's song about chrysanthemums—he had probably not even sung it yet. However, a gardener friend told me that picking the flowers encourages the plant to put out more of them. There you are, I thought. The defendant was not harming the flowers, he was helping them to grow more beautiful. I called the U.S. attorney's office and spoke to the assistant who would be handling the case. When he finished laughing, he agreed to nolle pros the ticket.

As another outgrowth of protests, the Secret Service and FBI became very concerned that somebody would try to harm President Johnson. Their fears led them to initiate prosecutions of alleged threats that were either patently ridiculous or clearly protected by the Constitution.

One day, another young man showed up in my office. Again, as seemed to be the fashion of the times, he was very slender, bearded, and somewhat ascetic in appearance. He had received a subpoena to appear before a federal grand jury, which, according to the subpoena, was investigating threats on President Johnson's life.

The young man explained that Secret Service agents had visited him a week before and told him they had intercepted a postcard sent to him from California that contained a threat on the President's life. He said he had not received any such card. The agents said they had intercepted it and were holding it as evidence. He told me he was a pacifist and a vegetarian who did not wish the President, or any other sentient being, harm. He did not know why anyone would send him a threat in the form of a postcard.

We went on the appointed day to the federal building and met Assistant U.S. Attorney Don Smith. I asked what this was about. Smith, sitting with the Secret Service agent, said that this was very serious indeed and that my client would find that out when he went before the grand jury. I said if that were all the information Smith wished to give, the client would invoke his privilege against self-incrimination. In that case, Smith said, he would indict me for obstruction of justice for giving that advice. I laughed and said he would do no such thing, as the client had the right to be silent and the right to my advice on that score. Smith yielded. He agreed to read me the text of the offending card. I could see it in his hands, a hand-printed message addressed to my client, but I could not read the words from across the table.

"It says," Smith began, "'Antonin Artaud had it right. Things are getting worse.'" Smith stopped to say that the Secret Service would be investigating this Antonin Artaud person. "'Lyndon's war is sicker and sicker. Murder is the name of the game.'"

Smith intoned this last bit sepulchrally. He added, "And the guy who wrote it does not even know how to spell 'murder.' He spells it M-E-R-D-E."

It took me a minute or so to control my laughter. I explained that *merde* is the French word for shit, and that Antonin Artaud was a writer. Smith withdrew the subpoena.

These two cases were, however, merely sidelights. On the main stage of national politics, Hubert Humphrey, who had served loyally as vice president, was anointed the regular Democratic candidate. Humphrey, long considered too liberal by the party machine, eagerly prepared to accept the nomination. The ferment that had caused President Johnson not to run was, however, unabated. Two major challengers emerged in the primaries. JFK's younger brother, Robert, had moved to New York and won a Senate seat. From that base, he mounted his campaign. Senator Eugene McCarthy of Minnesota, literate, articulate, and dovish on the Vietnam war, declared his candidacy.

In June 1968, Robert Kennedy was assassinated in Los Angeles. McCarthy's campaign could not best the tide of money and fixers that was sweeping Humphrey along. The Democratic National Convention in Chicago became a battleground of many skirmishes. Groups of protesters from the civil rights and anti-war movements massed in Chicago to demonstrate against the rigged nomination process and the political views it was designed to vindicate. Chicago Mayor Richard Daley put the police on the streets to help keep the convention on its appointed track.

The results were on national television for all to see. Inside the convention hall, objections to the Humphrey nomination and the process leading to it were gaveled down. Outside, police and demonstrators clashed. I watched it on television.

The Chicago police had arrested many hundreds of demonstrators for disorderly conduct and related offenses, and had mercilessly beaten those arrested and others as well. The state court cases filled the dockets. More ominously, U.S. Attorney Tom Foran convened a federal grand jury to investigate the leaders of groups that had come to Chicago to demonstrate. This was my first personal involvement in the process.

I knew some of these leaders, and had represented them and their organizations in various ways. This was 1968, and I had been a member of the bar for a little more than a year. But I was in Edward Bennett Williams's law firm, and was therefore assumed to know something about federal criminal law and procedure. In the fall of 1968, therefore, two activists who had helped plan the convention demonstrations called me. Tom Foran had subpoenaed them to the federal grand jury.

I went to Chicago and met with the two—let's call them Joe and Jim. Bill Kunstler had flown in from New York. Bill was famous; I was not. Bill had been a lawyer for two decades; I had not. I had met Bill when I first came to Washington. His brilliance, commitment, and charisma at first enveloped me. All the rest of his life, until he died in the 1990s, I never lost my admiration for him, his work, and his courage. There were, however, times when he was simply the most brilliant unprepared lawyer I knew. His tactical judgments were sometimes innocent of any study of the applicable law. Then there were those cases for which Bill recruited me, and then somehow had a schedule conflict as the trial date approached, so I was left to fend for myself. All that said, there were so many ways in which Bill inspired and delighted all of us.

I think this Chicago trip was the first time that all of these notions began to come together. Foran's grand jury was, we all knew, forerunner to a prosecution of movement leaders. The Chicago police excesses were not in Foran's sights. So Joe and Jim, with their subpoenas, were a test case, the canaries in the mine.

Tactically, however, we were in a weak position. A federal grand jury has a wider power to investigate than the government has to prosecute. Although the Supreme Court's 1970s cases reaffirming that power were some years off, I doubted our chances to derail the grand jury investigation, even though it was provably politically motivated and designed to invade First Amendment rights. Bill proclaimed a different vision, far into the night. This was, for young me, heady stuff. Bill's vision was of motions to quash, and a court hearing that would expose Foran's political agenda.

I kept pushing at the edge of this vision, to the time when the judge would rule, and perhaps refuse to quash these subpoenas. Late at night, we all confronted that prospect. If the judge ruled against us, and Joe and Jim refused to testify, they would be jailed for contempt of court. Maybe the court of appeals would let them out—and maybe not.

As the vision moved from courtroom postures to an image of Joe and Jim being led away in handcuffs, they took a more active role in the discussion. "Are you fucking crazy?" was their opening strophe. Joe and Jim felt they would be more useful to the movement for change outside, rather than inside, jail. With their concurrence, our strategy was this: We would move to quash the subpoenas, raising all the First Amendment issues. If the motion was denied, Joe and Jim would go before the grand jury but refuse to answer any questions beyond their names, citing their privilege against self-incrimination.

Taking the Fifth might seem dishonorable to some misguided souls, but it guaranteed they would not spend much time in front of the grand jury. It was clear that Foran was bent on indicting somebody. The grand jury is secret and inquisitorial. The prosecutor usually runs it, and Foran was certainly running this one. A potential defendant almost never gains anything by letting the prosecutor question him before the grand jury. The prosecutor gets a preview of the defense case, and often indicts not only for the main offense but also for perjury for telling an allegedly false exculpatory story.

The next morning the federal judge heard and denied the First Amendment claims. Joe and Jim went into the grand jury and gave their names. When asked their addresses, they invoked their privilege. I had a quick heated discussion in the hall with an assistant U.S. attorney who claimed that it was improper to plead the privilege against compelled self-incrimination to a question about one's address. There were in fact two federal court of appeals cases right on point. One's address could be a link in a chain of incriminating evidence and the Fifth Amendment is therefore available.

Perhaps because of this initial experience, I got another phone call when Foran finally obtained indictments in the spring of 1969. The main charge was that the eight defendants had conspired to travel in interstate commerce to foment civil disorder. The statute under which they were charged—the federal Anti-Riot Act—was vague and broad in its definition of disorder, threatening protected expression. The eight were a disparate group—aging anti-war activist David Dellinger, Black Panther leader Bobby Seale, SDS cofounder Tom Hayden, Youth International Party leader Jerry Rubin, peace and student activist Rennie Davis, irrepressible madcap leftist Abbie Hoffman, and two surprise additions. The two were chemistry graduate student John Froines and organizer Lee Weiner. The other six were all nationally known figures in the anti-war, student, and civil rights movements. John and Lee were less well known and the trial evidence would hardly connect them to the major events of that Chicago summer.

It is not unusual for a conspiracy indictment to include some relatively minor players. Conspiracy law is so sprawling and elastic that prosecutors can make a credible case against many a marginal figure. "The darling of the prosecutor's nursery," Justice Robert Jackson called conspiracy law. Conspiracy—the word has a sinister sound. The original conspirators gave themselves that name. *Conspirare*, in Latin, means to kiss or to breathe together. In the eleventh century, the Catholic church abolished the ritual embrace and kiss among parishioners at the end of mass. Rather, the senior prelate would kiss a ritual object. The more general kissing was regarded as denying the hierarchy of the secular and religious feudal order.

Those, such as the nascent bourgeoisie, who did indeed deny those hierarchies, embraced, kissed, and breathed together to symbolize their belief in equality. Their heresy was the symbol of their treason against things as they were. For centuries, ecclesiastical tribunals railed against this and other apostasis, masking their inability to understand with cries for punishment.

When I look at the government's 1960s and 1970s assaults on the movement for change, I am reminded of the centuries-earlier official reaction to heretics. The Nixon administration, in particular, brings to mind that earlier time. It re-established an independent Internal Security Division in the Department of Justice, and multiplied its resources four-fold. Internal security prosecutors and their FBI outriders were caught breaking the law again and again: illegal wiretaps, opening people's mail, burglary, putting informers into legal defense teams, and so on. All this was done with a perfect sense of rectitude and a naïve vision that youth-ful protest was dangerous to the republic.

The Chicago indictments were brought, and then prosecuted, with a fervor of this flavor. The defense camp—and camp was more than once the word of the day—resisted with displays of law and theater that fur-ther taxed official patience. The defendants, or some of them, thought of me as contributing to the legal defense, not the theatrical one. I had known Tom Hayden since 1960, when he was editor of the *Michigan Daily* and an undergraduate student leader. I had met the other defen-dants, except for Froines and Weiner, at meetings concerned with war, the draft, and racism.

Ironically, Froines was the first to call me. He respected the defen-dants' decision to mount a joint defense, but he wanted me to make sure that all the legal issues were raised. He and I knew that Arthur Kinoy, Bill Kunstler, and a host of others would be working on the same issues, so I was flattered that somebody thought I had something to contribute.

The case was assigned to Judge Julius Hoffman, Chicago's most eccen-tric and irascible judge. Now, I do support life tenure for judges, but robe fever quickly infects many of those appointed. Thomas Jefferson became so angry when one of his own appointees ruled against him that he had Attorney General Caesar Rodney write a philippic that decried "the leprosy of the bench." Jefferson had himself written of judges as "a subtle corps of sappers and miners." But when a judge appointed under the Constitution's article three sees and seizes the legitimate power to protect individual rights, there are few sights more magical. I have seen it happen, as judges and justices thought to be predictable followers of this or that line have proven courageous and independent. Warren, Brennan, Stewart, Stevens, Souter all come to mind. Judge Hoffman suffered from no such contradictions. He was arrogant and usually sure that threats to his established order of things were dangerous.

I sat at my typewriter and wrote motions addressing all the legal issues of which I could think. One basic theme was that the indictment did not clearly describe the defendants' conduct in terms that showed it to be beyond First Amendment protection. This was, of course, to be a theme of the trial. But there were quite a few judicial decisions holding that an indictment touching on areas protected by the First Amendment must be detailed and precise, so that a reviewing court can determine that the prosecution is not seeking to punish free expression. It became important, though at the time I did not know it, that I wrote and signed these motions on behalf of all the defendants. Each defendant had his own chosen lead counsel: Bill Kunstler for some, Len Weinglass for others, and Charles Garry of San Francisco for Bobby Seale.

I also filed a motion, sanctioned by the recent wiretap case in which I had participated, for disclosure of any electronic surveillance that might have been done on these defendants. In that summer of 1969, I had resigned from the *Selective Service Law Reporter* and Williams & Connolly to join the law faculty at UCLA. With the children, we were driving coast to coast in our VW van. At the Berkeley post office, there was a general delivery with the government's responses to the pretrial motions. Among these was the first ever Justice Department effort to justify warrantless electronic surveillance conducted for alleged national security reasons. More on this issue in chapter 9.

That summer, I flew to Chicago to argue the pretrial motions. This was my second appearance before Judge Hoffman, the first having been to get me admitted pro hac vice. Arguing to Judge Hoffman was the most bizarre courtroom experience of my life up to that time. At one point, I was inveighing against the secrecy with which the government sought to shroud the wiretap issue, in the name of national security. I had cited Jeremy Bentham's well-known opposition to secret proceedings, not only because it had a literary flavor but also because the Supreme Court had approved of it.

To see this episode in the mind's eye, visualize Judge Hoffman: short, bald, wearing rimless glasses—patrician of mien. Yet for all of this, like a cranky old man impatient with the inadequacies of all his underlings, and with nobody in sight but underlings. As I argued, he interrupted:

> *Judge Hoffman:* Mr. Tigar, now *I* know who Jeremy Bentham is, and I know that *you* know who Jeremy Bentham is. But as you can see, your presence here has drawn the attention of many people from the *media*. Perhaps *they* do not know who Jeremy Bentham is. So why don't you turn around and address your argument to them, and tell them who Jeremy Bentham is?
> *Me:* If it is all the same to Your Honor, I would like to argue to the court, because only you have the power to grant relief here.
> *Judge Hoffman:* Oh, very well!

Judge Hoffman denied all the motions and set the case for trial in early September. Sometime in August, Bobby Seale's lawyer, Charles Garry, fell ill and needed gall bladder surgery. He moved to continue the trial. Hoffman denied the motion. Seale protested that Garry had been his counsel in several cases, and alone among lawyers was prepared to take on the defense. Denial of a continuance, or a severance and continuance, denied him counsel of his choice.

Hoffman responded by observing that four lawyers, me among them, had entered appearances for the pretrial motions. The other three were Dennis Roberts and Michael Kennedy of San Francisco and Gerry Lefcourt of New York. We four had, for that limited purpose, represented all the defendants. Hoffman therefore held that the four of us would represent Bobby Seale. So he entered an order that we come to Chicago and try the conspiracy case, which was expected to last several months. Len Weinglass called me from Chicago to tell me of the order. I was getting ready to teach my classes at UCLA law school, and later in the fall to argue my first Supreme Court case.

"Len," I said, "Bobby Seale's chosen lawyer is Charlie Garry. I am not going to participate in some charade that has the effect of denying Seale counsel of his choice. Hoffman's order is clearly wrong. He is crazy. Will he really provoke a confrontation over this? Won't Foran and his assistant, Dickie Schultz, warn him that he is making a fool of himself?"

"Well," said Len, "on the front lines here we are not so sure. Hoffman does not appear to have many limits, and the Foran-Schultz team is more interested in goading him on than in trying to keep him within the law."

"Well," I said, "I am not going to come to Chicago. Hoffman has no lawful power to order me."

I, of course, knew that anybody ordered by a federal judge to do something must comply, or else get the order set aside by an appellate court. Unlike the situation in many state courts, one cannot disobey the order and defend a contempt citation on the basis that the order was invalid. There are some exceptions to this rule, but they are few and narrow. This order seemed exceptional enough to me and, in any case, I had not been served with it.

The next day, Weinglass called again. "Hoffman has issued a warrant for your arrest."

"What!"

"He has ordered that Kennedy, Roberts, Lefcourt, and you be arrested and brought to Chicago to represent Bobby Seale."

I called my friend Neil Herring and asked him to represent me. Neil quickly drafted a writ of habeas corpus attacking the arrest warrant, which we had not seen. Kennedy and Roberts were doing the same thing in San Francisco and Lefcourt in New York. I told the law school dean's office that I would likely miss the first meetings of my civil procedure class, and my seminar on repression of dissent.

Neil and I went downtown to the U.S. district court on Spring Street to file the petition for writ of habeas corpus. As we entered the clerk's office, a beefy cop-type approached and asked, "Which one of you is Michael Tigar?" (Ah, the joys of youthful anonymity!)

Neil and I stepped up to the clerk's counter. "File this, please," Neil said.

"I am a deputy United States marshal," the cop repeated. "Which one of you is Tigar?"

The clerk stamped the petition as filed. "I am," I said.

"I am Deputy Marshal Ray Smock. You are under arrest. You have the right to remain silent," he began, and continued with the rest of the Miranda litany. Smock agreed that I could remain with Neil while the paperwork was being done. An assistant U.S. attorney showed up and took the service copy of the petition. We all went upstairs to the courtroom of Judge Harry Pregerson, to whom the case had been randomly assigned.

I knew Judge Pregerson by reputation. He was a veteran of the Marine Corps who had been decorated for valor. He had been a storefront community lawyer in the San Fernando Valley. The story was that he had presided over a draft case when fairly new to the bench, convicted the defendant, and sentenced him to prison. Before the time to reduce the sentence expired, Pregerson began to think about the defendant's claim of conscientious objection. So he got in his car and drove to the prison in Lompoc, 200 miles away, to talk to the young man. He came back and reduced the sentence to probation on condition that the defendant do community service.

Neil presented our case: The order was illegal and Seale has the right to counsel of his choice. Assistant U.S. Attorney Brosio argued that Hoffman was just trying to hold unruly defendants in line. Judge Pregerson then got all technical, and when that started I knew that no good was likely to come of this. Habeas corpus, he said, is a limited remedy. (Where have you been, I said to myself, while the Supreme Court has been deciding a series of cases saying that habeas is a powerful tool in defense of liberty?)

"Mr. Tigar," Pregerson continued, "your remedy is before Judge Hoffman. My only duty is to see that the arrest warrant is valid on its face."

(Judge, my internal monologue continued, in American history the first major use of habeas corpus involved one court testing the validity and motivation of process issued by another court. I was thinking of Thomas Jefferson's failed efforts to round up alleged associates of Aaron Burr and hold them in military custody. The analogy was not perfect, but in my internal monologue there was no adversary to point out weaknesses.)

"So, Mr. Tigar, you can obey Judge Hoffman's order or be arrested."

I thought about this, and was to rethink my decision over and over in the ensuing 48 hours. First, I was disappointed that Judge Pregerson would not look behind the paperwork and see what was happening in Chicago. I knew that Charles Garry had brilliantly defended Bobby Seale in one politically motivated trial after another. I did not know, but would later find out, just how many illegal steps the federal government was even then taking against Seale and the Black Panther Party, but I had a sense that this was going on. All right, so I would be arrested. Being arrested in defense of a principle is not so bad. I spent much of my law practice defending people who had made that choice or had it thrust upon them. I thought about Pete Seeger and the Quaker hymn, "How Can I Keep From Singing."

In prison cell and dungeon vile
Our thoughts to them are winging
When Friends by shame are undefiled
How can I keep from singing.

This is a long internal thought process, but I had gone over some of it in my mind on the way to court. I stood up at the lectern.

"Judge Pregerson," I began, "the order directed to me is invalid. It is an effort to deprive Bobby Seale of his right to counsel of his choice. I do not think I can be part of any such effort, or contribute to it by any action of mine. You tell me that there are risks to me if I take this position. I am moved to think of Lord Brougham's defense of Queen Caroline, when he was reproached that his defense might endanger the British crown itself."

I quoted from memory a passage I had often read:

I once again remind your lordships, though there are some who do not need reminding, that an advocate in the discharge of his duty knows but one person in all the world, and that person is his client. To save that client by all means, and at all hazards and costs to all others, and among all others to himself, is his first and only duty. And in performing this duty he must not regard the alarm, the torments, the destruction which he may bring upon others. Nay, separating the duty of patriot from that of an advocate, he must go on, reckless of consequences, though it should be his unhappy fate to involve his country in confusion.

Judge Pregerson was not moved and, in retrospect I was taking myself rather too seriously. The marshals were to take me to Chicago. Deputy Marshal Smock recruited a retired Los Angeles police detective to help him. That's right. Two armed guards. They left the handcuffs off, based on my promise not to escape. We took the red-eye flight to Chicago on TWA, me in the middle seat with the these two beefy guys on either side. When I had to take a pee, one of them would go with me. The flight attendants averted their eyes at the sight of an older guy taking a younger guy into the toilet.

I had wanted to call home and let my family know where I was going and when I would arrive. This was, Smock told me, forbidden. It seemed that in the 1930s, somebody let Baby Face Nelson tell somebody where the marshals were taking him and the John Dillinger gang intercepted them. I did find out that the federal judge in San Francisco had held Hoffman's arrest warrant invalid, and liberated Roberts and Kennedy. Still no word on Lefcourt.

In Chicago, other marshals met us and drove me to the federal building. The lockup is on a high floor. The cells adjoin a corridor and out the windows I could see boats riding on their moorings at the marina as the sun rose. Sometime later, Bobby Seale was brought in from wherever they kept him overnight. Then Lefcourt arrived. The judge in New York had refused to quash the warrant but told Lefcourt to go to Chicago on his own.

So there we were, Seale and the two lawyers, sitting in jail together waiting for court to begin. The marshals took us all down into the crowded courtroom. The media people whispered back and forth about what must have happened. Gerry Lefcourt and I sat flanking Bobby Seale, and the other defendants sat with Bill Kunstler and Lenny Weinglass. They all smiled at us.

I don't remember much about that day in court. It seems there were pretrial proceedings, and that Judge Hoffman was irascible. I wasn't sure what I was supposed to do. At first, I thought that I must be a lawyer in the case because the judge had ordered me to be that. So I started to participate in conferences with the other lawyers and the defendants. A marshal looked at them all sternly and said, "Don't talk to the prisoner," meaning me. So I just sat there, and the marshals took us back to the cell at each recess. Lunch was bologna on white bread. "Tigar," Seale told me, "this ain't no gourmet restaurant."

Sometime in the afternoon, Tom Sullivan showed up. Tom is a hero. He was a partner at Jenner & Block, a big Chicago law firm. Years later, in the Carter administration, he was U.S. attorney for the Northern District of Illinois and he enforced the highest standards of professionalism and decency you would ever find in a prosecutor's office. His written policy on providing exculpatory evidence to the defense remains a model.

Late in the afternoon, Tom, Gerry, and I were seated in Foran's office, along with Foran's acolyte, Dickie Schultz. "It's easy," Foran said to Lefcourt and me. "You get Seale to waive his claim about being denied counsel of his choice, and then you go free."

Sullivan said it was outrageous to hold us hostage to force Seale to waive a perfectly good constitutional argument. Lefcourt and I said we wouldn't be a party to such a thing.

"Up to you," Foran said. "In a couple of hours, court will be over for the day. We don't hold prisoners in this building. You will go to the Cook County jail for the weekend, and we'll see what happens to your white ass over there." I found this a little scary.

Next stop was the courtroom. At the courtroom door, I spotted Irwin Weiner, a Chicago bail bondsman. He called out that Vince Fuller from the Williams & Connolly firm had asked him to be ready to post a bond. I waved and said thanks. In the courtroom, Tom Sullivan introduced himself as our counsel and moved that we be released on bail. Hoffman flew into a rage. He appeared demented in his fury, like the Red Queen.

"No lawyer who tries to horse this court," he intoned, his voice rising in pitch and volume with every syllable, "will *ever* be granted bail! Mr. Marshal, take them away!" I looked around at the spectators, the lawyers, and the defendants. Everybody seemed frozen in time and space, arrested (as it were) by what they had just seen and heard. As the marshal put a hand on me, I raised my right arm with my fist clenched, a spontaneous gesture of defiance.

Upstairs in the cells, Lefcourt and I sat and let the adrenaline dissipate. In a few minutes, Bill Kunstler came along the corridor and the marshal let him into our shared cell. "Well," Bill began, "they are filing an emergency application for bail in the Seventh Circuit, so let's hope we can get you out of here." We nodded our agreement. "Gerry," Bill continued, "I have to get back to New York. Did you leave your car at LaGuardia?"

"Yes."

"Well, just in case you are in jail over the weekend, I could pick up your car. You don't want it in the parking lot all that time."

"Thanks, Bill," Gerry said. He fished in his pockets and handed over the car keys. It occurred to me that the marshals had not searched us or taken our stuff away from us.

"And, Gerry," Bill continued, "I really need to be in the city this weekend. Could I camp out at your apartment?"

"Sure, Bill," Gerry said, handing over another set of keys. Bill embraced us both and called for the marshal. Then he was gone. Gerry cocked his head after a long, thoughtful pause.

"Do you know what just happened?" he asked me.

"Yeah," I said.

"I am in fucking jail. That's one of my lawyers. He is going to get in my Mercedes convertible and drive to my apartment. He is going to take off his pants and probably get laid in my bed, and I am going to spend the weekend in Cook County fucking jail."

I was agreeing that things did not look good for us when the marshal came along to the cell door. "Tigar," he said, "there is a man named Irwin Weiner here to see you."

"Oh, great," I said.

The marshal looked surprised, then said in a voice tinged with respect, "You know him?"

"Yes," I said.

"Well, it is really past the time when we are supposed to let anybody in here, but come this way." He unlocked the cell door and led me to an interview room. On the other side of the wire mesh screen were Irwin Weiner and a younger man who looked like a bodyguard.

"Irwin," I said, "thanks for coming. I really appreciate it."

"Vince Fuller called. I came right over. Mike, this is Angelo Pugliese." Angelo said "hi."

Some explanation may be needed. While at the Williams firm, I worked on the case of Ruby Kolod, "Icepick Willie" Alderman, and Felix Antonio "Milwaukee Phil" Alderisio, as I recount in chapter 9. Phil was from Chicago, and for some reason he often traveled with Irwin. There are more details on that case in another chapter, but I remembered Irwin and he and Phil apparently remembered me.

"Listen, Mike," Irwin continued, "if the court of appeals sets a money bond, it will be posted no matter what the amount. And Phil says that you can come to his house and have dinner, because he is cooking fettucine. Or you can have an airline ticket to wherever, and I mean wherever, you want."

"Thanks," I said. "If I get out of here, I will catch the first plane home. I don't think I need to run from a contempt citation."

"OK," said Irwin. "Now if you don't get bail, they are going to take you to Cook County jail. I guess you heard some bad things about that place, huh?"

"You could say that."

"Well, don't worry. Some people we know are already waiting for you if you show up there. Now, when you get there, a guard will come and ask you what you want for dinner. Steak, quail, lobster—you name it. They'll bring you dinner and make sure you are OK. Only thing is, when they do something for you, give them a tip. You got any money?"

I reached in my pocket. "I've got some twenties," I said.

"Oh no, that's too much. Use ones and fives. Angelo, ones and fives!" Irwin snapped his fingers. Angelo pulled out a roll of bills and peeled off a few. He handed them to Irwin who slipped them through the wire mesh.

"You smoke?" he asked. I said yes, because at that time I did.

"Regular or menthol?"

"Menthol."

Again Irwin snapped his fingers. "Angelo, menthol," he said. Angelo came up with a pack and Irwin pushed it through the mesh. "Good luck."

The marshal came and led me back to the cell. About half an hour later, a judge of the court of appeals signed an order releasing us, on condition that we show up Monday morning for court. So I never found out what would really happen at Cook County jail. I just went to the airport and paid what Continental Airlines charged to take me home to Los Angeles.

Sunday night, I flew back to Chicago. Michael Kennedy and Dennis Roberts had flown in from San Francisco, and Lefcourt from New York. Monday morning, there were picketers in front of the federal building, and I saw that they included law professors from several schools including Harvard. Over the weekend, Judge Hoffman had apparently reflected on the excesses of his position. He seemed, at any rate, to be an entirely different person. The four of us—Kennedy, Lefcourt, Roberts, and Tigar—stood before the bench. Tom Sullivan was beside us. Judge Hoffman entered the room. The clerk called the case.

"Well," said Judge Hoffman, "the court has considered the matter over the weekend. In view of the fact that all four of those that I ordered to attend are present, I am going to vacate the orders of commitment."

Michael Kennedy, standing next to me, spoke up. "I am not here in response to your order. That order was invalid. I am here in solidarity with my brother lawyers."

I kicked Kennedy, hard. "Shut it," I whispered. "Some of us have been inside the jail already, and would like to go home." Hoffman took no notice. "Therefore, you are all free to go."

Apparently, our sideshow was threatening to overtake the main event. The trial itself began and continued for months. I rejoined the team to assist with the appeal brief, for all defendants were convicted and Judge Hoffman held all of them and their lead lawyers in contempt for outbursts during the trial. Due to my momentary burst of fame, I was invited to speak at programs addressing the trial and the conduct of the defendants, their counsel, the prosecutors, and the judge. Stalwarts of the bar inveighed against defense counsel. I could not then agree and, with the perspective of years, still do not.

Sure, some of the defendants' antics were silly and counterproductive. But I see this in context. First, the politics of Vietnam and the civil rights movement had sapped confidence in the political and judicial systems. The prosecution was designed from the beginning as a show trial, not by the defendants but by U.S. attorney Foran and, as January 1969 dawned, the Nixon administration. Judge Hoffman not only ruled against every significant defense position, but also derided the defense and made clear that he was not paying attention to any of its contentions. He adopted this supercilious and mocking attitude from the first moment of being assigned the case. I was there for the pretrial motions, before any defendant or defense counsel had uttered a single disrespectful word, and I saw and heard it.

Hoffman's treatment of Bobby Seale was particularly horrific. Eventually, because Seale continued to protest his counsel's absence, Hoffman had him bound and gagged. The escalating disorder of the trial was mostly a reaction to the continuing provocations of Hoffman and Foran. I was reminded again of Queen Caroline's trial, this time of Lord Erskine's speech, as a decider and not as counsel: "Proceedings of this kind, my lords, have never been tolerated save in the worst of times and have afterwards been not only reversed, but scandalized."

Judge Pregerson went on to become a court of appeals judge, appointed by President Carter. He and his wife Bernice, a college teacher, love to take car trips. One day in the 1990s, as I was teaching civil procedure in Texas, the classroom door opened and the Pregersons strode in. The judge looked nearly the same as decades before, but in a leather jacket and chinos. I smiled and introduced my class to "Harry Pregerson, a wise and principled federal judge who once threw me in jail." The class applauded the judge, who retorted, "It was your own fault, and you know it." He was—is—right, and I would do it again.

My sense of resolution is enforced when I consider the law under which the Chicago prosecution was brought. The statute, passed in 1968, was known as the Rap Brown Act—named after the civil rights leader who had traveled from state to state. Some said that he was a powerful leader against racist political and social institutions. Others, including those who sponsored this law, said he was a carpetbagging troublemaker who stirred up riots. The Rap Brown Act was simple in design: Whoever traveled in interstate commerce or used any facility of interstate commerce such as the mails or telephone with intent to incite or carry on a riot, and who during that travel or "thereafter" performed or attempted to perform any overt act in furtherance of the illegal intent was guilty of a felony and could go to prison for five years.

So, somebody who traveled to Chicago with intent to stir up trouble and who did anything at all to further that design, even if the actions were perfectly legal, was a felon. The statute did not require that the traveler's actions pose any clear and present danger of illegality. The statute punished the desire to participate in unlawful conduct. It therefore flunked the Supreme Court's clear-and-present danger test as reaffirmed in *Brandenburg v. Ohio*, where the Court overturned a venerable criminal syndicalism statute.

Because the Rap Brown Act was so broad, it put a formidable weapon in the prosecutors' hands. Of course, this is always the danger with overbroad and vague laws that inhibit freedom of expression. Such laws permit overcriminalization, and enforcement by zealous prosecutors chills the exercise of protected speech because speakers cannot tell if their words and actions are inside or outside the law.

The Chicago case was a perfect example. Most of the defendants had planned demonstrations, and had even participated in them. Some of their plans and even their actions might be termed disorderly conduct. The reaction of Chicago's police to demonstrations at the 1968 Democratic convention—even lawful demonstrations—was more violent and unlawful than what the demonstrators were doing. Local authorities would not and did not prosecute police officers. Federal officials could not use the Rap Brown Act against the police, if only because that act punished only those who used an interstate facility. That is, the act burdened the right of interstate travel as well as the right of free expression. Of course, the U.S. attorney was not interested in prosecuting the police in any event.

The events of Chicago, like many pieces of history, were replayed in different versions in other cases. The most immediate of these were the student and youth demonstrations to protest the guilty verdicts of the Chicago conspiracy case itself. The trial, which had begun in September 1969, dragged on until the jury's verdict of guilty on February 18, 1970. The trial would have been even longer if Judge Hoffman had permitted more of the defense witnesses to testify.

In college towns across the country, student groups had been preparing for TDA—the day after—the verdicts. Given Judge Hoffman's rulings, everyone expected that the defendants would be found guilty. In Seattle, the local SDS chapter and affiliated groups picketed the federal courthouse in protest against the trial and verdicts.

The Seattle demonstrations turned violent. Demonstrators painted slogans on the federal building and broke windows. U.S. Attorney Stan Pitkin responded by indicting eight young activists under the Rap Brown Act. Since none of these young people had been born in Washington state, they all had to have traveled interstate to get to Seattle. The fact that some of them had arrived years before, and could not conceivably have had the forbidden intent at that time, did not deter the government. These were the leaders and the violent demonstrations would be blamed on them.

The indictment came down in mid-1970, while I was teaching at UCLA law school. One of the defendant's friends called me and asked if I would head the defense team. This woman was married to a draft resister who had benefited from the Supreme Court's decision in *Gutknecht v. United States*. I was four years out of law school, three years a member of the bar. With youth's arrogant sense of knowing all the answers, I agreed. I learned a great deal in the months that followed.

Our defense team included a prominent African-American lawyer from Spokane, Carl Maxey. Seattle lawyers helped out. The local American Civil Liberties Union made some office space available to us in an old downtown building.

Defending a complicated conspiracy case, or a complicated case of any kind, requires a team devoted to organizing the files and exhibits. We also needed legal research help. Law students came aboard to help us, and members of the defendants' organizations provided paralegal help. We did not find out until later that one of these youthful paralegals was in fact funneling all our defense information to the FBI and the Justice Department. This infiltration was organized by the local FBI, abetted by a senior Justice Department lawyer named Guy Goodwin. Goodwin, who had a lot of responsibility in those Nixon administration years, was caught pulling similar stunts in several prosecutions of political dissidents. He was a slightly stocky, shortish chap with salt-and-pepper gray hair. He was always impeccably dressed, and spoke softly and in a slightly affected way. Behind his back, his prosecutor colleagues mocked him as effeminate and regarded his work as sloppy.

I will give Goodwin this—he was witty. When I criticized him in the Seattle case for a shotgun approach to the evidence, he said evenly, "With your clients, I would use a squirrel rifle." Some years later, Goodwin was removed from any role in political prosecutions for having repeatedly invaded defendants' rights in such cases. I met him again years later in an ordinary case, as I recount in chapter 13.

Our trial judge in Seattle was George Boldt, an aging conservative jurist with no sense of humor and very little patience with the exuberance of youth. He put the case on a fast track for trial, but did agree that the trial would be set for December so that I would not have to miss many of the law school classes I was teaching. Despite meeting all my classes, I was back and forth to Seattle a lot. Ronald Reagan, then governor of California, seized upon these absences to demand that the chancellor fire me. At the monthly meetings of the University Board of Regents, he never failed to urge my dismissal.

The trial team was organized so that two defendants would represent themselves, while Carl Maxey and I would alternate in lead roles as defense counsel for the others. Maxey left the pretrial preparation to the team we had assembled in Seattle.

U.S. Attorney Stanley Pitkin was one of those Republican civil lawyers who get appointed to that kind of position when the Republicans have the presidency. He appeared to have swallowed whole the Goodwin/ FBI theory that my clients were dangerous revolutionaries. In the end, this delusion was the government's undoing. Pitkin had lost that essential skeptical detachment from the evidence.

An example came early. Pitkin called me one day and said that he had an item of evidence to show me and asked if I would please come to his office immediately. I rounded up two of the defendants, Michael Abeles and Jeff Dowd, and we went along to the federal building. Pitkin was in his office with the FBI case agent. In hushed tones, they said that they wanted to show us this evidence before they considered bringing more serious charges. They led us to a room. The FBI agent carefully opened a wooden box. "This," he intoned, "was found at the scene of the demonstration."

This was a World War II hand grenade body, the classic pineapple shape. It was empty of any explosives, no doubt having come from a war surplus store. It was painted baby blue. An alligator clip, such as electricians use, was soldered to the top of it.

Abeles and Dowd began to giggle. "It's a roach clip," one of them finally sputtered.

"What's a roach clip," Pitkin asked, mystified.

"Ask your teenagers," Dowd replied.

The harmless grenade body had been configured by some unknown person to hold the fag end of a marijuana cigarette—known as a roach— so that the smoker could get the last hits from a joint.

As the trial date approached, the defendants made public speeches about their views and activities. We were getting discovery from the government in the form of video footage of the demonstration. Some of this had been taken from an FBI van. The case agent told us, humorlessly, that the van was known in bureau lingo as a "creepy peepie."

The actor Donald Sutherland took an interest in the case. He and his wife, Shirley, were outspoken supporters of dissident individuals and groups. At a party in their Beverly Hills home, Don and I talked about the Seattle case. He arranged for me to join him on Dick Cavett's late-night television show to talk about the issues. On the day set for my appearance, ABC censors tried to bully Cavett into keeping me off the show, but he courageously held to his position. On the show, we bantered about possible uses of the Rap Brown Act. I imagined an elderly woman collecting radical literature sent to her post office box and exclaiming "right on!" in the post office. That would satisfy all the elements of the crime.

I am sure that Judge Boldt began to wonder what a Seattle jury would do about these defendants, when the evidence turned out to be rather less inflammatory than the indictment suggested and the government had loudly and publicly stated. He responded by ordering the case to be tried in the Tacoma division of the western district of Washington. This meant that we would have to commute 30 miles each way during rush hour in the wet weather of a Washington December. It meant that instead of the diverse urban jury we would see in the federal courthouse in Seattle, we would have more suburban types, government employees, and people from rural areas. We filed a petition for mandamus challenging Judge Boldt's unilateral and unexplained action, but lost 2 to 1 in the court of appeals. The Sixth Amendment guarantees only a trial in the state and district wherein the alleged offense was committed. Many larger districts are divided into divisions. The potential jury pool in each division can be quite different. We thought, and the dissenting judge agreed, that the trial judge should not have unlimited discretion to move a case.

As we prepared for trial we faced the most significant issue in any conspiracy case—the element of agreement. Our eight defendants were from different political groups and held different political views. They were activists. They strongly believed that if their message about civil rights, the Vietnam war, and free expression were repeated enough times in enough forums, the listeners would demand social change. Their belief ran headlong into two canons of criminal defense.

First, evidence that the defendants met together many times would tend to support an inference that they were discussing illegal objectives.

If the defendants took the stand and with other defense witnesses described how they had worked together, the jurors might not see this as simply a lot of protected associational activity. There was, that is, a tension between the desire to help the jurors understand these defendants and the tactical risk of seeming to support the government's conspiracy theory.

This was not an insoluble dilemma. Jurors will accept counter-intuitive propositions. They will come to analyze the facts without regard to their own preconceptions. In a long trial, such transformations are more likely, because unfamiliar ideas become commonplace as the trial wears on. There is no guarantee of this happening, however. Consider Atticus Finch in *To Kill a Mockingbird*. He summed up to a white jury in a sexual assault case. He was not simply asking the jurors to disbelieve the complaining witness. He was asking them to accept a proposition that contradicted their deeply held racial prejudice: that a white woman could genuinely desire a black man. In our case, a Tacoma jury would be less likely than a Seattle one to accept our invitation to see the world through the defendants' eyes.

The second issue involved public statements. There is no such thing as a public forum any more. Public forums existed in fourteenth century towns, where it was possible to reach almost the whole populace by standing up and shouting. By the eighteenth century, one might reach a fair number of people through broadsheets and leaflets. Today, our information is filtered through the media, whose editors decide what to print and broadcast. People congregate in shopping malls, which are privately owned and unreachable by picketers and leafleters. The Seattle case began in 1970, so there was no Internet to speak of. Even today, however, we are seeing a concentration of market power in Internet access. And the most disadvantaged Americans don't have Internet access at all. The majority of Native American homes, for example, do not even have telephones.

For our Seattle clients, therefore, my message was that their actions and activities would be seen by the public only to the extent and in the manner dictated by dominant print and broadcast media in our market. We had to think about the content of our messages, and the way in which they were presented. Did I think about the legal ethics of media contacts? Of course. But this was not an ordinary case. It involved a number of public issues, including but going beyond the right to demonstrate for one's views. The fact that the government had chosen to try these defendants did not rob them of their first amendment rights. Nor

could the charges be a valid reason to halt their participation in the ongoing debate over the Vietnam war, racism, and government accountability
for its misdeeds.

The defendants' and my views were soon to be tested. I learned a great
deal, and I think they did as well. During jury selection, defendant Chip
Marshall, who was representing himself, was questioning a prospective
juror.

Q: What do you do at that company?
A: I make nuclear missiles.
Q: (With genuine surprise.) What do you do that for?
A: About fifteen dollars an hour.

We did seat a jury in Tacoma, and the prosecution lost no time in
branding the defendants as interlopers who had come from the east to
disturb the tranquil precincts of Puget Sound with their radicalism and
disorder. Where had these prosecutors been, I wondered to myself. The
entire state of Washington had been the organizing ground of radical
unions from the Industrial Workers of the World (the Wobblies) down
to Harry Bridges' International Longshoremen's and Warehousemen's
Union.

In my opening, I took a page from Clarence Darrow's opening in a
Wobbly case in adjacent Idaho.

Yes, members of the jury, it is true that I am not from here. I am
from Los Angeles, California, where I live and work. And, like most
of you, I would rather not be here today. I would rather be sitting
by a quiet and free-flowing stream near my home. But I am here
because hundreds of people gave what little money they could afford to see that this case was defended. Now there is injustice being
done in many courtrooms across this country, and I would be in
every one of those if I could. But I cannot. I am here, in this courtroom. And I do not apologize for that, because I know that together we are going to find out the truth about what happened in
Seattle on that day.

After some preliminaries, the government called its first major witness, Red Parker. There was a frisson of shock as the bailiff announced his
name and he came into the courtroom. Red Parker had joined the local
Students for a Democratic Society chapter. He was a part-time student.

He worked in a paint store. He always had a more radical, violent suggestion about proposed action. He spoke often of imminent violent revolution, and tried to persuade others to join him for practice in shooting a
rifle. He had brought cases of spray paint to the demonstration and urged
people to deface the federal building.

On direct examination, and then on cross, he owned up to all of this.
Our defendants were at the center of youth and student radical activity in
Seattle, but their organizing had been lawful. Red Parker had been recruited by the FBI to join the SDS, and to try and set it on a different
course. He got regular payments for his work. The FBI told him to
encourage violence, to see who would rise to the bait. They told him to
see who would want to practice with a rifle. And because the FBI did not
approve of theft, they gave Red the money to buy the spray paint for the
demonstration.

Chip Marshall waited for his turn to cross-examine Parker. In a multi-
lawyer case, you always hold your breath because the other lawyers are
bound to ask questions that you deliberately did not ask. You did not ask
them because you didn't want to give the witness a chance to explain an
answer, or to curry favor with the jury with a self-serving speech. Marshall
was innocent of this lore. And he was having a good time questioning his
old buddy Red. So Chip plowed on where few lawyers would dare:

Q: You don't like us at all, do you, Red?
A: No I don't.
Q: You would do anything to see us convicted and sent to jail,
wouldn't you?
A: Yes, I would.
Q: You would even lie under oath, wouldn't you?
A: Yes, I would.

The government's case was coming apart. Fearful that they would not
win on the merits, the prosecutors changed tactics. They began to com-
plain bitterly that the defendants were speaking to the media and were
making too much noise in court. Every morning at trial, one or more
defendants would saunter in late, so the judge and prosecutor began to
make more of an issue of this tardiness. As the evidence revealed more
government dirty tricks, the defendants' comments became louder and
more frequent. The judge's impatience also increased, leading to this exchange between us:

The Court: Mr. Tigar, this gentleman is one of the deputy marshals. Tell him what you have.

Mr. Hanson (deputy marshal): I watched Jeffrey Dowd [one of the defendants] place this on the wall and asked him to take it off and he gave me the finger, and on the elevator and on the walls we have seen them. They don't come off when they dry. [This was a broadsheet about the trial events.]

The Court: Mr. Dowd is your client, Mr. Tigar, and I expect you to take appropriate action to see that this does not occur.

Mr. Tigar: The only evidence we have is this one label and I take the position that I am this man's lawyer and I have an obligation to explain Your Honor's wishes and I have an obligation to explain what the law is, but I don't believe I have the obligation to control his conduct or behavior, even assuming that I wanted to or that I could. He is his own man and will take the consequences.

Later, the exchange went on:

Mr. Tigar: My thinking is that I represent two defendants in these proceedings, Jeff Dowd and Roger Lippman, and we will have conversations throughout the course of this trial about their legal liability and obligation for things they have done. Those conversations are covered by the lawyer-client privilege. My job is to advise those defendants about consequences of actions they may contemplate taking and actions they may have taken in the past.

The Court: I take it that you will do that now in connection with this incident?

Mr. Tigar: Judge, the conversations I may have with them you may be assured will be in accord with my consideration of my responsibilities. I cannot talk to you about my professional client-attorney relationship.

The Court: I only ask you to advise them about this type of conduct and what it may lead to.

Mr. Tigar: I will inform them of Your Honor's views, certainly.

The Court: If you will do that, that is all I am asking you to do.

As Norman Dorsen and Leon Friedman said in their book *Disorder in the Court*, I was trying to express the lawyer's duty not to abandon his client by becoming an associate enforcer of the judge's ideas of decorum. As they note, "A criminal lawyer should no more be obliged to announce that he has cautioned his client against disruption than an antitrust law-yer should be obliged to announce that he has cautioned his corporate client against price-fixing." Whatever one may think of rules, we owe our clients undivided loyalty within very broad limits. As the Dorsen/Friedman book documents, courtroom disorder was a major topic of discussion in the 1970s. I thought the debate somewhat overwrought, but I was sure about my own stance. I had accepted the representation of these defendants, against whom all three branches of the federal government had set their hands. I was not going to become an agent for one of their assailants.

A day or so after Parker self-destructed on the witness stand, some of the defendants were late again. They were late because some of their number tried to see the judge before court to protest the treatment of spectators who had come to see the trial. Word of Parker's appearance had got out, and many people with the look and dress of those who might support the defendants had lined up outside the courthouse to gain admittance to the trial. The marshals refused to process them, claiming security problems. Marshals randomly took people out of the line and searched them. Outside where this was happening, a freezing rain was falling. The defendants took umbrage.

When court began, their remarks about the unfairness of the trial became more obvious. Judge Boldt took the bench and read a generalized and somewhat rambling critique of their conduct and held that all but one of them had been in contempt. He set sentencing for four days later. There was to be no trial, he said, because he had seen enough of their actions that he needed no other information. And since the contempt occurred in his presence or nearby, he was, so he claimed, entitled under the rules to proceed summarily.

Some of the defendants tore up their contempt citations. Others made their displeasure known. The judge also declared a mistrial in the case, which meant to him that the government could begin again at its pleasure. The defendants' reactions to all of this led to a second round of contempt citations.

Let us pause to consider this state of affairs. These young people—Lerner, Marshall, Dowd, Abeles, Stern, Lippman—had no doubt engaged in a demonstration at the federal courthouse. Television footage showed it. Some of them arguably had done some property damage during that demonstration. For this they were charged with conspiracy to commit and committing several felonies carrying heavy potential prison terms. They were required to post bail, and to incur heavy expenses of trial preparation. Their own resources being insufficient, they raised money from other sources. When they got to trial, they found that the FBI had planted an informer in their midst who tried to provoke unlawful activity. The prosecution was directed from the Justice Department of the Nixon administration, by personnel later found guilty of felonies for their unlawful actions, and who used methods later denounced as part of the impeachment hearings against Nixon.

In a broader context, the President and his men were continuing a war of which the majority of Americans disapproved, and were plotting in other ways—as Senate hearings later disclosed—to undermine the democratic process.

In this setting, what were these young people to do? Were they to remain silent and powerless as the system that calls itself justice unwound itself, and to wear the badge of accused felon all the while? Their courtroom comments, and their marks of disrespect for the process, seemed to me defensible. I choose that word carefully. I would have welcomed contempt citations from Judge Boldt that offered the defendants a trial where they could defend their courtroom behavior. The conditions would be these: The case would be tried before a jury in Seattle, where their political base existed. There would be full discovery of the government's ignoble role in invading the defense camp. There would be full discovery of government infiltration of their lawful political activities. Then, let a jury representative of the community decide the issue. By "defensible," I mean just this: I would defend them in a fair fight on fair terrain.

I saw firsthand how the marshals manhandled the defendants' supporters who sought entry to the trial. And the chief marshal of the district singled me out as well. One Friday night I walked down the jet-way with other passengers to board the plane back to Los Angeles and home for the weekend. There stood the U.S. Marshal for the Western District of Washington, Charles Robinson. He put me up against the jetway wall in full view of all the passengers and did a thorough search, making sure to feel all my pockets and squeeze hard where he knew it would feel uncomfortable.

Thinking of Judge Boldt, I am reminded of meeting my mentor Edward Bennett Williams one night at The Palm restaurant in Washington, D.C., just after he had lost a jury verdict in front of Judge Gerhard Gesell. He was later to win a new trial and an acquittal due to jury misconduct. I asked him how he had gotten along with Judge Gesell. He replied: "I will meet that SOB on any field of human endeavor, in a contest of his choosing, and under rules of his devising. As long as the SOB is not also the referee." Williams was, in his own eloquent way—both of us being somewhat the worse for drink—saying what Lord Coke had held in 1608: No man shall be judge in his own cause.

In any event, the mistrial and contempt scene were dramatic. In a few days we would go back to hear the sentences the judge was to mete out. But that afternoon, Carl Maxey and I and the other lawyers repaired to a bar near the airport, so that Carl could be ready to catch a flight back to Spokane. I got riotously drunk.

With all the bravado of the truly squiffed, I decided to drive back to the home of Michael Rosen, the ACLU lawyer who had lent me a bedroom in his house. I was doing just fine with all the controls and such, but I did not see a stop sign near Rosen's house. A Seattle policeman pulled me over and asked for my driver's license. I saw him register who I was, and I thought I was in serious trouble. The cop looked from my license to my face, and said, "You're the lawyer for those defendants in that trial, aren't you."

I said yes.

"Well," he continued, "is it true what they said in the paper, that the FBI bought the spray paint for people to use in the demonstration, and all the rest of that."

"It's all true," I said. "Their witness admitted it on the stand."

"I'll be damned," the cop said. "That really pisses me off. You know, we local cops had to go down there and wrestle with that crowd, trying to protect that federal building. It was really crappy duty, let me tell you. And now we find out that the goddamn feds were actually helping make it happen. I'm glad you were able to bring that out."

I felt better, but he continued. "Sir, you not only went through a stop sign but you appear drunker than owl shit, if you don't mind me saying so. How far do you live from here?"

"A couple of blocks." I gave the address.

"OK, I want you to follow me, real slow. There are no stop signs between here and there, but I want you to watch my taillights and take it easy. I'll get you home before you hurt somebody."

A few days later, Judge Boldt had all the defendants back for sentencing. This was before the days when all federal and many state courtrooms feature metal detectors. The courthouse scene was ominous. More deputy marshals than I could count patrolled outside and inside the courthouse. In the courtroom itself, more than a dozen deputy marshals sat or stood, all in black turtleneck sweaters, some with black jackets and some also wearing black gloves. Outside and inside, the marshals hassled potential spectators who looked like supporters of the defendants, by intrusive searches and by pushing them around.

Carl Maxey sat beside me at one of the counsel tables. The judge took the bench and called upon counsel to speak. We had agreed that Carl and I would split the argument. Our main contention, then and on the appeal that we later won, was that the judge could not proceed summarily and was so personally embroiled in the dispute that he should turn the case over to another judge. Whatever these defendants might have done, and with whatever intent they might have done it, the determination should be made in a hearing before a neutral tribunal with all the rights that the adversary system guarantees.

The judge called twice for counsel to speak. Carl Maxey looked at me and at the judge, and pointedly lifted his file and put it in front of me. He was bowing out. So I stood and argued. Judge Boldt ruled against us.

Then one by one the defendants exercised their right of allocution, to say why they should not be sentenced. It came to be Susan Stern's turn to speak. Susan was about five feet tall, and weighed perhaps 100 pounds. She was no physical threat to anyone, and she had to stand on tiptoes to be seen over the lectern.

She began quietly enough talking about what young people had come to feel about a government that was distant, hostile, and uncaring. She rebuked those who stood aside and would do nothing about injustice. Evoking the passivity of those who watched Hitler's rise to power and did nothing, Susan spoke of "good Germans." Judge Boldt either did not understand the reference or chose to feign ignorance, for he said heartily: "Well, let me tell you something. There is not a drop of German blood in my veins. My people are all Danish, 100 percent Danish!"

Susan could not resist. "Well, then, Your Honor," she said, "there is something rotten in Denmark." Perhaps the Judge had not read Hamlet, but he snapped that Susan should stop talking and sit down.

"I am not finished with my statement," she said. "We are entitled to be heard."

Again came the order to sit down, and a very large deputy marshal stepped up and grabbed Susan from behind. He pinned her arms behind her and she grimaced in pain. I lost my temper at this. I stepped behind the deputy and tried to pull him off Susan. This was not a particularly wise move. Another deputy stepped behind me and grabbed me. He tossed me against the wall, and my head snapped back against the unyielding paneling. As I opened my eyes, the deputy sprayed something in my face. I got dizzier and my eyes burned. I am not sure what happened next, but I can remember being carried out of the courtroom by two deputies. I opened my eyes as we all reached the courtroom side door and saw U. S. Attorney Pitkin standing there agape.

"Mike, what's going on," he said—unnecessarily, as he had been there all along.

"Tell these guys to put me down," I said.

He did and they did. The courtroom melee soon quieted down. The judge had retired to his chambers to write up more contempt citations.

I have reflected many times on that day's events. I used to hear rumors that the whole episode was captured on videotape and that some judges had seen the tape. I could never pin that down. I am not a violent person. I thought then and think now that the marshals showed up spoiling for a fight, and that they had begun the day with gratuitous exercises of force against relatively harmless civilians. Somebody in power must have evaluated the case and concluded it had no merit, for I never heard so much as a whisper that I might be prosecuted for an unjustified assault on a federal officer. Of course, maybe they concluded that since I was out for the count ten seconds into the first round, it was not worth pursuing.

Notes

1. Some history of conspiracy law is in the TEXAS LAW REVIEW essay cited in the notes to chapter 6.

2. On the Chicago case, see JASON EPSTEIN, THE GREAT CONSPIRACY TRIAL (1970); United States v. Dellinger, 472 F.2d 340 (7th Cir. 1972).

3. The exchanges with Judge Boldt are quoted in Norman Dorsen & Leon Friedman, *Disorder in the Court: Report of the Association of the Bar of the City of New York, Special Committee on Courtroom Conduct* 147, 48, 245-48 (1973).

4. The opinion reversing the Seattle contempt citations is *United States v. Marshall*, 451 F.2d 372 (9th Cir. 1971).

Chapter 9
LIKE A BIRD ON A WIRE

In his book *One Man's Freedom*, Edward Bennett Williams traced the history of unlawful electronic surveillance. He had argued some of the Supreme Court's leading cases on the constitutional protection against seizing the spoken word. When I came to Washington in 1966, he was representing several Las Vegas hotel executives in lawsuits against the FBI for unlawfully wiretapping and bugging their premises.

The Communications Act of 1934 forbade wiretapping. Bugging with the consent of one of the parties was generally thought legitimate under the Fourth Amendment, although the laws of many states prohibited it. Most of the electronic surveillance cases until 1967 were resolved under traditional search-and-seizure principles. In that year, the Supreme Court decided *Katz v. United States*, and held that a bug in a telephone booth violated the Fourth Amendment even though the telephone user had no traditional property interest in the booth. The Fourth Amendment, the Court said, protects people, not places.

Bugging a telephone booth was, however, inefficient unless a particular individual used the booth regularly. Usually, the police or FBI or IRS had to enter someone's home to install a bugging device. Until the Crime Control Act of 1968, there was no federal legislation that permitted tapping and bugging, even with a warrant. A tap or bug sweeps much more broadly than a traditional search for tangible objects such as guns or narcotics or even private papers. Thus, an authorization for tapping or bugging would resemble a general warrant that did not—as the Constitution requires—particularly "describe the persons of things to be seized." The 1968 act attempted to get around this problem by requiring an exceptional degree of probable cause for issuance of a warrant to bug or tap, or else the consent of one of the parties to the conversation.

The lack of legislative authorization did not trouble several government agencies. The FBI had been doing unlawful electronic surveillance at least since the 1930s. When Robert Kennedy became attorney general in 1961, he vowed to continue his crusade against Mafia influence on legitimate business. One of his targets was Las Vegas, and the FBI set up a dummy corporation there, Henderson Novelty Corporation, to handle its extensive campaign of unlawful surveillance.

With the telephone company's cooperation, FBI agents set up bugs and taps. To install bugs, the phone company would induce trouble on a customer's line. When the customer called for service, the service crew included an FBI agent who would take the opportunity to plant microphones. All of this led to Ed's civil suit against the FBI agents and the telephone company. The cases dragged on for years, but were finally settled on good terms.

The Las Vegas cases were clear instances of illegality because the agents had actually invaded protected premises to install the devices. Before the 1967 *Katz* decision, this sort of invasion was the touchstone of Fourth Amendment analysis. In fact, Ed Williams had argued the leading case on this issue, *Silverman v. United States*, which was decided in 1961. Julius Silverman was a gambler. I breach no lawyer-client communication in saying this because he was caught more than once in the act of running a gambling operation. In the case that went to the Supreme Court, the police had installed a spike mike through the party wall connecting Silverman's premises to the adjoining house. From that house, the police could listen in and gather plenty of evidence that gambling was going on. Using this evidence, they got a warrant and raided the place. It soon became clear that the warrant was based on the overheard conversations. The Supreme Court held that a one-quarter-inch trespass with a spike mike was enough under traditional Fourth Amendment analysis to be unlawful.

The Silverman story was already legend by the time I got to Washington, but I heard it over and over because of the Saturday lunches at Duke Zeibert's restaurant. Julius walked with a limp and was therefore known to his buddies as "Cripple Julius," just as another gambler was known as "Fifi," though for reasons I never knew, and yet another as "Lefty," which was fairly obvious. The Silverman legend goes like this. Julius called Ed from jail. Vince Fuller from Ed's office went out to the alleged crime scene and found evidence that the spike mike had made a dent in the heating duct on Silverman's side of the party wall. Indeed, the duct helped the microphone pick up sounds from all over the house.

Ed told Julius: "You will be convicted in the district court, though you will probably get bail. The court of appeals will affirm your conviction. But the Supreme Court will hear the case and unanimously reverse the conviction and set you free."

Julius shook his head: "I don't think so. I think this time I am going to prison. Thank God this is a federal rap here in D.C. so I maybe get to Allenwood or something instead of at Lorton with the schwarzes."

At this point, Joe Nesline, who had a record of allegedly running illegal card games in suburban Maryland and even one time right over a liquor store on Pennsylvania Avenue, chimed in, "Julius, if Eddy says he can do this, he can do it."

"Oh yeah?" said Julius, "how much you want to bet?"

"$10,000," said Joe. "Duke here can hold the money."

"OK," said Julius, and then added, smiling, "but it has to be what Ed said, unanimous."

Nesline winced at this condition but agreed. Duke held the money. The case dragged on for several years, through the district court and court of appeals, and then the Supreme Court granted certiorari. Ed argued, brilliantly as always. Every Monday, Julius would drag himself up the marble stairs of the Supreme Court to hear if the opinion had come down. One Monday, the Court decided. Julius ran out to a pay phone and called Duke Zeibert. "Duke, Duke, I won, I won!"

Duke paused and asked, "Yeah, Julius, but was it unanimous?"

"No, Duke, I am sorry for Joe's money, but it was not. Two of them did something they called 'concurred.'"

Because Judges Clark and Whittaker had indeed joined the Court's holding without reservation, legal experts called it unanimous and Julius paid off. Or so the legend had it.

These stories were not simply the stuff of lunchtime conversation. They were part of the fabric of legal education. Ed would always punctuate the story with citations to cases and bits of doctrine. In this, by the way, his biographers have never got it right. They captured the Irish *bon vivant* and *raconteur*. They mostly missed the legal theorist, mentor, and educator. The day I first heard the Silverman legend, Ed turned it into a discourse on the history of FBI illegal electronic surveillance. Ed saw where this law had been and where it was headed. All the electronic surveillance cases that came to me later seemed like a continuation of those conversations.

I have preached that lawyers must develop a structured sense of the law. In that way, when some new doctrine comes along, you have a place to put that knowledge. This was Williams's idea of the law as well.

There was another wiretap-related case in the Williams office when I arrived, and it wound up making law that remains a solid basis for the right to a hearing on government illegality. The United States had prosecuted three Las Vegas and Chicago figures, Ruby Kolod, Willie "Icepick Willie" Alderman, and Felix "Milwaukee Phil" Alderisio. Kolod was an executive at the Fremont Hotel in Las Vegas. Alderman had the reputation of being a hit man who dispatched his victims with an ice pick in the ear. Phil Alderisio was in business in Chicago. Kolod believed that he had been swindled by a Denver promoter named Robert Sunshine. He sent Alderman and Alderisio to Denver to explain to Sunshine that he should refund Kolod's money. The explanation, according to Sunshine, included death threats—in person and by telephone.

Sunshine went to the FBI, and Kolod, Alderisio, and Alderman were prosecuted in Denver federal court for using interstate commerce to make extortion threats. Williams tried the case. Among his theories was that there were not in fact any threats. If there had been, and if Kolod had indeed met with Alderisio and Alderman to discuss plans, at least some of this illegal activity would have been recorded on the FBI-installed bugs. For that reason, Williams reasoned, the defense needed copies of all the bugged conversations. If there was no incriminating evidence in these, then that fact would be admissible as tending to show that no such conversations took place.

So the case stood when I joined the firm in the summer of 1966. My first research project was on "negative evidence to prove a proposition." There are a number of good cases on that issue. For example, if the witness was at a party all evening and did not see Bill there, that is some evidence that Bill was not there. This is not a surprising idea, and perhaps not very interesting. The witness can be impeached by all manner of cross-examination about how big was the party, in how many rooms, how much alcohol was consumed, and so on. Williams was hoping that the judge would order the wiretaps produced, that the FBI would refuse, and that the case would therefore be dismissed.

This hope was founded on another line of case law that was to prove significant in the electronic surveillance cases. In criminal cases, the government is required to produce certain of its evidence for the defense to inspect, copy, and use in hearings or at trial. Sometimes the government can avoid this obligation by a valid claim that the evidence is privileged and not relevant or important to the defense.

For example, the government need not always tell the identity of an informer on whose word a search warrant has been obtained, or a warrantless search conducted. Because of this informer privilege, the FBI often called illegal wiretaps and bugs by code names such as "Confidential Informant C-1." But this privilege goes only so far. A leading case, on which we were to rely, shows how this works. In the late 1940s, the FBI wiretapped Justice Department lawyer Judith Coplon and a Soviet agent. These illegal wiretaps allegedly showed Coplon helping the Soviet agent prepare to commit espionage. Coplon's lawyers moved that the taps be produced, so that they could show the government's case was tainted by this illegal evidence. Coplon was convicted. The court of appeals reversed, in an eloquent opinion by Learned Hand. He held that to discharge its burden of coming forward with evidence and of proving that there was no taint, the government would have to produce all the wiretaps. If the government was unwilling to disclose its illegal taps, then the court would dismiss the prosecution. The Coplon case was part of Ed Williams's basic understanding of wiretap law, and he would rely on it again and again. The Supreme Court has expressly adopted Learned Hand's reasoning in that case.

Williams's legal arguments (and my research on them) did not do well before the trial judge or in the U.S. Court of Appeals for the Tenth Circuit. Williams filed a petition for certiorari in the Supreme Court. While that petition was pending, Peter Taft—a lawyer in the office—was talking one night to an FBI agent in connection with the civil case in Las Vegas. The agent let slip that in addition to the wiretaps and bugs in Las Vegas, the FBI had a bug in a Chicago store where Alderisio was known to hold meetings.

On October 9, 1967, the Supreme Court denied certiorari. The case was over, unless we could think of something else to do. I drafted a motion to stay the Court's mandate pending the filing of a petition for rehearing. Such motions are rare. Rarer still are cases in which the Supreme Court grants a rehearing after denying certiorari. In the motion, I repeated that counsel had good, and new, evidence that Alderisio had been the subject of illegal electronic surveillance, which might have tainted his conviction. Citing Coplon, I argued that the government had to disclose this surveillance and submit to a hearing on it.

I took the motion to the Supreme Court clerk's office personally and met with Deputy Clerk Cullinan. He gruffly asked, "Does Edward Bennett Williams know you are filing this thing?"

"Yes, sir," I said. "That is his signature."

"I know it's his signature," he said. "I'm asking you if he read the thing before you got him to sign it. We don't grant these."

I assured Cullinan and he file-stamped the motion. I asked Ed about the experience and he told me that Cullinan was famously belligerent and famously bibulous, to the point of losing exhibits and misinforming lawyers about scheduled arguments.

A few days later, Acting Solicitor General Spritzer answered our motion. He did not deny that there had been illegal electronic surveillance. However, he revealed for the first time that there was a committee in the Justice Department that reviewed all electronic surveillance cases and would permit disclosure to the defense only if the committee concluded that the illegal surveillance was arguably relevant to the case.

This response set in motion a fundamental change in criminal procedure. We replied to it, noting that prosecutors could not determine whether surveillance had tainted a case. Our criminal justice system is adversarial. In every comparable situation, judges and not litigants are the arbiters of what is legal and what is not. Whatever privileges government may possess, it cannot foreclose inquiry into its own illegality by the secret deliberations and Delphic pronouncements of its own servants.

Our rehearing petition, filed in mid-October, was in the same vein. On December 4, 1967, the Court entered a brief order directing the Solicitor General to file a response to the rehearing petition within thirty days. Our optimism was fueled.

Newly installed Solicitor General Erwin Griswold filed the response, and we did a brief reply. We had expected at most a briefing schedule, but on January 29, 1968, the Court issued a brief per curiam order, granting rehearing and certiorari, and directing the government to disclose electronic surveillance so that there could be a hearing on whether the government's case was tainted.

The Court's order cited little authority, but its message deeply disturbed the Department of Justice. Perhaps the Court did not know just how many bugs and taps the FBI, IRS, and other agencies had installed, without any legal basis. The use of these devices was not limited to a few so-called "organized crime" investigations. Rather, wiretapping and bugging were the norm in national security cases, and even before the Nixon administration they were extensively used against all manner of dissidents.

The Justice Department—including the FBI—was sitting on a cache of illegally obtained material, with targets as diverse as Martin Luther King, Jr. and white anti-war protesters. The short opinion in *Kolod*, read literally, would require wholesale disclosure of that material anytime the federal government prosecuted somebody who had been picked up on a tap or bug. This point became clearer to the government as we got the chance to turn up the heat.

In the fall of 1967, Ed and I met with Martin Popper, a lawyer for the Soviet Union. He sought counsel for a Soviet citizen, Igor Ivanov, who had been convicted of espionage. Ivanov, a chauffeur for the Soviet trading company Amtorg, was arrested along with two Soviet diplomats at a meeting with an American engineer for ITT, John Butenko. The government's case was that Butenko had been passing secrets to the Soviets. The two diplomats, because of their official immunity, were simply kicked out of the United States. Ivanov had no immunity, so he was prosecuted, convicted, and sentenced. The court of appeals affirmed the conviction. I was assigned to write the petition for certiorari, which was due the first week in December 1967.

Because the Kolod case was pending, I put a footnote in the Ivanov certiorari petition, saying, "No question is presented concerning electronic surveillance, on the assumption that if there was any, the Solicitor General will disclose it," with a cite to our Kolod pleadings. Solicitor General Griswold, in his response, included a footnote citing the government's Kolod pleadings and saying that surveillance not found by the Justice Department committee to be arguably relevant would not be disclosed.

I had hoped for such a response. The odds were against any Supreme Court review of the criminal procedure issues in a case where the Soviet spies were caught red-handed (as it were). The electronic surveillance issue had potential. The Supreme Court had decided that electronic surveillance, with a warrant and under strict safeguards, might be consistent with the Fourth Amendment. In the 1968 legislation, Congress had tried to meet those standards.

So I invoked a little-used Supreme Court rule, and moved to amend the petition for certiorari to add an additional question presented. This procedure permits a petitioner to add an issue that arises after the certiorari petition is filed, and avoids what would otherwise be an untimely presentation. If the motion is granted, the petition with its amended issue is deemed to have been filed on the original filing date. The question I added demanded disclosure of any illegal electronic surveillance.

Thus, when the brief *Kolod* opinion came down, its literal language would require the government to own up to surveillance in the *Ivanov* case and in untold others. The Solicitor General, assisted by senior Justice Department lawyers and by the department's Internal Security Section, moved to modify the *Kolod* order. By this time, Kolod had died, so the case became *Alderman v. United States*.

In his motion, the Solicitor General obliquely conceded that electronic surveillance had become a favorite government pastime. He claimed that national security would suffer if the government had to disclose surveillance in espionage and internal security cases. He said that a surveillance of a Mafia boss might record two underlings plotting against their chief; disclosure to the chief might endanger lives. He hinted, with little subtlety, that government agencies might resist disclosure or even be less than candid about what they had done. This last argument might lead somebody to ask, "Who is really in charge here?" but one might not want to hear the answer. To deal with these issues, the Solicitor General suggested that disclosure in camera to a district judge was the preferred way to proceed.

The issue was thus rejoined. Whenever government has done wrong, the temptation is to bury the illegality in the bureaucracy. The fox, which remains in charge of the henhouse, will then assure everybody that all is well. When that gambit fails, the government's next position is that it should present its views to a judge, in secret and ex parte—without the other side being present or being able to respond—and let the judge decide how to proceed. This suggestion has the allure of reason, for judges are institutionally neutral. But nobody can decide anything fairly without hearing both sides. The danger of a one-sided presentation is particularly acute in these cases, where the opening premise is that the government was right to violate the law deliberately.

By the spring of 1968, I had already participated in enough wiretap cases to share the Williams firm's institutional knowledge. In one income tax evasion case, the prosecutor resisted disclosing the surveillance logs, saying that an informant's life would be in danger. The judge asked to review the logs. He then asked the prosecutor how the conversation could possibly endanger anybody. "Well," the prosecutor backtracked, "disclosure would harm a financial interest, so it is an economic life." Even when honest prosecutors eschewed this kind of sophistry, the FBI would often hide relevant information from its own lawyers. In case after case, I have seen prosecutors double-crossed by FBI agents who failed to make relevant and required disclosures.

So we knew the value of adversary inquiry, in open court, firsthand. The Court responded on March 18, 1968, and set the motion to modify for oral argument. In a later order, the Court also asked the parties to brief and argue the issue of standing to suppress illegally obtained evidence.

On June 17, 1968, we received another piece of good news. In *Ivanov*, the Court granted the motion to amend the petition for certiorari and granted certiorari limited to electronic surveillance issues. Our strategy had paid off, helped by the Solicitor General sweeping *Ivanov*-related concerns into his motion to modify the *Kolod* order.

On October 14, 1968, Edward Bennett Williams presented oral argument in *Alderman* and *Ivanov*. I reproduced his argument, in annotated form, in *Persuasion: The Litigator's Art*. The keystone of it was this:

> Now, first of all, it is our position, if the Court please, that the Fourth Amendment to the Constitution does not make a division among the various kinds of crime. It does not draw a line of demarcation, and the founding fathers, when the Constitution was written and when the American Bill of Rights was forged, understood quite clearly that there is a difference in the various types of crime.
>
> They gave recognition to this in Article 3, Section 3, of the Constitution when they defined treason, and they prescribed the quantum and quality of proof necessary for a treason conviction, but they didn't make any exception in the Fourth Amendment with respect to spy catchers or subversive hunters.
>
> It is next our position, if the Court please, if the Attorney General of the United States certifies to the Court that there is a national security consideration which should excuse the United States from making a disclosure with respect to the nature, the time, the place, or the fruits of an electronic surveillance illegally conducted, we say he should be excused provided he consents to a dismissal of the prosecution under the time-honored principle of *Coplon* against the United States, which was decided in 1950, in an opinion by Judge Learned Hand, which was foursquare with the facts in the case, an alleged spy, a convicted spy, and the premise was articulated that there the government had a choice of making a full disclosure to the defendant for the vindication of her constitutional rights or dismissing it. The government dismissed.
>
> Now, that case, and I think it is significant to note, has stood unassailed by the government for 18 years until argument was heard in this case last term. . . . So, if the Court please, it is reduced to essence that the concept of national security should not be the talisman for a pro tanto suspension of due process of law or of any of the rights guaranteed to an accused in a criminal case.

If, in the conduct of relationships between governments in our time, it has become the custom or it has become a necessity to engage in wiretapping or eavesdropping or dissembling or purloining or burglarizing or even killing, it is not our argument in this Court today that the Executive Branch should be manacled or impeded or harassed in the conduct of relationships with other governments. It is our argument here today that at least the federal courts should be a sanctuary in the jungle, and that these morals and mores should be not be imported into the American judiciary system, and that the fruits of this kind of conduct should not become evidence in a criminal case brought by the sovereign power against an accused, nor should those [fruits] derived from these kinds of conduct be available to the prosecutor in a criminal case brought by the sovereign power.

In essence, as I understand the government's position in this case, it is asserting its right to be let alone and to that we say amen, as long as the evidence is not offered in a federal criminal proceeding.

The Court's decision in *Alderman* required a court hearing in any case involving unlawful electronic surveillance, so that the government could discharge its duty of showing that its evidence was not "the fruit of the poisonous tree."

Tapping and bugging issues were at the center of other cases in the firm. Robert G. "Bobby" Baker, secretary to the Senate Majority, was convicted of tax and theft crimes, an important loss for Ed as well as for Baker himself. However, the court of appeals held that the trial judge had not conducted a sufficient hearing on possible taint from electronic surveillance, and it remanded to the trial judge for those hearings. Ed assigned Peter Taft and me to conduct those hearings, a real introduction to cross-examining FBI agents based on their own records. In the end, we lost, and Baker served a couple of years at a minimum security prison. I still see Bobby around Washington, and have worked on a few post-conviction motions for him. In that work, Ed was helpful. He had the same idea that I did. Once you have represented a client, it is relatively easy to be drawn back in even if the money is not there.

The battle against uncontrolled electronic surveillance took a new turn in the summer of 1969. In the Chicago conspiracy case, the Justice Department filed an admission that it conducted electronic surveillance of at least some of the defendants without a warrant. This was the first of these admissions. The government's claims were remarkable. Beginning in 1941, President Roosevelt had authorized the FBI to wiretap people suspected of endangering the national security. FBI Director Hoover had seen to it that these general authorizations were continued from president to president. Of course, the original FDR position was based on the imminence of war, which made it understandable if not entirely in harmony with the Constitution.

However, over the years the FBI had taken this original mandate and expanded it all out of proportion to its origins. It routinely tapped and bugged foreign diplomats and other aliens on the premise that it was protecting national security. FBI Director Hoover also thought that domestic groups that he considered subversive were dangerous to national security, and so the FBI tapped and bugged them as well. From that summer of 1969 until the 1972 Supreme Court decision holding domestic national security electronic surveillance unlawful unless done with a judicial warrant, the Department of Justice admitted tapping and bugging in dozens of cases involving domestic dissident people and groups.

But Chicago was the curtain raiser. I drafted a brief on which we all worked, and I argued the issue to Judge Julius Hoffman. The result was predictable in that court. He held that the government had the power it claimed. But we had laid the basis for litigating the issue elsewhere. The argument was not complicated, and was based on the same separation-of-powers analysis that backed our challenge to the Vietnam war. The President is commander in chief, but nothing in the Constitution authorizes him to usurp functions that are constitutionally committed to another branch of government.

The Fourth Amendment gives judges, and not executive officers, the power to issue search warrants. Behind the amendment's text lies important history. In 1772, two cases from England held that executive warrants were unlawful. These cases involved political dissidents, so those who drafted the Fourth Amendment had recent experience upon which to draw when they insisted on judicial warrants. There are some exceptions to the warrant requirement, for exigent circumstances and in public places. There are even instances where the Fourth Amendment probable-cause standard is relaxed, such as border searches. But nothing in our history seemed to justify as sweeping a rule as that for which the government contended.

This issue finally found a favorable forum in the case of Melvin Carl Smith. Smith was convicted in Los Angeles federal court of weapons charges arising from the activities of the Black Panther Party. When the wiretap issue arose in his case, his lawyer, Jean Kidwell Pestana, called me. Jean and her husband, Frank Pestana, were progressive lawyers of the old school: principled, resilient, and careful students of the theory and practice of legal ideology.

The facts and argument in *Smith* followed the pattern established in the Chicago case. The Department of Justice disclosed that the FBI had picked up Smith on warrantless electronic surveillance, justified by an asserted national security exception to the Fourth Amendment warrant and probable cause requirements. This time, however, the case was before Warren Ferguson, a principled and studious judge. Judge Ferguson's opinion was the first judicial ruling that warrantless national security electronic surveillance violated the Fourth Amendment. Judge Damon Keith in Detroit made the same holding two weeks later, relying on Judge Ferguson's reasoning, and the *Keith* case was affirmed by the Supreme Court. Ferguson held that the government must disclose the contents and details of its surveillance and submit to a hearing on taint, or else suffer dismissal of its case.

Judge Ferguson recognized the national security interest the government was asserting, but held that it could not displace the clear constitutional command that searches must, with few exceptions, be based on a warrant granted by a judicial officer. The executive branch cannot be both law decider and law enforcer. The fox cannot be in charge of the henhouse.

I argued that the government should be given a week to make its decision and, failing that, should suffer dismissal. As the law then stood, this might not have been an appealable order and Smith would be released. Judge Ferguson wanted to give the government an opportunity to seek appellate review. I could understand, and even support, the idea of having an appellate court decision uphold our position. However, Smith's welfare was my primary duty.

And so, the Department of Justice took the case to the Ninth Circuit, by way of mandamus. A mandamus is technically directed to the district judge whose rulings are being challenged, and at that time courts of appeals were quite liberal in encouraging the district judge to be heard. So Judge Ferguson asked Warren Christopher to represent him, thus setting the stage for a three-part oral argument featuring Warren, a Department of Justice lawyer, and me.

The department was represented by Robert Mardian, Assistant Attorney General for Internal Security, who was later prosecuted for his role in the Watergate scandal. The Nixon administration had greatly increased funding for internal security matters in the Department of Justice and in the FBI. It had set up the internal security function under a separate assistant attorney general, rather than keeping it within the criminal division. This independence meant that, in practice, the Nixon White House agenda of unlawful surveillance of political enemies went on unchecked. In later years, when Nixon resigned and Gerald Ford installed a new attorney general, FBI agents who had participated in illegal break-ins were prosecuted.

Mardian's oral argument was surreal. He apparently dwelt in a world where everyone shared his paranoid vision of enemies hiding everywhere, and his view was that only a secret and unaccountable government establishment could protect us. He began by holding up a sealed cardboard box and telling the judges that it contained national security information that would show why these taps were necessary. Judge Browning, presiding, asked, "What are we supposed to do with that?"

"You should receive it and read it, and you will see," Mardian replied.

"Mr. Mardian," Judge Browning said patiently, "is that material part of the record?"

"Oh, no, Your Honor, it is for this court's eyes only."

"Mr. Mardian," Judge Browning continued, "as an appellate court, we review the record below. We are not in the habit of receiving ex parte communications that the other side has not seen, and that even the district judge did not have before him. We will not receive your box."

Mardian continued his argument, mostly reading it from a prepared script. Judge Shirley Hufstedler asked him a question. He looked at her impatiently and said, "Ma'am, I'll be getting to that later on."

All of us at counsel tables, and the judges, visibly caught our breath. Judge Browning, always ostensibly affable but with a steely edge to his voice, said, "Mr. Mardian, you will answer *Judge* Hufstedler's question, and you will do it now."

I had been gratified that Judge Ferguson was not hypnotized by the invocation of national security and that the court of appeals did not seem to be. I am sometimes reminded of Lord Coke's dictum: "God send me never to live under the law of conveniency or discretion. For if the soldier and the justice sit on the same bench, the trumpet will not let the crier speak in Westminster Hall."

Once the Supreme Court decided *Keith*, the Ninth Circuit had only to follow suit. The government would not disclose how it had invaded Melvin Carl Smith's privacy, and so the case was dismissed. In the wake of *Keith*, dozens of cases against dissidents were dismissed because the government never wanted to make an accounting of its wrongful conduct. One such case was that of Leonard, who had been a fugitive for almost a decade and had been working as a nurse in Washington. He was arrested in the 1970s and faced state court charges in Illinois dating from 1968, and federal charges in both Chicago and Cleveland.

When Leonard and I went to the Chicago criminal court for arraignment on the old state charges, two FBI agents met us along with the state's attorney. They all said that Leonard had better make a deal to testify against his old comrades, or else it would go badly for him. We almost laughed. All the charges against him were tainted in one way or another by illegal government surveillance. The possible exception was a minor charge of scuffling with a police officer, and even then there were eyewitness issues.

When the bluff did not work, the state's attorney agreed that Leonard could plead to one count of nonviolent disorderly conduct and get 24 months' unsupervised probation, freeing him to go to medical school. This plea bargain became the pattern for returning fugitives from the insurgency of the 1960s. Leonard is today a doctor.

Melvin Carl Smith and Leonard were only two of the victims of FBI bugging and tapping. We had the issue in the Seattle conspiracy case. I went to New Orleans in 1970 to try the wiretap motion in the case of the civil rights leader H. Rap Brown, where we proved that the Louisiana authorities had consciously sought to intercept lawyer-client communications. The federal judge refused to find that the FBI had known of or encouraged the state authorities in doing this. This was, however, my chance to try an issue in the old federal courthouse in the French Quarter, where the district courts and the Fifth Circuit sat for many years. The judge was Lansing T. Mitchell, known as "Tut." Imperious and always impeccably dressed, he was the figure of a jurist.

I had the FBI agent on the stand and was about to pin him to an inconsistency in his report when Judge Mitchell interrupted. "Mr. Tigar, I don't know if you know this, but I consider my years as an FBI special agent to be the proudest of my life." I had not known, but asked my questions anyway—to no great effect.

The statutory authorization for electronic surveillance became law in 1968. It contained a provision forbidding the government to use illegal electronic surveillance in any trial or hearing, and requiring prosecutors to affirm or deny the existence of illegal surveillance if asked. These two provisions proved to be important in unexpected ways.

The Nixon administration and Justice's Internal Security Division decided to go after dissidents using federal grand juries. After all, the federal grand jury is only nominally independent of the prosecutor. It meets in secret, and a witness's lawyer must stay outside the room. If the grand jury is investigating an alleged conspiracy, its subpoenas can go anywhere provided a credible argument can be made that some overt act, however slight and whether legal or illegal, in furtherance of the possible conspiracy took place in the judicial district where the grand jury is sitting. The list of procedural protections for grand jury witnesses was already short in the late 1960s, and has become shorter with the passage of time.

The Nixon administration tactic was simple. Subpoenas would go out to a number of dissidents, on some flimsy theory about a conspiracy to violate the law. In the Philadelphia area, the targets were nuns, priests, and lay workers involved in peace demonstrations. In Arizona, people involved in an organization allegedly connected to a bomb plot were subpoenaed; this alleged plot turned out to be a figment of the FBI's imagination. The Arizona grand jury directed most of its subpoenas to people in the Los Angeles area on the theory that the conspiracy being investigated held some light connection with Arizona. Predictably, those subpoenaed refused to testify on First Amendment grounds. When these objections were overruled, they invoked their privilege against self-incrimination.

Using a provision of the 1968 law, the government gave use immunity to those who refused to testify, meaning that their Fifth Amendment privilege evaporated but their answers could not be used against them, except in a prosecution for perjury if the government disagreed with their version of events. So the witnesses had a dilemma. If they testified that they and their friends were innocent, they might be prosecuted in Arizona, far from home, for allegedly lying. If they implicated their friends, then the latter would be prosecuted.

Many of these folks refused to accept the immunity and went to jail for contempt. Those who decided to testify quickly learned about the perjury trap. The prosecutor would ask question after question about the smallest details of their conversations and activities. It became clear that the prosecutor had access to electronic surveillance, and thus could keep asking questions about conversations that the witness might only dimly remember but of which the prosecutor had a transcript.

It appeared, therefore, that prosecutors were using unlawful electronic surveillance to formulate grand jury questions, hoping by this means to obtain indictments that would be arguably based on evidence independent of the illegality. The U.S. Court of Appeals for the Ninth Circuit held that this tactic was proper, and that grand jury witnesses had no standing to challenge the basis of a prosecutor's questions. The Third Circuit held the contrary, in a case involving an activist nun, Sister Jogues Egan.

As it happened, leftists were not the only ones interested in this issue. In Los Angeles, a long-running investigation of alleged interstate gambling focused on clients I had been representing. I had helped draft a certiorari petition for two grand jury witnesses who had worked for Caesar's Palace casino. The Supreme Court granted certiorari on my petition, and on the United States' petition arising from the Philadelphia investigation. Thus, in one case the defendant was petitioner, and in the other case the United States was. This meant that I would argue first for Gelbard, then the Deputy Solicitor General would have two back-to-back half hours, then Sister Egan's counsel would argue.

When certiorari was granted, I was traveling in England, working on the book that became *Law and the Rise of Capitalism*. I had a publisher's advance and a small foundation grant but little else. I agreed to brief and argue the case from the Ninth Circuit, for an up-front fee of $25,000 plus expenses. That plus the advance and grant was enough money to live in France for a year and do research and writing on the book. I wrote the brief in the American law section of Oxford's Bodleian Library.

In the brief and in oral argument, I needed to show that this case involved at least two stories. The government's story was based on a narrow statutory reading, bolstered by decisions that sharply limited judicial control over prosecutorial discretion in running a grand jury.

Our story was quite different. We had a literal, textual argument, but I have never thought that such arguments are enough, standing alone. When the text supports you, by all means argue it. You may pick up a vote or two. But the self-styled textualists have proven ready to abandon their faith to reach a result. Textualism permits results without regard to their consequences. It can therefore become a mask the law puts on to commit some indignity. As we all know, in daily speech and writing the same words may carry quite different meanings depending on the intention with which they are written or spoken, or the context in which they are used. I agree with those who say that the process of communication always depends on a connection between the speaker and the hearer, or the writer and the reader. In fact, my book, *Persuasion: The Litigator's Art*, explores this premise at some length. Although I was arguing for David Gelbard and Sidney Parnas, I wanted the Court to inquire how a gambler, an accountant, and an outspoken nun all came to be making the same contentions.

In short, the four years since the 1968 act was passed illustrated how one should never accept just a little erosion of due process to catch a clearly dangerous enemy. This theme has been sounded again and again, in literature and in law, but it is often and easily forgotten. I wanted to show how an expansive view of the grand jury's power permitted prosecutors to avoid limits on the legality of government conduct.

As I said, we won 5 to 4. Several years later, in *Calandra v. United States*, the Court held 6 to 3 that the grand jury could hear unlawfully obtained evidence that did not involve electronic surveillance. And in 1992, the Court held that the prosecutor was not obliged to present exculpatory evidence to the grand jury. So our 5 to 4 win was precarious, and represented an outer limit of judicial control of the grand jury.

I had thought that the case would be 5 to 4 or at best 6 to 3. In the days before oral argument, I met with Peter Westen to map out a strategy. Peter was then at the Paul Weiss firm's D.C. office, and had just obtained certiorari in *Chambers v. Mississippi*. With Peter's help, I found a case authored by each of the five Justices whose votes I really needed, and resolved to cite each case in the opening minutes of oral argument. Justice White caught on to this tactic. As I cited the second case, he whispered in Justice Brennan's ear and held his hand with fingers outstretched. He then counted off the remaining citations, and when I got to five, he reached out and gave Justice Brennan a playful tap on the shoulder.

When arguing to an appellate court, the judges' or justices' interaction can often give valuable clues. Sometimes the judge may use a question to argue with a colleague, or even to help an advocate who is in trouble. In the *Egan* argument, Deputy Solicitor General Friedman noted in an aside that the government had searched its records after the court of appeals decision and that there had in fact been no electronic surveillance of Sister Egan. One Justice wondered aloud if this mooted the case, but of course the answer was no because the issue was bound to recur in the same grand jury investigation.

When Sister Egan's lawyer was arguing, one Justice asked him to comment on the government's denial that there had been electronic surveillance. The lawyer was being driven to concede that if there had been no surveillance, then Sister Egan was not justified in refusing to answer questions. Therefore, she was properly held in contempt and properly committed to jail. Sister Egan was in the front row of spectators in her habit. At the mention of jail, she took out a handkerchief and dabbed at her eyes. Seeing a nun cry was too much for Justice Brennan. He quickly asked the lawyer "just to clarify" if in fact Sister Egan was entitled to a new opportunity to go before the grand jury, and did not face any risk of jail. The lawyer agreed.

In the *Gelbard* majority opinion, Justice Brennan wrote that the statute required the government to disclose electronic surveillance, and that its language therefore trumped the historic disinclination of court to interfere with grand jury proceedings.

My experience belied the government's assurance that wiretapping and bugging would be used only in carefully limited circumstances. The judicial controls on surveillance warrants were, in practice, loose. In case after case, I was confronted with surveillance tapes made over months, involving thousands of hours of conversations. Inevitably, these tapes swept up lawyer-client communications, innocent social conversations, and moments of intimacy. In one celebrated case, the defendant achieved a kind of hat-trick record by (1) having an innocent social conversation (2) about a lawyer-client-privileged issue (3) while engaging in a sexual act.

The ubiquity of electronic searches points up their inherent character as general searches. The application for surveillance may describe in detail what the government hopes to overhear, but the actual search is a kind of strip-mining. The gleanings represent only a tiny fraction of what the listeners amass. The pervasive sense that the government, or big business, can collect and use so many details of our private lives erodes our sense of independence and freedom.

Even after the Supreme Court held that warrantless domestic national security electronic surveillance was unlawful, the Justice Department continued to think that it could wiretap and bug at will as long as its target was a foreign national or the case involved foreign national security. The courts of appeals took inconsistent positions on the issue, and in 1978 Congress passed the Foreign Intelligence Surveillance Act, which set up a special court to issue judicial authorization for foreign electronic surveillance within the United States' borders. Had this act not been passed, the Supreme Court would probably have agreed to hear one of the foreign surveillance cases, perhaps one in which I was counsel.

One of those cases involved David Truong, a student from South Vietnam who had opposed the United States' involvement in the Vietnam war and after the American withdrawal from Vietnam, had worked to normalize relations with the Socialist Republic of Vietnam. David was part of a group against which the FBI and the CIA directed its investigative activity. The CIA was, in this respect, violating the mandate that limited it to foreign investigation. Its justification was that the investigation involved a foreign country. So it recruited a Vietnamese woman to pose as a friend of those seeking to normalize relations with Vietnam. This agent urged David and others to try to obtain secret United States documents about American policy.

There was no question that David developed a friendship with a lower-level State Department employee, or that the employee copied State Department cable traffic and gave it to David. The factual issue was whether this cable traffic, consisting of what I termed "diplomatic chit-chat," could legitimately be termed secret or involve any risk to national security. I came in second on that issue in the jury trial; I could share the loss with my partner, Sam Buffone, and our co-counsel, Marvin Miller, but I accept the responsibility. The court of appeals expressed some concerns about the overbroad use of espionage laws, and especially about the government's failure to fulfill its discovery obligations. But it eventually affirmed the conviction and sentence.

The government had manipulated events to have venue in the Eastern District of Virginia. This meant trial in Alexandria, on the "rocket docket" and to a conservative jury. In the District of Columbia, it would have been a different case, at trial and on appeal.

David's case had several interwoven stories. The United States, unrepentant for its errors in Vietnam, had turned against those who had opposed its policies. Rather than opening debate about matters affecting national security, it invoked draconian laws on espionage and classified information to maintain the wall of secrecy. Even if one thought that David had strayed over the line and had no right to the documents he obtained, punishing him under laws designed to protect vital state secrets represented a dangerously overbroad reading of those laws. The CIA's agent had befriended several well-known activists to create the basis for prosecuting them.

The Truong investigation had begun while Gerald Ford was President. Ford's attorney general, Edward Levi, was a well-known legal scholar who during his brief tenure brought real reform to the Justice Department. We learned that Levi resisted the FBI's efforts to conduct warrantless searches directed at David. When Jimmy Carter became President in January 1977, he named Griffin Bell attorney general. Bell was a partner in an Atlanta law firm and had been a judge on the old Fifth Circuit. He had written an opinion for that court upholding the exclusion of civil rights activist Julian Bond from the Georgia legislature. Bond had been elected, but the legislature refused to seat him because of his outspoken though lawful opposition to the Vietnam war. The Supreme Court reversed, but Bell's insensitivity to constitutional values soon became apparent in his new job.

In May 1977, having returned from a weekend at the Kentucky Derby, Bell approved the FBI burglary of David's home to install a hidden microphone and a tap on David's home telephone. The tap and bug operated for 268 days, all without a warrant. Bell also approved warrantless searches of David's mail. We filed motions to suppress illegally obtained evidence and subpoenaed Bell. The trial judge refused to quash the subpoena, and Bell testified that he had approved these searches because "I was trying to catch me a spy." He appeared innocent of any Fourth Amendment understanding.

The electronic surveillance did not produce much evidence of consequence, and so the issue did not make much headway. And, as I said, given that a new system for judicial warrants was being established under the Foreign Surveillance Intelligence Act, the Supreme Court did not take up the issue.

In the early days of the case, however, we learned again just how powerful national security can be. In the earlier cases, district judges seemed to abandon their power of independent thought when the government pronounced this talismanic phrase. In American law, in cases as diverse as the World War II Japanese relocation and Cold War loyalty-security proceedings, the supposedly independent judiciary seemed timid. The battle for judicial independence must be fought over and over. In David's case, the trial judge denied bail, although David was not a flight risk. We took the matter to the court of appeals. The law clerk for one of those judges later told me that he thought I had made a winning argument. He told this to his judge, who said: "You don't understand. This is a spy case. He stays in."

Throughout the trial, we constantly battled for disclosure of prior witness statements, and almost every day the prosecutors would present another batch of discovery material that they had just received from this or that secret or semi-secret agency. We were at the bench one day, with the jury out of the room, quarreling over one such late disclosure. The prosecutors were saying that they had trouble getting the CIA to give up documents. I turned to the courtroom and said in a loud voice, "Would the CIA lawyer please stand up." A lawyer stood up, realized he had been found out, looked sheepish, and then sat down. Judge Bryant called him to the bench to explain the agency's position. Despite the searches and the discovery fights, we eventually lost the case after several rounds of appeals.

I can remember around that time having lunch with Justice Brennan, and telling him of Griffin Bell's arrogant and somewhat incoherent performance under adverse examination. Brennan laughed and remembered the Julian Bond case. "When Hugo Black saw Bell's opinion," Brennan said, "I thought he was going to come out of his tree." As it happened, when we sought review of the court of appeals' bail denial, the circuit justice for the Fourth Circuit, Chief Justice Burger, was out of town. We therefore presented the application to Justice Brennan, who granted it in an opinion that still carries a powerful message about the constitutional right to bail. This meant that all during our long trial and many appeals, David was out of jail.

I am at times chagrined to see the extent to which we have accepted electronic surveillance as a fact of investigative life. I am more concerned when I see the cavalier way in which investigative agencies undertake it, and the extent of its invasions. Consider, for example, the prosecutions of leading Mafia figures. The massive electronic surveillance in those cases generates tens of thousands of pages of transcript. Prosecutors and investigators become careless in handling the material and create procedural error. Defense counsel cannot possibly wade through the material to find possible exculpatory evidence. And because the major figures know they are being overheard, the tapes do not yield much useful investigative product. Cases continue to be won or lost based on the testimony of witnesses and the presence or absence of documentary and other physical evidence. The net result is that all this snooping invades privacy without any arguable corresponding benefit.

There are exceptions to this observation, to be sure. In a celebrated prosecution of Irish-American supporters of the Irish Republican Army, a wiretap revealed that the defendants were trying to use code words to hide their arms dealings. But being forgetful, perhaps as a result of advanced age, they sometimes mixed their signals. One transcript went like this:

"Paddy!"
"Yes, Michael?"
"Paddy, did you do any good with the fellow today?"
"I surely did. I bought a machine."
"You bought a machine? Where the hell is it?"
"In me garage."
"Jesus, Mary, and Joseph, you've got a tank in your garage? In the middle of New York City?"

"No, Michael, I've got a bazooka in me garage!"
"Paddy, how many times have I got to tell you. A bazooka is called a pencil. A tank is called a machine."

As if to mock the alleged value of this sort of electronic intrusion, these defendants were acquitted by a federal jury.

Notes

1. *Katz v. United States*, 389 U.S. 347 (1967), traces the history of electronic survcillance law and cites all the relevant cases up to that time, including *Silverman*.

2. Alderman v. United States, 394 U.S. 165 (1969); United States v. Coplon, 185 F.2d 629 (2d Cir. 1950).

3. Judge Ferguson's opinion is *United States v. Smith*, 321 F. Supp. 424 (C.D. Cal. 1971) *See also* United States v. U.S. District Court, 407 U.S. 297 (1972). Both opinions contain accounts of Fourth Amendment history.

4. The Rap Brown district court opinion is *United States v. Brown*, 317 F. Supp. 531 (E.D. La. 1970).

5. *Gelbard v. United States*, 408 U.S. 41 (1972), discusses the 1968 Crime Control Act in some detail.

6. Justice Brennan's bail opinion in *Truong* is reported at 99 S. Ct. 16 (1978).

7. *United States v. Williams*, 504 U.S. 36 (1992), is the case on exculpatory evidence before the grand jury. The opinions contain a review of grand jury law after *Gelbard*.

Chapter 10

BY ANY MEANS NECESSARY

Justice Brandeis told us that "government is the potent, omnipresent teacher. For good or for ill, it teaches the whole people by its example . . . If the government becomes a lawbreaker, it breeds contempt for the law; it invites every man to become a law unto himself; it invites anarchy."

I think government is the most dangerous criminal around. When government commits offenses, or more exactly when people commit crimes in the name of government and with its power, they can wreak more harm than any individual. Government is also a recidivist. If not stopped, it repeats its crimes. It seldom repents for wrongs; its spokesmen think up new justifications and excuses.

Suing the government civilly for wrongdoing is daunting. Government agents have qualified immunity from suit. The state and federal governments as entities claim a broad and absolute immunity. The Supreme Court has made it harder for lawyers to get legal fees when they sue the government and win. Public officials and sovereign entities can move to dismiss the complaint on immunity grounds, and if the trial judge rejects their legal position, they can take an immediate appeal. The Supreme Court has held that the official defendants may be able to appeal more than once in a single case, putting the day of reckoning off even further. The government is a repeat player in the legal system; it has a staff of lawyers skilled in managing litigation and keeping the plaintiff from bringing it to closure. The marginal cost of one more lawsuit is relatively small compared to the resources that a plaintiff must expend.

I believe that the criminal process provides significant opportunities to expose and correct government overreaching. I wish this were not so, because that process provides those opportunities only when the government has behaved badly by prosecuting an innocent person or by using foul tactics. The defendant in such a case endures torments that can often never be redressed, and risks economic and other losses, jail, or even death. The costs of victory can be high.

I have tried to pick cases that permitted me to litigate government accountability, and particularly that of the intelligence services such as the FBI and CIA. These agencies' conduct and operation not only threaten democratic rights of individuals, but also can undermine the right to organize and to participate in public decision making. Many of the cases I talk about in this book are examples. And it may well be that government misconduct affects well-heeled clients as well as poor ones. This is in one sense a good thing, for I have been able to pay my rent all these years and put my children through school.

Some of these cases are studies in judicial courage or the good sense of juries. Cameron Bishop, Francisco Martinez, and John Demjanjuk are three examples.

In the middle of 1975, I was visiting John and Nellie Connally on their ranch south of San Antonio. It was just after John had been acquitted, and I took the chance to ride with him on horseback and by jeep over the Texas hill country. Somehow, a lawyer in Denver managed to get the ranch number and track me down. Cameron David Bishop, who had been leader of an anti-Vietnam war student group, had been arrested. Cam was charged with having used dynamite to blow up four electrical power towers in the Denver area in 1969. He had, however, been unavailable for trial—a fugitive, in the government's words—until he was arrested in Rhode Island in 1975. He was charged with four counts of sabotage, on the theory that these power towers supplied electricity to defense facilities. Would I come to Denver and discuss representation?

I said I would come. I went back to Washington and told Ed Williams that I was thinking of doing the case. The family could pay expenses, but not a fee. Ed peered over his glasses and said, "How about I get you a Communist bomber in Baltimore to represent, then maybe you could come back and bill a few hours on weekends?" I demurred and he gave his rueful blessing.

Cam Bishop was from a southern Colorado farm family, sheep ranchers by trade. He had been part of the student movement against the Vietnam war in college, and active in the Students for a Democratic Society. The indictment charged the dynamiting of power towers as four counts of sabotage, each carrying a 30-year jail term; 120 years was a long time, but of course he would not be able to do it all.

The case brought at least one stroke of good fortune. I met Hal Haddon, who agreed to be co-counsel, along with my friend John Mage and me. Hal had just started in private practice after heading up the public defender's office. He is one of the world's great trial lawyers and a champion friend.

Our judge was Chief Judge Albert Arraj, stern but practical. It is ironic that when I stepped into the Denver federal courthouse to try the Nichols case, that was the second bombing case tried in that building, and again the presiding judge was chief judge of the district.

The government's evidence that Cam had assembled a cache of dynamite and had blown up the towers was extensive. We did have one miraculous scene in which the FBI said it had found his fingerprint on a piece of dynamite wrapper found at the scene, right near the center of the blast. We did not have the forensic resources to debunk this evidence completely, although one expert said it was impossible for a latent fingerprint to be preserved on dynamite wrapper in that way. The fingerprint debate went on at the edges of the case, rather like the dispute over the shroud of Turin.

We also had experts jousting over whether blowing up one power tower in an entire grid could pose any danger to power supplies, given the way in which the system was interconnected. The government proved, without contradiction, that defense facilities were located near Denver and did use electricity from this power grid. And because one of Cam's former friends had been given immunity to testify against him, we had the standard sort of cross-examination about testimony obtained in such a way.

Given that Cam made his own opening statement, and given all the small doubts that we might sow, we thought it possible to get a hung jury. In the end, we did get acquitted on one count.

At the core of the case, however, was that sabotage required the government to prove that the defendant had acted during a time of war or of national emergency declared by the President. This element escalated the case from a property crime punishable in state court to a major-league federal case. In 1969, no war was in progress, for Congress had not declared one. What was the national emergency? Government exhibit 600 provided the answer. It was a beribboned and gold-sealed copy of a proclamation by President Harry S. Truman of a national emergency with respect to Korea in 1950.

1950? Yes. No president had "undeclared" the national emergency, and therefore it was still pending. This could not be, I thought at first. Then, I began to look at the statute books. Dozens of federal programs and presidential activities were continuing under various authorizations that depended on the continued existence of a national emergency. Presidents Truman, Eisenhower, Kennedy, Johnson, Nixon, and Ford had not wanted to issue a new proclamation of national emergency, and Congress had not taken action to require them to do so.

Such a fiction might serve to preserve funding for executive branch programs or maintain an executive prerogative to authorize some military action. But it seemed ludicrous that this old proclamation could provide an element of a federal felony. I went to see Adrian "Butch" Fisher, then dean of Georgetown University Law School. Dean Fisher had been law clerk to Justice Brandeis and to Justice Frankfurter. He had begun his career in public service in World War II, and by 1950 was legal adviser to the State Department. I liken this job to being solicitor general. The legal adviser is not, or should not be, simply an instrument of administration policy. He or she must given independent advice about the powers and duties of the United States.

Fisher agreed to be a witness for the defense, for he thought it absurd to claim that the Korean war was still somehow going on. Then the question arose, on what basis could he testify? He had personal knowledge of exhibit 600, and the events that led to it. He had maintained his role as a leading international law scholar, teacher, and practitioner.

But was the pendency of a national emergency a fact element of sabotage that the jury would decide? Or was it a jurisdictional element on which the judge would make a finding and instruct the jury. The law on this subject has moved in the ensuing years, and today it seems more likely that the Supreme Court would hold that this element is for the jury. We were, in 1975, ready to argue it both ways.

Dean Fisher came to Denver. With the jury in the box, he took the stand. Government counsel looked at each other, and at their FBI case agent, but none of them knew who he was or why we might be calling him.

Q: Will you tell the jury your name, sir?
A: I am Adrian Fisher.
Q. What is your business or occupation, sir?
A: I am dean of Georgetown University School of Law, in Washington, D.C.

We continued, through his clerking, his public service, his tenure as general counsel of *The Washington Post*, and his teaching and scholarship.

Q: I show you know what has been received in evidence as government exhibit 600, and I ask you, sir, if you have ever seen it before?
A: Yes, I have.
Q: Who wrote it?
A: I did.
Q: How did you come to write this, sir?
A: President Truman decided that the Korean hostilities required that he declare a national emergency. I researched the precedents concerning the various military conflicts short of actual war in which the United States had been involved, and I drafted this for his signature.

The prosecutors were looking at each other like deer in the headlights. Judge Arraj, knowing incipient road kill when he saw it, leaned forward and said to them, "Don't you want to object now?" The lead prosecutor obediently stood and said, "I object," without stating a ground.

"Sustained," said Judge Arraj.

I then asked that we be permitted to make an offer of proof of what Dean Fisher would have said, but in the form of questions and answers out of the jury's presence. Judge Arraj excused the jurors. Dean Fisher told us a brief history of the Korean conflict and how the proclamation came to be. He then said that the Korean war was over no later than the mid-1950s. Up to that point there had been some stray shots over the border.

Hal, John, and I tried the case to conclusion. The jury convicted on three of the four counts. The prosecutors moved to revoke Cam's bail, citing the fact that he had been a fugitive for nearly six years before being captured in 1975. We then saw a human side of Judge Arraj unseen before. I cited to him Justice Jackson's opinion as circuit justice in the Communist Party Smith Act cases. These leaders had been denied bail, but Jackson set them free. His main argument was that the case involved core issues of political freedom, and what a reproach it would be to our system if the defendants were jailed and it turned out that their first amendment challenge to their convictions was sustained on appeal. The opinion, which I cite often, is classic Justice Jackson—patrician, eloquent, thoughtful, and humble, all in a single document.

Judge Arraj heard our arguments, including that Cam's family would put up property to secure his presence. He granted bail, saying:

One of the impressive sights in this trial has been that Mr. Bishop's family has been here every day. Some days, his children have been here as well. It is heartening to see this kind of family support, and I believe that Mr. Bishop would not disappoint his family by running out on this case and causing them to lose almost everything they own. There is something else. I am confident that my rulings in this case are correct, but suppose the court of appeals thinks otherwise? These young people would rightly suffer some loss of confidence in the judicial system.

I returned to Washington and wrote the appeal brief. The court of appeals argument foreshadowed its decision. The morning of argument, I was having coffee with Hal Haddon and his partner Bryan Morgan. Bryan rode the bus to work, and he told us that two young men, whom he assumed were law clerks, were talking about our case on the bus. The tenor of one clerk's remark was how ridiculous it was to contend that a national emergency declared in 1950 could still be going on.

Some oral arguments seem to turn on a single question from the bench. The prosecutor argued that a national emergency lasted until it was undeclared. A judge asked:

Q: If President Lincoln had declared a national emergency for the Civil War, and no later President had revoked that declaration, would that emergency still be going on, so as to permit a sabotage prosecution instead of one for simply destroying government property?

The prosecutor hesitated and that deer-in-the-headlights look came over him again. The judge continued, "That has to be your position, doesn't it?"

"Yes," the answer finally came.

The court of appeals could have approached the issue from a number of perspectives. If it had held that Judge Arraj erred by excluding the evidence, we would have been back for a retrial, perhaps on some lesser charge. It held, however, that the statute as applied violated due process of law, for how could anyone know that the Korean war was still going on? In effect, the court held that there was a knowledge requirement with respect to the element of national emergency that could not possibly be satisfied. We took this as an acquittal on appeal, foreclosing a retrial, at least in federal court. Given that the statute of limitations had run on any state charges, Cam was almost free.

We were not, however, quite finished. The United States has the right to petition for certiorari from an adverse court of appeals judgment. I called Andy Frey, the deputy solicitor general who handled criminal cases. He was agitated. "This decision is indefensible. Maybe you can argue that the evidence should be admitted, but declaring the Sabotage Act unconstitutional is really too much."

"Andy," I said, "this is all because the government decided to use a draconian law when it could have used a milder one that did not create these problems. And when you think of it, the government's theory about the Korean war looks a little silly."

Our conversation turned to pending legislation, soon to pass, that did away with any pending national emergencies and regulated how future ones might come and go. Andy was sure that since Congress was soon to solve the problem, the Supreme Court would not want to inject itself into the issue. And the United States does not like to petition for certiorari unless it is pretty sure the Court will take the case.

So Cam was truly free. It was a story like the fable of the fox, which had a bird in his mouth and was walking over a bridge. He saw his reflection in the water and thought that there was another bird down there. So he dropped his real bird and went for the reflection, thus losing everything.

I hear from Cam now and then. He remains an activist, working on issues in his community.

Francisco "Kiko" Martinez grew up in Alamosa, Colorado, near the New Mexico border. This is ranching country on the lower elevations, and then you get into the magnificent San Juan Mountains over by Pagosa and Durango. Alamosa is about 200 miles west of Rocky Ford and La Junta, where Cam Bishop had grown up.

Kiko attended the University of Minnesota Law School, and went to work in a legal services program back near his hometown in the early 1970s. Kiko's legal efforts for farm workers, and his radical politics, angered a lot of people. Somebody torched the legal services office. As conflict escalated, somebody sent letter bombs to a right-wing biker group. The government alleged that Kiko had sent the bombs and indicted him. Fearing that he would not receive a fair trial, Kiko fled to Mexico, where he lived under the name of José Reynoso-Diaz for seven years. In 1980, he was crossing the border at Nogales, Arizona, when a guard became suspicious and began to question him closely about who he was. Kiko attempted to leave the crossing point, but was arrested and jailed. He gave the name, José Reynoso-Diaz. The government held him in custody, and was about to deport him to Mexico in the belief that he was not a U.S. citizen. However, a routine fingerprint check revealed that Francisco Martinez and José Reynoso-Diaz were the same person. He was sent to Colorado to stand trial on the bombing charges. The defense obtained a severance of the counts of the indictment, so that there would be three separate trials, one for sending each explosive device.

The trial had generated such publicity that U.S. District Judge Winner moved it to Durango, Colorado. After the third trial day, Judge Winner met secretly one night in his hotel room with the prosecutors and the FBI case agent. He said that he thought the case was being badly tried and that the government should provoke a defense motion for mistrial. Judge Winner said he would grant the motion. The judge and the others discussed strategies to provoke the defense. Sure enough, the defense made a motion, the prosecutors feigned reluctance but consented, and the judge granted it.

However, a television reporter had seen the prosecutor and FBI agent going into Judge Winner's room, and told the defense. This led to a lot of litigation to find the facts. The court of appeals for the Tenth Circuit held that since the defense mistrial motion was provoked by government and judicial misconduct, the motion was not a valid waiver of Kiko's double jeopardy rights. In short, the government was barred from retrying Kiko on the first set of severed charges. The government persisted, however, and brought the severed charges on for trial. Kiko was acquitted on the second set of charges. The government then dismissed the third set, and Kiko and his family thought the case was over.

Two weeks later, however, the government brought a new case, this time in Tucson, Arizona. They resurrected the border-crossing incident, and indicted Kiko for falsely telling the border guards his name was José Reynoso Diaz, and for falsely swearing to a magistrate that this was his name. The magistrate charge related to the hearing at which he was given appointed counsel and had to tell his name.

That's when Kiko called me. Would I represent him? I recruited some student help and went to Tucson. Judge Browning dismissed the indictment as vindictive retaliation for the government's loss in the earlier case. The Ninth Circuit reversed, and sent the case back for trial. In Tucson, Antonio Bustamante and Fernando Fajardo agreed to help. A new team of students stepped forward as well. We all thought that Judge Browning would be angry at having been reversed and would still harbor good feelings about Kiko. We therefore prepared a statement waiving a jury, thinking that Judge Browning would see how flimsy these charges were.

The morning of trial, we looked at the waiver. There is this old story about the trial lawyer who said he knew jurors were prejudiced, but so is everybody in one way or another. He said he would rather have twelve prejudiced people than just one. If Judge Browning wanted to help Kiko, he could do so with jury instructions and in a dozen other ways. So we did not file the waiver, at least for the time being.

Judge Browning took the bench. The government moved to exclude all evidence that we might present that Kiko faced unfair government tactics in Denver, so that we could not tell the jury why he took the name of José Reynoso Diaz. To our surprise, Judge Browning quickly granted the motion. I put the jury waiver form in my briefcase. This judge was not inclined to do us any favors.

The trial took only a few days. Kiko had indeed used the name José Reynoso Diaz, and had identification permitting him to live lawfully in Mexico under that name. So what, we said? Leonard Sly had become Roy Rogers, Marion Morrison was John Wayne, Gary Hartpence was Gary Hart. Kiko was not charged with trying to deceive the Denver authorities, for there would have been no venue for that. And by claiming to be a Mexican citizen, he was not deceiving the border guards with an intention to gain unauthorized entry into the United States, for he was entitled to come in because he was in reality a U.S. citizen.

The prosecutor sought to suggest that Kiko was an international terrorist, taking advantage of our inability to show the facts of the Colorado cases. He tried to introduce evidence that Kiko had been to Cuba, even stapling a document to that effect to the back of another exhibit in the hope we would not see it.

The jurors figured that something odd was going on, even if they did not know exactly what it was. In the end, we were probably helped by the judge limiting our proof, because we tried a tight, focused case. The jury was out for three days and came back with a split verdict. Not guilty of false statements to the border guards, but guilty of perjury for swearing to a false name before the magistrate. There was a reason for this split verdict. The false statement charges required the government to prove that the statements were material, and the jurors no doubt concluded they were not. However, in those days, before the Supreme Court decided to the contrary, the issue of materiality in a perjury case was for the judge to decide. Judge Browning told the jurors that they had to assume the statements were material in the perjury charge. The Supreme Court has since held that the jury decides this issue.

In my summation, I stressed the jury's role. The prosecutor had said the case was quite simple. Kiko was not José Reynoso Diaz and therefore he was guilty.

I said something like:

> You know, members of the jury, when I was young my sister and I would sometimes share a cupcake. That worked out because she liked the frosting and I liked the cake. I was reminded of this when I heard [the prosecutor] talking to you. He wants to tell you about just one little part of the judge's instructions to you—the frosting. He wants to tell you about whether or not Mr. Martinez's name was really José Reynoso Diaz or not. He doesn't want to get down into the main issue here—the cake. He doesn't want you to ask the hard question of whether it made any difference what name Mr. Martinez gave at that border.

Then a little later, I suggested that the jurors might wonder what was really going on, and that I was sure they would try to figure it out. I returned to this theme of the prosecutor's air of calm confidence:

> [The prosecutor] talks to you like this case is open and shut, like there is nothing really for you to decide. Then when the lawyers are done arguing, the judge will give you instructions, in a very matter-of-fact tone. Don't be misled by all that. We all take an oath to do what we do here. The prosecutor takes one to uphold the law. I took one to be a lawyer. The judge takes one to be a judge. You took two oaths. One to tell the truth when we talked to you on voir dire, and another one to well and truly try this case. So don't let the attitudes that you might think the prosecutor or the judge have keep you from doing your job. This case is too important for the prosecutor to decide. It is too important for the judge to decide. It is so important that we asked you to give up time from your work and family and come in here and decide it.

Our textual argument was that the hearing before the magistrate had been addressed to a single issue—whether the defendant was indigent and therefore entitled to appointed counsel. A defendant might say, "I have ten cents and my name is Mickey Mouse." The only relevant matter was whether he had only ten cents, for if so a lawyer would be appointed no matter what his name was. Our real argument was that this case was part of a dishonorable agenda, mostly hidden from the jurors, but that they could infer from all they saw and heard.

Kiko had been out on bail pending the trial of these charges. But now the judge, without much urging from the prosecutor, revoked Kiko's bail and ordered him committed to jail while an appeal was pending. He set bail at $250,000. We were stunned, and glad indeed that we had not waived a jury given this judicial attitude. Kiko's wife was crying quietly.

At that moment, a Tucson lawyer who was in the courtroom and had been watching the trial came forward. I had met him briefly in a coffee shop, but knew him only by reputation as a civil trial lawyer who litigated pro bono cases. "Your Honor," the lawyer said, "you know me. I have a firm downtown. I'll put up the bail." The judge argued with the lawyer for about ten minutes, saying that there might be an ethical problem putting up bail for a client.

"Mr. Martinez is not my client and never has been, Your Honor. I am putting up bail money because I think there was error here and because I trust him."

So Kiko spent a few hours in the marshal's office while the lawyer got the money together. On appeal, the court of appeals noted that the trial judge had not received, nor had the government offered, any evidence of how the Diaz name was material to the magistrate. Conviction reversed, with directions to acquit.

Thus, after 15 years Kiko was free and within the year readmitted to the bar. He works pro bono for prisoners and for people in his community. He and Cam Bishop are among the tens of thousands of young men and women dealt with unfairly, to one degree or another, or chilled in their activism by an atmosphere of repression. I grieve sometimes at how much America lost by silencing and punishing the energetic, though at times misguided, desire of these young people to help make a more just society. That has been a major theme of the work I have tried to do. By litigating test cases, by defending those accused, I hoped to be doing more than helping these clients. I wanted to free up their power to make change.

A similar, and perhaps more dangerous, form of repression is at work today in the criminal justice system. In the past ten years, the rate of incarceration in the United States has increased geometrically, so that we now imprison five to eight times as many persons as a percentage of our population than do western European countries and Canada. This toll falls most harshly on people of color. The atmosphere of repression and the attitude of overcriminalization that produces these statistics also results in decimating families and communities. Young people caught up in this system for relatively minor first offenses are shunted into overcrowded prisons and derailed from meaningful participation in society. They face great hurdles resuming a productive life. We are wasting that energy.

The Demjanjuk case was not about youthful energy, but about government fraud and vindictiveness. In 1977, the United States sued John Demjanjuk, a Cleveland auto worker, claiming that he had fraudulently obtained his citizenship when he immigrated to the United States after World War II. The government sought to denaturalize him. It claimed that Demjanjuk, born Iwan Demjanjuk in the Soviet Ukraine, had in fact been the notorious "Ivan the Terrible" of the Treblinka death camp. According to the government, Ivan was a Soviet soldier, captured by the Germans and recruited into the Nazi guard forces. As Ivan, he allegedly supervised the murder of tens of thousands of concentration camp victims—dissenters, gypsies, homosexuals, and Jews.

There was never any question that such a person existed, and that he was savagely cruel even by death camp standards. The camp survivor stories, corroborated by postwar Soviet interviews of other collaborators, proved that beyond doubt. But was this man, living in his suburban home with his children, that Ivan?

The case was brought by the Office of Special Investigations (OSI), a unit of the Department of Justice Criminal Division, established and funded for the express purpose of hunting down Nazi collaborators and denaturalizing them. It was clear in 1977 and, as a result of government studies is clearer now, that tens of thousands of Nazis and Nazi collaborators gained entry to the United States and were helped to gain entry to other countries after World War II. It was official U.S. policy to exclude such people. It was also official U.S. policy to help some of them gain entry. If a Nazi could help us build rockets, root out leftists, or otherwise be useful, he or she would be assisted. Stories of American complicity in protecting Nazis are legion. American intelligence services protected Klaus Barbie, known as the butcher of Lyon, from capture for many years until finally the U.S. helped the French bring him to trial. In the process of admitting and protecting Nazis, many agencies generated millions of pages of classified documents, which are only now beginning to be reviewed and released.

OSI was set up to correct some of those past errors. However, like many other single-purpose agencies, it sometimes lost sight of its broader obligation to make sure that its work was done fairly.

John Demjanjuk came to trial in 1981. A federal judge in Cleveland accepted the government's proof and held that he had been Ivan the Terrible. The Court of Appeals for the Sixth Circuit affirmed. OSI was not finished. It began deportation proceedings, and at the same time cooperated with Israeli authorities to extradite Demjanjuk to Israel for trial. All his appeals done, Demjanjuk was sent to Israel in 1987. The Israelis put him in a solitary confinement cell where he remained for nearly seven years.

The Israel trial was televised to the world. Treblinka survivors gave emotional testimony that they recognized Demjanjuk as Ivan the Terrible. The court rejected arguments that these eyewitness identifications were tainted by suggestive photo arrays that had been shown to the witnesses. The court rejected Demjanjuk's testimony that after he was captured by the Nazis he spent the war in various POW and work camps. It discounted the testimony of an expert that the German identification card claimed to be his did not bear his signature and was irregular in appearance. The court sentenced him to die by hanging, and he waited in his cell while a scaffold was being built in the prison yard.

After the Israel conviction, Demjanjuk's son-in-law, Ed Nishnic, and his son, John, Jr., called me and asked if I would go to Israel and handle the appeal. In Israel, an appeal of such a case could take months, for the Supreme Court would review all the evidence over many days of proceedings. I said no. I was not interested in going to Israel for that length of time, and the issues of eyewitness identification and forensic testing did not seem to me as important as some of the other cases I was working on. That is, everyone is entitled to counsel, but not everyone is always entitled to the counsel of a particular lawyer.

A lawyer may not, the ethics rules wisely say, decline a case for personal reasons, which would include an ideological opposition to the defendant or a feeling that taking the case would cause the lawyer some bad publicity. But a lawyer who is already overloaded with pro bono cases is free to decline to take on just one more.

Within months, however, the Demjanjuk case changed. Ed and John, Jr. had from the beginning known that their best hope was to find the real Ivan. Against the combined forces of American and Israeli prosecutors they stood little chance with a reasonable doubt defense. They therefore invested all their energy in trying to find that person. They went to Europe to interview people. They became suspicious that OSI had not turned over all its evidence during the American proceedings. They started a Freedom of Information Act proceeding that yielded clues to exculpatory evidence. Thinking that perhaps the OSI lawyers were discarding material that might be relevant, they stationed themselves outside the OSI offices in Washington, D.C., and raided the trash cans. When the former Soviet Union began to fall apart, they gained increased access to investigative files located in that territory.

From all this effort, they pieced together a story that led the Israel Supreme Court to acquit Demjanjuk, Sr., and an American court to hold that the OSI had defrauded the courts. Ed and John, Jr. proved, by witnesses and photographs, that Ivan the Terrible was a man named Ivan Marchenko.

Demjanjuk's Israeli lawyer, Yoram Sheftel, introduced the new evidence before the Israel Supreme Court. As the media covered this story, the court of appeals judges who had upheld sending Demjanjuk to Israel became concerned that OSI had misled them. After all, some of the new evidence consisted of Soviet interview reports, called protocols, that had been in OSI's hands from 1979 onwards.

In January 1992, the Sixth Circuit judges directed the court clerk, Len Green, to send a letter to the Department of Justice asking for an explanation of how exculpatory evidence had been withheld from the defense and the court. When that happened, Ed and John, Jr. called me again. I said that I knew something about U.S. federal procedure, and that sending an innocent man to his death based on false evidence was an issue on which I could work. I asked them to call me if the court of appeals took further action, and even if it did not we could discuss what other proceedings might be filed to help restore the old man's citizenship and contribute to a good result in the still-pending Israel appeal.

By June 1992, the Department of Justice had still not answered the court's letter. The judges—Chief Judge Merritt and Judges Lively and Keith—were irked at being ignored. So they issued an order directing Justice to produce evidence and to file a brief explaining its position. They appointed the federal public defender for the northern district of Ohio to represent Demjanjuk and directed his office to file a brief as well, with whatever evidence had become available to the Demjanjuk family. Ed and John, Jr.—"the boys"—called me.

I had been scheduled to try a major antitrust case, on leave from the University of Texas Law School, but it settled during jury selection. I had been working with students on appointed criminal appeals, but those involved supervising briefs and an occasional oral argument. I was winding up my responsibilities as past chairman of the American Bar Association's Litigation Section. I want to be candid here. I won't take a case if it goes against my grain, but sometimes I am moved by restless energy. I said I would join the team of appointed counsel and would recruit law students to help me with the briefing.

It is difficult to describe the love and devotion that John and Ed lavished on this case. John, Jr. was 11 years old when it all started. Ed had married into the family in 1980. By the time I met them, they had put their careers firmly in second place. No sacrifice of time or energy was too great for them, even as the media reviled the old man as a mass murderer. They were never the most efficient paralegal assistants you could find; their filing system sometimes left me frustrated. But they were there in this case, without complaint and without limit on time or resources. It was one of the most rewarding relationships of my life.

In June and July 1992, the federal defender and I worked on a brief with the help of law students. The court set oral argument for August 8. On August 7, I was in San Francisco at the ABA annual meeting, planning to take the red-eye overnight to Cincinnati. I ran into Ken Starr, who was then U.S. solicitor general, at a meeting. We were standing with Myron Bright, a judge on the U.S. Court of Appeals for the Eighth Circuit, and author of some really good articles on appellate argument. I asked Ken whether he would be arguing in Cincinnati.

"Oh, no," he said. "Patty Stemler will be arguing for us. Bill Bryson and I have been getting her ready for weeks now. Our case is solid. We are going to clean your clock."

Myron Bright rasped, "Ken, if your case is so goddamn good, why don't you argue it yourself."

I stumbled off the Delta red-eye and went to a hotel in Cincinnati to shave and change clothes. Patty Merkamp Stemler was and is a formidable lawyer. That day, she had a hard time with a tough panel of judges. And she made what I think is a fatal error for an advocate. She refused to concede the problems with her own position. "Mistakes were made" was the best she could do, and the passive voice and halfhearted tone simply annoyed the judges.

When it was our turn, Ed Marek, the federal defender, did the first part of the argument. He focused on factual detail. When it was my turn, we did not have much scheduled argument time left, but the court let me present a full position. Yes, I said, you can recall your mandate. You have jurisdiction regardless of the passage of time because fraud on the court can always be redressed under Federal Rule of Civil Procedure 60(b)(6). And you always have what the Supreme Court called "jurisdiction to determine jurisdiction." That is, you can compel parties to produce evidence and argument to determine if there was fraud that you would in turn have the power to recognize and remedy.

"What should the court do?" the judges asked. I said that a panel of three appellate judges was not the most efficient fact-finding body. You should, I said, appoint a special master to take testimony and make recommendations. The argument then turned to the more general subject of fraud on the court. Why, Chief Judge Merritt asked, would government lawyers do the things that we accused them of? Why would they hide documents, mislead witnesses, and tell lies to the court and their adversaries? In my mind, I thought of the self-righteous attitude of these lawyers. Nazi hunting was a just cause, but the more heinous the crime we seek to punish, the more careful we must be that the accused is not convicted out of some feeling of collective culpability.

I answered Judge Merritt this way: "I do not know why these lawyers did these things. I only tell the court what they did and how they did it, based on the evidence we now have and that we confidently expect to produce. Perhaps this case illustrates Ruskin's maxim, 'There is no snare set by the fiends for the mind of man more dangerous than the illusion that our enemies are also the enemies of God.'"

I heard that quote uttered by Konni Zilliacus in a 1963 parliamentary debate. He attributed it to Ruskin, but I have been unable to find it in Ruskin's work or in any collection of quotations. No matter. Our oral tradition of advocacy is full of unattributable bits of purloined eloquence.

A few days later, the court of appeals named Judge Thomas Wiseman of Nashville as special master and we embarked on the next phase of our adventure. For the next 10 months, our team took depositions and held hearings in Nashville, Boston, Los Angeles, and Washington, D.C. We exchanged thousands of documents.

The key witness was George Parker, who had been an OSI lawyer in 1979 and 1980 in charge of the Demjanjuk litigation. In early 1980, Parker wrote a memorandum to his superiors. He typed it himself. He reviewed the evidence, including some recently obtained Soviet protocols. Despite eyewitnesses who placed Demjanjuk at Treblinka, documentary evidence cast significant doubt on that claim. Parker wondered if the OSI's position would be a "ruse on the court." The boys had heard about this memo in the past, and had repeatedly asked the Department of Justice to produce it. The department had officially denied that such a memorandum existed.

We put a subpoena on George Parker, and he called to say that he had kept a copy of his memo when he quit, or was removed from, the

Demjanjuk case. That had happened in the spring of 1980, after his proposals about the case were largely rejected. In our 1992 hearings, the Justice Department lawyers at first tried to say that Parker's copy was not authentic, or that he had not in fact sent it. They retreated from this position as the evidence mounted.

The Parker memo centered on several Soviet protocols that the United States had received in 1979. The Department of Justice first took the position that these had simply been misfiled, and never intentionally withheld from the Demjanjuk defense. This version paled when a former assistant U.S. attorney took the stand. He had kept copies of the protocols when he left government service. I pause here to say that the Xerox machine was a wonderful invention, for it made copying quick and easy. The xerographic fusion of powder to paper has got more people in trouble than many other inventions, for the human desire to keep a memento has frustrated many efforts to get rid of difficult documents.

This witness admitted that the protocols were not in some file cabinet during the 1981 Demjanjuk trial, but in a government lawyer's briefcase in court. So when the government lawyers told the federal judge they had turned over all the exculpatory material, and that the only documents they had further inculpated Demjanjuk, they were not telling the truth. These documents included information about someone who was of a different description and at different places than the person who was Ivan the Terrible.

Another, though not the only other, item of significant evidence concerned one of those eyewitness identifications. In December 1979, OSI attorney Norman Moskowitz went to Germany and interviewed a former camp guard named Otto Horn. Initially, Horn could not identify a photo of Demjanjuk as Ivan the Terrible. Moskowitz then presented Horn with another set of photographs that was different, except that the Demjanjuk photo was also included. He left that set on the table before Horn with Demjanjuk's photo on top. Horn, after Moskowitz prodded him, got the idea and identified the Demjanjuk photograph. Horn had a motive to cooperate because he had clearly collaborated with the Nazis. Later, Moskowitz noticed Horn's deposition in Germany and with Demjanjuk's counsel present asked him if he could identify Demjanjuk from a photograph. He did so. Moskowitz then asked him if he had previously identified the same photograph, and Horn said yes. When Parker resigned, Moskowitz became lead trial counsel in the 1981 denaturalization case.

On that first trip to Germany, Moskowitz had been accompanied by two OSI historian/investigators, Garand and Dougherty. They saw this suggestive identification procedure and each made a separate memorandum noting it. Moskowitz was shown as receiving a copy of these memoranda although he denied ever reading them. Somebody at OSI threw a copy of them in the trash in the late 1980s when the Demjanjuk case was still going on in Israel. "The boys" recovered them, and the memos became important items of evidence in our proof that the OSI had defrauded Demjanjuk and the courts.

During the year of hearings on our fraud claim, I went to Israel with Deputy Public Defender Michael Dane to see Demjanjuk and get his signature on interrogatories posed by the government. At that point, the government was still clinging to a theory that there were two Ivans at Treblinka, one of which was Demjanjuk. Later, it conceded that this variant was untenable.

Knowing and working with Mike Dane was one of those unalloyed pleasures in this kind of law practice. There are lawyers with whom I would share a counsel table, and those with whom I decidedly would not. This decision, for me as for any lawyer, is quixotically personal. But the decision to be co-counsel involves the kind of camaraderie that one also hears about in military campaigns.

I went to Israel by flying to Paris and then catching a Delta flight to Ben Gurion Airport. It was January 1993, during a cold winter in Paris, but staying there overnight was nonetheless a kind of inspiration. Of all the cities I have visited, Paris has magic for me. Walking the streets of the Left Bank, peering into and visiting the antique booksellers, sometimes buying an old edition of French law books, having dinner at Allard, are all a connection to the history of those principles of struggle and ideology by which our views on human rights are shaped.

Mike Dane and I arrived in Israel in the afternoon. That night, I walked up to the Arab city of Jaffa and had dinner. The next morning, Mike and I breakfasted at the hotel with Yoram Sheftel, then went to see Demjanjuk. He was under the sentence of death that would not be lifted until July 1993. He was in solitary confinement. His cell was perhaps six feet by 12 feet, and included a partially partitioned area with a shower and toilet. The entire length of the cell's front was barred. On the other side of the bars, at a desk, sat a guard. Against the wall on the guard's side was a cot. A guard sat at that desk at all times. Facing the guard, on his desk, was a small television set. To speak to Demjanjuk, we sat in his cell with the bars locked. He had pasted on the walls many of the cards he had received in the nearly six years he had been there. He had by some means fastened a cardboard box about 12 inches cubed to the wall in the corner of the cell. He had drawn on the front of the box the image of a TV screen and tuning knobs. It seemed that Demjanjuk had asked for a television set in his cell or at least visible to him. Not only was his request denied, but also a TV set was issued to the guards, who pointedly watched it with the screen turned in their direction. The cardboard TV set was a silent protest.

When he arrived in Israel, Demjanjuk had been repeatedly interrogated by Israeli police and lawyers, who used sleep deprivation and threats among other measures to seek a confession. None ever came. Demjanjuk always denied collaborating with the Nazis. To try to establish rapport with his guards, Mr. Demjanjuk taught himself basic conversational Hebrew .

Mike Dane and I talked to the old man at length. At times, there were tears in his eyes. At one point he looked at us and said, "Not for you, I am a long time hanging in the yard," gesturing towards the area where a scaffold was to be built to hang him. Our business done, the old man insisted we stay for lunch. He had been afraid to eat the food prepared in the prison kitchen, and had therefore conducted a hunger strike until the authorities agreed to let him prepare his own food. So the guard brought a table and set it just outside the cell. On the table were cans of food, a can opener, bowls, and eating utensils. Demjanjuk could reach between the bars and laboriously open cans and prepare a simple meal. We shared what he made for us.

After that day, I did not want to stay in Israel. I went the next morning early to Ben Gurion Airport. A security guard opened my suitcase and my briefcase, and called over a more senior guard who had a big gun and some insignia of rank. She began to take file folders from my briefcase and read the contents. I said, "I am a lawyer. Those are private legal files."

She said, "I know. I can see that." And kept on reading. After what seemed a long time, she looked up and said, "These are about this man Demjanjuk."

"Yes," I said.

"You are his lawyer."

"One of them."

She looked at me appraisingly. "You are going to clear his name?"

"I hope so," I said.

"Good!" she replied, and snapped my briefcase shut.

After we held all the hearings before Judge Wiseman, he wrote an opinion that disappointed us greatly. While agreeing with almost all of our factual submissions, he held that the government's conduct was not so bad as to require any relief. So the matter stood as the summer of

1993 began. We challenged Judge Wiseman's findings in (to use a locu-tion that only lawyers can use with a straight face) lengthy briefs.

Then in late July, the Israel Supreme Court issued its opinion acquit-ting Demjanjuk. A few days later, the court also upheld the Israeli Justice Ministry's decision that the evidence was insufficient to prosecute Demjanjuk for having served at camps other than Treblinka. In our view, such charges would also have been barred by the doctrine of specialty, which says that if you are extradited to stand trial on one set of charges, you may not then be tried for something else.

Demjanjuk's acquittal raised a further problem. The judgment denatu-ralizing him was still in effect. He was not a U.S. citizen. The USSR had fragmented, so perhaps he could claim Ukrainian nationality. He did not want to go to the Ukraine. A Department of Justice spokesman told the media that Ukraine was his most likely next stop, and that he would prob-ably be tried there and shot. In Israel, crowds had gathered to protest the court judgment and the Demjanjuk family feared for the old man's safety.

Our team prepared and filed an emergency motion in the court of appeals. For more than 200 years, American law has given the executive branch nearly complete power over the admission and exclusion of aliens. We thought it unwise therefore to seek an order directing that Demjanjuk be admitted to the U.S. Rather, we requested an order that the govern-ment not interfere with him entering the country. We also feared that if he were to stop in a third country between Israel and the United States, he might be held there and tried.

Our efforts to get him back into the U.S. drew publicity. My teaching colleague at Texas, Michael Churgin, an expert on immigration law, told me we had little to no chance in the court of appeals. However, the court set us down for argument the afternoon of August 3, 1993. I flew to Cincinnati. As our team had lunch, I had a message to call Alan Ryan. He had been my colleague at Williams & Connolly, then went to the solici-tor general's office, and in 1980 had become head of OSI. In that last capacity, he had negotiated a deal with the Soviets whereby they were supposed to produce all relevant material on Demjanjuk. Alan was by 1993 in private law practice, but he had been a witness in our proceed-ings and kept track of the case.

Alan asked if we would be willing to accept a deal, if he could broker it. The deal was that Demjanjuk would be admitted to the United States. The government would consent to restoring his citizenship. The govern-ment might then file a new suit seeking to denaturalize him, alleging service at other Nazi camps. If he lost in the district court and on direct appeal, he would leave the United States without taking further legal action. If he won, that would be it.

The deal sounded good to us. It would get him reunited with his family, would put an end to the litigation over fraud on the court, and would give him a clean shot at clearing his name for good. We talked it over and said we thought we could convince the old man to accept it. Ryan promised to call Deputy Attorney General Philip Heymann and try to get him to consent.

We walked across the plaza from the hotel to the federal courthouse. Members of the media were on hand. We sat in the spectator section of the courtroom waiting for the clerk, Len Green, to tell us the judges were ready. As we sat, we chatted with *The New York Times* reporter. The reporter then recognized a Justice Department lawyer and asked him, "Hey, Bob, are you going to argue this today?"

"No," said Bob, "Doug Wilson will argue it. I am just here to help out."

"How do you think it's going to turn out," the reporter asked.

"I don't know," Bob said. "But whatever happens, you will have a decision before 5. Chief Judge Merritt wants to see his kisser on national TV."

At that moment, a woman sitting just ahead of us turned around and looked at Bob. "Excuse me," she said, "I am Mrs. Gilbert Merritt. And my husband will not be pleased when I tell him what you said."

I was reminded of the bumper sticker, "Be sure brain is fully engaged before putting mouth in gear," a remnant of the days before automatic transmissions.

The oral argument was in a sense joyous. Everybody knew the procedural facts. The issue was whether the court had any authority to get Demjanjuk out of danger and back into the country. Oral argument on the merits of the case was a month away.

I began by noting that we had an uphill battle, and cited a new Supreme Court decision that the government had not mentioned, that might seem to strengthen its position. You might ask why I did this? If the court of appeals ruled for us, the government might well have challenged its ruling in the Supreme Court. I wanted the court of appeals to take account of all the adverse precedent, so that the government could not later argue that it had missed something.

The case turned, I said, on the historic power of federal courts to control the custody of those who were seeking relief. Chief Judge Merritt asked if this referred to habeas corpus ad subjiciendum, known as the

Great Writ. This version of habeas corpus is the one we hear most about. This is the writ federal courts use to liberate state prisoners from unlawful confinement. It can be used to enforce an order for release on bail. But the scope of this writ has been limited by Congress and the current Supreme Court.

No, I said. We are seeking a writ of habeas corpus cum causa, which has a narrower function but is equally enshrined in English and American legal history. This is writ that compels the jailer to bring a litigant to court so that his case may be decided, and so that no harm comes to him while the court is considering his fate. This writ does not require a decision on the merits, on whether the litigant is ultimately entitled to relief. Again, I thought this narrower ground of relief more defensible. I noted that, of course, the executive branch had said that the court had no power to do anything at all.

Judge Keith interrupted to say, "Well, Mr. Tigar, they come in here and say that several times a week, but that doesn't usually stop us."

As the argument continued, Judge Merritt asked me what kind of an order I thought the court should enter. At that point, I felt the panel was really with us. Judge Lively, in questioning the government lawyer, seemed particularly concerned that he had written an opinion sending Demjanjuk to Israel, but that the government had misled him on the facts.

Late that afternoon, in a decision reported only in Westlaw, the judges granted our request. If we could get Demjanjuk to the border of the United States, the government would have to let him in. Ed and John, Jr. got the old man on an El Al flight to New York and then by plane to Cleveland. He was home. Picketers assembled on the sidewalk in front of his home, shouting epithets, but he was home.

On September 3, 1993, I argued the merits of his case. On November 17, the court ruled that the United States had defrauded the courts by concealing exculpatory evidence and creating false trail. The government sought to have all the Sixth Circuit judges hear the case, but was rebuffed.

Now the question was whether the government would go the Supreme Court to overturn the decision. If it could do that, then Demjanjuk would likely be expelled from the U.S. yet again. I called Solicitor General Drew Days, and asked for a meeting in Washington, D.C., so that we could argue that the United States should not seek Supreme Court review.

Our team met with Solicitor General Days, Deputy Attorney General Heymann, and a couple of other Department of Justice lawyers. I began by saying that I was surprised that the government was still litigating this case. I reminded everyone that Alan Ryan had proposed a deal that would have avoided the Sixth Circuit excoriation of the government. Solicitor General Days said he had not heard of any such proposed deal. Heymann looked flustered and mumbled that he had not thought the deal worth pursuing and had not told anybody about it. He had simply rejected it. This news seemed to upset Days. My friends in the media told me that Heymann's penchant for going his own way was angering Attorney General Reno and that his tenure as deputy attorney general would not be long. This turned out to be true.

Turning to the merits, I argued that the government should now simply leave this case alone. Its position was surely arguable, but using Demjanjuk as the means to test the law seemed unfair after 16 years of litigation that had impoverished and taken a great emotional toll on the family.

Our arguments did not work. Days sought certiorari, which the Supreme Court denied, but only after a further complication. I ran into Days a year or so later, at a memorial service for Justice Brennan. I had been talking with Jack McKenzie, who had just retired from *The New York Times* editorial board, and Days came to sit beside us. He had returned to teaching law, and I remarked that our last meeting had been about the Demjanjuk case.

"Tell me about that," Jack said.

"Well," Days said, "I thought the Sixth Circuit had the wrong standard—a kind of reckless fraud on the court—and that the Supreme Court should set them right. So I went ahead and petitioned for cert." It should be said that an impressive number of the solicitor general's petitions are granted.

"Then," Days continued, "we routinely distribute the printed petition to all the lawyers in our office. So a couple of days later, one of the lawyers came to see me. He had been in the SG's office for nearly 20 years, a specialist in tax. His eyes were rimmed with red. He had not slept and he had been weeping. He laid the petition on my desk and said, 'I know about this case. In 1980, I think it was, I talked to a lawyer in this office who was about to go to work at OSI.'"

Days continued: "So this lawyer went on, 'I asked what cases he would be working on and he said Demjanjuk. But that there was some evidence they had the wrong man. I asked him if he was going to reveal this to the other side and the court and he said no.'"

McKenzie, ever even-tempered and even-spoken in public, said, "Oh, my goodness. That is what Max Frankel used to call 'a turd in your pocket.'"

Days smiled. "A turd in my pocket? A turd on my table. A big one. Here I am litigating against Tigar and now I get this news."

I cut in. "Drew could have kept this to himself, but instead he told me about it and wrote a letter to the Court. He probably doomed his chances for certiorari, but in my book his candor set him apart from the other lawyers who worked on this case."

After the Supreme Court denied certiorari, I was deeply involved in other cases. I tried to find a law firm that would represent the family in the next phase, getting the denaturalization judgment overturned. It seemed obvious that this should be done, and that seeking this relief would not be expressing a view for or against the OSI as an institution or Nazi hunting as a process. But no law firm I approached would touch the case. Partners at the big firms candidly said they wanted nothing to do with it. They knew I had been attacked for representing Demjanjuk, and that I had replied forcefully that exposing government fraud that almost sent someone to his death did not seem even controversial.

Federal defenders Mike Dane and Debra Hughes stepped back into the case, and won a ruling restoring the old man's citizenship and dismissing the denaturalization, though without prejudice. So matters stood until December 1998, when OSI wrote to the Demjanjuk family and said it planned to sue the old man again to take away his citizenship. This time, OSI said, it had solid evidence that after he was captured by the Nazis he agreed to be a camp guard and had served at several concentration camps. No live witness had ever seen him serve as a guard. The records on which OSI based its case were contradictory and fragmentary.

The family called me again, and I agreed to help. The federal defender could no longer serve. For more than two years, we sifted through more than 100,000 pages of documents and a dozen CD-ROMs, each the equivalent of several boxes of material. With a couple of law students, another volunteer lawyer and the boys, Ed and John, Jr., we went to trial in May 2000. The judge ruled we were not entitled to a jury trial. By the time you read this, the judge will have ruled, and the losing party will perhaps have taken an appeal.

As the trial preparation wore on, I became more and more convinced that the government's case was too thin to meet the standard of "clear and convincing evidence," almost beyond a reasonable doubt, that the law requires. More seriously, I voiced a concern with what I called "trial by archive," that is, digging up old documents from ill-maintained Soviet archives and dispensing with proof that could be cross-examined. The tactic reminded me of the loyalty-security purges of the 1950s, when FBI archival files were used indiscriminately. Indeed, although I did not share this with the court, I was reminded of the FBI's false reports to Justice Brennan about my alleged political activity in an effort to prevent me having a Supreme Court clerkship.

On February 21, 2002, a federal judge in Cleveland ruled in the government's favor, accepting its patchwork of challenged evidence. Mr. Demjanjuk is over 80. He and his family will once again trudge to the appellate courts. In the 25-year history of this litigation, every trial court has ruled against him, and every appellate court has eventually vindicated him. Regardless of the outcome this time, he will have participated in helping us learn some basic lessons about government misconduct.

Notes

1. Olmstead v. United States, 277 U.S. 438, 485 (1928) (dissenting opinion).

2. Justice Jackson's opinion on bail for the Communist Party leaders is *Williamson v. United States*, 184 F.2d 280, 95 L.Ed. 1379 (1950)

3. United States v. Bishop, 555 F.2d 771 (10th Cir. 1977), reversed Cam's conviction.

4. *See* United States v. Martinez, 667 F.2d 886 (10th Cir. 1981). The reversal of Kiko's final conviction is reported at 855 F.2d 621 (9th Cir. 1988).

5. A candid assessment of official complicity in bringing Nazis to our shores may be found at www.fas.org/sgp/news/1999/11/naraiwg.html.

6. The history of habeas corpus is chronicled in *Fay v. Noia*, 372 U.S. 391 (1963), which was overruled later, but remains a solid contribution to American legal history.

7. The Demjanjuk case is chronicled in *Demjanjuk v. Petrovsky*, 10 F.3d 338 (6th Cir. 1993), *cert. denied sub nom. Rison v. Demjanjuk*, 513 U.S. 914 (1994). The Sixth Circuit's grant of habeas corpus is not reported, but is available at 1993 WL 394773 (6th Cir. 1993).

Chapter 11
SPEECH PLUS

Freedom of expression was a dominant theme from Berkeley days onwards, from Jacobus ten Broek's class to KPFA and through law school. Because KPFA was so conscious of the free expression issue, the discussions we had there were better and deeper than any academic study of free speech could have been. Alexander Meiklejohn had been a commentator on the station, and I even met him once. As part of my thesis study of J. Robert Oppenheimer's loyalty-security investigation, I had delved more deeply into the history of McCarthyism. I recount in this kaleidoscopic way to invoke again an approach to issues in the law. Legal rules are ossified history, to be studied as an anthropologist would, seeking to understand not only their shape but also their origins and the social context in which they came to be.

Because KFPA was interested in free expression, I had a front row seat at events—such as the House Un-American Activities Committee hearings—that put that issue to the test. One of those was the San Francisco trial of Lenny Bruce, the comedian, for having said "cocksucker" during a nightclub performance. The California statute under which he was prosecuted was later held unconstitutional, in a case involving a young man who wore a jacket that proclaimed, "Fuck the Draft." Bruce's lawyer was the formidable Al Bendich. But the star of the show was Bruce, who kept up a running, drug-induced patter throughout the trial. When asked whether he had said to the arresting officer, "Eat it! Eat it!" he replied, "No, I said 'Kiss it! Kiss it!'" Bendich asked, "Do you apprehend a difference?" Bruce said, "Oh yeah, man. There is a big difference between kissing your mother good-bye and eating your mother good-bye."

Although I had only a marginal role in the Free Speech Movement (FSM) of 1964-65, I was drawn into a case that sprang from it during my last year in law school. UC Berkeley's post-FSM chancellor, Roger Heyns, issued new rules on students' rights of free speech. These were drafted with the help of law professors, and I commented on the various drafts. The rules permitted students to speak from the steps of the university administration building, but provided that a given student or group could do so only once in any calendar week, even if nobody else wanted to speak there during that week.

One week, President Johnson escalated the Vietnam war twice, and a student protest group wanted to hold a second rally. The administration said no, so the students set up a microphone and spoke anyway. A law professor, representing the chancellor, told them to desist. They did not. So three students, Bettina Aptheker, Susan Stein, and Harold Jacobs, were charged with a violation of the rules and ordered to submit to a disciplinary hearing. They called me and asked if I would represent them.

I suppose this was my first real trial. I wrote a brief arguing that the once-a-week rule was an unreasonable restriction on speech. UC was a public university, and the administration building space had historically been a public forum—indeed, the FSM had been concerned with recognizing and preserving its status as such a forum.

The hearing officer was John Hetland, a very conservative law professor who taught property. The chancellor's choice in this respect did not augur well for our side. Facing me as prosecutors were one law professor, one political science professor, and one portly lawyer from the firm that represented the university. As part of my case, I called the law professor-prosecutor to testify and examined him about the various drafts of the proposed speech rules. He had written a note on one such draft doubting the wisdom of the very rule my clients were said to have violated.

The administration building steps were suitable for public expression, and had historically been used for that purpose. No other group wanted to speak at that time, and the speakers were orderly and not unduly amplified. In short, the restriction swept broader than necessary to ensure fair access to the forum, and could not therefore be justified as a valid time, place, and manner rule.

In the end, of course, the three students were found guilty, as Hetland rejected our constitutional argument. The university demanded a heavy punishment. Professor Hetland said that although the students had violated a rule, he thought that having a two-day hearing with all these lawyers was a colossal waste of time and money. He sentenced the students to one semester of ineligibility for intercollegiate sports and banishment for that period from the hamburger stand in the Student Union.

Since none of the three played sports or ate hamburgers, this punishment reflected Hetland's view of the whole affair.

When I began law practice the next year, these free expression issues followed me. Defending civil rights usually involved securing the right to protest. The Vietnam war protests dealt as much with the right to oppose the war by various means as with the wisdom and legality of the war itself. The Chicago and Seattle cases dealt with First Amendment issues arising from the congressional statute that sought to punish interstate travel for the purpose of protesting. When government wishes to pursue a policy without interruption, it often seeks to chill expression by its opponents, and to that extent speech is bound up with all sorts of substantive policy issues.

I have not often been asked to advise the government about such matters, but one case makes the point. During the 1970s, the Federal Trade Commission was considering restrictions on advertising directed at children. Lawyers there asked my law partners and me to help in this endeavor. We declined. We thought that such ads were quite improper. But we reasoned that rules to restrict them were inherently overbroad and subject to abuse. This has proven, in my view, to be so. Enforcement of kiddie-porn laws has swept up exploiters of children, but has also led to prosecution of researchers and those people whose private conduct poses no public threat. And like all censorship laws, enforcement techniques drift quite easily into entrapment, as the Supreme Court has noted. We also thought, for example, that high school students' free speech rights should not be curtailed, and that the First Amendment problems in drawing lines between different types of speech directed at minors were insurmountable.

This is not to say that I have always defended free expression that affects children. When I was at Williams & Connolly, we represented Georgetown University Hospital. In one of several such cases, I was counsel for the hospital when a young mother refused on religious grounds to authorize a blood transfusion that was necessary to save her newborn baby's life. We drafted papers to have the hospital appointed legal guardian, and got Judge Robinson to go with us to the hospital room. We dressed in hospital gowns and argued. We won. Whatever rights the parents had to practice their religion stopped short of the right to make that kind of decision for their children.

There is another issue of choice here. I don't have the time or resources to defend everybody's speech, so I choose the battles in which I will engage. In America today, those without money have a hard time having their voices heard. I have preferred to represent progressive folks who lack access to a money-controlled market in expression cases. And in the same vein, I do not agree with the current Supreme Court teaching that money is speech. As I have written elsewhere:

> The First Amendment to the United States Constitution guarantees freedom of speech and press. Today, moneyed interests dominate electoral politics, drowning out less-well-financed voices. The sensible citizen wonders if campaign finance reform would help even things out. That citizen even asks whether the dominance of money so erodes the freedom of speech that government has an affirmative duty to see that all voices can participate in the process.

That citizen, reading current Supreme Court decisions, will be disappointed. The Court has held that limits on individual contributions to influence elections and contributions to officeholders for increased access are forms of speech protected by the First Amendment. Only few and ineffective restraints on money in politics are found to be constitutional.

Thus, the Supreme Court sees the First Amendment through the prism of bourgeois ideology. Money, the universal commodity, enables speech. It pays for the means by which a message is delivered. Therefore, money and speech are in a sense equivalent. The Constitution places no inhibition on people spending their own money. By this reasoning, money is speech. The wealthy person does not want to talk, or hand out leaflets. But because money is the equivalent of all things, he or she can pay for others to do those things.

My choice of free speech cases means that I get to meet all manner of very interesting people. If making a pile of money is not your first concern in law practice, this is a very good organizing principle. Think about it. I have already listed some of the protesters whose paths crossed mine. The gay beat poet Allen Ginsberg retained me for a time on a matter that I don't quite remember; he sent me a little money and an autographed collection of his poems with a nice drawing and a long inscription. People interested in getting political material from abroad lived interesting lives and had interesting stories to tell.

Then there was Karl Dietrich Wolff. He was leader of a German student group in the 1970s. On a visit to the United States, he was served with a subpoena to testify before the Senate Internal Security Subcommittee, then chaired by Strom Thurmond. Someone told Wolff to call me and we appeared on the appointed afternoon. The idea of a congressional investigating committee with a roving commission to investigate leftists was strange to Wolff, who became increasingly restive as the afternoon wore on. I was reminded of Bertolt Brecht's appearance before the House Un-American Activities Committee, a transcript of which I had heard. Brecht's English was not very good, and neither was that spoken by the translator he brought with him. An additional complexity was that the Dixiecrat committee chairman also had a limited vocabulary, and at one point wanted to know if Brecht believed in the "class struggle between the petroleums and the bergwarsie."

As our hearing began, committee counsel Jay Sourwine asked Wolff if he swore to tell the truth. Wolff whispered that he preferred to affirm than to swear to a deity. I repeated this. "What?" Thurmond exclaimed. "He won't take the oath? He has to take the oath!"

"Senator," I said, "he would prefer to affirm. He has the right not to invoke a deity."

Thurmond persisted: "He is in contempt if he won't take the oath."

I asked for a recess and Jay Sourwine and I talked. Sourwine then chatted with the senator and we resumed. Wolff affirmed.

Sourwine then went through a series of questions about Wolff's visit to the United States and his speeches to student groups. Wolff deflected the questions with complaints about being harassed, as he was simply exercising his right to speak and respecting his listeners' right to hear. At one point, Wolff spoke of the legal problems that the Black Panther Party was having, and blamed the committee for helping cause those troubles. Sourwine interjected: "You mention panthers. You have been talking about people, and now you talk about panthers. Panthers are an animal species, are they not?"

This was too much for Wolff. He replied: "I tell you one thing, Mister. I prefer panthers to pigs." The dialogue became even less informative from that point on.

The First Amendment also led me into the world of New York politics. In late 1975, New York Governor Hugh Carey authorized an investigation of New York Democratic Party Chairman Patrick Cunningham, who was also party leader in the Bronx. The investigation was to be conducted by the notorious Office of Special Prosecutions, and was clearly an effort to unseat Cunningham from his party positions.

The regular Democratic Party in New York was politics in the old style, with an organization that rewarded the faithful with public jobs. Over the years, I came to respect Pat Cunningham's political judgment and to value his friendship. I litigated and won half a dozen cases for him, and lost the last one when the action moved to federal court and the jury found he had evaded tax on his income. In the earlier skirmishes, however, I thought that regardless of my disagreements with the regular Democrats, the use of state criminal charges to settle political fights was a bad idea.

In the first act of this drama, the special prosecutor summoned Pat to a state grand jury, and demanded that he waive his Fifth Amendment privilege against self-incrimination before testifying. Under New York law at that time, unless he waived he would have immunity from prosecution for whatever he disclosed. Pat refused to waive. The special prosecutor then invoked New York Election Law Section 22, which said that if any party officer refused to waive the privilege, he or she was automatically stripped of his or her party position.

We convened a three-judge federal court, which held that this statute violated the First and Fifth Amendments. A political party had the right to choose its leader, within certain broad limits, and the politician had the right to serve as leader. Conditioning political participation on giving up your Fifth Amendment rights violated settled Supreme Court law and trespassed on the First Amendment.

The state appealed the decision directly to the Supreme Court, and I argued the case in the spring of 1977. As I prepared for oral argument, I was conscious of some parallels between this case and my own situation. If a Supreme Court Justice could reject a law clerk for a good reason, a bad reason, or no reason at all, why could New York not regulate who would be a political party officer? The answer was obvious, because political parties are voluntary associations with rights of their own, and this law was dictating to them who they may and may not have as a leader.

The parallel had also occurred to Chief Justice Burger, who referred to it in oral argument. I said in reply, "The power of public officers with respect to those whom they choose to be their confidential aides may be greater" than what the Constitution permits states to exercise in this context. Justice Brennan smiled and I went on. The Court held, with only Justice Stevens dissenting, that New York Election Law Section 22 violated the First and Fifth Amendments.

Back in New York, however, Cunningham was charged with having wielded his political power in violation of the law. He was charged with extortion for allegedly telling a newspaper editor that the Democratic Party would not run ads in the paper if the editor continued to attack Cunningham's policies. He was charged with an offense akin to bribery for favoring a judicial candidate who had contributed to the party's coffers. There were other, similar charges. We won them all. Politics is not polite, and heated controversy is not extortion. The First Amendment shields decisions about candidates, or newspaper advertising, or many other things, from attack by means of criminal statutes. The use of criminal sanctions in the arena of speech is fraught with special dangers, for general criminal laws tend to be so vague and broad that they sweep protected conduct within their terms and fail to give fair warning of what is prohibited. This is, as the cases teach, the vice of vagueness in the First Amendment context.

Pat's law partner was also indicted in some of these cases and was represented by Louis Nizer one of the great trial lawyers. Even in his later years, he was a formidable negotiator. When I represented the producers of *One Flew Over the Cuckoo's Nest* in a threatened antitrust suit against United Artists, Nizer took personal charge for UA. We held a meeting in his New York office, and he showed an impressive command of the issues in our case and in the movie business. He also made clear from the beginning that he had authority to settle. In a single meeting, we resolved the dispute and walked away with serious money and major concessions— as well as preserving a valuable business relationship. This last point may bear emphasis. Often, litigators forget that the clients may have good reason to deal with each other in the future, and that too much hostility can destroy that prospect.

In our criminal case, however, Nizer should not have appeared. He had written his argument out in longhand, with red pen marks on it for emphasis. As he stood at the lectern, his associate crouched beside him so that when he lost his place the associate could help him find it. As litigators, we should pray that someone will be kind enough to tell us when to hang up our guns.

Freedom of expression also helped me to get back in touch with labor organizing. In the fall of 1973, my work on *Law and the Rise of Capitalism* was going well. I could foresee the book being done. I was restless. Some years later, I was talking to therapist Anya Rylander-Jones in an effort to save my marriage and maybe understand what drove me so hard. Anya tried to get me to focus on what was happening now, and what was possible to make happen. I still carry some little sayings around that address this issue:

Don't push the river; it flows by itself.
I am doing this now and it's enough.

Anya's other way of describing my condition was to talk about two archetypes—the warrior and the scholar. The warrior battles; the scholar ponders. I have both of those in me—maybe we all do. I am convinced that the great litigation lawyers think deeply about the context and consequences of their work. The warrior and the scholar need to talk.

So my scholar was under some serious pressure from my warrior. As though my discomfort went forth on the ether, I got a call from New York. David Scribner, a longtime labor lawyer, a surviving hero of the labor movement, wanted to visit me in France to talk about a case. A week later, Dave arrived, energetic and rubicund, with a trimmed white beard and spectacles. We sat on my front porch, looking down some 20 kilometers to the bay at Cannes, drank coffee, and talked.

Dave was representing a group of rank-and-file steelworkers. The steelworkers' union president, I.W. Abel, had signed a new contract with the ten largest steel companies, the key feature of which was an Experimental Negotiating Agreement (ENA). Under the ENA, the union and management would negotiate for a time after the contract ran out and then submit any differences to binding arbitration. The right to strike would be a thing of the past.

One could argue the merits of such a proposal. To me, it seemed foolish for the union to give up its heftiest bargaining tool. In labor history, the right to take concerted job action had been won at great cost. Merits aside, however, the ENA was wrong because it had been forced upon the membership without any semblance of democratic procedure. There was no membership consultation, much less a vote. The deal looked like another high-handed action of Abel and his group, who were already being challenged for leadership positions by people who had more support among the rank and file. Abel would note that the companies gave up the right to lock out the workers, but even this was lopsided; the companies could still lock out on local issues, while the workers could not strike on such issues.

Dave said he was going to file a lawsuit challenging the ENA. We discussed theories. The plaintiffs would be rank-and-file leaders from the big steel towns—Gary, Cleveland, Pittsburgh, Youngstown. We knew the story of the case, but we needed a legal theory. For that we turned to the Labor-Management Relations Act of 1959—the Landrum-Griffin Act. This was a difficult choice, because Landrum-Griffin was enacted to curb union power, and to impose more limits and restrictions than its predecessor, the Taft-Hartley Act of 1947. Taft-Hartley, in its turn, was an attack on the union rights conferred by the

Wagner Act of the New Deal era. Indeed, Taft-Hartley was enacted over President Truman's veto.

Some parts of Landrum-Griffin, such as those regulating union elections, did not confer a right to sue on individual union members. Only the Secretary of Labor had standing in the first instance to bring a lawsuit. But other sections gave our clients claims we could litigate. The law guaranteed freedom of expression in the context of union democracy, and it required union leaders to be fiduciaries for their members.

I was not a labor lawyer, but I had done some work for unions and had a general idea of what this was all about. Union democracy and members' rights echoed familiar themes from other parts of my practice and experience. Dave had brought some of the basic legal material with him. We roughed out a lawsuit, sitting there on my terrace overlooking the bay at Cannes. Several weeks later, I was sitting in Dave's office in New York ready to begin work. In the office was a lawyer my age who was also volunteering to work on the case—John Mage. John and I became friends, and later law partners.

For the next few weeks, my warrior and scholar personae lived in happy harmony. The scholar met Staughton Lynd and his wife, Alice, in Chicago. Staughton was a social historian, son of famous sociologists. He had moved to Chicago and was attending law school, so he brought legal theory together with economic history into our discussions. When he graduated from law school, he began practicing labor law in Youngstown, Ohio. In Pittsburgh, I met Jim Logan, a labor lawyer and activist who would play a key role in the case. We decided to file in Pittsburgh, in the U.S. District Court for the Western District of Pennsylvania. This was the historic steel town and was in the Third Circuit, where court of appeals precedent seemed to favor us.

And in New York I met Robert Gordon, of the New School for Social Research. Bob died a few years later, very young. He was among the most articulate and progressive scholars of labor economics of his generation. I sat and listened, sometimes contributing a thought or two, with Mage and Scribner and Gordon. We ranged over the history of American labor, from the Cordwainers' Case of 1807 through the statutory reforms of the 1930s, and down to 1974.

In the Cordwainers' Case, Pennsylvania courts upheld the convictions of striking workers for a "conspiracy in restraint of trade." All concerted job action was, under this view, a crime. Throughout the nineteenth century, this idea held sway. Union organizing was incitement to lawlessness. As America became an industrial nation and its work force was increased by European immigrants schooled in a radical tradition, the antistrike rhetoric of establishment forces increased in fury. During the 1887 Chicago strikes that led to the infamous Haymarket trials, Tom Scott, the president of the Pennsylvania Railroad, proclaimed, "Give those strikers a rifle diet for a few days and see how they like that kind of bread." The *Indianapolis News* proclaimed, "If the workingmen had no vote they might be more amenable to the teachings of the times." The *Chicago Times* thundered: "Hand grenades should be thrown among these union men who are striving to obtain higher wages and less hours. By such treatment they would be taught a valuable lesson, and other strikers could take warning from their fate." Not until 1930, with the Norris-LaGuardia Act, did federal law limit the judicial role in union busting.

If a major industrial union were to abandon the strike as a weapon, such a concession should be made only after the membership as a whole had been consulted, informed, and had made a deliberate decision. Gordon agreed to be our expert witness, to present a historical panorama about worker rights. At the same time, we did not want to embrace a theory that would weaken the power of union leaders to confront powerful management. We did not want to make law that would permit management to fracture the fragile unity of the union membership. Union decisions were entitled to membership respect, and were not a means for disruption or "dual unionism." But the only decisions entitled to such respect were those arrived at democratically.

Our legal theory had to incorporate these historical truths. Union democracy, as somewhat guaranteed by Landrum-Griffin, was only a part of the story. The abstract entity known as the union represents the members in name only—the "representing" is done by the union leaders. On the shop floor, the union rep who will present your grievance is the shop steward. That name, blessed by long history, says a lot. Union leaders have an obligation of stewardship.

To express this theory, we turned to Title 3 of Landrum-Griffin, which simply stated that union officers have a fiduciary obligation—they are trustees. There was some case law holding that this statute applied only to union financial assets. The better view, or so we thought, was that Title 3 applied to the whole range of union member rights. This would include the right to fair representation, the right to strike, and the right to be consulted. We were expressing, that is, what later came to be known as a theory of intangible rights. Our view of fiduciary duty had good support in decisions concerning the obligations of corporate officers and directors to the corporation and its shareholders. Working through this issue—uniting historical insight with legal theory—made my scholar happy.

The soldier in me was enlivened by meeting the clients. Gary, Indiana, is a depressing town. Many of the mills were already closing down. The town as a whole suffered the malaise of so many industrial cities in what came to be known as the Rust Belt. I will always remember my first meeting with the group of rank-and-file activists who were to be our Gary clients. Their leader was Alice—Brother Alice, as she was fondly known, for in steel union lingo your fellow workers were your brothers, and in 1974 little attention had been paid to finding a gender-neutral way of speaking.

We met at the mill, and then went on to a Catholic social hall. A local priest—who seemed young even to my 30-something self—let us in. He spoke to us of the social problems of the decaying city. The struggle to reclaim the union from I.W. Abel was, it seemed, part of some larger idea to revitalize this community.

In Cleveland, George was our host—a tough and gray veteran of the mill. For George, the right to walk off the job was central to his way of thinking. George even pointed out how wildcat strikes—those not authorized by the contract or (at least openly) by union leadership—were playing an important role. He recounted how worker protest had ended some unsafe working conditions in several plants.

My soldier and my scholar were united in Youngstown. There, rank-and-file candidates committed to union democracy had won elections and were running the local. John and Jim and the others were not only going to help us in this lawsuit; they regarded it as part of a broader strategy to democratize the union as a whole. We spent long evenings talking through short- and long-term strategies.

We filed our complaint and asked for a preliminary injunction. This was the quickest way to get our case into court and put the maximum pressure on the other side. Our defendants were Abel, the union, and the ten steel companies. With adversaries like that, we could not afford to have the case turn into a major discovery battle. We needed to find out quickly if the case would have staying power.

But staying power in the courts was not our only objective, and for many of our clients was not the major objective. This case could be a rallying point for Abel's opponents, for those who wanted to democratize the union and return it to core principles in which they believed. The ENA had been adopted in a hurry, and after negotiations that were mostly secret. The case was a focus for publicity and protest.

I do not know directly, but have a clear sense of what happened in Cleveland, Gary, Baltimore, Los Angeles. In Pittsburgh, rank-and-filers stood every night at the plant gates passing out leaflets about the issue. Our case plan was simple. We would present the testimony of rank-and-file leaders about how ENA was adopted, and then the expert overview from Dr. Gordon. Staughton Lynd helped with research and worked with witnesses.

There was no jury. We wanted, however, to impress on Judge Teitelbaum and the media that we represented a genuine union member voice. Every day of the hearing, the courtroom was filled with steelworkers. Since they were all our clients, directly or as members of the plaintiff class, we subpoenaed them to appear as potential witnesses and asked the judge to waive the rule and permit them to remain in the courtroom. Their union contract provided for days off with pay as long as they remained under subpoena.

Our witnesses included rank-and-file leaders who showed a greater understanding of steel company finances and organization than our opponents thought possible. Our witnesses withstood condescending cross-examinations. In the end, Judge Teitelbaum ruled against us. But we had helped to organize rank-and-file activity and opinion in the union locals and in the international union, which led in turn to election victories for our clients in union politics. We had served our purpose.

When I came back to the states in January 1974 to work on the steelworkers' case, I took the time to hunt around for a longer-term job. I met with Edgar and Jean Cahn at Antioch Law School, and thought about teaching there. The school, based as it was on clinical legal education, was a fascinating and challenging place, though riven by internal dissension even then. I also had reservations about full-time teaching.

Coincidence helped to resolve the matter. I called Ed Williams to say hello and he invited me to lunch. We sat at Duke Zeibert's restaurant with some of the lawyers I had known in the firm and talked inconsequentially about memories. A lawyer who had joined the firm since I left, Earl Dudley, was working on a bribery case, and we batted around First Amendment issues about the difference between lawful campaign contributions, which are a form of protected expression, and illegal bribes and gratuities.

Ed and I walked out together, past the headwaiter's table where Mel Krupin alternated with Duke as captain of the place. Ed turned and spoke softly. "We've got a new case coming in. It would be nice if you and I could work on it together." We parted, and only later did I wonder if I had just been offered a job.

The next day I called and asked what he had in mind. Did I want to come back to the firm, on a fast track to be a partner? And, by the way, the case was the impending indictment of John Connally, former Texas governor and Treasury Secretary, for allegedly accepting an illegal gratuity from the milk producers. So when the steelworkers case was over, I returned to France to pack up.

I was back in the old firm, in the same building at 17th and I streets Northwest. I had a corner office and freedom to work on draft cases left over from the Vietnam war. The firm, which was Williams & Wadden when I joined it in 1966 and then became Williams & Connolly, had become Williams, Connolly & Califano. Joe Califano had jumped from Arnold & Porter.

The law firm had changed in five years. I had left in 1969 to teach at UCLA, when there were about 12 lawyers occupying three floors of the Hill Building at 17th and I, looking on to Farragut Square. By 1974, not only were there 35 lawyers and a lot more office space, but also the atmosphere had changed. Lawyers my age were concerned that the old, informal way of doing things would give way to a bureaucracy that would change working relationships. More important for many, Joe Califano seemed to be seeking clients whose cases would change the firm's approach to the law.

The governance issues were being debated by the lawyers of my generation. Williams, Connolly & Califano each had super-percentages of revenue. For all the partners after them, the younger lawyers wanted to have a lockstep system that would prevent year-end fights over money. They wanted to encourage retirements by capping profit shares by the time a partner had been practicing a certain number of years. They hoped by this to preserve the camaraderie of the place. After all, we were accustomed to dropping in to each other's offices to talk about cases and issues. We would head out for lunch together in small groups. By 1976, the new plan was in place. I don't know how all of that has fared since Ed Williams died and the firm has grown to more than 100 lawyers.

This sort of informal discussion is essential to any litigation practice. Every well-run law firm encourages it. I think of public defender offices with their regular meetings to talk about cases. When Sam Buffone and I opened our law firm, we vowed never to be larger than would fit a table at the Palm Restaurant, and that we would meet at least once a week while everyone talked about every case in the office.

A firm grown as large as Williams, Connolly & Califano could not fit every lawyer at a restaurant table, but it could maintain something nearly as useful. The firm had installed a lunchroom on the first floor, open to all the lawyers. Ed Williams's idea was that in that room you could talk about a case without being overhead by a potential adversary. The food was pretty good, too. There were a couple of smaller rooms where you could lunch with a client in privacy.

The lawyers my age were right to be concerned about the firm's future. Its present showed signs of tension. Joe Califano had joined the firm on condition that he get a bigger share of the pie than Paul Connolly was getting. Ed Williams retained his even larger share, but it seemed to me that in a law firm where there was plenty of money for everybody, Joe's need to show that he could outdo Paul was unseemly. Paul was a founder of the ABA Litigation Section and a first-rate trial lawyer. We often disagreed on ideological issues, but despite our disagreements he went out of his way to help me make a name in the profession. He did this for many others as well.

There were other ways in which Joe's view of law practice seemed at odds with what this litigation law firm ought to be doing. Joe had attracted a major client that had other issues as well as litigation. Joe pitched the idea of fully servicing this client by helping to draft administrative regulations concerning batteries or some such thing. Drafting regulations is good lawyer work, but litigators might not be good at it. If you hired lawyers to work on the regulations, then you would need to keep that regulatory work coming in to feed those lawyers.

Joe's other innovations were continual sources of frustration. He hired two retired noncommissioned officers he had known during his days in the Pentagon to be office managers. He had originally named their quarters on the fifth floor "the control module," but Williams balked at that. By the time I got there, the operation was called executive services and included a typing pool, central file repository and retrieval, office supplies control, and related functions. That name was dropped as well, after some of us saw leaflets posted near the office advertising a downtown massage parlor called Executive Services. Among the organizational innovations was off-site file storage. In one test, some of us asked for retrieval of 14 case files related to an issue on which we were working. Executive services was able to find only five of them.

Of course, litigators are famously antagonistic to bureaucracy. They prefer a kind of organized chaos. We count on good people and not the assumed perfection of systems. Joe Califano did not understand that if you bureaucratize a litigation law firm, you will kill its spirit.

More significantly, the delegation and sub-delegation inherent in Joe's organization model may produce a lot of billable hours, but it plays hell with effective litigation strategy. My disagreement with Joe on this issue surfaced soon after I rejoined the firm. His secretary called and said that Mr. Califano wanted to talk with me. I said, "I'll be in the office all day." She politely said that this was not the point, and made clear that I had been *summoned*. I went.

Joe began by saying, "Williams says you are pretty good. We need to see about that." Not a good beginning. "I've got a case for you. The other side is being handled by my old firm, Arnold & Porter. This is sort of a grudge match for them." And for you, too, I thought. He told me about the case—a libel suit against *Army Times*, a publication for people in military service. *Army Times* had published an exposé of insurance sales directed at military people; the insurance company had sued. If the company were a public figure—which it surely was—then whatever minor errors were in the article were no doubt protected by *New York Times v. Sullivan*.

Joe and a team of firm lawyers had drafted a motion to dismiss the complaint, which the district judge had denied in a scathing opinion from the bench. Judge John H. Wood, Jr. was a crusty, opinionated autocrat. Now a discovery battle loomed. I winced. In civil cases, you don't need much detail to state your case. Had Joe and his team fixed the judge's mind that this case needed to be tried?

Joe told me how he thought the case should be handled. "I can give you one fourth of the time of one lawyer, one half of another one, and maybe one half of yet another." He kept on, until the total reached about two and one-half lawyers.

"I don't want that kind of help," I said. "I would like the full-time help of one lawyer, Kevin Baine. I don't want any paralegals from downstairs. Kevin and I will use our own secretaries for any paralegal work. That is the way I would like to do it."

Joe seemed mystified by this approach, but acquiesced. "Well, this is your case now, so handle it the way you want."

I leapt into the facts. The reporter had done a valuable service, based on months of investigation. The story had merited an artist's drawing on the cover, depicting a smooth con man bilking a GI. At the same time, the other side alleged that the story was flawed in both concept and details. This promised to be an exciting trip, defending one voice in an important debate.

There is a temptation to over-lawyer complex litigation, especially on the defense side, when the client is paying by the hour. It happens on the plaintiff's side too, when the lead lawyers are taking on too many projects, handing off too much work, or are insecure about their own abilities. Using too many lawyers makes case preparation unfocused and unwieldy. It leads quickly to overuse of discovery devices, which runs up the cost even more.

In this case, the plaintiff's counsel were being paid by the hour, and they staffed the case that way. At our first meeting with them, two junior partners and an associate showed up. A senior partner and more associates were available if need be. They presented a list of *Army Times* employees whose depositions they wished to take. As to some senior executives who had nothing to do with the challenged story, we said nothing doing. From the remaining names, the plaintiffs' lawyers proposed a punishing schedule that would set all the depositions in a row over a three-week period. We agreed to that.

The author, editor, and illustration artist gave their depositions first. At each one, the plaintiffs were represented by at least two partners and one associate lawyer—the combined bills just to take those depositions must have been enormous. The lawyer asking questions followed a detailed script that was in a notebook that had no doubt been prepared by a paralegal. The questioning was long, tedious, and antagonistic.

From the author's deposition:

Q: You use the word exposé to describe your story. Isn't that a loaded word?
A: It doesn't seem so to me.
Q: Well, have you ever heard of an exposé that was favorable to somebody? [The interrogator's voice rose to a crescendo.] Have you ever heard of an exposé of a *saint?*
Mr. Tigar: In the answer, would you like the standard elements of sainthood—temptation, miracle, and martyrdom?
Q: I withdraw the question.

The other side also deposed the cover artist, who was a skilled painter but nearly incoherent when asked to explain the reason why he depicted characters in a certain way. All communication requires some connection between speaker and hearer, and in this deposition there was next to none.

Q: And did somebody from *Army Times* call you?
A: Yes.

Q: Did they ask if you were free?

A: What?

Q: [impatiently, reading from the deposition notebook] Did they ask if you were free?

A: They wouldn't do that. I don't work for free.

After the initial three depositions, the other side called and said it would not be taking any others for the time being. Not so fast, I replied. We want to move this case, and you told us you wanted that also. We promptly noticed the depositions of all our witnesses, on the same schedule the other side had set and then abandoned. We made the complete record of how the story was conceived, researched, written, and edited. The other side's lawyers showed up and said each time that they had no questions now but would have some at some indefinite future date.

If we had to try this case to a jury, however, I wanted a way to get inside the head of an investigative journalist. People in that line of work tell harsh truths, if they are doing a good job. If they are sloppy or out to malign, they tell harsh and hurtful falsehoods. I am not a friend of libel law. Once, at a dinner with Justice Hugo Black late in his life, I listened as one of the other guests at this small gathering went on and on about his libel suit against *Time* magazine, and the harm the offending article had done him. The lawyer's rant was discourteous to the Justice, who bore it politely, interrupting only to repeat his long-held credo that the First Amendment was designed to forbid private libel actions as well as government suits alleging seditious libel or libel on government.

I have often thought Justice Black's view was right, and cannot think of filing a libel suit myself, at least against the media. My view is often tested in practice by the spectacle of irresponsible journalism. In my line of work, however, the fault is as much or more with the government sources who use their journalistic contacts to plant false stories in an effort to influence pending cases.

In the *Army Times* case, the issue was intensely practical for our summary judgment motion to the judge and for an eventual jury trial if we lost that motion. I have believed, and written for trial lawyers, that a good expert witness is like a mid-trial summation. But what expertise would we need here? Not an insurance expert, I thought. The plaintiff's case was about insurance. Our case was about journalistic integrity and freedom of expression. The plaintiff was an insurance company; let it get the jury to identify with its problems. Our client was a newspaper; we wanted the jury to identify with us. *Army Times* had only recently turned to investigative journalism to serve its readers by discussing such issues as insurance targeted at the captive military market. This was our story.

I asked around. Where could I find a journalism professor who really understood how reporters think and work? I wanted somebody who identified with investigative journalists. I wanted somebody who had done that for a living. I thought first of my old journalism teachers, Pete Steffens and Alan Temko. Neither one seemed right for a San Antonio jury. I called Sidney Roger, a labor journalist of the old school who had been a commentator on Pacifica Radio, and had taught at Berkeley. Sid might not be the best person for San Antonio either, although in the waterfront towns of East Texas I would have used him in a heartbeat.

Sid told me of Roy Mac Fisher, who had been editor of the *Chicago Sun-Times*, a tabloid, and was now dean of the School of Journalism at the University of Missouri. This was an education for me. Sid told me that Missouri and Columbia were the best journalism schools in the country, with Missouri having an edge in print journalism and Columbia in broadcasting.

I got Fisher's résumé and made an appointment to see him. I asked him to sit with the reporter who wrote the story and pretend that he was the senior editor. I asked the two of them to take the challenged story and number every factual statement in it, sentence by sentence and paragraph by paragraph. There were more than 1,000 statements.

Then, I asked Fisher to interrogate the author about the source of every statement and decide whether the author's use of sources was in accord with good journalistic practice. In journalism, as in the rest of life, we are often less than entirely sure about things. Journalists, like anybody else who is talking in public about other people, have a responsibility not to monger unreliable information. Indeed, they have a special responsibility to their readers because of the position of authority they assume. Did this journalism meet those standards? And could Roy Mac Fisher say that it did based on his decades of practical experience and the best academic standards he could use?

He could, and did. If we ever tried the case to a jury, I wanted to tell two stories. The first would be about the plaintiff's insurance business, for that was what we had been sued about. But I also wanted to tell the story of how an investigative reporter works, researches, uses sources, and then puts it all together. If the jurors identified with the reporter as a working person trying to do a job, then we would win even if the jurors thought he made an error or two. That said, we stood by the story.

We finished up the discovery we wanted to take and moved for summary judgment. There was, we claimed, no genuine issue of fact. I finally got to meet Judge Wood. The courtroom was full of lawyers. It was a calendar call for all pending motions. Wood took the bench in a foul mood, living up to his reputation.

When our case was called he said, "I see that the defendants have filed one of these motions for summary judgment. It looks like the same sort of thing that this fellow California, or whatever it was, put before me months ago."

"Oh, we agree entirely," said the plaintiff's lawyer.

"If Your Honor please," I ventured, "we filed this motion only after a lot of discovery. It is a new motion. The plaintiffs don't like it, and maybe you won't like it either. But we feel about our motion like the mountaineer said about his pancakes: 'No matter how thin I make 'em, there's always two sides.'"

Lawyers in the courtroom laughed. That really scared me. Most judges like to originate the humor. Wood smiled. "Oh, you mean it's like the little boy who was asked what was the score in the baseball game and he said, "we are behind 25 to zero,' and the man asked him, 'And you ain't worried?' And the boy said, 'No sir, we ain't had our ups yet.'" The courtroom lawyers laughed again, thankfully louder this time.

Judge Wood set a hearing, and the other side argued that it needed more time to take additional discovery before making a full response to our motion. Judge Wood was only mildly impressed. "You say there is something out there that gives you a case. All right, you have 45 days to take discovery and find it. If you don't, I am inclined to grant this motion. Now, court is adjourned, so come back and let's have some coffee in my chambers."

In those days, Braniff Airlines had a one-stop flight from San Antonio to Washington, D.C. But you had to get it about 3:30 in the afternoon, and the airport was on the outskirts of town. The other side's lawyers said they had to leave to catch a plane. We said we could use some coffee. No, we did not talk about the case ex parte, but we did visit with the judge about my representation of his friend John Connally, and he showed me his signed picture of Connally. This litigation had been hard fought, and I think the judge resented the other side's rejection of his efforts to get the lawyers in his chambers. Of course, he had just finished rejecting their position, but that is the very time when one should seem ready to continue the fight.

Judge Wood was controversial. He had even made some remarks from the bench showing that the racial and ethnic biases of his south Texas upbringing were alive and well. But he had been a superb jury lawyer, representing defendants in civil negligence and product liability cases. He no doubt thought the "liberal media" needed policing. So our task was to explain our case as a principled, fact-based defense. If we could do that, we might introduce cognitive dissonance into Judge Woods's pre-formed views about the media.

This is the same approach one always makes to a decider. The decider carries around a bundle of preconceptions. Some of these represent fundamental values about fairness and hearing both sides. Others are less benign. A trial lawyer tries to find a reason that appeals to that decider why he or she should win the case. This is not pandering, it is simply recognition that humans decide cases and that all humans have prejudices.

By Monday of the next week, the other side was ready to extend an olive branch, and to reach a settlement that was acceptable to our clients. Joe Califano was pleased, and I got another libel case.

Ed and Joe asked me to represent the *Washington Post* and its investigative reporter, Ron Kessler. The *Post* story had alleged that Charles "Bebe" Rebozo, a friend and confidant of many political figures and owner of a Florida savings and loan, sold stock that he knew had been stolen. The stock had been stolen, but Rebozo denied knowing this. The story had run in the aftermath of Richard Nixon's resignation as President. Rebozo's name had figured in the investigation that resulted in Nixon's resignation, and there had been allegations that Rebozo helped the Nixon campaign raise and spend money in questionable ways.

Ron Kessler was then and is now a formidable investigative reporter with interest and expertise in financial matters. He was proud of his story. However, Rebozo had filed suit on his home turf in Miami, and had beaten back the *Post's* claim that it was not subject to suit in Florida. In addition to Ron Kessler, I had the chance to work with the *Post's* legendary editor, Ben Bradlee, and even to meet Katherine Graham. In Florida, we had the help of Sandy d'Alemberte, the great Florida lawyer who was later ABA president.

I worked the same basic theory as with *Army Times*. I retained Roy Mac Fisher to interview Kessler. In the meantime, we confronted Rebozo's claim that he was not a public figure within the meaning of the Supreme Court's cases beginning with *New York Times v. Sullivan*. Public figures cannot collect for a false and defamatory story without proof by clear and convincing evidence that the author knew the story was false or acted with reckless disregard of its truth or falsity.

To prove Rebozo was a public figure, I asked a researcher to copy and clip every media reference to him, beginning about 1950. In that year, Rebozo had first come to press attention as a friend and supporter of George Smathers, a conservative Florida political figure. This was before the Internet days. The researcher pasted each reference to an index card and I arranged these in some sort of order. We then noticed Rebozo's deposition. The deposition began affably but went downhill. I turned over card after card and asked Rebozo to acknowledge that he had been at this or that public function, or played this or that public role in business or politics. He became increasingly irritable as the second deposition day began and I was still turning over cards. Ron Kessler sat beside me and passed notes.

Several hours into the second day Rebozo turned to Kessler and said irritably: "Who are you? I don't know you."

Kessler introduced himself. Rebozo looked stunned. "You mean you are the hooligan who wrote that story?" He turned to his lawyer, "Why do I have to sit in this room with a hooligan like that?" From this exchange, I had the sense that having Rebozo under examination during a jury trial might be fun.

Even after being confronted with all of this, Rebozo refused to concede he was a public figure. We filed a motion for summary judgment nonetheless, based on his deposition and on the factual research that showed a basis for Kessler's story. I wanted, however, to nail down that public figure status, and I thought there was one person who could confirm it authoritatively—Richard Nixon.

I told Ed Williams I wanted to notice Nixon's deposition. He doubted the wisdom of doing this, and said I would have to get Katherine Graham's personal approval. So we made an appointment. Ed and I sat in Ben Bradlee's office with Ben and Mrs. Graham. I outlined the situation. Ben said, "Kay, do you really want to take the heat for picking on Nixon like this?" Mrs. Graham smiled and recalled what Nixon's Attorney General, John Mitchell, had said when the *Post* first broke the Watergate story, that Mrs. Graham would have her "tits in the wringer."

Mrs. Graham gestured toward the front of her dress and said sweetly: "What's he going to do, Ben? Put my tits in a wringer again? You know, maybe I could use a little more up here." I saw in that moment the managerial style of this courageous and brilliant woman. Her tone was soft, but her air of command was unmistakable. And she would make this decision, as she had so many others, based on her principles and not on any idea of convenience.

As it happened, I did not get to take Nixon's deposition because we got summary judgment from the bench shortly thereafter. Then I left the Williams firm, and the judgment was reversed in part, though not on the public figure issue. The court of appeals noted that the First Amendment–based preference for summary judgment in libel cases had been disfavored by the Supreme Court, and the case was decided before the Court clarified the law and tilted it back toward the media. The case dragged on, and later I heard it was settled without Rebozo collecting any money.

As I said, the folks whose speech gets the authorities worked up make interesting clients. In Texas, I helped a group of protesters charged with inciting a riot. Jury instructions that Sam Buffone and I drafted, but that the judge refused to give, laid the basis for reversal of their convictions on appeal. We were defending two basic ideas in those proposed instructions. First, you can join a group, some of whose members violate the law, without necessarily associating yourself with the unlawful purposes. Second, speech that incites and stirs people to anger is protected unless it poses a clear and present danger of imminent lawless action. It galls me when somebody intones "You can't shout fire in a crowded theater," because of course you can—if there is a fire. You can't falsely shout it to cause a panic.

When a group of demonstrators occupied the president's office at the University of Texas to protest the university's investments in apartheid, I appeared as an expert witness to say that apartheid was an international crime and maybe the students were justified in their peaceful protest. The judge excluded my testimony, but it helped to make the demonstrators' point.

Lawyers have often been in trouble for speaking. Sometimes they are held in contempt for sassing judges, as with Erskine's comment: "Your lordship may proceed in any manner he wishes. I stand here as advocate for a fellow citizen." Or the nineteenth century Irish barrister John Philpott Curran, interrupted by an English judge who said, "Mr. Curran, if you continue in this vein, I shall be obliged to commit you for contempt." To which Curran replied with a bow, "In that event, your lordship and I will have the satisfaction of knowing it won't be the worst thing your lordship has ever committed."

I have myself said things in and out of court that I regretted or was made to regret.

George Pratt was a superb judge with a remarkable sense of humor. I once argued before him in the Second Circuit, the day after I had played the role of Andrew Hamilton in the Zenger play at the New York Historical Society. That morning, *Newsday* had a picture of me in 1735 regalia with powdered wig. My opponent began his argument by saying with mock respect, "It is always difficult to follow Professor Tigar." Judge Pratt interrupted and said, "Oh, but you should see him when he is dressed up like Andrew Hamilton."

Before being appointed to the Second Circuit, Judge Pratt was a judge in the U.S. District Court for the Eastern District of New York, with chambers in Brooklyn. He tried the ABSCAM cases, involving members of Congress caught in an FBI bribery sting operation. In the sting, an FBI agent claimed to represent a wealthy Arab sheik who would pay congressmen to induce them to introduce special legislation to regularize his immigration status.

For my client, Congressman Murphy, who was the only defendant acquitted of racketeering, bribery, and conspiracy, it was important to me that a defendant in another case testify for us. But this defendant had his own troubles, and his lawyer said he would invoke his Fifth Amendment privilege if we called him. I therefore moved that the government be ordered to give this man, Howard, use immunity. These were the days before the Supreme Court ruled that such a motion had no chance at all.

The judge and I argued back and forth about this. Finally, seeing that maybe Howard's testimony might be double-edged for my defense, Judge Pratt inquired mildly, "Mr. Tigar, if I order the government to give Howard immunity, and you call him to testify, will you agree to be bound by everything he says?"

I heard a voice. The voice was mine, rushing out without my brain filtering its words. And I said, "Oh, Your Honor, I'm not into bondage."

Judge Pratt was unfazed, so maybe it went right by him. My son and his college friends, who were in court because this was the day before Thanksgiving, suppressed their giggles.

Nothing I have said or could say can match the combative eloquence of my friend Michael Kennedy. I will not tell his entire story here, for it belongs to him. His mouth should be on retainer, in more ways than one. One night in California, Kennedy and I were sitting in my rented home in Laguna Beach with a client when the police battered in the door and took the client away in handcuffs. Kennedy followed the police into the street shouting, "You honky dog motherfuckers, when I get through

with you, you'll wish the alligators had eaten you." He was charged with
disorderly conduct a few days later, though the charges were dismissed
shortly thereafter.

Some time later Kennedy told me that he had tried a case in Trenton,
New Jersey, which ended with a hung jury. He had talked to some of the
jurors to see what he might do to improve his case if there were a retrial.
He was not aware of a New Jersey federal court rule that forbade contact-
ing jurors without court approval. That posed a fairly simple issue, because
contempt requires proof that the contemnor intentionally violated a known
legal duty. I assembled some authorities on this subject. Unfortunately, my
plane was late and I arrived in court after Judge Debevoise had already
called the case. I sat next to Kennedy and listened as the prosecutor began.
I noted that there were two court reporters, one taking down the proceedings and the other sitting calmly at her Stenotype.

"Your Honor," the assistant U.S. attorney began, "we had some concern about Mr. Kennedy interviewing jurors but we are not going to
pursue that, and we don't think the court should either. However, I would
like the court reporter to read what happened after Your Honor declared
a mistrial in this case."

I was not prepared for this. I glanced at Kennedy, who looked about as
innocent as an altar boy caught gulping the communion wine. The court
reporter intoned from her steno tape, something like:

> *The court*: Members of the jury. I thank you for your service and I
> declare a mistrial in this case. The court is adjourned.
> (Judge leaves the bench.)
> *Prosecutor*: Well, Mr. Kennedy, it looks like we will be trying these
> clients of yours all over again. We'll do better next time.
> *Mr. Kennedy*: Is that what you think, shithead? Why don't you and
> I step outside right now and let's settle this.
> *Prosecutor*: See you later.

Judge Debevoise made some appropriate tut-tutting noise and said
that lawyers should behave more civilly in the future. I couldn't be angry
at Kennedy. His rhetoric was milder than what he sometimes used. I did
wonder why he had not told me this was coming, but I wondered more
that the prosecutor would need to tattle to the judge about it.

Of course, lawyer speech has often had loftier expression than some of
these stories would suggest. In 1761, the British colonial authorities used
general warrants called writs of assistance to search for goods on which

protesting colonists had not paid tax. John Adams was at that time a young lawyer in Boston. Another lawyer, James Otis, made a speech on the Boston Common against the writs of assistance. Of those events, Adams later wrote, "then and there was the child Independence born." When the young Adams was retained to represent John Hancock in a forfeiture proceeding, his contentions and later a text of his undelivered argument were thoroughly aired in the press of the time, along with running commentaries on the legal issues. When John Adams was in Philadelphia on July 3, 1776, waiting for the next day's events, he looked back at those times and said that these court cases and the controversy around them were "the Commencement of the Controversy, between Great Britain and America."

Lawyers are qualified by training to speak on public issues. Their participation in major litigation qualifies them further. As my friend John Mage has written, "In the U.S. system, all significant legal and political questions are given legal form." For this reason, lawyers are valuable participants in public discourse, even when they are also litigating about the judicial resolution of the same issues on which they are speaking in public.

Because I think about things in this way, I was honored when a Las Vegas lawyer named Dominic Gentile called me and asked if I, along with Sam Buffone, would take his case to the Supreme Court. Dominic was a successful defense lawyer, former faculty member of the National Criminal Defense College, and published author. His client was Grady Sanders, who owned a private storage company. The Las Vegas police rented lockboxes from Sanders's company, and used the boxes to store money and narcotics for a sting operation. The police neglected to tell Sanders what they were doing.

The money and narcotics disappeared, and the ensuing public outcry occupied the media for months. Eventually, the police having denied guilt, the district attorney indicted Sanders. Dom went to court and got a trial date six months in the future. The night before, he had carefully studied the rules of professional responsibility to see what public comment he could make about the case.

After the arraignment, Dom held a press conference, which he had the good sense to videotape. He kept within the bounds of proper comment as he saw them, and he said that the evidence showed that the Las Vegas police were probably the ones who had stolen the money and drugs. At the trial, no prospective juror remembered Dom's press conference, although some jurors recalled public statements by the police and the district attorney. Dom presented evidence to support his theory and the jury acquitted Sanders.

Shortly after the trial, the Nevada bar sent Dom a letter saying that his press conference violated the disciplinary rules and that he was subject to discipline. A justice of the Nevada Supreme Court had initiated the complaint. Dom put on a thorough defense at the bar disciplinary hearing, including testimony on his own qualifications and the opinions of a media expert and a criminal defense lawyer.

The bar found him guilty and the Nevada Supreme Court affirmed. The punishment was a private reprimand, which would do no great harm to Dom's reputation, but he chose to challenge what the Nevada authorities had done. And so we filed a petition for certiorari, making three basic points. First, we said that lawyer speech should be protected unless it poses a clear and present danger to the administration of justice. Second, we argued that the rule under which Dom was punished, based on an ABA Model Rule, was unconstitutionally vague and broad—indeed, contradictory. Dom was found to have violated section 2(d) of Nevada Rule 177, which proscribes uttering "any opinion as to the guilt or innocence of a defendant or suspect in a criminal case." Section 3(a) of the same rule, however, states that, notwithstanding the prohibitions of sections 1 and 2, counsel "may state without elaboration: a. the general nature of the claim or defense." Third, we argued that on the facts Dom's press conference was not only harmless but also a public service.

This third point, being factual, is not the sort of thing that the Supreme Court is said to care about. Its jurisdiction extends only to deciding federal law issues when reviewing a state court judgment. It was clear to me, however, that one's attitude toward lawyer press conferences in general, and this one in particular, could well drive this case. The story here was the relentless media barrage from the police and the district attorney, and Dom's modulated response, undertaken only after careful study. As we looked at the cases on lawyer speech and gag orders, an interesting pattern emerged. The only lawyers who were disciplined for comments prejudicial to the fair administration of justice were defense lawyers. Prosecutors and police never seemed to be sanctioned, even though in my own experience alone they are the most potent and deliberate source of prejudicial media leaks.

Few defense lawyers have a pipeline to media sources. On the other hand, in every media market there is a police beat that keeps in daily contact with the prosecutors and police. Over time, reporters develop relationships with these law enforcement sources. In every major criminal case in which I have been involved, the prosecutors have been responsible for prejudicial media comments. These comments have ranged from premature release of information to prejudicial rumor and speculation. In a case that continues to excite media attention, by the time of the trial the prospective jurors have internalized the media reports, and it is difficult if not impossible to unearth and examine their preconceptions on voir dire.

We did find one celebrated case where a prosecutor was disciplined. He had tried a murder case that was then reversed. He said publicly that the case should not be retried, and the district attorney brought disciplinary charges.

We could not know how Dom's story would impress the Justices. The case would be close either way, and it was Justice Souter's first term on the Court, so he was an unknown entity. So we had another story, rooted in the writings of John Adams and James Madison and other lawyers whose public speeches had fueled the drive for American independence. After all, I argued, if the Las Vegas police had stolen money and narcotics, that was a matter of public concern quite beyond the Sanders trial. The public's business may be done in one forum at once. To restrict lawyer speech because a trial was pending in one forum would cripple the debate in the forum of public opinion.

I thought that an argument based on this constitutional history might interest the originalists and textualists on the Court, principally Justices Scalia and Thomas. As it turned out, I was much too optimistic. In the final tally, five Justices held that lawyer speech about a pending case could be restricted or punished if it posed a substantial threat to the fair administration of justice. The Court rejected cases holding that only a clear and present danger standard was proper, saying that those rules applied only to non-lawyers, including clients and the news media. This holding did not do us much harm, for reaffirming the client's right to speak has proven valuable in high-profile cases.

The tone of this part of the majority opinion was quite hostile to Dom and his actions. These Justices had, it seemed, taken this case to clamp down on lawyers, and the opinion reflected that view.

A separate five-Justice majority, led by Justice Kennedy, held that the disciplinary rule under which Dom had been punished was unconstitutionally vague and overbroad, in that it provided no discernible standard for determining what speech was permitted. This opinion contained helpful language about the lawyer's right to speak. Justice Kennedy also noted, but did not have five votes for doing so, that once the Court had decided that Dom's punishment and the rule under which it was imposed were unconstitutional, it had no business reaching out to decide the broader issue.

Even with that split outcome, *Gentile* has put a barrier in the way of those who would draft restrictive rules for lawyer speech, for drafting narrow and precise rules in this area is difficult.

At oral argument, I was soon struck by how much opposition the Court's members had to my position. The historical argument simply was not resonating with Justices Scalia and Souter, and Justice Thomas was quiet as usual. Justice White was positively hostile. In any case involving a constitutional rule, the battle is usually over when you decide who has the burden of proof. That is, if my opponents had the burden of justifying a restriction on speech, in light of history and the decided cases, they would probably lose. On the other hand, if I were compelled to find a case that upheld a clear and present danger standard for lawyer speech, I would lose.

Justice White clearly thought that I had the burden. I resisted these suggestions, and in my rebuttal argument he returned to the attack. "Has this Court ever held . . . " his question began, his voice rising with each word. My daughter Elizabeth, then eight years old, was sitting in the front spectator row and her little voice said, "Why is that man yelling at Daddy?"

It became clear to me that Justices O'Connor and Kennedy were the keys to a majority here. Justice Kennedy has taken a consistently pro-First Amendment position, and I thought it likely he would do so again here. Justice O'Connor was going to be a key vote. She asked whether it was true that every state bar had a rule somewhat like that in Nevada. I said yes. She asked what significance that had. I said that every state bar would need to learn that the First Amendment did not stop short of its door, particularly when the speech was truthful, and on a matter of public concern. I sought by this answer to distinguish the lawyer advertising cases, on which Justice O'Connor has been rather restrictive.

Arguing the *Gentile* case helped me to put my own views about lawyer speech into perspective. I am not a fan of lawyer advertising, because I think it cheapens the profession, but I can't see a constitutional basis for barring it. I was called for jury service in Austin, Texas, some years ago and the lawyer asked if anyone on the panel knew him or his name. One juror said, "I saw your TV ads." The lawyer brightened and said, "What did you think?" The juror replied, "I think that sort of thing makes a piss-poor impression."

I also think that restrictions on lawyer solicitation should be limited by the First Amendment. In the civil rights days, the Supreme Court struck down such restrictions as they applied to the NAACP and to labor organizations. Today, in the wake of a mass disaster like an air crash, insurance company and airline representatives are on the scene talking to victims and their families, to get statements and make settlements. That is the time when those folks need lawyers, and there must be some way to let them know that they have that right.

The major lawyer speech issue remains the one I have faced in almost every case I talk about in this book. What to say to the media and when? I will routinely seek a gag order preventing discovery material from reaching the media. This material is often not admissible in evidence, and it can have a prejudicial impact on prospective jurors. We got such orders in the *Nichols* case, and I successfully argued in the court of appeals that they were valid.

In general, I don't trust the media. Reporters have their own agenda. They may tape or interview for 30 minutes and choose a snippet or two that fits the theme of their story of the day. I also think that jurors do not appreciate lawyers who grandstand for the media. Lawyers who do that hurt themselves, often by creating expectations that the admissible evidence will not fulfill. It has been said of a lawyer I know that the most dangerous place to be is between him and a TV camera. Actually, it has been said of more than one lawyer I know.

That said, media people have been very helpful over the years. Often prospective witnesses will talk to a reporter when they will shut the door on an investigator. Media people have resources to run down leads. Their reportage can help us prepare. Then, there are media forums where the public interest aspect of a case can be discussed in an intelligent way. I learned to trust certain reporters and certain forums. In some cases, the decision to prosecute or appeal may be in the hands of public officials. These officials pay attention to media coverage. There are, in short, no iron-bound rules, only the exercise of judgment.

If I am lead counsel in a case, then I must be in charge of media contacts. I will respect media confidences and expect mine to be respected as well. In most cases when there is a phalanx of reporters on the way to court, I will confine myself to a brief statement on what we expect will happen, and be sure to say something like, "We respect the jurors so much that we think they should be the first to hear the evidence." If I am representing a political figure, the rules may be different. Politicians must explain their conduct to the media, to maintain contact with the electorate. Case law firmly holds that the defendant, particularly one who holds or aspires to public office, has a broad right to speak. However, this right and opportunity can too often be misused. If a case is pending, we can often put the client's position into pleadings filed in court, which the media can then have and from which the client can read.

It is important to keep those media contacts short and controlled. I remember in the early 1990s representing Congressman Ron Dellums. The Reagan Justice Department had leaked a false story that somebody in his office was dealing narcotics. The leak was timed to hit the evening news. I had only a limited chance to confer with Dellums and his staff before the news deadlines, so I was surely not going to spin some story that later events might contradict. I stepped before the cameras and said, "We deny the allegations and we are trying to find the allegators," and then went back inside Dellums's office. After six months of investigation, an official report concluded what we had found within 24 hours—there was no evidence to support such allegations and none was uncovered in a diligent investigation.

Because the media are insatiable, they will keep on hammering at the story. Letting your client make an initial denial before you know the facts is therefore almost always fatal. One of our duties as lawyers is not to believe our clients. We are supposed to have our crap detectors strapped on and working. Letting our public figure clients lead with a story that later proves false can do more harm even than confessing. If President Clinton and his lawyers had followed these precepts, the course of history would have been quite different.

The final media debate concerns televising trials. Some states do it, and the Supreme Court has given the practice its constitutional blessing. The Court has refused, however, to allow the televising of its own proceedings. I oppose television of sensational trials. Even though the camera may be hidden, it has a pervasive influence. Jurors are aware it is there. Witnesses know they are on television, and their celebrity status can influence their testimony. Direct and cross-examination is by nature intimate, a relationship among witness, lawyer, jurors, and judge. When the witness feels that he or she is performing for a larger audience, this intimacy is broken. Then, too, television broadcasts of snippets on the evening news add to the sensationalism of media coverage. A juror can resolve not to look at newspapers, but television sets are so ubiquitous that it is hard to avoid hearing or seeing broadcast trial coverage. We have enough trouble convincing judges not to sequester juries into the hands of obliging pro-prosecution bailiffs without this added distraction.

In sum, when one thinks about the First Amendment and trials, it is important to distinguish between what the Constitution may permit and what it might be wise to do.

Notes

1. The Texas riot case is *Hirschi v. State*, 683 S.W.2d 415 (Tx. Ct. Crim. App. 1984).

2. The labor case is reported as *Aikens v. Abel*, 373 F. Supp. 425 (W.D. Pa. 1974).

3. The affirmance on public figure and reversal on actual malice is *Rebozo v. Washington Post Co.*, 637 F.2d 375 (5th Cir. 1981).

4. Freedom to import political material from abroad was the subject of *Williams v. Blount*, 314 F. Supp. 1356 (D.D.C. 1970).

5. Gentile v. State Bar of Nevada, 501 U.S. 1030 (1991). Our briefs, which are on Westlaw, contain a detailed history of lawyer speech in the United States.

6. On trials and media, see Panel Discussion, *What to Do When Your Case Is Front Page News*, 14 REVIEW OF LITIGATION 595 (1995) (with Dom Gentile, Scott Armstrong, William Colby, Walter Cofer, Judge John Onion, and me).

Chapter 12
DEATH—
AND THAT'S FINAL

Hardly anyone who supports the death penalty does so without reservations of some sort. Few will admit to wanting innocent people executed, and most will argue that the system for trying capital cases should be fair. These thoughts sometimes get in the way of arguments in favor of death. Or so it has seemed to me.

Over the years, I have debated capital punishment, and other issues of criminal justice, with William F. Buckley, Jr. several times. In a 1989 program, he intoned, "A society that takes 10 years to execute Ted Bundy is a society whose legal processes are not working well enough." We could start there.

Bill Buckley is an impassioned, eloquent spokesman for his ideology. He lives just off Park Avenue in a lovely duplex apartment, where one is greeted by sounds of him playing the harpsichord. Before one taping of his program "Firing Line," he invited me to lunch with him. This is an honor, I was made to believe, accorded to few. I arrived at the restaurant a few minutes early to find it shuttered. Apparently, Buckley and I were to be the only lunchtime guests. The Buckley limousine arrived, and he greeted the owner in a flurry of Italian conversation. Inadequate linguist was I.

Seated at the table, Buckley and the owner continued their discussion. At last, in English, the owner asked me what I would like to eat. "I only caught a word or two of that," I said, "but if you indeed have risotto, I would like that. Perhaps risotto con funghi," thus nearly exhausting my knowledge of menu Italian.

A few minutes later, lunch was served. Mine was a lovely-looking rice with mushrooms. Buckley was served a plate of plain white rice. He looked pained, and asked in English why his rice was different from mine. "But, signore," the owner protested, "that is what you ordered."

The battle of egos continued during the taping of *Firing Line*. Buckley was at his most arch, and at one point he interrupted my argument to say, "Oh, Mr. Tigar, now you're being fatuous." I replied, "Well, I thought it was my turn."

Later, Buckley summed up by saying that laws passed by legislatures mandated a death penalty for cold-blooded murder. He continued: "Those laws, in my judgment, are now being frustrated as a result of the cool resources of very bright people who walk into the situation with an ideological predetermination to render the law nugatory."

I argued: "If I'm retained as a lawyer and there's a human life at stake—one of course is gone, that's why there's a murder charge—the question is, shall the state be entitled to take this other life, this life, now deliberately. As a lawyer I've got the obligation to go out and walk the mean streets and find the facts, to check that alibi out, to check the defendant's mental condition, to hire an investigator. How can I do that if I'm in, for instance, a state like Georgia, where I can get only $500 for my fee... and where the pressure of my other business makes it impossible for me to do a decent job?"

Over the years that I have known Bill Buckley, he has often spoken up on behalf of people convicted of murder when he thinks they have been treated unfairly and if there is evidence they were wrongly convicted. On occasion, he has been mistaken in his judgment, but he has shown the courage to speak his mind. One such case was that of Charles Culhane and Garry McGivern, convicted of murdering a deputy sheriff. They were at first convicted and sentenced to death, won a retrial and were again convicted but given long prison terms. I represented them on appeal and in post-conviction proceedings, though without success. Eventually, they were granted parole. They have become spokesmen for prison reform and against the death penalty. Buckley was even a member of a support committee that also included Pete Seeger. I claim to have brokered that deal by getting Bill to agree not to sing progressive folk songs and Pete to agree not to espouse right-wing politics.

This admirable quality of compassion points up the contradiction in Buckley's point of view and in that of others. He began the television program of which I speak by talking about a notorious confessed multiple murderer. Yet I had with me a newspaper clipping recounting that he had asked the archbishop of New Orleans to intercede on behalf of a Louisiana man who had been on death row for nine years. Had the law acted with the celerity for which Buckley seemed to contend, his act of charity would have been impossible, for its object would have been killed.

In that same program, Buckley excoriated New York Governor Hugh Carey for vetoing a capital punishment bill, saying that Carey was wrongly frustrating popular will. Carey said that if the bill passed and anyone were sentenced to death, he would feel duty-bound to commute the sentence. A week later, Buckley wrote: "You were your usual brash brilliant self, but plainly wrong on the Hugh Carey matter. How does it feel to be wrong every now and then?" I wrote back: "Given other experiences with him, I would be pleased to see proof that Hugh Carey did something wrong. Proof that he promised to spare someone from the executioner in the manner provided for by the New York Constitution doesn't quite do it for me." I went on: "I will plead guilty to being brash. I am taking your letter home tonight to show my mother, and she will thank you for 'brilliant.'"

Tucked into this debate are almost all the issues in the death penalty debate as I have observed it. As I said, summing up on the television program, "If we're going to have this penalty, which I acknowledge I oppose and you acknowledge that you favor, I take it that it's common ground between us that the state should never be able to exact it without making sure that the system that led to it is fair and just and decent and right and accurate. . . . "

In the years since we taped that program in 1989, almost nothing has changed in the way capital cases are tried. The Supreme Court has reaffirmed that a defendant must be given expert assistance. It has clarified what the sentencer must be told about the aggravating and mitigating circumstances that may move the sentencer toward or away from death.

A Columbia Law School study found fundamental legal error in two-thirds of the capital cases tried in the United States since capital punishment was upheld by the Supreme Court in 1976 subject only to certain broad limits. Most of those errors involved police officials hiding exculpatory evidence, prosecutors and police denying the accused basic rights in the criminal justice system, and judges who overlooked those errors. Many of these judges, particularly in the Death Belt states of the American South, are elected, in campaigns designed to fire up the vengeful spirit of the majority community. This Columbia study reaffirmed what has been clear for so many years, and is borne out by looking at the racial composition of death rows. Crimes committed against whites by African-Americans are far more likely to be prosecuted as capital than those committed in any other combination of victim and killer. It is easy to see why a system so dominated by racial disparity would tolerate the other errors that the Columbia study found.

As for the right to counsel, the *National Law Journal* did a study of appointed counsel in capital cases in 1990. Given what is at stake, one would expect that only the most qualified lawyers would be found adequate to the task. By now, almost everyone has read the anecdotal evidence that this is not so. The classic story of the Texas appointed lawyer who slept during his client's capital murder trial has made the rounds. The trial and penalty phase lasted just 13 hours, and the lawyer did not even object when the prosecutor said the jurors should sentence the defendant to death because he was gay.

Here is a short summary of what the *National Law Journal* found:

- The trial lawyers who represented death row inmates in the six states were disbarred, suspended, or otherwise disciplined at a rate three to 46 times the discipline rates for lawyers in those states;
- There were wholly unrealistic statutory fee limits on defense representation;
- There were no standards for appointment of counsel; and
- Some capital trials were completed in one to two days, in contrast to two-week or two-month-long trials in some states . . . where indigent defense systems were operating.

In short, the right to effective counsel is ignored in the cases where the stakes are highest. In capital cases, the incidence of constitutional error is higher than in non-capital ones. The idea that a capital case can be well-tried in one or two days is laughable. In the Oklahoma City bombing trial of Terry Nichols, jury selection alone took five weeks to get a panel that was willing to swear it could overcome the media barrage. The trial itself took nearly three months. The defense called more than 100 witnesses. The jury acquitted Nichols of murder, finding him guilty of lesser charges, and voted not to impose a death penalty. This result was achieved only because defense counsel had the dedication and resources to combat the government.

My first capital case was that of Angela Davis. Within months after she was arraigned, however, the California Supreme Court struck down California's death penalty law. I recall, however, how the prospect of death hung over the courtroom. I had argued a motion to dismiss the charges for want of evidence, pointing also to the state's deliberate refusal to present exculpatory matter to the indicting grand jury. The case was being run by Albert Harris, a special prosecutor named by Governor Ronald Reagan. Although our hearing was devoted only to legal motions, he made a grandstand play by wheeling in a shopping cart laden with guns connected to the crime, but not necessarily to Angela Davis. Since neither side could present evidence at this hearing, the shopping cart was simply a prop.

I thought that if posturing were the order of the day, the court should be reminded that this prosecution, on this evidence, had a political motive. So I began my argument: "May it please the court. I am going to show that with Albert Harris as the engineer, the Marin County grand jury is America's only working railroad." I then went over the evidence and law in detail and at length.

Harris made his argument, and as he finished he walked across the small courtroom to stand in front of Angela. He concluded, "In short, Your Honor, not only is there enough evidence to send this case to trial, there is enough to take this young woman and lock her in a green gas chamber and drop cyanide pellets into the acid and put her to death."

At the time, I thought this was conscious rhetorical excess. Now I am not sure. I remember the last morning of the Terry Nichols trial. Terry was charged with conspiracy, arson, use of a weapon of mass destruction, and eight counts of murder of federal agents. The jury acquitted him of arson, use of a weapon of mass destruction, first-degree murder, and second-degree murder. It convicted him of conspiracy and involuntary manslaughter. The judge held that he was eligible for a death sentence on the conspiracy count, so we had a penalty trial.

After days of deliberation, the jurors announced that they were deadlocked on the threshold question of Terry's intent toward resulting death. We read the federal death penalty statute as requiring jury unanimity for every phase of a penalty trial. In the ordinary criminal case, if the jury fails to agree, there is a mistrial and the defendant may be retried. However, we argued that this federal law provided that if the jury were not unanimous, then there could not be a death sentence. Put another way, every juror had to sign the verdict sheet for death, if such a sentence were to be imposed.

The government saw it differently. It argued that a jury deadlock meant that we would impanel another jury and the government could once again seek a death verdict. The lead prosecutor moved for a mistrial. The judge said he had not decided how to read the statute. This presented us with a classic dilemma, made more painful by the fact that Terry's life was at stake. We thought the jury would never agree to a death penalty, but we could not be sure. If we were wrong, the stakes were too high. So we joined the motion for mistrial, but expressly requested that the judge decide here and now that the jury had rejected death.

That was in the late afternoon. The next morning Judge Matsch called counsel to the bench. He said he had thought about the issue overnight and "I am going to take this verdict." He was calling a halt, ruling that the non-unanimity was a vote for life. The Supreme Court later held unanimously that this is the proper reading of the statute. Two of the prosecutors, as they heard this ruling, embraced each other and wept. They were weeping because they had not been able to get a death sentence. They had bought into the ideology of what they were doing.

I do not necessarily fault them for that. I simply observe that for many prosecutors, seeking a death penalty is not the performance of an unpleasant duty but part of a righteous crusade. I think it dangerous to wield the power of the state with such fervency, for one is more easily led into the serious errors that scholars and lawyers and judges have found in capital cases. Prosecutors and defense counsel play different roles in our system. A prosecutor is not simply an advocate; he or she represents a sovereign that has a duty to administer justice impartially. As the Ninth Circuit has said, "A prosecutor has a special duty commensurate with a prosecutor's special power, to assure that defendants receive fair trials."

The Supreme Court has held that the death penalty must be reserved for homicide cases where the defendant intended to cause death or acted so recklessly with respect to resulting death as to manifest depraved indifference to human life. Even in such cases, however, a death sentence can never be automatically imposed. If a defendant is convicted, there must be a separate trial on punishment, to a jury in most jurisdictions or to a judge. At that trial, the sentencer must make a "reasoned moral response" to evidence about the offense and the offender.

For this response to be reasoned, the offender must have the right to present mitigating evidence and to have the sentencer pay attention to it, by jury instructions or other guidance. This set of procedures is designed, so the Supreme Court has held, to narrow and rationalize the capital sentencing decision. That expressed hope proves illusory.

The Supreme Court has stepped away from trying to regulate prosecutorial discretion to seek the death penalty, with the result that racial bias is rampant. Then, there are the cases mentioned above, fraught with legal errors including inadequate counsel. The right to present evidence and make arguments is illusory unless a lawyer is prepared and willing to do that.

At a more fundamental level, the crimes for which the death penalty is sought disturb the community. They tend to be the more sensational and scary murders. When such a disturbing event happens, political leaders want to reassure people that everything is all right. As I said in Chapter 1, there is great pressure on police and prosecutors to announce that the case is solved and the suspect in custody. In such a rush to judgment, exculpatory evidence may be overlooked. Police and prosecutors may fail to perform scientific tests that would exclude the defendant from suspicion.

Certainly this was the pattern in the Nichols case. Once the FBI had decided that Terry Nichols helped Timothy McVeigh plan and carry out the Oklahoma City bombing, senior officers sent memos shutting down all other avenues of investigation. More than 1,000 latent fingerprints suitable for comparison were cast aside unchecked. The FBI ignored evidence about McVeigh's activities and associates and directed all its field offices to stop looking. When Ron Woods and I were appointed, our first task was to assemble a team of investigators to try and follow those leads, and to seek information from the government that would permit us to do so.

We were lucky in one sense. The federal death penalty statute provides a modest but adequate hourly fee for counsel, and funds for investigators, experts, and paralegals. That statute also provides a death penalty for dozens of crimes. It shuts off federal court review of state capital sentences, in the very circumstances where such review can be so important. As such, there is much in it that is a monstrous step backwards. To top it off, the statute was called the Anti-Terrorism and Effective Death Penalty Act.

The term "effective death penalty" makes me wonder. I had thought the death penalty was effective, in that nobody executed had come back to life. But that is probably not what is meant.

When Chief Judge Russell of the Oklahoma federal court called me in 1995 to tell me he was going to appoint me counsel for Terry Nichols, there was a sense in which I welcomed the appointment. I am opposed to the death penalty. I know that polls show most voters are for it. And yet, I have thought that in a well-tried capital case jurors might turn toward life when they saw the human side of capital punishment up close. And if we can begin convincing jurors to vote for life, maybe we can influence prosecutors not to seek death. At least, I thought, this would be so in a publicized case.

In talking to jurors about death, I think we should remember that almost every religion practiced in the United States preaches forgiveness of sin and redemption. People don't always follow those beliefs, but they are there. We really do value all human life, if we think about it. If a friend of yours called up and said he was going to commit suicide because of something he had done, you would probably try to talk him out of it.

Judge Russell had several versions of why he chose me, all of which could be true. Experienced trial lawyers in Oklahoma had all demurred, saying they knew victims or relatives of victims and could not stand the community pressure or felt a conflict of interest. Judge Pat Higginbotham of the Fifth Circuit had recommended me. There is a list of potential appointed counsel, kept in a defender services office in Washington.

Judge Russell's most colorful story of the appointment recalled his visit to the Smithsonian Institution in Washington, where he saw a videotape of my closing argument in a mock death penalty case. Every summer, the Smithsonian holds a folk-life festival on the Washington Mall. In 1986 the American Trial Lawyers' Association set up an outdoor courtroom and held a program on lawyers as storytellers. They invited 32 lawyers and judges from around the country to hold forth, a few at a time. We told stories, did mock direct and cross-examinations, and summed up to juries composed of spectators. We got good crowds and good media coverage, letting folks know what trial lawyers do. Later, Jud Best got the ABA Litigation Section to replicate this sort of thing at state fairs.

I was assigned to give a penalty summation in a mock murder case, where the mentally retarded defendant had beaten an elderly woman to death. The defense had plenty of evidence of child abuse growing up and other mitigating matter. Judge Russell said he remembered my concluding words and was motivated to appoint me to the Nichols case. I had finished up saying:

> Members of the jury, I am about done now. I will go home tonight and my daughter will ask me, 'Daddy, what did you do today?' I will say, "I tried to spare the life of one of God's creatures." And members of the jury, what will you say when you go home?

This was, as I say, 1985. At the University of Texas Law School, I had begun to work with Rob McGlasson, a talented capital case lawyer. Congress had provided for death penalty resource centers, and Rob was setting one up in Austin. I became chair of the center's board of directors from then until Congress abolished the centers several years later. In that job, I helped a dedicated team of mostly-young lawyers advise capital case trial lawyers and litigate federal habeas corpus petitions for death row inmates. Along with the ABA, the center recruited private lawyers to help with the tide of litigation.

From the beginning, the center drew hostility from politicians who wanted the death penalty carried out more surely and swiftly and from judges who, for one reason or another, resented the effort the center made in every one of its cases. Some judges spared no chance to criticize center and volunteer lawyers, sometimes in published opinions. When a lawyer for a large corporation, with lots of money at stake, takes every procedural step to protect his or her client's interest, that is called aggressive lawyering and is praised. When these lawyers invoked every procedure to forestall executions, they were blamed.

The Supreme Court and the court of appeals had made clear that if a capital defendant did not raise a given argument at the earliest possible moment, the argument might well be waived. Knowing this, I often spoke to groups of lawyers and said that capital case representation in the court of appeals was different from other cases. In the ordinary case, one must choose among arguments, rejecting weaker ones to focus on the main chance. But in a capital case, who would want the responsibility for jettisoning an argument that might turn out in later case law to be victorious? Therefore, I said, put all your arguments in. After one such talk, a court of appeals judge stopped me in the hall and said, "Goddamn it, Mike, why do you tell these lawyers to gum up the works with all of these arguments?" I said I thought their doing so was the fault of a system that penalized their clients if they did not do so.

At every Fifth Circuit judicial conference, the attorneys general of Texas, Louisiana, and Mississippi would circulate written attacks on the resource centers and their work. I would meet with supportive judges and try to organize responses. To this day, our opponents on the bench remember my advocacy for the resource centers, and there is a decided chill when we meet or when I appear for argument and they are on the panel.

Even our supporters at times expressed anger at the youthful enthusiasm of some center lawyers. One lawyer had made a media statement after an adverse ruling from a district judge, doubting that the judge had paid attention. I confess I have picked public fights with judges, but have tried to do so only when there seemed to be some point to it. This sort of remark did not seem to serve any purpose, but the lawyer surely had a right to make it.

I got a call from a court of appeals judge. "Come to my office," he said. I did. He showed me the offending newspaper article. I began to say, "Well, of course, this lawyer had a First Amendment right. . . . " That was as far as I got. The judge thumped his desk. "I am not talking about the First Amendment! I am talking about what people are supposed to say!"

The center helped make some good law, and lost its share of cases. I lost three that I can remember. A young mentally retarded man named Marquez had been on trial for murder. Every day, the deputies led him past a phalanx of TV cameras and lights on the way to and from court. Resenting a remark one TV reporter made, he spat. The judge responded by ruling that this gesture meant young Marquez was dangerous, and ordered him shackled in the jury's presence during the penalty phase of his trial. The jury sentenced him to death. The court of appeals rejected arguments based on mental retardation and the evident prejudice of being shackled by court order when the jury is deliberating whether you are "dangerous." It did so not on the merits, but because trial counsel had not made an adequate record.

I twice argued in the Supreme Court on the issue of whether youthful age is so clearly a mitigating factor that jurors must be instructed to consider it. Most states provide for such an instruction, but Texas does not. I lost both cases 5 to 4. In the first one, *Graham v. Collins*, the majority held that the issue had not been raised by trial counsel and therefore could not be raised on appeal. The next term, in *Johnson v. Texas*, the Court had the issue squarely presented and rejected my argument 5 to 4. I thought Justice Kennedy's opinion failed to keep the promise of what he had earlier written, about the need to guide the jury's decision. After all, as even Justice Scalia has said, jurors have life experience that permits them to evaluate evidence. They have no life experience with legal concepts, including concepts about what they are to do with the facts as they find them to be.

At oral argument, I knew which Justices would not vote for me. I said at one point that youthful age has been a mitigating factor since antiquity. "What in antiquity?" Justice Scalia interjected. I noted a Roman law principle from several centuries before the Christian era. Justice Scalia asked a question about this principle, more to see if I knew what I was talking about than from any interest in the issue. Justice Scalia, after writing at least one solid opinion on the importance of mitigating evidence, came to reject the entire Supreme Court doctrine of special procedures for capital cases. He did not, in this instance, care what history might teach us, even though in other cases he has been assiduous to discover rules for today in the experience of the distant past.

Justice White was also plainly hostile. He had written an opinion reversing the death sentence in *Morgan v. Illinois*, holding that a juror must be willing to listen to mitigating evidence and give it effect to sit on a capital case. I thought that *Morgan* said something important about the principle we were asserting. So I cited *Morgan v. Illinois*. Justice White said, "Flattery gets you nowhere." I replied that I was taken aback. Justice White said that was his intention.

At that point Justice Stevens, seated to White's right, chimed in, "Mr. Tigar, I know that some of us would like to hear how Justice White's opinion supports your position, so why don't you tell us?"

I was traveling in England when I heard news that I had lost *Johnson*. I wept in my anger and frustration, as much for myself as for the young African-American whose life I had not been able to save. I could not think of a way to protest, except to stop eating the flesh of dead animals, so I did that for several years.

I had, as these stories show, been deeply involved in death penalty work for several years when the call came about the Nichols case. I can remember, when we finally came to trial in September 1997, wondering if I was right about the potential of jury justice in a publicized case. Our defense was simply that Terry Nichols had not played any culpable role in the bombing. At one point, we were told, the jurors were 10 to 2 for outright acquittal and their split verdict was surely a compromise. But we spared his life.

In terms of making our arguments, we had begun by deciding that we would try our case to the jury and not in the media. As trial approached, Judge Matsch decided that the clerk of court would draw 1,000 names for potential jury service. The jurors would go in groups of 500 to the Colorado fairgrounds on the outskirts of Denver, to fill out questionnaires on their qualifications, attitudes, and media exposure. Both sides had submitted draft questionnaires and the judge had crafted one from parts of both submissions.

I took the view that these mass gatherings were part of jury selection, and that Terry therefore had a right to be there. The law provides that he could not be shackled or in prison dress. So the jurors saw him seated a few feet from the judge, with Ron Woods and me, wearing a sport jacket, slacks, and an open-neck shirt with a turtleneck under it.

At trial, Ron and I flanked Terry at counsel table. We had individual voir dire, and it went on for nearly five weeks. Every time Judge Matsch displayed impatience, we would be able to convince him to go on, by finding some important bit of information about jurors from just a few more questions.

The prosecutors, of course, wanted the jurors to identify with the victims and adopt the victims' calls for vengeance. This is the myth of solidarity, making the jurors feel a part of something just and right. This is the most dangerous and yet I think the most powerful appeal to jurors. Bertolt Brecht wrote a poem, *All of Us or None*. But he did not mean everybody or nobody. He meant "all of us oppressed anti-fascists" must stand against "them," or else none of "us" would be left standing.

In death penalty cases, prosecutors invoke this myth regularly and with dramatic results. Think of what a capital case juror is being asked to do. One will not sign a piece of paper that requires the state to take a human, strap him to a gurney, and put poison in his veins until he is dead unless one is convinced that this particular human has somehow become the "other," the not-human. And so prosecutors use, with the Supreme Court's blessing, words like dog and cur and animal because they understand solidarity. The more polite defenders of the death penalty, like some Supreme Court Justices, say the same thing by opining that there is a social contract, the breach of which will place you outside—very, very far outside—the rest of humanity.

The myth of solidarity, as a tool of influence, can be good or malignant in its effects. We can see the excesses committed in its name—in Kosovo, Ireland, Palestine, and in our major cities. Solidarity can short-circuit reason, for as Shimon Peres said of a political adversary, "We would all prefer to remember than to think."

There is, however, a countervailing myth to use when solidarity is invoked as a means of stirring passions for vengeance. That counterweight might be called an aspect of equality, but is better seen as transcendence. We want the jurors to think beyond the result in a particular case, to think about what principles of judgment ought to guide not just this result but all of human society. We try to help them understand that both they and the defendant are now living in this human society, along with all potential accusers and all potential defendants. Transcendence is abstraction taken to a plane of socially determined myth.

In the penalty phase of the Nichols case, I struggled with this idea of transcendence, in the wake of more than 50 witnesses who described their ordeals in emotional and graphic terms. Here is what I said:

> I feel now, when I think about that evidence, as though I'm standing before you and trying to sweep back a tide of anger and grief and

vengeance. And I'm given pause by the fact that I feel that way, and I wonder if sometimes you might feel that way. But when I think that, then I think also of the instructions that the judge is going to give you, because those instructions, as we contemplate this tide of anger and grief and vengeance, can get us all to higher ground, because the instructions will tell you that neither anger nor grief nor vengeance can ever be a part of a decision reached in a case of this kind.

I am, when I say this, not attacking these victims. We know their sacrifice. But we know that with the centuries of our civilization piled so high that we have come a very long way from justice based on vengeance and blood feuds.

This trial was moved from Oklahoma City because, I submit to you, it was thought that even the neighbors of those who lost so much would not do to sit in judgment. And to them, therefore, we can only say when we hear their grief and their anger and their desire for vengeance, "Bless those in need of healing."

But when I talk about this process, I want to say that I believe something else. And I don't want to say it in an effort to reach into a place that I'm not entitled to be but to share with you some thoughts about a concept of justice, to share with you some thoughts that suggest that if you come to this point, you would turn your face toward the future and not toward the past.

Later in the summation, after talking about the evidence and the judge's instructions, I said:

But, of course, even then, an eye for an eye, conscience of the community? Well, the words do appear, I know, in the Old Testament. They appear at a time when God is instructing the people of Israel about a system of blood feud and vengeance. But later on even at that time, when a court was convened to decide who should live and who should die, called a Sanhedrin, it was decided that a judgment of death could only be pronounced in the temple. And so the Sanhedrin stopped meeting in the temple.

And why? Because in the earliest stages of the development of our cultural tradition, it was recognized that when the law in its solemn majesty directs that life be taken, that can be crueler than deliberate vengeance because it teaches, because it is a voice that comes from a place that is at war with a reasoned and compassionate system of social organization.

I suggest to you that the government wants to drag you back to a time of vengeance. I suggest to you that the FBI agent who said to Lana Padilla on the 21st of April, 1995, before a jot of evidence was in his hand, "Those two guys are going to fry," symbolized a rush to judgment that is at war with what the conscience of the community ought to do and ought to think about. I submit to you that to surrender your deliberations to vengeance is to turn your back on lessons that we have all learned with great difficulty and a great deal of pain.

Nobody knows the depths of human suffering more than those who have been systematic victims of terror; and yet in country after country, judicial systems are saying that in each case, the individual decision must triumph over our sense of anger. . . .

Well, I've gone through the form and I've gone through the instructions. And if I've said anything that makes you think that I'm trying to tell you what you've already decided or what you ought to think in terms of your deepest convictions, please disregard it. . . .

When I concluded my earlier summation, I walked over to Terry Nichols and said, "This is my brother." And the prosecutor got up and reminded all of us, thinking that he would remind me, that there were brothers and sisters and mothers and fathers all killed in Oklahoma City. Of course, when I said, "This is my brother," I wasn't denying the reality of that. I hope I was saying something else. I was talking about a tradition that goes back thousands of years, talking about a particular incident, as a matter of fact. You may remember—most of us learned it I think when we were young—the story of Joseph's older brothers, Joseph of the many-colored coat, now the *Technicolor Dream Coat* in the MTV version. And they were jealous of him, cast him into a pit thinking he would die, and then sold him into slavery. And years later, Joseph turns out to be a judicial officer of the pharaoh, and it happens that he is in a position to judge his brothers. And his brother Judah is pleading for the life or for the liberty of the younger brother, Benjamin, and Joseph sends all the other people out of the room and announces, "I am Joseph, your brother." That was the story, that was the idea that I was trying to get across, that in that moment, in that moment of judgment, addressing the very human being, his older brother Judah, who had put his life at risk and then sold him into slavery, he reached out, because even in that moment of judgment he could understand that this is a human process and that what we all share looks to the future and not to the past.

Members of the jury, we ask you, we suggest to you, that under the law, your judgment should be that this case go back to Judge Matsch and that he reach the just and appropriate sentence under the law and under the verdict that you've already reached.

I won't have a chance to respond to what the prosecutor says, but I know that after your 41 hours of deliberations on the earlier phase, you're all very, very accustomed to thinking of everything that could be thought.

My brother is in your hands.

I have turned that summation over and over in my mind, wondering what was in it that I might say at some other trial. In the summer of 2001, a New York federal jury refused to give a death sentence to two men convicted in the Kenya embassy bombing that took more than 200 lives. In one of those cases, a defendant named Mohamed had been arrested in South Africa on his arrival there from Tanzania. A South African immigration officer and an FBI agent cooked up a story that Mohamed had demanded to be sent to the United States to stand trial on the bombing charges. He was quoted as saying that he wished to be with his comrades even if that meant facing a death sentence.

The South African authorities obligingly put him into the FBI's hands and deported him. Had he demanded formal extradition, South Africa would have imposed a condition that no death penalty be sought. Such a condition is mandated by South Africa's constitution. The same condition was imposed on another defendant extradited from Germany in the same case.

David Ruhnke, Mohamed's lawyer and a superb advocate, helped start proceedings in South Africa for a declaration that Mohamed's removal was unlawful. Given Supreme Court authority, a favorable decision would not bar the United States courts from trying him. Our courts, with some cogent dissents, still hew to the now-discredited view that it does not matter how the prisoner is brought to the forum, even if doing so violates international law.

However, Ruhnke argued that a declaration that Mohamed should not as matter of South African law face the death penalty would be a mitigating factor on which the judge might instruct the sentencing jury. Mohamed's lawyers lost in the South African trial court and lodged an appeal with the constitutional court. As it happened, my wife Jane and I were in South Africa the week the case was to be argued. We had been scheduled to have lunch with Justice Goldstone in his chambers.

Justice Goldstone asked me to read Ruhnke's affidavit and the rest of the appeal record, and to help his clerks research whether a South African decision would make a difference in the American courts, or whether the case was mooted by Mohamed having been deported. I did as he asked.

In late May 2001, the constitutional court decided the case. It recognized that South Africa would have attached a condition to any formal extradition. It held that when a country sends someone from its borders—by deportation, extradition, or whatever—into the hands of another country, the sending state bears a responsibility to ensure that the person will not be subjected to invasion of his or her rights in the receiving state.

I e-mailed the decision to Ruhnke as soon as it arrived. He convinced Judge Sand to instruct the jury that as a matter of South African law Mohamed would not face a death penalty, and that the jurors must consider this as a mitigating factor. The jury deadlocked, resulting in a life sentence. This was not such a stretch of mitigation law. The statute and the constitution give the defense wide latitude. In *Nichols*, we asked Judge Matsch to tell the jury that it is a mitigating factor that "Terry Lynn Nichols is a human being." The government argued that we were trying to smuggle anti-capital punishment sentiment into the case. Judge Matsch gave the instruction.

Publicity about innocent people on death row, the circus around the execution of Tim McVeigh, and other events have begun to cast a shadow on the death penalty. United States foreign service officers filed a brief in one case noting that our use of the death penalty embarrasses the United States in the eyes of other countries. There is some reason to think that the utility and fairness of this penalty are being rethought, and that all the publicity about excesses and abuses has something to do with that. As Shelley wrote in his own time: "The cloud of mind is discharging its collective lightning, and the equilibrium between institutions and opinions is now restoring, or about to be restored."

Notes

1. My essay on defending Terry Nichols is at 74 Tex. L. Rev. 101 (1995), and is reprinted in Persuasion.

2. The book containing my mock death penalty summation is Sam Shrager, The Trial Lawyer's Art (1999).

3. The Supreme Court cases I argued are *Johnson v. Texas*, 509 U.S. 350 (1993*); Graham v. Collins*, 506 U.S. 461 (1993).

4. The *Marquez* case, concerning the shackled defendant, is *Marquez v. Collins*, 11 F.3d 1241 (5th Cir., 1994) (No. 92-5642).

5. Material from the *Nichols* summation is available online, including in a Westlaw database, OKLA-TRANS. See also *The Power of Myth: Justice, Signs & Symbols in Criminal Trials*, LITIGATION 25, Fall 1999.

6. The South African constitutional court judgment is *Mohamed v. President of South Africa*, CCT 17/01 (May 28, 2001).

7. The Ninth Circuit quotation is from *United States v. LaPage*, 231 F.3d 488, 492 (9th Cir. 2000).

Chapter 13
POLITICS NOT AS USUAL

Thinking about most of the cases and issues in this book, you may wonder how a lawyer can make a living with so heavy a pro bono docket. There are several answers to this question. Once I was representing a corporate executive during a grand jury investigation. He said, "I heard that you represented Angela Davis." I said yes, I had. "Well, how is it that you can represent me and her, given that politically we have nothing in common?" I asked him what his biggest problem was at the moment. He said, "This prosecutor seems hell-bent on messing up my life."

"That's interesting," I said. "That was Angela's problem too."

He then said, "Yeah, but did you charge her what you are charging me?" I thought this uncharitable of him, because his legal fees were being advanced by the corporation as permitted by Delaware law. But I answered, "I represented her without a fee."

"How does that work?" he asked.

"She was an underdog. I represent a lot of underdogs. I make it up by charging market rates to the overdogs. That's you." He seemed happy to be an overdog.

In the same vein, a congressman under indictment sat in my office with his longtime friend, a very conservative lawyer. Indeed, this lawyer had been a prosecutor of whom Ed Williams had said, "He gets up every morning and pisses on the Bill of Rights."

The lawyer said to the congressman: "OK, you don't have to worry. I'll protect your right wing and Tigar here will protect your left wing."

"Wings, hell," the congressman said, "it's my ass I want protected."

291

The lesson there is that you can represent controversial clients and still get straight business. The smart clients, and the firms that refer litigation, want a certain kind of representation and they respect those who battle for underdogs. There are exceptions. Two days after the media reported that I had been appointed to represent Terry Nichols, a major corporation for whom I had been litigating fired me.

When Sam Buffone and I started our law firm in January 1978, we made sure that one-third of our billable hours were pro bono. We still made a good living. That brings up the next point. If you wish to get rich beyond your dreams, then sell cocaine or become an investment banker. Of course, if you make that career choice, you stand some chance of going to Club Fed, as the minimum security federal prison is sometimes called. By the same token, I am saddened to see our very best law graduates opting for large law firms where they will be required to bill inhuman hours and will have neither meaningful pro bono work nor great responsibility for litigation. That sort of environment provably leads to burnout and alienation, or puts you on a ladder that you need to keep on climbing to support the lifestyle you achieve.

I find it hard to sympathize with the young lawyer, let's call him Bob Cratchit, told by the partner to stay in on Christmas Day to draft 100 more interrogatories, if young Cratchit is making six figures and signed up for this with his eyes open. I am not condemning Cratchit's choice, only saying that there are other choices out there.

Smaller litigation firms still get good business and do a good job, often better than the leviathans. When a major client asks me to head up a litigation project, I like to keep the team as small as possible. When I think of the behemoth law firms and their approach to litigation, I am reminded of a story. A Texan got off the airplane at Shannon Airport in Ireland and rented a car. He drove into the countryside and stopped to talk to a farmer who was standing near the roadway. "Tell me," the Texan asked, "how big a spread do you have here."

"Well," said the farmer, "it goes along this stone wall to that hedgerow, and then up to the top of that rise where the sheep are standing, then along over to that line of trees."

"Is that all?" said the Texan. "Back where I live, I get in my car in the morning, and I drive and I drive and I drive, and by sundown I still haven't got to the edge of my ranch."

"Oh," said the farmer, "I had a car like that once."

In sum, it is possible to do well enough and to do enough good. It is possible to practice law, or at least the kind I like to do, in a setting that satisfies. Indeed, over the years I have managed to blend practice and teaching in this sort of way. Candidly, it is harder to find a job that includes a heavy dose of public service than it used to be. The cuts in legal services funding have seen to that, as have law firms' reluctance to take on pro bono work. On that latter point, I used my position as ABA Litigation Section chairman to lobby firms along these lines: Doing pro bono helps your bottom line. It tunes up your associates by giving them challenging work. It gives you good publicity.

All of this fails, however, to answer the question, "what kinds of cases ought one to take and what kinds should one shun?" I have made many mistakes along these lines, but have tried to develop a working answer to this question. My answer will not be right for every one. That is as it should be. The personal decision to take or decline a case resides with the lawyer.

For the representation to work, the lawyer and client have to connect at some point. You must find the client's story compelling at some level of abstraction. As I once wrote, in litigation as in love, technical proficiency without passion is not wholly satisfying. Law practice should be fun, in whatever forms you do it. "How is it to be a federal judge," I asked my friend Bill Wilson. "It's like getting paid to eat ice cream," he said.

You can think of this from the standpoint of the jurors (or judge) who will try your client's case. If you are suing for $100,000, the jurors don't think of their decision as a zero-sum matter in which $100,000 is subtracted from one side's assets and placed with the other. They believe that they are adding to the net store of justice in the world, and they should be helped by the lawyer to see it that way. So you have to ask at the first moment, where is the justice in this case? If you can't answer that, maybe some other lawyer can, and that case should go to that lawyer and not to you. When Ed Williams joked that the ideal client was "rich as Croesus and scared as hell," he captured the image obliquely. Whatever has scared that client must be seen as a kind of actual or prospective injustice.

In law practice, as in the rest of life, we may not be presented all at once with a cosmic decision as was Faust, or Jabez Stone in the American version, where the devil offers us a bargain for our soul.

The image of the devil fighting for the soul pervades our literature. Images from Steven Vincent Benet's *The Devil and Daniel Webster*, or the cadences of Milton's *Paradise Lost*, enliven our speech and our perceptions. The devil, we say, is in the details, or in the bottle in front of us. For, as we know:

[M]alt does more than Milton can
To justify God's ways to man

In lawyer circles, there is the story of the young law student standing in front of the career services bulletin board and shaking his head. An older gentleman appears beside him. "Why the frown?" the older man inquires.

"There are no jobs in public service," the young man laments. "To make money and pay off your law school debt, you have to sell your soul."

"And what," asks the old man, "is wrong with that?"

"Well, for one thing you go to hell when you die."

"That's not so bad."

"Oh, come on!"

"No, really. I'm the devil, and I know."

"Oh, sure! The devil."

"You don't believe me. Come with me for awhile. I'll have you back before your next class."

And with that, the young man was spirited away to a sort of paradise. Soft breezes blew. There were refreshing drinks and good things to eat. Beautiful young men and women swam in the lagoon. The young man spent several days there, and then by some magic was back where he had been standing—and hardly any time had passed.

So he sold his soul. He became successful and wealthy. Unlike some who followed in the same path, the United States attorney never bothered him, and he certainly did not go to Club Fed.

As it must to all mortals, death came to him. And he went to hell. It was a fiery furnace. The noise and stench were unbearable. The cries and groans of eternal anguish rattled around inside his head.

After a few days of this, by his reckoning of time, he demanded to see the devil. There was a wait, but his wish was granted. There in an air-conditioned office sat the older gentleman who had recruited him.

"Look," the fellow said. "When you and I made the deal, I came down here. It was beautiful, peaceful—nothing like what's out there."

"Ah, yes," said the old gentleman, "you must have been in our summer associate program."

No, I don't worry too much about that kind of bargain, though it has in various forms been the subject of popular literature, including the movies. As a lawyer, I may make metaphorical use of the Faustian legend, as I defend the life or liberty of someone committed to my care.

But in my life, my own piecemeal bargains, the legend lives as well. I say to myself, fearful of my own failures to heed my fellow creatures' calls for justice: What if I wanted some day to sell my soul to Mephisto? I might see him at a distance, that old gentleman. Quickening my step, I catch him by the shoulder and he turns to look me in the face.

"Mephisto, old man. Remember me? I am ready to sell you my soul."

And he looks at me, finally recognizing who I am. "Your soul?" he says with that smile of his. "I already have it."

Wishing therefore to find cases that enrich in all the right ways, including the way that pays the rent, I have been led down some wond'rous paths.

In 1973, I took a break from writing *Law and the Rise of Capitalism* and came to California to represent Michael Randall, who had been charged in state court with a batch of felonies for possession and distribution of marijuana and other drugs. He was said to be a leader of the Brotherhood of Eternal Love, a group of hippie dope-smokers who more or less followed the teachings of Dr. Timothy Leary. Indeed, Leary had dwelt among the brotherhood until his arrest and imprisonment on California state marijuana charges.

By early 1973, however, Leary had escaped from his California prison and was rumored to be in Algeria, or Gstaad, or somewhere. I packed up and moved into a rented house in Laguna Beach, California, and drafted a batch of motions to suppress the evidence against Randall and his co-defendants.

The state's investigation of the brotherhood had been sloppy. The police had seldom bothered to get warrants, and the probable cause was thin for their warrantless searches. Why should I get involved in all of this? I never tuned in to the dope culture. I thought drop out was a copout. The social problems of racism, poverty, and war were not going to be solved by living up the canyon and tending marijuana gardens. These folks even lacked the sort of coherent world view that characterized intentional communities like the Quakers, Shakers, and utopian socialists.

But defending the Fourth Amendment against police misconduct seemed a good fight, and ultraconservative Orange County seemed the right place to do it. At that time, California law conferred standing to challenge an illegal seizure upon any defendant against whom the evidence was to be used, even if the search was of somebody else's person, car, or house. The federal law limited standing to the actual victim of the

illegal search, and the Supreme Court had expressly rejected the California rule. The liberal standing rules in California state court meant that I
could file more than 100 motions to suppress evidence for Randall, based
on almost every conceivable Fourth Amendment issue.

We were lucky. Our trial judge was Raymond Vincent, who thought
it was his job to enforce the Constitution, even on behalf of unpopular
defendants. We were winning about two-thirds of the motions to suppress. I was working with my friend Michael Kennedy. While we were
litigating these motions, Timothy Leary was arrested in Kabul, Afghanistan, and brought back to jail in Orange County. He would face federal
passport charges, in addition to charges in Orange County for his alleged
role in the brotherhood and, of course, for his escape from prison. I had
met Leary only once, back in 1966 when he came by radio station KPFK
in Los Angeles for an interview with another staff member. Michael
Kennedy had represented him in the California courts. Leary, through
another lawyer, asked that Michael and I come to see him.

This was a lawyer-client conversation, but Leary's later behavior has
blown the privilege, so I can tell the story. Leary looked gaunt, but his
blue eyes sparkled. He began to talk. He had been in Switzerland, and
some member of the Afghan royal family had urged him to visit Afghanistan where the narcotics were plentiful. Before Leary could get there,
the old royal family had been displaced. He was met at the airport by
American drug enforcement agents and escorted back to the United States.

Simply put, Leary wanted Michael and me to represent him in the
Orange County case. I was, bluntly, a little leery of Leary, but said that
we already had a client, Michael Randall, and could not do that. Leary
tightened his lips. His expression became slightly demented. He looked
at Kennedy and said, "Michael, if you don't represent me, I can make
things very tough for you." Michael shrugged and we left.

A couple of years later, Leary struck a bargain with the federal and state
authorities and offered to give testimony against his former wife Rose-
mary, his former lawyers, and others. For a time, the Justice Department
tried to sell those cases to local U.S. attorneys in various parts of the
country. Nobody was buying. I represented one of the targets of Leary's
proposed testimony.

"You know," the Justice Department lawyer said, "Leary has waived
his attorney-client privilege, so we can subpoena all his former lawyers if
we want to."

"Where did he send in the waiver from," I asked, "Pluto?"

One of the proposed cases landed on the desk of the William Browning, U.S. attorney for the Northern District of California. Browning was a Republican appointee, a civil trial lawyer from the peninsula. He had prosecuted Patty Hearst and had bested F. Lee Bailey.

I sat in his office with the Justice Department lawyer. "You know," I said, "this DOJ lawyer has never tried a major case in his life. I want to talk to you about his idea that you should use Leary as a witness. Leary has written a book admitting that he has told 17 different stories of his prison escape. So if your direct examination takes two hours, I have 34 hours of cross. In one of his stories, he said that he was having LSD flashbacks and that he thought he was a Buick and that every other prisoner was a Chevrolet, and he just had to get away. Leary is so far out that his testimony would really be a story from the center of Uranus."

Browning smiled, but did not commit. Two weeks later, he sent word that the grand jury had refused to indict based on Leary's story. Rumor was that Browning had frankly told the grand jurors the problems with these cases. I respected Browning for his actions. Unlike so many prosecutors, he saw the weakness of the bargained-for testimony and evaluated the case without yielding to the political pressure to charge somebody.

I have a picture on my wall, drawn by a courtroom artist, of the John Connally defense table. Ed Williams sits next to Connally, who sits next to me. Connally had been Treasury Secretary in the Nixon administration. He was a Democrat, and had been governor of Texas. Most people recognized him because he was riding in the car with President Kennedy on the day Kennedy was assassinated, and was himself seriously wounded by the gunfire.

Connally had always supported the cause of agribusiness, and openly opposed plans to cut milk price supports. The issue arose in 1972 and the dairy farmer associations were awash with well-paid lobbyists. One of these, an Austin, Texas, lawyer named Jake Jacobson, was Connally's longtime friend.

When the congressional and special prosecutor investigations of the 1972 Nixon re-election campaign uncovered the milk lobby's financial records, suspicion focused on the Jacobson-Connally relationship. The milk lobby group, Associated Milk Producers, Inc. (AMPI) had given Jacobson $10,000, and its records suggested that this money was for Connally, as a thank you for his support.

Jacobson admitted he had received the money. He said he offered the money to Connally, who refused it. Jacobson repeated this story several times under oath. He said that he had kept the money in his safe deposit box, and he indeed opened his box and produced $10,000 in cash. This gesture simply increased suspicion, because several of the bills bore the signature of George Schultz, who had succeeded Connally as Treasury Secretary. It was, of course, impossible for Jacobson to have received those bills from AMPI while Connally was Treasury Secretary.

The Watergate special prosecutor indicted Jacobson for lying about Connally refusing the money. The indictment was dismissed because the prosecutor's grand jury questions had been inept and Jacobson could plausibly claim that he did not deny giving the money. Jacobson was asked, in effect, "Is it your testimony that you did not give the money." He answered, "yes." And indeed, that was his testimony. It might have been false, but it was his. So he had told the literal truth, and under Chief Justice Burger's opinion for the Supreme Court in *United States v. Bronston*, that meant he could not be a perjurer. The prosecutors persevered, however, and Jacobson eventually pleaded guilty to giving Connally two unlawful gratuities. In exchange, the prosecutors forewent any more perjury charges, dismissed Texas indictments charging Jacobson with looting three savings and loan associations of millions of dollars, and agreed to help Jacobson keep his law license.

The Watergate special prosecutor's office had achieved a formidable reputation for integrity and success. The prosecutors had won all their cases but one. That one, an acquittal of agribusiness magnate Dwayne Andreas, had come in a case defended by Ed Williams.

By the time the Connally case was brought, Leon Jaworski had become special prosecutor. Although Jaworski recused himself from the Connally matter, his years-long antagonism to, and rivalry with, Connally and the Vinson Elkins Connally law firm fueled some suspicion that this was a grudge match. That suspicion was not, however, widespread. Members of the media were nearly unanimous in putting the case in the best pro-prosecution light.

That attitude palpably changed during the trial. Ed's cross-examination of Jacobson was classically brilliant. I had traced every one of the bills that Jacobson had turned over, and the government's theory came apart. Jacobson had indeed received $10,000 to give to Connally, and soon afterwards had applied just that sum to his mounting pile of debts. To secure his testimony, the government had dismissed Texas indictments against him for stealing nearly a million dollars from savings and loan associations he controlled.

Connally's testimony showed all the characteristics that had brought him success and that commended him to me as a friend in later years. He was measured and firm, and radiated a sense of confidence. This was difficult, for the trial bore down upon him, as he struggled to maintain his air of command in the face of family and friends.

Character witnesses took the stand one after another, including the expected strong white males, such as Ambassador Robert S. Strauss, Jack Valenti, Robert McNamara, and Dean Rusk. Barbara Jordan, the African-American member of Congress who had led the impeachment proceedings against Richard Nixon, surprised us all by appearing for Connally. When she had been a state senator in Texas and he was governor, he had behaved honorably and she was there to recognize that, despite the passage of time and Connally's defections, first to Nixon and then to the Republican party. Reverend Billy Graham was a character witness. Ed asked him, "What is your name?" "I am the Reverend Doctor Billy Graham" came the booming reply. "What is your business or occupation?" "I preach the gospel of Jesus Christ all over the world," the witness declaimed. "Amen!" exclaimed Juror No. 5, an African-American woman who carried a Bible in her purse and read from it during breaks in the action.

My favorite character witness was Lady Bird Johnson. We sat one weekend in the eighth floor conference room just off Ed's office and talked about her forthcoming testimony. Bob Strauss, a longtime family friend and counselor, sat with us. Mrs. Johnson said she was nervous about testifying.

"It really is a formula," I said. "Ed will ask you how you know John Connally, and then put the two questions permitted of character witnesses. He will ask your opinion of his character for integrity, and then what you know of his reputation for integrity. Then he will ask the same two questions about the attribute of truthfulness, since Connally has testified and his honesty is relevant."

"Yes," Mrs. Johnson said, "but I am not sure how I should *be*, if you know what I mean."

"Mrs. Johnson," I said, "when I first came to Washington in 1966 and your husband was President, you were very active in establishing parks where children could play. I lived on Capitol Hill then, in a racially-mixed neighborhood, and I remember you coming to dedicate these parks. The people on this jury are just like the parents of those children who came to hear you speak."

On the stand the next day, Mrs. Johnson was her usual poised self. She answered the ritual questions, and then, with no question pending, turned and looked right at the jury. "You know," she said, "there are a lot of people who don't like John, but there's nobody who says he isn't honest." This was a perfect comment in so many ways. It was heartfelt and counterbalanced Connally's evident arrogance, a quality that turned off voters.

When the case went to the jury, it was early afternoon. Bob Strauss was there, and he predicted that the jury would be back in time for dinner. He had ordered all the ingredients for a victory party delivered to his Watergate apartment. Strauss was right, and we celebrated that night.

Back in 1967, when I first came to Washington, I had been junior lawyer to Ed Williams in the defense of Robert G. "Bobby" Baker, the secretary to the Senate majority. We lost. As the Connally jury came in, I was sitting next to Ed at counsel table. The foreman stood to announce the verdict. Ed's hand tightened on my leg. "Not guilty." Twice. Ed had tears in his eyes. "Well," he murmured, "that makes up for the last time."

I got a lot of criticism for participating in the Connally defense, from old friends and comrades on the left who wondered how I could represent somebody like that. I liked Connally personally, and thought the deal for testimony that had been struck with Jacobson was an abuse of prosecutorial discretion, given Jacobson's motives to lie. The case was worth defending. As Connally's personal fortunes declined, and I had moved to Austin, Texas, I continued to help him and his family.

In a more general sense, there is something pleasing about representing conservatives charged with crime. Indictment gives them cognitive dissonance, for their previous suspicion about defendants' rights is first challenged and then evaporates. One can only hope they hold on to the lesson.

In a related vein, during one trial of a political figure, we were sitting in the office after court one day. The client suggested that we call as a defense witness a once-powerful but now disgraced and convicted political ally to establish a fairly marginal point. Ed and I argued against this course. The client persisted. Finally, Ed said with some exasperation: "It will create a diversion. It will be like blowing up the courthouse." The client replied heatedly: "Well, you know, they have done everything they can to get me in this case. They have spent ten million dollars if they've spent a dime. They have gone to every one of my clients and friends. I am sunk even if I'm acquitted. I say let's blow up the courthouse." I looked at him and said, "You know, you are the second client I've represented who said he wanted to blow up the courthouse." Ed chimed in, "Yes, but the other one said it before he was indicted."

In Orange County, California, early in the 20th century, James Irvine assembled more than 90,000 acres into the Irvine ranch. By 1975, there were some 88,000 acres left, but control had drifted into the hands of a foundation controlled by major corporate interests, with the Irvine family holding only a 22 percent stake. The foundation proposed to sell its interest to Mobil Corporation for $123 million.

For years, Joan Irvine Smith, the founder's granddaughter, had battled against the foundation. Indeed, she had lobbied for the legislation that forced it to divest. She thought the Mobil deal grossly undervalued the ranch, and she did not like Mobil. She wanted to see a sort of leveraged buyout whereby the family could regain control. In fact, due to our litigation victories she was able to make that deal.

I got the case early in 1975. Chuck Robb, who was later served as governor and senator in Virginia, was the associate initially assigned. Our job was to enjoin the proposed deal, whereby the foundation would sell its stock in the Irvine Corporation. The foundation was a California entity. The corporation had been formed in West Virginia. Joan lived in Virginia. We could piece together a diversity action to be in federal court, though we did not have a federal question that would survive analysis.

In those days, there was no federal courthouse in Orange County. We would be litigating in downtown Los Angeles before a judge who might or might not know or care about the impact of 88,000 Orange County acres—including prime beachfront—passing into the hands of an oil company. So we filed our lawsuit in Orange County Superior Court, during a month when the regular probate judge was handling preliminary injunctions. He was careful and scholarly, and understood fiduciary duties from several perspectives.

Lawyers sometimes choose a forum automatically, marching into federal or state court, or filing in a state with only marginal contacts, without thinking through the consequences. A hasty forum choice can condemn the client to years of litigation that never touches the merits. We needed to get this case heard.

Our theory was that a dominant majority shareholder in a closely-held corporation owes a fiduciary duty to the minority shareholders to get a fair price when it sells out. The law in support of this view was not uniformly in our favor. However, this majority shareholder was a non-profit corporation, subject to regulation by the state of California. We convinced the attorney general that the price was inadequate, so the state joined us as plaintiff, in its capacity as parens patriae. Not only did we get a valuable ally, but I also was able to argue that the court should consider denying our motion for preliminary injunction and granting the state's motion. The state did not have to post a bond.

Mobil invited Joan to a meeting to lay out its real estate plans for the property, hoping to gain her support. The meeting was on February 14, 1975, and when the Mobil lawyer wished her Happy Valentine's Day, Joan said between her teeth, "Yeah, the massacre."

In discovery, we found that the corporation did have enough cash flow and liquid assets to make a leveraged buyout possible. But that merely meant that we were not asking for a remedy that would do no good. Our story was that the Irvine family was being frozen out of their patrimony, and a big chunk of Orange County was passing into the control of Mobil. The foundation's lawyer argued at length that the case law did not support us.

When it was my turn, I discussed the cases that were on our side, then turned to a broader theme.

> This court sits, as Your Honor knows from long experience, in equity. The consolidation of law and equity in code pleading has not abolished the unique role of the court of equity. The chancellor of England got his legal principles from a different source than did the common law judges. He relied on rules derived from the canon law and ultimately Roman law. Indeed the term fiduciary is a corruption of a Latin word, *fideijussor*, meaning bearer of rights.
>
> Now, Mr. Privett has cited a lot of cases, essentially arguing that because in certain older cases majority shareholders could behave in a certain way, it must be all right here. I am reminded of Pope Gregory VII, of the 11th century, who received a letter from a peasant complaining that the lord was grinding him down by unfair exactions. Gregory asked the lord to explain, and he said he was doing no more to these peasants than was permitted by the custom of that place. Gregory replied, and I would say to Mr. Privett, "The lord thy god hath said my name is Truth; he hath not said my name is Custom."

A few weeks after the argument, the judge granted a preliminary injunction to block the sale. After some wrangling, Joan Irvine Smith was able to arrange a deal that valued the property somewhere near what she claimed it was worth and preserved her family's leadership in developing it.

Edward Hudson was an engineer by profession. He and his company had built major oil and gas projects in the United States and abroad. He was honored by the French and Algerian governments for his role in building pipelines in North Africa. Politically, he was somewhere over on the right. He had been a good friend of old H.L. Hunt, the reclusive and unorthodox Dallas oil magnate. This friendship brought him into touch with Hunt's two sons, Herbert and Bunker. These two were later to amass and then dramatically lose a fortune in a foolish effort to corner the silver market.

But back in 1975, the Hunts were mainly in the oil business. Like their father, they tended to be secretive and suspicious. Apparently, their suspicions led them to hire investigators to wiretap some of their employees. This was illegal. The investigators were clumsy. One of them was caught climbing down a telephone pole on the outskirts of Dallas, where he had been servicing a wiretap recording unit.

The government charged and convicted the investigators under the federal wiretap statute. But the prosecutors suspected that the Hunts had paid the wirtapping investigators and pursued this suspicion before a federal grand jury. The Hunts were apparently worried about this government effort. Ed Hudson entered the picture.

According to the government's evidence, the Hunts asked Hudson to retain famed criminal defense lawyer Percy Foreman to represent the wiretapping investigators, in the hope that Foreman would induce them to refuse to testify about who hired them. Hudson was not a lawyer, and saw nothing particularly wrong with carrying money and instructions from the Hunt boys to Foreman. After all, the investigators were going to get a lawyer, and they wouldn't have to pay Foreman's fees. This sort of thing often happens in the pro bono world, where an organization pays legal fees to someone under government attack.

The difficulty arises when the payer wants to influence the choice of lawyer, or worse yet, wants the lawyer to represent the payer's interests rather than devote his undivided loyalty to the true client. The government obviously thought that the Hunts were paying Foreman to keep the investigators quiet rather than simply provide representation. Ed Williams tried to talk the Justice Department lawyer, Guy Goodwin, out of putting Hudson into the indictment but Goodwin refused. Ed handed the case off to me. The government indicted the Hunt brothers, their general counsel, one of their lawyers, Ed Hudson, and Percy Foreman. The case was assigned to Judge Halbert Woodward, whose chambers were in Lubbock but who also sat in Dallas, which is part of the same judicial district.

One joy of working this case was that I met lawyers with whom I formed lasting friendships. Representing Ed Hudson along with me was

Mort Susman. Mort had been U.S. attorney for the Southern District of Texas, and was one hell of a trial lawyer. We were co-counsel in other cases.

The Hunts' general counsel, Ralph Shanks, was represented by Pat Higginbotham of Dallas, but when Pat was appointed to the district bench, Shanks' case was severed and never tried. I have kept in touch with him all these years; he recommended me to Chief Judge Russell as appointed counsel for Terry Nichols.

The Hunts were interesting co-defendants. Bunker in particular seemed a little out of place, no matter where he was. The first day in court, he took care to introduce himself to everybody inside the bar of the court, including the marshals, clerks, and prosecutors. As he made the rounds to the astonished court personnel, one lawyer on the team drawled, "Bunker's pancakes never did get quite done."

Even though Guy Goodwin had obtained the indictment, he showed up only for the first few months of pretrial wrangling. U.S. attorney Jim Rolfe and assistant U.S. attorney (and later U.S. attorney) Mike Carnes represented the government, though with some diffidence because they thought little of the case and less of Goodwin.

One major item of government evidence was the notes that Ed Hudson had made of his conversations with the Hunts about the reasons for hiring Foreman. These might be viewed as suggesting that Foreman would be more loyal to the Hunts than to his clients. Hudson had the habit of making notes of conversations as a reminder of what he was to do. He kept these notes in his desk drawer.

In addition to hiring a lawyer for the investigators, the Hunts had tried to find the investigators jobs in their chosen fields. Investigator Kelly had worked as a security guard; Hudson needed a guard at his plant and offices and hired Kelly. Kelly's other chosen field had, of course, been obtaining evidence illegally; his wiretap conviction was his résumé builder on that score. Kelly spent part of his night shift at the Hudson company rifling the files. When he found the notes, he took them to the government and traded them for a reprieve on his wiretap conviction.

Guy Goodwin eagerly agreed to use the notes and to give Kelly the benefit he sought. In so doing, Goodwin doomed the entire case against all the defendants. The notes were ambiguous, but they clearly referred to dealings among the Hunt brothers and Hudson. Under the Supreme Court's decision in *United States v. Bruton*, these written statements by Hudson could be used against him in a separate trial, but not in a joint trial with the Hunts and the other defendants.

I filed a severance motion for Hudson, seeking a separate trial. The government was hard put to oppose the motion, given the *Bruton* decision. As the prospect that the case would become untriable loomed, Goodwin sought to salvage what he could. He offered Hudson a free pass if he would testify against the Hunts.

Hudson scoffed at the idea. The case was ridiculous, he said, and he would not cooperate with somebody like Goodwin. It was interesting. I disliked Goodwin because he had planted an informer in our Seattle conspiracy defense camp, and because he had been caught doing the same thing in other cases. Hudson simply didn't trust him. But Goodwin asked that Hudson come to the U.S. attorney's office and hear the offer in person.

One Dallas morning, we paid that visit. Goodwin, down from Washington, had borrowed an office. He said that if Hudson would testify against the Percy Foreman and the Hunts, he would drop all the charges against him. Hudson, gruff and blunt-spoken at age 72, said no thank you and prepared to leave.

"Just a minute," Goodwin said primly. "Mr. Hudson, didn't Percy Foreman represent your wife in your divorce case? And didn't he get the largest cash settlement in Texas history from you?"

"Yes," Hudson said carefully. "So what?"

"Well," said Goodwin. "This is your chance to get back at Percy Foreman."

Hudson looked at Goodwin with a mixture of puzzlement and distaste. "You don't understand a thing about it," he began. "I had been trying to divorce that woman for years. Every time we would get close to settlement, she changed lawyers. So one day I read in the paper that she has hired Percy Foreman. That morning I went down to the Rice Hotel where he always had breakfast and sat at his table. 'Percy, how much?' I said. 'Thirteen million,' he said. I said, 'Done!' And he kept his word. So I have nothing against Percy Foreman, even assuming I wanted to make a deal with you to take care of it." Then, turning to me, he said, "I've had enough of this. Let's get out of here."

As we walked out, Hudson turned to me and said in a voice that could be heard in Abilene, "Tigar, am I wrong or is that man a damned faggot?"

So there you had Ed Hudson, reactionary and homophobic, but targeted by the same government in the same unfair way that had befallen my politically correct clients. There was no social harm in freeing him, and a great deal of social good in confronting and beating the government.

How did it turn out? Goodwin abandoned the case. Rolfe and Carnes prepared to try a case that did not include Hudson, who had been given a separate trial. They would also be without Percy Foreman, who was always too ill to come to court and whose brilliant lawyer, Mike Johnson, got him severed out as well.

Carnes and Rolfe were no strangers to Texas juries, and they knew their case was looking a little thin. On the eve of trial, under pressure from Judge Woodward to get the matter settled if possible, they offered the Hunts a deal. The charge was obstruction of justice, a felony. If the Hunts would plead guilty to "aiding and abetting misbehavior so near to the court as to obstruct the administration of justice," that would settle the case. Nothing doing, said the Hunts' lawyer. Carnes and Rolfe then agreed that the Hunts did not have to admit they were guilty of anything. They could plead nolo contendere (literally, I do not contest it) and pay a $1,000 fine each, making clear that this was a petty offense on a par with a traffic ticket. The deal was done.

I went off to Los Angeles for the premiere of a movie that had been made by Fantasy Films, another one of my clients. I had a message to call Judge Woodward. He was cordial, but he asked frankly, "Mike, were you thinking of forcing the government to try Mr. Hudson?" I said that had crossed my mind. He said that it was none of his business, but that Mr. Hudson could have the same deal that the Hunts had received, and that it was surely not a big deal to pay a fine. I got the message. Ed and Mort Susman and I flew to Lubbock one fine day—in Hudson's plane— to plead nolo contendere. In recognition of Hudson's alleged lesser involvement, his fine was only $500. This is what Guy Goodwin's case had come to.

One night in my Dallas hotel, while working on the Hudson case, my friend Seagal Wheatley came to see me. Seagal is a trial lawyer in San Antonio and he had once upon a time been U.S. attorney. I have done a few cases with Seagal and we have come out on top in every one. We had met in the *Army Times* libel case. That night, Seagal brought with him Robert Mann, a banker from Waco who was charged with conspiracy to misapply—which is a polite way of saying steal—the funds of his bank, the First National Bank of Waco. This case gave me a fascinating journey through the Texas banking system. There were plenty of good reasons to be involved in it.

I had litigated in Texas beginning with the *Wingerter* draft case in 1969, which had been referred by one of San Antonio's oldest law firms. But from the Connally acquittal and the *Army Times* libel case onwards, I built a reputation in Texas that gave me good trial experience, brought business to Williams & Connolly, and when I started my own firm, put us on a solid pay-the-rent foundation.

The Mann case was right for me, because it raised issues that needed to be aired. I also got to work with my friend John Mage, whose knowledge of economic theory proved decisive in our trial. It was a chance to learn an entire field of law, economics, and regulation. The year was 1975, long before national banks leapfrogged across state lines. Texas prohibited branch banking, which meant that every bank stood by itself, limited to one place of business plus a remote location for banking by automobile. In such a banking system, small banks needed to form relationships with larger banks to service their customers. If the small bank had a customer who wanted a larger loan than the small bank could provide, it could enlist the aid of its big city associate. These small bank/bigger bank arrangements were known as correspondent banking relationships.

Typically, the relationship was cemented, and the small bank's customers assured of a warm welcome in the big city, by the small bank putting a fairly large demand deposit in the larger bank. The larger bank could use this money to increase its lending power. At that time, demand deposits of this kind did not draw interest. This state of affairs produced something called the compensating balance bank stock loan.

A compensating balance loan is a familiar phenomenon. Almost anybody who borrows substantial sums of money, for example for a mortgage, has one. If you keep a balance on deposit at the bank, it is more willing to lend you money because it is making a profit two ways. First, the bank lends out the money you deposit at a higher interest rate than it pays you. Second, of course, the bank charges interest on what you borrow.

The bank stock loan, in 1975, was a variation on this theme. Mann, who already owned a couple of small banks, purchased more than 90 percent of the stock of the First National Bank of Waco. To finance the purchase, he pledged the stock as collateral for a loan from Bank of the Southwest in Houston, which was one of Texas's major banks. He paid only 2.9 percent interest on this loan. The day that deal closed, Mann caused the First National Bank of Waco to place a $4 million demand deposit in the Bank of the Southwest, which was about the amount of his bank stock loan.

The government indicted Mann and the corporate entity, Bank of the Southwest. The theory was that Mann had appropriated for his personal benefit the financial leverage/advantage of the demand deposit. That is, it was alleged that he personally got a lower interest rate because the bank's money was up there in Houston at no interest. There were several ways one could analyze this transaction from the government's point of view, but they all focused on Mann gaining a personal benefit from corporate assets.

The case had been brought by a Justice Department prosecutor who was following up on a Treasury Department study of these bank stock loans and congressional hearings concerning them. This was a test case. I think the way we approached it, and our eventual jury acquittal, points up some interesting ideas about trial strategy and preparation.

A correspondent banking relationship, we found, was full of intangibles. Sure, you could look at the demand deposit that the little bank put in the big bank and figure the lost opportunity cost to the little bank—that is, the amount it could have made by lending the money at interest. You could then add up the other side of the balance sheet and compute a value for the services the larger bank gave to the little bank and its customers—handling foreign transactions, arranging loan participation, and so on. John Mage and I read a batch of articles on correspondent banking. It was impossible to put a value on these services. Should you price them at average cost, marginal cost, or the fully-distributed cost, which would include a share of everything including the polish on the bank's front door?

In addition, there were intangible aspects of the relationship that could not be measured at all. If a Waco customer wanted tickets to a Houston football or baseball game, the Waco bank could call somebody at the Houston bank and get some help obtaining those. This little service might ensure customer loyalty in Waco, the value of which is impossible to measure. In one study, the author found that the big bank had helped one of the little bank's customers buy a pet alligator.

These small-town, one-location banks in Texas were usually closely held by one or two families. Their stock was not publicly traded, and hence it was difficult to value for estate or resale purposes. The bank stock loan inevitably put a value on the stock, because the big lending bank had to determine value in a way that satisfied federal regulators that its loan was backed by sufficient collateral. The compensating balance bank stock loan was therefore a principal means of making bank stock marketable.

This research was fascinating, but I would rather be lucky than smart. I was lucky. One author of articles that supported the value of these loans to depositors and shareholders was Dr. Edward Knight, who worked at the Federal Reserve Bank in Kansas. Another author, who had written an article that was even better for us, worked with Dr. Knight. We found out that Dr. Knight was in Houston, helping the prosecutors put their case together. So we devised a strategy to force the government to put him on the stand.

The case was assigned to Judge John V. Singleton, a fair-minded but combative and cantankerous judge. The court of appeals decision that remanded the Mann indictment for trial had been written by Judge John R. Brown, who had chambers in the federal courthouse building in Houston. One day early in the trial, Judge Singleton called the lawyers into chambers after lunch and said, we thought jokingly, that he had seen Judge Brown at lunch:

> "I asked him right out if the court of appeals intended to say that your clients were guilty. And you will be relieved to know that he said no, they could still be acquitted and it would be all right with him."

Robert Mann had been indicted along with the corporate entity known as the Bank of the Southwest. Mort Susman represented the bank, along with a lawyer from Leon Jaworski's firm. We had a little trouble with jury selection because the corporate lawyers from Jaworski's firm did not understand that this was a criminal case and that we wanted jurors whose outlook would make them suspicious of the government's actions and motives. I remember one shouting match among lawyers, as Mort Susman and I explained to one of Jaworski's partners that we would not exercise peremptory challenges to exclude all the African-American jurors. Our general reasons were two. First, it was racist and we would have nothing to do with it, even though that partner said it was his practice to do it. Second, the backgrounds of African-American jurors give them insights into police and prosecutorial behavior that may not be shared by whites. We had a specific reason as well. One African-American juror, whom this lawyer wanted to exclude because of his race, held a Ph.D. in economics and would be uniquely qualified to interpret the evidence we planned to present.

For the trial, the bank chose to have a vice president sit at counsel table as its representative. I wished it had chosen somebody else, for he looked too much like the archetypal heartless banker, austere in his three-piece, pinstripe suit that seemed out of place in a warm Houston summer.

Mort Susman delivered his usual ebullient and brilliant opening statement. I was listening to it most impressed until he said, "And, members of the jury, all these things I have told you will be shown to you by Mr. Mann's counsel, Michael Tigar."

I didn't need the plug, and winced at the idea that jurors would expect me to carry a burden of proof that we did not possess in this criminal case. But I understood that we did have a story to tell, even though we would try to tell it by cross-examining the government's witnesses. We did not put Mann on the witness stand, and had not planned to do so. This was not a reflection on him. Robert Mann was and is an articulate and honorable banker. In fact, when I was appointed to represent Terry Nichols in 1995, I had not seen Robert for nearly 20 years. The Oklahoma federal judge to whom the case was initially assigned, Wayne Alley, said we would try the case in the little town of Lawton, Oklahoma. We, of course, won a change of venue to Denver when Judge Matsch was assigned to replace Judge Alley. But we were plenty worried about how that Lawton community would receive us. One day, Robert Mann called me to say that he guessed that I was concerned about Lawton. I said yes. He said he had spoken to a banker friend of his in the community and that, while there was a lot of sentiment about our client, this banker would make sure that the trial team was welcomed and could find the facilities and services it needed. This sort of gesture arose no doubt from Robert's own experience, which back at trial time in 1976 weighed upon him.

As I noted, there had been thousands of these loans. The government targeted Robert Mann as a test case. This test was to consist of convicting him of a felony and putting him in jail. His civil lawyers had sought to head off the attack, and by the time I came aboard he had been battling for several years at great financial and personal cost. Waco is a small enough town that when the bank president is charged with a felony everybody knows about it. Living under that cloud had taken its toll on the Mann family.

In the end, and without revealing confidences, I can say this. Often somebody who has been targeted in this way is unable to be the most persuasive witness for himself or herself. The person's anger and frustration seem ready to burst out and overwhelm the jury. A solid merits case then becomes personalized in a way that diverts attention from the real issues. And so I have been economical about defendants taking the stand, often against the advice of my mentor, Ed Williams.

The government's case would have to include a summary witness who would describe the transaction and try to show how the compensating balance loan benefitted Mann personally. The government had to prove an agreement to injure or defraud the First National Bank of Waco. The government had also said we would hear from at least one senior official of the Federal Deposit Insurance Corporation. Our defense was that Mann did not intend to injure or defraud his bank and that he relied on the fact that this was the normal method of financing small bank acquisitions in Texas. This latter point gave us a fine line to walk. It is never a defense to say that "everybody else did it too," although a jury that hears that fact may acquit from a sense of fairness. Rather, we needed evidence that Mann was *aware* of this common and lawful practice and of its approval by regulatory authorities until the Treasury Department switched its outlook. But if Mann were not going to testify, how would we do that?

We assembled speeches and articles about compensating bank stock loans, and managed to get government witnesses to admit that these were widely circulated among bankers. Mann had to have seen them.

The government's first major witness was a senior Treasury Department accountant named Shockley. His direct examination at the hands of prosecutor Hank Novak seemed wooden. As is our custom, Mort and I moved for production of any of Shockley's prior statements before we began the cross. The government resisted, saying that one key document was not Shockley's prior statement at all, but government lawyer work product, done while preparing him to testify. We cited the Supreme Court's then-recent decision in *Goldberg v. United States*, and Judge Singleton ordered the paper turned over.

The document was in question and answer format. It contained the full, literal text of each direct-examination question and each of Shockley's answers. We had witnessed a memorized recital. The document was entirely typewritten. There was, however, no answer typed in to the first question. Mort went first, so he got to spring that trap.

Q: Mr. Shockley, this whole thing contains all the questions and all the answers that the jury just heard, is that right?
A: Yes.
Q: Except that for the first question, there is no answer, do you see that?
A: Yes.
Q: The first question is, "What is your name?" Correct?
A: Yes.
Q: Well, my question is, did they not know who was going to be

the witness, so they left it blank and that way anybody who showed up could read off these answers?
A: No, that's not it at all.

In the general merriment, the answer went unheard.

In my cross-examinations, I kept seeking ways to build our factual record on the ubiquity of these loans. And I asked every witness whether he knew the work of Dr. Knight. If the witness said yes, I went on to ask if he thought well of that work. They all said yes. And I asked if it wasn't true that Dr. Knight was right here in Houston, working on this case. Would Dr. Knight appear as a government witness?

Whether this pressure led the prosecutor to call Dr. Knight I do not know, but he did. Dr. Knight was a scholarly and rather smug fellow, but he clearly knew the theoretical side of banking. Mort Susman, in his cross, dwelt on the doctor's lack of practical experience at lending money and protecting bank assets. That had been one of our themes. Building a correspondent relationship is not, we kept asking the government witnesses to affirm, just a matter of counting and calculating. There are intangible aspects of customer service and financial stability, and these pose decisions that a community-oriented banker is best qualified to make.

On my cross, I took Dr. Knight carefully through the literature on compensating balance bank stock loans, and on the larger subject of correspondent banking. You might think this sort of thing is not cross-examination fodder in a jury trial, but I would disagree. Our job as lawyers is to help the witness teach the jurors. Even when cross-examining an opponent's expert, we want to keep the witness at a level of discourse that bridges the gap between his or her discipline and the jurors' experiences.

Finally, I reached for the articles that Dr. Knight and his colleague had written. He explained how these bank stock loans promoted liquidity of bank stock and helped the small bank's customers. He acknowledged that it was hard to give a numerical value to a demand deposit on one hand, and the services provided by the correspondent bank on the other. I took a risk:

Q: Doctor Knight, in sum you are saying that the transaction for which Mr. Mann is on trial here was in fact beneficial to the stockholders and depositors of the First National Bank of Waco?
A: Yes.

Dr. Knight and the prosecutor tried to qualify or minimize that answer on redirect, and the jury did take more than two days to acquit. But the deliberation time was due, we later heard, to the stubbornness of a retired railroad engineer from Conroe who didn't like us.

Dr. Knight was the last witness that day. As we got into the elevator to leave the building, the junior prosecutor on the team stepped in with us. My massive ego treasures this moment. He looked at me with wide eyes and said, "How in the hell did you do that?"

I tried the Mann case barely ten years out of law school. Its lessons were important to me. Jurors care when the government is unfair to people. Jurors care that the defendant tried to do a good job in whatever profession he chose. Jurors' desire to do justice leads most of them to be intellectually curious, and to welcome the chance to follow you into a complex area to understand it.

Ben was from San Antonio, and dealt in watches and jewelry. He was an accomplished gemologist. Richard sold oil-field pipe, and was damn good at it. As far as I know, they never met, but they are joined together in my mind. In both of their cases, I had to explain to a jury how a responsible business person could become so befuddled by alcohol that he lost track of what he was doing. Their cases taught me valuable lessons, some of which I did not appreciate at the time. The trial lawyer lesson in each case was how difficult it can be for jurors to put themselves in another person's place, and how hard we must work to make that happen.

Ben made a trip with business associates to Hong Kong. While there, he bought $300,000 worth of gemstones. He called back to his office in Texas and had them put on his insurance policy, which was some evidence that he did not intend to conceal them. He became ill in Hong Kong and started taking medication. He was also emotionally troubled by a telephone quarrel with his wife. On the flight from Hong Kong to San Francisco, he drank at least 12 ounces of vodka, a bottle of wine, and some cognac. He had the gems in various pockets of his clothing, consistent with his practice of not carrying them all in the same place. When he stepped off the plane in San Francisco, he handed the customs agent a partially filled-out form that he had not signed. The agent asked him to sign the form, which did not include the gems. The agent then ordered a search and the gems were found.

At this point, Ben's traveling companion, a corporate lawyer, advised him to cooperate with the customs agents. Ben obligingly sat down and wrote out a statement admitting to smuggling the gems. He was, of course, indicted. The trial judge refused to suppress the confession.

It was clear to me that Ben had been in an alcoholic haze, that he had begun to fill out the declaration on the airplane but had lost track of things. The customs agents testified at the suppression hearing, and would at trial, that he appeared normal and in control of his faculties. I asked Dr. Bernard Diamond, the founder of modern forensic psychiatry, to examine Ben, to help the jury understand how he had not been in charge of his own thoughts and actions. But fearful that jurors would react negatively to "shrink" evidence, I also called Dr. Arthur Burns, professor and chair of the department of pharmacology at the University of Texas Health Science Center.

Dr. Burns was a magnificent witness. He explained the synergistic effect of alcohol, medication, and altitude on people. He said that there is a state of intoxication, at about three times the minimum legal definition, in which a person can appear normal and go through an entire evening talking and interacting with people. He or she will then go home to sleep and the next morning not remember a thing. It is fugue state. Burns turned to the jurors and said, "This has happened to one in three Americans. I know it has happened to me." Three jurors nodded in agreement.

We had Ben's friends as witnesses as well, to help the jurors know about what he drank and how he felt. When the customs agents took the stand, I tried to get as much evidence as possible of Ben being somewhat "out of it," but also stressed his entirely cooperative demeanor. In summation, I asked the jurors how they thought the customs service should behave. Several of them were working-class folks, and several were people of color who had shown some suspicion as the customs agents testified.

This is not just an issue about the airport in San Francisco. It deals with the border crossing at Tijuana and the roving checkpoints along the highways. When they stop you, should they try to trick you into signing something, or try to help you make sure that all the items are checked and the proper duty paid? If they cared about the revenue, and not about just making cases, the taxpayers would sure come out ahead in cases like this one.

Now the prosecutor points a finger and says that our witnesses are Ben's friends. Sure they are. If ever it happens to you, and I pray that it does not, that you are 1,500 miles from home and a bunch of cops take charge of you, you will give thanks that you had some friends or family with you so that they can tell what happened.

The jury hung 9 to 3 for acquittal on the main charge. The three dissenters were women from the suburbs, about Ben's age. I thought they had probably heard the, "honey, I got drunk and screwed up" story in their own lives and were not prepared to be charitable. That view, for which I had no particular evidence, influenced me in preparing for Richard's case.

Richard was charged with understating his income by about $7 million on his personal returns over four years. He had been in the oil field pipe business with an offshore corporation, but bad tax accounting resulted in all the income being taxable to him personally. We could and did show that he paid tax on all the income that he actually spent. He lived fairly modestly. As a matter of the government's tax accounting, he was liable for half the total business income. His business partner, who had made a deal and was not indicted, had simply taken the money and spent it on airplanes, fancy homes, and other pleasures. Even if tax accountants might say Richard should pay tax on half the money, fairness in this criminal tax evasion said Richard did not intentionally violate a known legal duty to pay.

Richard was a recovering alcoholic. For the four years of the business, he was someone who functioned very well during the day and was drunk every night. He sold a lot of pipe, but did not keep track of the money.

To tell Richard's story, we asked a psychiatrist who ran a treatment center to help us. In this way, we could show the jurors that he was seeking help and not simply hiring some doctor to try to beat the rap. I did not think the defense would be credible unless Richard acknowledged his problem enough to seek help for it. The doctor had never testified for a criminal defendant. He had testified in favor of suspending the licenses of impaired doctors, and had twice been appointed by courts to examine defendants in celebrated cases. He looked and sounded credible and qualified.

To introduce the themes of his testimony, I borrowed from a suggestion made by Chief Judge David Bazelon to come up with this line of questioning:

"Doctor, when someone like Richard here comes to you as a patient, do you find that his family has a hard time understanding why he is behaving as he is? Do you ask the family to come in so you can discuss the condition that Richard is suffering from, and what can be done about it? Do you sometimes find that family members are fearful, or skeptical, or even maybe a little hostile, about what you do, and about Richard himself? Doctor, I want you to imagine that the jurors and I are Richard's family, and that we have come to ask you for an explanation of why he has been behaving as he has. Would you do that?"

However, in line with my experience with Ben, we also had a scientist who presented pictures of brain scans showing what alcohol had done to Richard's brain.

This medical evidence would never have carried the day with a skeptical jury. We called Richard's former wife, a nurse, to say with dignity and compassion that she had loved him but that his drinking drove her away. The jurors told us later that they voted her best witness. They were told not to deliberate about the case until it was over, so they kept a score sheet on witnesses.

We also presented evidence of Richard's partner's profligacy, to such an extent and effect that the government did not dare call him as a witness. A Nieman-Marcus employee told of the fur coats the partner bought for young women; an accountant told of hauling cash in suitcases; an oil company employee ruefully confessed to receiving bribes and kickbacks. The government ought willingly to have produced this evidence of its witness's wrongdoing, but it did not. Every day, we would file a motion seeking more such information, and every day the judge would turn us aside. But as we were able to piece together some of the story, the judge finally relented. One afternoon he said:

A federal judge is supposed to listen. And sometimes a bell goes off. I have denied repeated defense requests, but today the bell went off. The defense motion for production of impeachment material is granted. Produce it tomorrow morning here in court.

The prosecutor said, "Your Honor, the documents are in New Orleans." The judge replied, "I am not talking geography, I am talking about my order. Tomorrow morning."

The jurors, however, reserved their worst witness award for the government's summary witness, an IRS special agent who had a chart of Richard's unreported income. He had, without apology, based his chart on the testimony of the liars and thieves on whom the government relied. This proved again the adage that "an expert is someone who was not there when it happened, but who for a fee will gladly imagine what it must have been like."

I hesitated at times to take on corporate clients. When it was a criminal case, there was a chance to move the law in a constructive way. In civil cases, I tried to be sure that I could embrace the issues with passion and concern. If I could not, then I would not be a good lawyer for that case.

The general counsel of an oil company called me. He told me that the company and others were defendants in an antitrust case. It had been to the court of appeals and back. It had been pending for 15 years and they wanted to get it over with. It seemed that so much discovery had been done that there was a database on Lexis, accessible by password. That must mean that every fact in the known world had been discovered, and just for this case. I said, "How about a trial?" The general counsel said that this idea had not been suggested. I said that in my experience, setting an early trial date would get the case over with by settlement or otherwise.

I am not exaggerating. Many corporations and their outside counsel buy the idea that when you get sued, the object is to prevent resolution as long as possible. I think this is usually a bad idea, for it keeps contingent liabilities alive. As a matter of policy, this tactic also chews up too many scarce judicial resources.

When I looked at the case, I thought the plaintiff's theory unrealistic. I quickly learned how some large firms spend the clients' money in high-stakes litigation. Of course, we had droves of lawyers at every meeting. The defendants had already, before I came on board, agreed to share the cost of mock mini-trials and jury research. We did a couple of those at a cost of hundreds of thousands of dollars, and got nothing I thought very useful. I hired jury consultant Hale Starr to help our team, for a modest cost, and sharpened our themes and theories.

The pressure of a quick trial date worked wonders. The plaintiffs agreed to a mediation process that was on a parallel track with the trial. This helped them to get a realistic view of their potential recovery.

I want to say that I do not believe in haste for its own sake. I say this partly because a judge may read this book and I don't want it cited against me when I move for a continuance. I am in this respect reminded of Judge Lucius Bunton. He is the image of the autocrat. In private gatherings, with the benefit of a little whiskey, he told what used to be called dirty jokes with great enthusiasm. On the bench, he became famous for moving the docket. A cleaning crew left a spray bottle near his bench. He filled it with water and aimed it at lawyers and witnesses who droned on too long.

He asked a lawyer in a civil rights case, "How long will this trial take." The lawyer did not know—or perhaps did not appreciate—Bunton's passion for speed. "Well, Your Honor, I would say about three weeks."

"Very well," Bunton replied, "we'll set it for a weekend in August in Pecos. It'll seem like three weeks."

This was not an idle threat. There is a federal courthouse in Pecos, Texas. There is also a small airstrip. My friend Gerry Goldstein reports that he could not use the phone booth there because there was a rattle-snake in it, trying to escape the sun.

In time, Bunton became the longest-serving judge in the western dis-trict of Texas, which stretches from El Paso to Austin, some 700 miles. That meant he was chief judge. He was fairly new to that title when Walter Smith was appointed a federal judge. At Judge Smith's first judi-cial conference, he was sitting with me and some others having breakfast when Bunton approached.

"Walter," Bunton said in a voice that could be heard all over the dining room," what the hell are you doing?"

"What do you mean?" Smith replied.

"Taking five days to try a half-day case," Bunton exclaimed.

"Well, Lucius," said Smith evenly, smiling as he said the first name, "if it's the case I'm thinking of, it was sent back for retrial by the court of appeals after you did it the first time. I think they call the other four and half days due process."

That is not the sort of haste of which I speak. In our antitrust case, just a few weeks before trial, the plaintiffs moved to have the courtroom wired up for CD-ROM video presentation of documents. I object to that sort of thing because I want the witnesses to handle the actual papers they wrote and the jurors to see them do it. Our plaintiffs said, "Judge, we need this because we have 20,000 exhibits."

I replied, "They are lying, Judge. Nobody has ever tried a jury case with 20,000 real documents since God was a little girl. I have read the exhibit list, and at least four out of five items on it are not admissible. So I think we should get a pretrial order on exhibits before we go wiring up the courtroom."

The judge agreed. As we kept the pressure on, we drove the case to a settlement even as we were selecting a jury. Over the years, using basic litigation moves has settled more than one complex case that was mired in discovery and motions.

Edward Bennett Williams gained national prominence in the 1950s for representing Frank Costello, the alleged Mafia leader. I met Costello in the late 1960s. He was wearing his trademark silk turtleneck and smoking English oval cigarettes. During Costello's defense, Ed honed his theory that everyone charged with a crime was entitled to a defense.

Over the years, I have represented people charged with alleged Mafia involvement. These cases seem to bring out the worst in prosecutor and police behavior. Reversals of convictions are rare in the United States Court of Appeals for the Second Circuit, which hears appeals from the New York federal courts, where many of the big cases are tried. Many years ago, reversing conspiracy convictions, that court of appeals warned against substituting a "feeling of collective culpability for a finding of individual guilt," but that warning has largely gone unheeded in later years. Indeed, conspiracy law has been stretched in Second Circuit case law further than in any other court I can think of. I say this ruefully because two of the most troubling cases involved my clients—the Puerto Rican independence leader and human rights lawyer Roberto Maldonado and alleged John Gotti lieutenant Frank Locascio. Thankfully, Roberto, whose case had political overtones, is back in Puerto Rico and has been readmitted to the bar, so he can continue his work.

One example of the way these cases are brought and tried was in what started as the Salerno case and became the DiNapoli case when Salerno died. My friend Gus Newman called and asked me to represent Vincent DiNapoli on appeal. Gus is one of the world's great lawyers and great friends. If he tries a case and loses, which is not often, he brings in another lawyer to do the appeal. That way, he says wisely, somebody can grade his paper and feel free to raise any issue that he might have overlooked. I have never found an issue that he did overlook, for a Gus Newman record is a pleasure to read.

Vincent DiNapoli was convicted of racketeering offenses after a 14-month trial involving many defendants. The case involved price fixing, union bribery, and other allegations. The evidence about Vincent and his brother, Louis, was all heard in about three months of trial. They sat there for the rest of the time without any visible or audible connection to the case. In such a mega-trial, fairness goes out the window. The most careful jury couldn't possibly keep all the evidence straight.

As is usual in cases like these, there had been months of electronic surveillance, resulting in thousands of hours of tapes. These had been mishandled when they were turned over to a retired police officer to study. There were dozens of issues on appeal, including a report by some jurors that the judge and the marshal had tried to pressure the jury into reaching a verdict.

The court of appeals panel was headed by Judge George Pratt, whose fair mindedness led him to schedule an entire morning of oral argument. All the lawyers could be heard, the court could ask its questions, and all the issues could be aired. After a remand for hearings on the jury issue, the panel reversed the convictions. It reached only one issue. The government had called two men, Bruno and deMattei, before the grand jury, where under grants of immunity they had given testimony that tended to exonerate the DiNapolis. When trial came around, the government refused to turn over the grand jury testimony to the defense, much less give a new grant of immunity so that Bruno and deMattei could testify to the jury.

The court of appeals acknowledged that the law forbade the trial judge from forcing the government to grant immunity, but noted there was something unfair about using the grand jury to find exculpatory evidence and then effectively burying it if the witnesses later decided to invoke a privilege. It held that the trial court should have admitted the grand jury testimony into evidence.

Having been denied bail on appeal and sentenced to 24 years in prison, the DiNapolis were now out on bail, at least for the time being. The government filed a petition for certiorari, which the Supreme Court granted. The court of appeals' theory for admitting the grand jury testimony was certainly arguable, although there were other theories on which it could have reached the same result. Therefore, my major tactic was to convince the Court that the result was fair, even if the Justices disagreed with the reasoning.

Mafia figures are not popular clients, however, and the Justices seemed skeptical. During argument, I held up the transcript of Bruno's and deMattei's testimony—which was in the record—and criticized the government for trying to suppress it. I was echoing Judge Altimari's criticism of government counsel during the court of appeals argument.

Justice White broke in and asked, "Do you expect us to read all that?" as though the content of this testimony were irrelevant to the result. I said yes, and noted that under the Court's precedents "you can affirm the court of appeals on any ground, even if it was not raised or considered below." To which Chief Justice Rehnquist remarked, "But only if we want to."

The Court, in an opinion by Justice Thomas, reversed the court of appeals. But as a clerk to the Justice explained to me, there was a paragraph in the opinion that held out plenty of hope for us on remand. The court of appeals was invited to reconsider how this testimony might be held admissible. The opinion rejected only the reasoning and not the result.

On remand, the panel again reversed the convictions, but the en banc court set that aside. However, the en banc court noted that there were a half-dozen issues yet to be resolved. In sum, the panel could reverse the convictions again. At that point, Gus Newman stepped in and negotiated an end to hostilities on favorable terms.

Representing alleged leaders of the alleged Cosa Nostra can have desirable side effects. One day in the 1990s, I was standing at 88th Street and First Avenue in New York, trying to hail a cab for the airport. As I waited, a garbage truck rumbled up the street with a dumpster hanging on its side. The dumpster broke loose and careened towards me. I pushed my companion out of the way, and jumped aside as the dumpster approached. It rolled over my laptop case and into a parked car. My computer was broken in half.

I gathered my wits and took down the names and addresses of witnesses. I copied the name and phone number of the garbage company from the side of the dumpster. Later, I called the number and told the man that his trash truck had ruined my laptop computer. He was quite rude, and said I could not prove that his truck did the damage.

I called a former client, and told him what had happened. The client said, "That's terrible. No wonder they say the garbage business is run by gangsters. I will call this gentleman and explain his obligations." I soon had a new computer.

Another Ed Williams legacy to me was the representation of political figures. Through this experience I gained an understanding of the First Amendment and speech and debate issues, media pressures, and the ways the public and, therefore, the jurors see such people. Those were good lessons when Sam Buffone and I represented Congressman John Murphy, charged in the ABSCAM cases with having taken a bribe in exchange for offering to help a fictitious Arab sheik. Of all those defendants, only Murphy was found not guilty of two-thirds of the charges, including bribery and racketeering. The trial judge gave him the same sentence as the others, however.

I make no apologies for losing one-third of that case. I am convinced, however, that two reasons we lost were that voir dire was compressed into a morning and that we were yoked for trial with another member of Congress whose lawyers pursued a different strategy. On the voir dire issue, I ran into one of the jurors a couple of years later at a restaurant. He said hello and reminded me that he had served, and then said, "We knew your client was guilty of something, but we had a hard time figuring out what it was."

Then in 1993, while I was on the University of Texas law faculty, I was propelled into another political case. I was at home one evening when Dean Mark Yudof called me. He said: "In a few minutes, you will get a telephone call from Senator Kay Bailey Hutchison. She is an alumna of this law school and played a very important role in reorganizing our alumni association. She will ask you a question. The answer is yes."

I had already read that Senator Hutchison had been indicted for misusing her office, charges dating from her tenure as treasurer of the state of Texas. The Travis County District Attorney, Ronnie Earle, had conducted a publicized raid on the treasurer's office to get computer hard drives that he said would show that Kay had used state employees to raise political funds for her candidacy.

Senator Hutchison did call and I did say yes, joining a defense team led by Dick DeGuerin, with Ron Woods as co-counsel. I have seldom agreed with Senator Hutchison's political positions, but this case did not smell right. I knew Ronnie Earle, and had seen the way his office cavalierly dealt with capital cases. I knew that he harbored political ambitions, and indeed had his eye on the Senate seat that Kay then held. I also knew that Texas law is wide open when it comes to raising campaign funds. I regret this latitude, but it had certainly well served some of my favorite people, like Ann Richards and Bob Bullock. The raid to get evidence that could just as easily have been subpoenaed was a grandstand play, and gave us a solid motion to suppress.

For months we litigated pretrial motions, finally forcing Earle to delete any allegation that Kay had destroyed documents and to admit there had never been any evidence of that. We moved to recuse the Travis County judges, as being political allies of Earle and opponents of Kay. We then had good fortune. Retired Judge John Onion was assigned to the case. Judge Onion was a scholar and teacher as well as a judge. He was regarded as nonpartisan and fair by everybody we met; this is quite a feat in a state that elects judges on partisan lines.

Judge Onion granted a motion for change of venue to Fort Worth, Tarrant County, Texas. As trial approached, we put subpoenas on state political officers for their fund-raising records, to establish that Kay's activity was consistent with the best political practices. These officers resisted the subpoenas and boxes of responsive records piled up in the courtroom waiting for Judge Onion to rule.

We brought our motion to suppress on for hearing, but Earle said he was not ready to try the issue. He consented that the motion would be deferred until the challenged evidence was offered at trial. This was a fatal error, for which he later blamed the judge.

In Fort Worth, we began jury selection. Kay sat with her husband, Ray, and was as attentive and skilled an analyst of prospective jurors as I have ever seen. At one point, the prosecutors objected to Kay and Ray holding hands in the presence of prospective jurors. Judge Onion thought this motion was nonsense, and underscored this by saying that they could hold hands but could not kiss.

Judge Onion also rejected efforts to televise the proceedings, citing some of the same analysis that I discussed in Chapter 10. After he ruled, the lawyer for the TV station asked him to hurry up and sign an order denying relief. Judge Onion smiled and said, "You're going to try and mandamus me, aren't you." The lawyer said, "It had crossed my mind."

"Well," said the Judge, "I am not going to let you take me up there without some findings on the record. Mr. Tigar and Mr. Earle, please submit proposed findings and conclusions so that I can do a short opinion." This was a good thought. In the Nichols' case, when we wanted a sealing order we always made sure to build a record so that Judge Matsch would be protected on appeal. Even then, the media argued, though unsuccessfully, that he should have made more detailed findings. I characterized this in oral argument as saying in effect that Judge Matsch should stay after school and write a hundred times on the blackboard, "I find that the balance favors nondisclosure."

A week before the trial, the *Fort Worth Star-Telegram* carried a big picture of Ronnie Earle, above the fold, with a story of how he planned to win this case.

Jury selection was almost finished one afternoon. The next morning, Earle asked to see us all in the judge's chambers. He said, "Judge, I move to enter a nolle prosequi in this case,"—that is a voluntary dismissal. If that were granted, he could start over again in Travis County and hope to get a different judge. He could then rethink his tactical decisions.

We said we opposed this, recognizing that the district attorney has discretion to discontinue a case. "Mr. Earle," Judge Onion said, "there are more than 100 prospective jurors out there and it is all over but the peremptories. If you have a motion, you file it on paper and I will hear it.

But I am not going to inconvenience those people that you have caused to be here."

We went into the courtroom and exercised peremptories. Earle presented a written motion. Kay, whose courage I salute to this day, stood firm that she wanted her case tried and not dismissed. Judge Onion called us to the bench. Dick stated our client's position. Judge Onion said: "I'll hear this motion later this morning. Right now we are going to swear the jury. Mr. Earle, I know you are ready for trial because I read that story in the paper." Earle looked stricken. When the jury was sworn, jeopardy would attach.

The jurors were in the box, the prospective jurors excused. Judge Onion gave them the oath, and his initial instructions. He looked over at the prosecutor's table and said, "Who will open for the state?" Earle and two other prosecutors looked down at their table. Judge Onion said it again, "Who will open the for the state? Mr. Earle?"

Earle stood and said, "Your Honor, we have a motion."

Judge Onion said, "I know you do. But this is the time for opening statement. Will you make an opening statement or not. The law requires that you do so."

"No," Earle said at last.

"Very well," said Judge Onion, "the state rests and closes." He turned to the defense table. "Counsel, approach the bench."

At the bench, Dick moved for directed verdict of acquittal. Texas practice, unlike that in federal court, ascribes real meaning to that motion. A judge cannot enter judgment, but rather must instruct the jurors and let them reach a verdict. In open court, Judge Onion said, "Members of the jury, in Texas the law requires that the prosecutor make an opening statement, setting out what the state intends to prove. If he does not, he rests without presenting evidence. Therefore, the part of the trial that I told you about, where the evidence comes in, is over. Please retire to your jury room while I prepare a jury charge and form of verdict."

Judge Onion then wrote out instructions to the effect that since the state had a burden beyond a reasonable doubt and had presented no evidence at all, the jurors should return not guilty verdicts on the charges. He prepared verdict forms for their use. Then, the jurors trooped back in to hear the instructions and receive the forms.

A new form of agony began. They were out five, ten, 15, 20 minutes. Finally they came back in. They had taken their job seriously, so they elected a foreperson and read all the papers carefully. The foreman read out the verdict. Kay was not guilty.

Earle blamed it all on the judge, saying that he had been sandbagged by the ruling that the legality of his search would be litigated only after the jury was sworn. But his own consent had created that situation. In truth, I believe, somebody with more political sense told him that it was dangerous to start this kind of a case.

Senator Hutchison has remained a friend. And she does have a piece of paper saying she is not guilty. The other 99 senators have to ask you to take their word for it.

Notes

1. Some of the material on the Faustian bargain appeared in LITIGATION magazine.

2. I have discussed Ed Williams' work in the *Connally* case in detail in *Persuasion*. In 1993, I did a mock cross-examination of a mock Jacobson, as I would have done it. That event is reported by James McElhaney in the January 1994 ABA JOURNAL, p. 94.

Chapter 14
LOOKING FORWARD— CHANGING DIRECTION

At the front of *Huckleberry Finn*, Mark Twain inserted this notice:

> Persons attempting to find a motive in this narrative will be prosecuted; persons attempting to find a moral in it will be banished; persons attempting to find a plot in it will be shot.

As I approach the last chapter of this narrative, stories tumble around in my head and will not arrange themselves by topic. I feel like the character in Christopher Fry's play *The Lady's Not For Burning*, who exclaimed, "I will not be the toy of irresponsible events." I could claim that I have not been trying to preach as well as tell stories, but that would not be true.

Those who deny that the present is as much a part of change as the past wrongly assume that things as they are are things as they will always be. To give just one example, it seemed in 1990 that South Africa was suddenly loosed from the grip of apartheid, as though some discontinuous event had occurred. The apartheid state seemed so strong, and then suddenly Nelson Mandela was free and things were changing at a fierce pace. "All revolutions are impossible," the South African jurist Albie Sachs said, "until they happen. Then they become inevitable." Yet for those around the world and in South Africa who had struggled all those years against apartheid, the change did not seem sudden at all.

More significantly, there were those who thought that the end of apartheid signaled an end to a host of South Africa's social problems, as though repealing the laws that mandated racial separation would entirely satisfy the black majority's demands for justice. That could not be, of course. South Africa was a country where the white minority lived fairly well, for they controlled most of the private wealth and most of the social services were devoted to their needs. When those services and wealth began to be spread around, white resentment flared. And when the spreading seemed agonizingly slow, black resentment flared as well. So the change was only one long step on the road, a qualitative change that would then require and set in motion hundreds of quantitative changes towards justice and equality.

I cite this example because I was in South Africa during some crucial times, and because it provides a lesson for us all. In our search for precedent and rules, lawyers sometimes forget to think about the ways that law might move forward to produce more justice. There are those for whom constitutional analysis consists of the futile search for original intent, as though one could know every thought of the Constitution's drafters. Even if one could know those thoughts, held as they were by wealthy white males, many of whom owned slaves, why would we choose to be bound by them? As I said in Chapter 4, I respect the framers of the Constitution, and can think of no greater insult to them than to imagine that they wanted us to see no further than they saw, to understand no more than they understood.

My book *Law and the Rise of Capitalism* was an effort to put today into its context. I wrote three plays on legal history with the same idea. The first was about the trial of John Peter Zenger, the colonial newspaper editor who was tried for seditious libel and acquitted by a jury in 1735. Andrew Hamilton of Philadelphia, who was Benjamin Franklin's lawyer, came to New York to provide a defense. Zenger had criticized an autocratic colonial governor. His trial was a celebrated step on the road to American independence from Britain. Governeur Morris, a signer of the Declaration of Independence, said much later: "The trial of Zenger in 1735 was the morning star of that liberty which subsequently revolutionized America."

I must admit that I liked writing the play because I was to perform in it at its opening during the ABA annual meeting in August 1986. A troupe of actors from Austin, Texas, played most of the parts. I was Andrew Hamilton. My daughter, Kate, played Hamilton's daughter, Margaret, and Scott Armstrong, the journalist, played Zenger. *The New Yorker* wrote up the performance in its *Talk of the Town* section, and dashed my hopes of an acting career by writing: "Mr. Tigar went well beyond ham. He went whole hog." But the exercise was fun, and led me to write a play about the Haymarket trial and Clarence Darrow, and another, with Kevin McCarthy as co-author, about Irish and Irish-American lawyers. I had learned my lesson and did not try to act in either of these.

These efforts to examine the past were ways of trying to see what I should do in the present and the future. For me, trying to see the future clearly requires an international perspective. This is not a surprising thought. In the daily practice of law, the North American Free Trade Area has exerted influence on commercial law practice. The tariff and trade agreements to which the United States is a party are at the front of national and international debate. Globalization is a weasel word, for it shifts meaning depending on context and speaker. But the debate over globalization has drawn labor, human rights, and environmental groups into conflict with governments and multinational corporations. The reasons for this conflict lie in the tendency of international capital to erode barriers to labor rights, human rights, and environmental protection.

My earliest struggles with international law were over issues of war and peace. Today and looking forward, I have been concerned with the globalization of human rights. As a journalist in England in 1962 and 1963, I covered the early work of Amnesty International and other organizations involved in the founding of the European Court of Human Rights. I covered the debates over third-world economic development, as the former colonies put forward ideas of social and economic rights. These two forces have today become much stronger. The basic rights to political expression, religious freedom, and due process have been expressed for more than 300 years. They are enshrined in our Bill of Rights. They are the first generation.

After World War II, such documents as the Universal Declaration of Human Rights recognized a second generation of rights—to subsistence, education, health care, and generally to a just distribution of national wealth for certain basic necessities of living. Today, there is a third generation of rights dealing with the environment and responsible development.

While the concept of rights, thought of as entitlements that every state must recognize and enforce, has developed, the autonomy of nation-states has eroded. That is, it was once thought that every sovereign could, within its borders, recognize or deny rights as it wished, without interference from other sovereigns or from international bodies. This positivist theory, on which Jeremy Bentham wrote extensively in the late 18th century, dominated legal thought in the 19th century.

Throughout the 19th century, however, the theory of sovereign right came under increasing pressure, first with international opposition to the slave trade and then in other areas as well. The two world wars changed the face of international legal thought entirely, and the Nuremberg trials firmly established that sovereigns, state actors, and individuals would not have immunity, or impunity, from crimes against humanity and crimes against the peace. In the years since World War II, there has been a growing consensus that sovereign states must also respect at least first generation rights.

I have been working in the context of this history for all of my legal career. The root principle is accountability, to be distinguished from immunity or impunity. I was propelled into a larger role by a terrible event.

I had watched with concern and horror the 1973 military coup in Chile that brought an end to the progressive civil government of President Salvador Allende. General Augusto Pinochet and his colleagues embarked on a pattern of killings, tortures, and disappearances, all with the apparent support of American military and intelligence agencies. I befriended Chilean exiles who were struggling to restore democracy in Chile. One such exile was Orlando Letelier, who had been foreign minister and ambassador to the United States in the Allende government.

On September 21, 1976, in Washington, D.C., a bomb exploded in Orlando's car, killing him and his assistant, Ronni Karpen Moffitt, and injuring Ronni's husband Michael. Orlando had been working at the Institute for Policy Studies (IPS), a think tank organization in Washington. The FBI quickly descended on IPS, demanding information and documents in a purported effort to see if leftists had killed Orlando.

It was obvious to Orlando's colleagues that the most logical suspects were agents of General Pinochet, who had publicly branded Orlando a traitor. Within hours of the killing, people at IPS called me and asked for my help. That help drew me into the Letelier case for the next 16 years, and then into the broader fight to bring General Pinochet to justice.

I called a friend at the Department of Justice. We set up a meeting with Attorney General Edward Levi within a few days. Levi took us seriously. I said that I thought the FBI was using the investigation as a pretext to investigate IPS and Orlando. A couple of years later, a congressional committee reported in detail that the FBI and other agencies did indeed keep track of foreign dissidents in the United States and report on them to their oppressive home governments. Finally, in 2000, the U.S. government released documents showing that the FBI had reported to Chilean secret police about the actions of anti-Pinochet activists, and that at least one such report had led directly to the arrest and killing of an activist.

Back in 1976, our concerns were based on experience and intuition. I said to the attorney general that I thought Chilean agents would not have done the bombing personally, and that the question was whom would they recruit in this country. The most likely suspects were Cuban émigrés. That group had already claimed credit for bombings at the Cuban United Nations mission. And where, I asked, would evidence of their actions be? At CIA headquarters in Langley Park in the custody of CIA Director George Bush.

"Tell you what, General Levi," I said, "you back one truck up to IPS and one up to the CIA. IPS will produce documents at the same rate as the CIA." He laughed and said he would take care of the CIA angle, and that the FBI would be reined in. For the next two years, the FBI investigation zigged and zagged, and I began to study what else might be done to redress Orlando's death.

By this time, I had met Sam Buffone, and we were planning the law partnership that we formally established on January 1, 1978. Sam proved to be the best friend and best law partner a person could have, and after I left Washington in 1984, he continued to pursue the Letelier case until our judgment was finally paid.

By the summer of 1978, the FBI had officially determined that Orlando was killed by Cuban émigrés recruited and paid by Chilean intelligence agents. It captured two of the agents and made plea bargains with them, and the government indicted the émigrés. Sam and I drafted a civil complaint on behalf of Orlando's widow, Isabel, his four sons, and the Karpen and Moffitt families. The Foreign Sovereign Immunities Act (FSIA) had been passed in 1976, and it contained a provision that foreign states were not immune from suit in the United States for certain torts committed in this country. This statutory language seemed straightforward to us, so we sued the individual perpetrators, the head of the Chilean secret police, General Contreras, the Chilean secret police agency, and the Republic of Chile.

Our suit provoked criticism from the established international bar. The FSIA tort provisions were, they wrote, designed for automobile accidents and not for alleged human rights abuses. It is hard to imagine in today's atmosphere that our suit would be controversial, but we were regarded as oddities for filing it.

The Chilean government filed objections, in the form of diplomatic notes. Some defendants chose not to appear. When the judge rejected Chile's official claims of immunity, we tried the case. Just as when one sues the United States, one cannot get a default judgment against a foreign state without proving the case to a federal judge. Judge Joyce Hens Green heard the evidence and arguments. She was clear and decisive. The Chilean government never quite admitted the killing, but argued that even if guilty, it would be a discretionary act from which they were immune. Judge Green curtly reminded the government that whatever discretion a foreign sovereign might possess, it did not extend to blowing people up on the streets of Washington. Her rejection of the argument could not mask the arrogance of the Chileans in making it.

We won a judgment against the Chilean government. Over the next few years, Congress passed statutes restricting American military and diplomatic cooperation with Chile until the judgment was paid. We sought to collect by seizing a LAN-Chile airliner in New York, but had to give the plane back because the court of appeals said LAN-Chile was sufficiently independent of the Republic of Chile that its assets could not be seized. Finally in 1991, President Pinochet stepped aside. The new civilian government agreed to set up an international tribunal that would look at the Letelier case. The American and Chilean governments took this step because Senator Edward Kennedy was about to introduce legislation that would have let us collect the judgment by seizing Chilean assets. Sam Buffone brilliantly handled this situation, and the judgment was paid—some $4 million. One must note that you cannot get punitive damages against a foreign sovereign. The tribunal awarded legal fees to Sam and me. I used mine to establish Letelier-Moffitt human rights scholarships at the University of Texas and Boalt Hall, the law school at the University of California.

Other human rights cases beckoned from time to time, including work on the suit to get at money stolen by Philippine President Ferdinand Marcos, and on amicus briefs about Palestinian rights. I visited Cuba several times to study conditions there and to work on normalizing Cuban-U.S. relations. However, when in 1987 I was named vice chair of the ABA Litigation Section, a new arena opened up for me.

Becoming vice chair of a section that had more than 40,000 members at that time was a surprising honor. The section, like most parts of the ABA, is not really based on grassroots democracy. Ben Civiletti, who was about to become chair, had a lot to say about who would be nominated, and he supported me. As soon as my name was announced, I knew that I had better start making discretionary appointments and planning whatever projects I wanted to bring to fruition. If I waited until I was actually chair, it would be too late. So in those next three years, vice chair, chair elect and then chair, I tried to advance a human rights agenda.

On the domestic front, this meant bringing women and people of color into positions of leadership. It meant starting the Litigation Assistance Partnership Project, to put law firms into contact with pro bono and legal services offices for impact litigation. It meant support for death penalty representation. On the international front, I wanted to make contact with groups fighting for human rights. Of course, we had to be careful not to step into territory claimed by other ABA entities, for there is nothing so fierce—nor so enervating—as a turf battle.

My friends Ken Broun and Jim Ferguson told me of their work in South Africa, holding trial advocacy training workshops for black lawyers. They not only used civil case files, but also taught techniques for defending political trials. I was enthusiastic and I wanted the litigation section to be identified with this work. The next summer, in August 1988, I flew from the ABA annual meeting in Toronto to Johannesburg to participate.

Our work was sponsored by the Black Lawyers Association, which was affiliated with the Pan-African Congress. The next year, we broadened our approach and also worked with the National Association of Democratic Lawyers, affiliated with the African National Congress.

Apartheid South Africa was chilling, but underneath the repression one could feel the pulse of change. I dined one night with a white South African lawyer who represented major oil companies. As we drove to his house, he pointed out the signs that the racial barrier was crumbling. When we met with the black lawyers in suburban Johannesburg, two white judges were there to participate and help with the teaching. The law school at Witwatersrand was integrated, as was that at Natal, in Durban.

The organized bar had managed to keep most blacks out of law practice, but we thought our work might increase the number. From Johannesburg, we went to Umtata, the capital of Transkei, which was one of the homelands established by the apartheid government. Blacks were to be citizens of a homeland and not of South Africa itself, where they had no social or political rights. The homelands were, in short, a cruel joke if said to be sovereign, and an instrument of apartheid policy. Only Israel recognized them as viable political entities.

One of the judges I met in Johannesburg was Richard Goldstone, who has remained a friend ever since. Richard had already decided a leading antiapartheid case called *Govender*. Mrs. Govender was prosecuted as a nonwhite living in a white group area, which was a criminal offense. Upon conviction, she was evicted from her home. Judge Goldstone wrote an opinion holding that under the statute as he read it, she could not be evicted unless there was equivalent housing available. Under this modest precedent, it became so difficult to evict nonwhites that housing segregation in Johannesburg began to break down. In later years, Justice Goldstone would head a commission to investigate police violence against antiapartheid activists and would serve as prosecutor at the International Criminal Tribunal for Yugoslavia. Today he is a justice of South Africa's constitutional court.

I recall sitting in a law office in Umtata and reading the official magazine of the South African Law Society. An editorial complained that domestic and foreign critics were urging the law society to take a stand against apartheid. The law society disagreed. Our job, it said, is to take and apply the law as we find it, and not to try to change things. This bit of nonsense was galling for several reasons. First, the system of apartheid was imposed in the early 1950s by the National Party, which changed things by purging the voter rolls of nonwhites and forcibly evicting nonwhites from their homes. Second, there were plenty of examples of progressive lawyers working to change things, if only to make rules that would ease the inevitable transition to a post-apartheid society.

In one sense, the editorial was only a symptom of the world in which the white rulers dwelt. The first day I arrived in Johannesburg, police were scooping up all copies of a newspaper that had dared to violate the law by printing a picture of police beating black protesters. I attended a public meeting on a possible new constitution for post-apartheid South Africa, but we could not publicly utter the name of Albie Sachs, the constitutional scholar who had written on this subject. Albie was in exile, a banned person. Indeed, the apartheid government had tried to kill him with a car bomb as he worked in exile in Mozambique. One of our Black Lawyers Association colleagues had been arrested and charged with a felony for having a book by Nelson Mandela in his car. He was acquitted when he explained that he needed the book because he represented clients charged with treason for supporting Mandela and the African National Congress (ANC). I was reminded of the Robin Williams routine, in which he portrays former Alabama Governor George Wallace, and intones:

P.W. Botha [the South African President] to a white courtesy telephone, please. P.W. Botha to a white courtesy phone. Say, P.W., this is George Wallace. Listen here, Sparky, do you understand that you got six million whites and somethin' like thirty million blacks in your country? Does the name Custer mean anything to you?

One of our mock trials for training advocates was a treason case. The case file assumed that the principal witness against our clients was tortured into confessing and then offered a life sentence in exchange for testimony. Torture was routine police behavior in South Africa, not to mention outright political killings. I was asked to demonstrate how one would cross-examine such a witness.

Q: Ms. Mqubele, do you want to die?
A: [Hesitantly.] Why, no?
Q: I want you to look around this courtroom and tell his lordship [there were no juries in South Africa] who it is in this room who has the most to say about whether you will live or whether you will be hanged by the neck until you are dead?
A: The prosecutor, I suppose.

The rest of the examination could go into the circumstances of her capture and questioning, but I thought this a good way to get the court's attention. It was important for all of us involved in the teaching to stress the need for vigorous advocacy, and that one must not be intimidated by the atmosphere of repression. In this we were supported by our South African colleagues, many of whom were living examples of such courage.

Godfrey Pitje had been a lawyer in the offices of Oliver Tambo and Nelson Mandela. When Tambo was exiled and Mandela jailed, Pitje kept on practicing law. One day, he refused to sit at the small table reserved for nonwhite lawyers. He insisted on sitting where white lawyers sat. For this he was tried and convicted. For some months, he was under a restriction that he must remain in his house, and could not meet with more than one other person at a time. His wife and children took turns having their meals with him.

On that 1988 trip, we went to Durban, on the east coast. My friend Charles Becton, an African-American judge and lawyer, was in the group. One morning, we walked out to look at the beach. There were signs restricting the best beach for the white racial group. Bec wanted to take a photograph, but there were also posted warnings that stated it was a felony to take a picture of the signs. Ken Broun said that the previous year, he had been walking along the beach and asked a passerby, "Is this the Indian Ocean?" The man replied in a shocked tone: "Oh, no sir! This is the white ocean. The Indian ocean is 200 meters farther on."

I came back to South Africa in 1989. On that trip I met Dullah Omar, who was one of Mandela's lawyers and was later to be minister of justice in the first nonracial government. Dullah confided that the summer of 1989 would see demonstrations against apartheid all over South Africa, led by an umbrella group called the Mass Democratic Movement. The MDM was new enough that the government had not got around to banning it. Dullah said there were to be mass arrests at these protests, and he wanted us to work with young lawyers and teach them what we knew about cross-examining police in such cases. He predicted that Mandela would be out of jail within a year. Seeing the repressive state of things, we doubted him—or at least I did—but he was right.

The next time I came to South Africa, Dullah was working with the ANC people who were drafting a new constitution for the country. We talked about the legal status of the homelands, and about the ANC's desire and promise to move from legality to legality. This form of transition meant, for example, that the life tenure of judges appointed during the apartheid era would be respected. Of the 100 or so judges on the higher courts, 99 were white and 99 were men. The new government would move as quickly as possible to diversify that group, as judges retired or died.

But, Dullah and others were thinking, can we really trust those old judges to interpret the new laws fairly? South Africa would have a constitution that included the most advanced bill of rights in the world. I gave a lecture at the University of the Western Cape entitled, "Old Judges and New Laws." I suggested that the ANC study the western European experience and establish a court with exclusive jurisdiction over constitutional issues. Such a constitutional court would have all its judges named by the new regime. This suggestion came from others as well, and was adopted. A multiracial constitutional court sits in Bramfontein, near Johannesburg, and its decisions are widely respected. Its members include Albie Sachs, Richard Goldstone, and Arthur Chaskalson, three white leaders of the antiapartheid struggle.

In my 1990 visit to South Africa, I lectured on constitutional principles at the historically black law schools in Umtata, Cape Town, and Fort Hare (where Mandela went to law school). I can remember my surprise at Fort Hare when my talk drew a crowd of about 600; there were only 200 law students. The evening began with the group singing a freedom song that had been a felony to sing only months before.

Even though a transition was in progress at that time, the old white government still ran things. The week after my visit to Fort Hare, 27 students were gunned down by the security police. And as I left Fort Hare by car for Umtata, with my two ANC comrades, uniformed military police with Uzi automatic rifles stopped our car. They asked us to get out and lie on the ground. We did so and they searched the car. My friends negotiated with them in Afrikaans and we were allowed to go on our way.

As I learned more about South Africa, I involved the ABA Litigation Section in the changes there. Richard Goldstone visited with us on a trip to the United States and Dullah Omar spoke at our annual meeting. A Black Lawyers Association representative attended a section council meeting. We began to send books to Fort Hare law school. We were invigorated by watching the changes being made in that society.

In that same period, the Soviet Union was crumbling and young people from the former Soviet bloc looked to American human rights activists for guidance. I did not support every initiative of the organized bar in that era. The deconstruction of socialism in the former eastern bloc was accomplished with a great deal of corruption. The social safety net in those countries has largely been dismantled, casting many people into poverty. I did and do support rationalization of the criminal justice systems in those countries, along with enforcement of all the first- and second-generation rights. Due process and free expression, along with mechanisms to protect them, are within the expertise of litigators. I went in 1991 to Siracusa to a meeting of jurists from a dozen or so eastern European countries.

From these experiences, I have tried to understand what path I must take to extend human rights in the afternoon of my life in the law. I see a great contradiction at work. While the rest of the world is discovering new ways to protect and extend democratic rights, the mechanisms for protecting them in the United States are under attack.

In South Africa, the day the justices of the constitutional court were sworn in, they heard argument on whether the death penalty was consistent with the new South African constitution. In the investiture ceremony, President Mandela remarked that his last time in a court, he had been there to hear if he would receive a death sentence. As Justice Goldstone later said, "I don't think he was consciously trying to influence us, but he surely did." In the wake of its liberation, South Africa saw an enormous upsurge in political violence, white against black, black against white, and black against black. There were holdover criminal cases involving defendants of all races. The constitutional court joined the majority of modern states and held the death penalty unconstitutional. The European Community had abolished it by decision of the European Court of Human Rights and by treaty. In this same period, the United States was condemning more prisoners to death and in 1994 the Clinton administration sponsored an enormous expansion in the number of federal capital crimes.

On another front, in 1998 a brave Spanish lawyer named Juan Garcés brought a private criminal action against former Chilean dictator Augusto Pinochet, and Spanish judge Balthazar Garzon began judicial proceedings on the application. In Spain as in many other countries, counsel for victims can commence a criminal prosecution. Garcés' clients were victims of Chilean military torture and their families. All in all, Garcés presented more than 1,000 cases of torture, disappearance, and murder, out of the thousands of such instances during the junta's rule in Chile from 1973 to 1991.

Garcés and Garzon fought back several legal challenges in Spain, and Garzon issued a warrant for the arrest of General Pinochet. In the fall of 1998, Pinochet went to London for medical treatment, thinking himself immune from trouble on these charges. The British authorities acted on the Spanish warrant and arrested him. He claimed immunity from prosecution and resisted extradition back to Spain. Many people in the human rights community thought that this case would go nowhere. I did not agree. I was therefore pleased to get a telephone call from the English barristers who were representing the British government, and by extension the Spanish judicial authorities, in the extradition proceedings as they made their way to Britain's House of Lords.

These lawyers asked if I could advise them on the immunity issues that we had litigated and won in the *Letelier* civil case. I said yes, and my law school approved travel for two student research assistants. My wife, Jane, and I paid our own way, and we were on the next plane to London. The main issues were two. First, was the president of a country, even one who had achieved power by military coup, immune from prosecution for complicity in tortures, disappearances, and murders? Second, did Spanish courts have the power to try to punish Pinochet for his crimes, since most of his acts were done in Chile? A subsidiary issue was purely factual: Did the evidence show that Pinochet either ordered these abuses, or knew of them and encouraged their commission? On that factual issue, the European Union treaty does not permit the prisoner to present evidence in the extradition court; the issue is to be tried in the demanding state if the prisoner is sent there. Nonetheless, it was important that the extradition court in Britain have a comfortable sense that this case was factually well founded.

Two main principles underlie most of the modern human rights agenda, at least for me. Today, no sovereign state and no official can claim immunity from civil suit and criminal prosecution for crimes against humanity. Indeed, the principle may be broadened to state that there is no immunity or impunity for any violation of a peremptory international law norm such as torture and genocide. This principle emerged in the wake of World War I, and was a main element of the London Charter, which established the Nuremberg Tribunal that tried the Nazi leaders. The United States, Britain, France, and the USSR all signed that charter. The British House of Lords in its Pinochet decision would not go so far, however. The majority held that Pinochet lost whatever immunity he may have had only when Britain signed the Convention Against Torture in 1990. This limited victory nonetheless paved the way for a full-blown extradition hearing.

Although the United States signed the London agreement, our government has continued to assert an expansive view of its own immunity, and that of its officials in lawsuits alleging human rights abuses. This position is, in my view, contrary to the dominant themes in transnational law today. Moreover, it is inconsistent with the position the United States takes with respect to other states. That is, we allow human rights lawsuits in our courts against foreign states, on a narrower view of immunity than our own government takes when it is the defendant. This imbalance needs to be corrected.

The second Pinochet issue was that of jurisdiction. Traditionally, a nation's criminal law is enforced against acts within its territory—the principle of territoriality. This principle may be expanded to cover actions done outside the borders but knowingly directed at the territory with the intent to cause a result there. For example, an illegal business combination in Central America may violate U.S. antitrust laws if it is designed to and does produce anticompetitive effects in our markets.

A nation may also, under a traditional view, punish criminal acts against its citizens and nationals, no matter where those acts occur—for example, by an attack on American citizens abroad. This is the principle of passive nationality. In Pinochet's case, some of the victims were Spaniards, and this principle might apply. The criminal law may be brought to bear on conduct by American citizens and nationals done anywhere in the world, if the legislature specifies that the law is to have extraterritorial effect, a principle known as active nationality.

However, some crimes are regarded as being committed against all humanity, and therefore may be prosecuted by any state where the alleged offender may take refuge. This notion was firmly established by the end of the 18th century, with respect to the offense of piracy. It is known as universal jurisdiction and today is applied to crimes against humanity, genocide, torture, and other violations of international peremptory norms.

A peremptory norm may be defined as one that is so well established that no nation may opt out of it and claim it is not applicable to its conduct. If a rule of international law is merely customary, a nation-state may or may not accept the custom. However, by this time in the history of civilization, and with the precedents of Nuremberg and the Yugoslavia and Rwanda tribunals, basic principles of humane conduct are binding on all nations.

Universal jurisdiction has been controversial. Henry Kissinger has denounced it, and the official U.S. position has alternated between caution and hostility. After all, conceding the principle would give a Chilean court the power to try Henry Kissinger for plotting the kidnaping of a pro-democracy Chilean general, or former CIA Director George Bush for supporting the tortures, disappearances, and killings done by the Chilean military intelligence apparatus with CIA support. One alternative to universal jurisdiction is creation of an international criminal court with broad powers, but the United States has also opposed that.

Of course, there is always the risk that the prosecutorial power conferred by universal jurisdiction will be abused, just as prosecutors abuse their power when using any other kind of jurisdiction. If prosecutorial abuse were the basis to shut down entire mechanisms of enforcement, most criminal justice systems would crumble.

In the Pinochet case, an aspect of universal jurisdiction was important. A state where the prisoner is found is obliged to try him or extradite him. Aut dedaere, aut judicare is the legal maxim.

After the House of Lords ruled, Pinochet was subjected to an extradition hearing in the Bow Street Magistrate's Court. Because Magistrate Roland Bartle was known to harbor conservative views, the Pinochet lawyers thought that he would rule in their favor. They went so far as to encourage leading conservative politicians to make public statements in favor of Pinochet's cause. This strategy backfired, as Bartle wrote a stinging denunciation of efforts to influence him, and reaffirmed the idea that the growing human rights movement was on its way to producing "one law for one world," an astounding sentiment from that source.

The extradition hearing, which Sam Buffone and I attended to assist Juan Garcés and the English lawyers, was quietly dramatic. Charge after charge detailed the record of Pinochet-directed oppression, and nothing in the rather stilted and boring speeches of his lawyers could change the evident course of things. For me, the most exciting moment was the procedurally routine testimony of a Scotland Yard inspector who had arrested Pinochet. He described going to the house where Pinochet was staying, being made to wait, and then being taken to a sumptuous drawing room where he was sitting, wearing a silk shirt and holding a silver-decorated cane.

> Augusto Pinochet Ugarte, I arrest you for the crimes of torture, genocide, and conspiracy. I caution you that anything you say may be taken down and given in evidence against you. Anything you may later decide to say may permit a comment on your silence. And he looked at me and said, "I do not recognize your authority. I will not respond to these charges."

After the extradition order, Britain's Home Secretary decided Pinochet was too ill to stand trial and sent him home to Chile, where courts there reached a similar result.

But in just under two years, international criminal law had been changed. On that first trip to London, people thought nothing would come of the case. Others worried that the Chilean right wing would be moved to support another military coup. Because of that latter worry, I met secretly with Chilean political leaders in London.

If we can see that immunity/impunity is under serious and principled attack, where should the next skirmishes be fought? I have tried to play a constructive role in more than a dozen countries. Officially, the United States has preached human rights rhetoric, sometimes backed by military power, all over the globe. It is time, I think, to bring the principles of accountability home.

In Chile where democratic institutions are being rebuilt, in Europe under the Convention on Human Rights, in South Africa, in decisions of the Inter-American Commission on Human Rights and Court of Human Rights, and in so many other places, the norms developed in the wake of World War II are being applied and expanded. Popular movements are challenging governmental and private multinational efforts to undermine democratic control of economic development.

In our own country, however, the challenges have become greater. We are, to be sure, the most litigious country in the world. We have more lawyers, more litigators, and more lawsuits. Of course, litigation is often a good means to adjust and resolve private differences, in a fair forum provided by the state. However, the most important function of litigation, time out of mind, has been to control governmental conduct, and more generally the conduct of the powerful toward the weak. And yet, access to that kind of justice was severely curtailed in the 1980s and 1990s.

The erosion began with provisions limiting funding for legal services for the poor. These underfunded agencies were then forbidden to help their clients with class suits to redress major problems, and even to give advice on denial of constitutional rights. This latter limitation was struck down in 2001 by a closely divided Supreme Court. As Justice Kennedy said for the majority, "An informed, independent judiciary presumes an informed, independent bar." That presumption, far too often, does not hold true.

Congress funded then abolished resource centers to help train and support lawyers trying death penalty cases. The pace of executions has increased even as scientific tests and old-fashioned investigation are proving that dozens of death row inmates were innocent. America's incarceration rate is five to seven or more times that of our major trading partners in Europe, North America, and Asia.

The Supreme Court and Congress are taking an expansive view of official immunity from suit, and a narrow view of the right to sue for redress against official wrongdoing. In the sector of private lawsuits, reactionary politicians proclaim hostility to litigation designed to compensate people for the wrong done by defective and dangerous products and substances, and they deride and attack the lawyers who do that kind of work.

Although women and people of color continue to lag behind everyone else in education and income, the current Supreme Court majority uses a technical analysis of equal protection to limit affirmative measures to redress that imbalance. The Court's majority seizes at times upon supposed original intent, and then conveniently jettisons history when analyzing it would serve a progressive agenda.

I am not so egotistical, or so energetic, that I can or should be tackling all of these issues at once. Several years ago in Austin, I went to the same eye doctor as Ambassador Ed Clark, who was in his eighties. One day, he had the appointment just before mine. As he came out of the doctor's office, I asked, "How are you doing?" He replied, "Well, Dr. Keys says I can see more than I have the energy to do anything about." I understand that comment more with every passing year.

I have been lucky in this past decade to be associated first with the University of Texas and now with Washington College of Law at American University in D.C. Law students are eager to join a team that will do impact litigation around human rights issues. In the Nichols trial, ten law students provided essential help, and now I supervise clinical students in a law school that has made clinical education in human rights a cornerstone of its mission and the basis for its high ranking in the fields of international law and clinical studies.

I will follow my own rule and not try my cases in print or announce them here before their time. But I can say this much: In spring 2001, the International Court of Justice rebuked the United States and the state of Arizona for executing two German nationals while Germany was contesting their death sentences before that international tribunal. In May 2001, the South African constitutional court held that a defendant in the Kenya bombing case had been illegally removed from South Africa by the misconduct of the South African authorities and the FBI. This ruling led to an instruction by federal judge Leonard Sand to the sentencing jury that as a matter of South African law this defendant should not have faced a death penalty. The jury decided on life imprisonment.

I have been speaking to refugees forcibly removed from their Indian Ocean island home so that the United States and Britain could build a military base. The tortures and disappearances in Chile have never been fully investigated, much less redressed. Death penalty litigation continues to need good lawyers, which means more lawyer training and more just plain lawyering.

In this work, I seek to harvest new ideas from the old lessons of the law. "From the old fields," Lord Coke wrote, "must come the new corne." More deeply, Karl Renner wrote:

Given that, like all else under the sun, norms have their causes, wherein do these lie? Given that they enjoy a real existence, what are its characteristics, what is the mode of their existence and how do they change? Given that their origin lies in the conditions of life of the human race, that they are nothing more than a means of preserving human society, what part do they actually play in the existence and development of our own generation?

After the Nichols trial, I said to friends, "I don't know if I have another trial in me." I am slower at 60 than I was at 30, which in some ways is a good thing. I don't jump up and make foolish objections quite so readily. My brain and my mouth are more often running at about the same speed.

Along with nurturing, and increasingly being nurtured by, my children, and giving and getting love, and sailing waters new and familiar, I am going to keep sensing injustice. In the middle of 2001, I was arguing a motion in a hotly disputed case. I remarked that "in this my seventh decade of life, time has dulled my fighting faith." The judge interjected, "Not much." I hope that's right. One truth in there is that the law now belongs to a generation or so behind me. To that generation, I can only say that this sense of injustice is a powerful thing. There is a world to be understood, and to be changed.

I cannot think that all the changes for which I wish will happen within my lifetime. I cannot believe that I will be invited to wield power in any significant way, in some new constellation of social relations. I am just a lawyer. I have my ticket to stand near centers of power, and to exercise whatever influence I can have. I am trying to push things so that those who can and will change the order of things are free to do so. Free in the old sense that the state does not try to crush them and their movement. Free also in the sense that second- and third-generation rights to social needs permit them and their children to flourish.

Afterword

I finished this manuscript on September 1, 2001. Ten days later, the mass murders in New York, Washington, and Pennsylvania caused every thinking person to address anew the questions of justice and injustice. As I write this Afterword, the threat of biological warfare hangs over us all. The FBI is rounding up suspects and holding them without bail, in secret, under arduous conditions, and without confidential access to counsel.

The principal task of lawyers is to remember. We are to remember past events so that we may learn from them. We are therefore called in times like these to take an unpopular stance in favor of preserving old liberties, and in favor of building a world based on respect for basic human rights norms.

I paraphrase the philosopher only a little when I say that those who do not understand history are condemned to repeat it. This is not a new insight. Every spring I say to law students, "Those who do not understand criminal law are condemned to repeat it." It was right to say this when they asked me to look back at the struggle for human rights these past 35 years. It is imperative to say it now.

The media and the politicians have said terror and terrorism so many times that the words are losing their power to shock us. They play sounds and show pictures of September 11, and conjure those images again and again with their words. They are beckoning us down a dangerous path. As Shimon Peres said of his political opponents, "They would prefer us to remember and not to think."

The idea of terror comes to our tradition in images of fear. As the Psalmist wrote:

My heart is in anguish within me,
The terrors of death have fallen upon me
Fear and trembling come upon me,
And horror overwhelms me.
And I say, "O that I had wings like a dove!
I would fly away and be at rest; yea, I would wander afar
I would lodge in the wilderness.
I would haste to find me a shelter from the raging wind and tempest."

In more modern times, however, we think of terror as organized but senseless violence, done in the name of an ideology.

For example, in the town of Beziers, near Marseilles, in the year 1209, 15,000 men, women, and children were slaughtered to root out the Albigensian heresy. "Whom should we kill?" asked Philip Augustus' general. "Kill them all," the papal legate replied. "God will recognize his own."

In Ireland, Bosnia, Chechnya, South Africa, and a hundred other places in the world, young people will point to this or that spot and tell you a story. Someone's grandfather's grandfather killed someone else's grandfather's grandfather right over there. And the killing is not yet fully avenged. Ruskin wrote, "There is no snare set by the fiends for the mind of man than the illusion that our enemies are also the enemies of God."

We have in our country been mostly spectators of this sort of thing, and must now catch up to the rest of the world in understanding its causes and remedies. I say we have "mostly" been spectators. From 1872 to 1920 there were more than 4,000 lynchings in America. Some of us remember the freedom summer of 1964, when thousands of young people went south to Mississippi and other southern states. In Mississippi alone, dozens of black churches were burned, and hundreds of civil rights workers beaten, brutalized, and even killed.

Calmly now, therefore, with as keen a sense of history as we can command, what are the causes of the kind of violence we have seen? In Ireland, to take an example close by, we can trace the path of English oppression, which robbed people of their homes and land and, in the interest of forced unity, forbade them to speak their language and practice their beliefs. Irish resistance is spoken of in songs and stories. The pent-up anger has for nearly two centuries taken the form of urban violence, of terrorism. If we can see the roots of that violence, we may more clearly understand what is now going on around us.

Our leaders' strident vow that terrorism is always illegitimate sounds cynical and hypocritical. After all, our own CIA has sometimes sought out practitioners of vengeful extremism. We have paid them and equipped them. We have sponsored them in the arts of assassination and bloodshed. Indeed, in the Islamic world many of the groups we today denounce as terrorist were funded and armed by the United States as counterweights to the Soviets. Many of the guns our troops face today were furnished to arm the opposition to the Soviet army.

Our leaders' failure to acknowledge this history puts us all at the terrible risk that it will be repeated.

The first duty of government is to protect citizens and to do so in ways that respect fundamental human rights. In this, our government failed us. Airport security was lax, because airlines had successfully lobbied to make it so. Airplane security was lax because airlines in our country had not heeded the lessons taught by, for example, El Al, in whose planes it is very difficult to get access to the cockpit during flight. Our CIA and Defense Department had developed dispersible anthrax strains and spores to use against enemies, and yet had not equipped our own populace to combat the anthrax. We knew that the former Soviet Union had stores of such biological weaponry, and that it was in the hands of other nations as well. The clamor for more law enforcement weapons, and the curtailment of civil liberties, comes in great measure from the very agencies of government that failed to use the means they had. To give an example from the news, our Agriculture Department screens incoming passengers for fruit flies at a cost of about 75 cents a person. There was no equivalent screening for instruments of terror.

There are two basic forms of terrorism, both equally criminal. One is state-sponsored terrorism, as practiced by the former repressive regimes in Chile and South Africa and still in use today in Afghanistan.

The second form of terror, which usually takes the form of urban violence, often begins with insurgent groups fighting injustice. Then, at some point, a group of insurgents loses touch with the imperative need to embrace human values even in the struggle against inhumanity. Frighteningly, to those of us who watch the angry crowds on television, desperate people give their support to that kind of leadership. When I say desperate, I mean the kind of poverty and deprivation which we in this country can scarcely imagine. I have walked in villages littered with the shards of shattered lives, and I have seen that anger.

The desperate followers of that kind of terrorist leadership are as much victims as those who perish in the attacks about which we read and hear.

Both state-sponsored terrorism and insurgent group terrorism are criminal. I have no doubt that there must exist the duty and the right and the power to investigate and to judge the killings of innocent people. But the legitimate right to conduct those investigations and to inflict that punishment lies only with those who accept the following obligations:

- To struggle against all forms of terrorism, by whomever committed;
- To use means that honor and do not trample upon the tradition of human rights;
- To understand the reasons people will follow the lead of those who sponsor terrorism; and
- To support the legitimate struggle of those people to live in dignity in accordance with those norms of human rights that have become norms of international law in the past three score years.

To put the matter another way, the only kind of justice worthy of the name is social justice. Social justice includes both process and legitimacy. It includes process because that has been the lesson of history for three millennia. It includes process because we have seen the cost of doing otherwise. We have seen how the arrogance of power has detained people without probable cause, refused or subverted impartial judicial review of detention, and drowned out calls for reason and proof with strident cries for vengeance. Hundreds of people, perhaps more, are being held right now while our government disregards these guaranties. The department that calls itself Justice is using this excuse to repeal dozens of guaranties of procedural fairness, not only in so-called terrorism investigations but also across the board.

As Justice Richard Goldstone has reminded us, American history teaches that fair trials are indispensable to public confidence in judicial judgments. As the Second World War drew to a close, Winston Churchill was in favor of summarily executing the Nazi leaders. It was the American government that insisted on trials. So we got a charter defining war crimes and crimes against humanity. We had public trials that placed beyond rational question the evidence of Nazi genocide.

Public and fair trials, by civilian domestic and international courts, of alleged human rights abusers and terrorists—whether their acts were state-sponsored or not—have served and will continue to serve a salutary function. The world will see the evidence, the wrongdoers will be publicly exposed, and if the proof is not there, those wrongly accused will be vindicated. The means by which evidence is obtained will be subject to adversary testing.

What has the FBI or CIA done to convince us that it can use responsibly the power to arrest at will, detain indefinitely, and interrogate without limit? In so many cases, including those in which I have been counsel, these agencies have leapt to wrong conclusions and then refused to admit their errors. In the meantime, the truly guilty are free to plot again.

Social justice includes legitimacy because the proper exercise of force can only be in the context of redressing the social ills that have led people to follow false echoes.

In the realm of foreign and military policy, I cannot imagine that raining bombs on a country filled with starving people will serve the long-term interest in discouraging people from following extremist leadership. From 1954 onwards, when we took over from the French in Indochina, our country sought to impose a military solution on a social conflict. Hundreds of thousands of lives and billions of dollars later, we had accomplished nothing of any value.

When we think of crimes against humanity, we must remember that governments and governmental groups are the most dangerous criminals. They have the most power to inflict harm, and are the most likely to be recidivists. State-sponsored terrorism is the most dangerous brand, especially when it masquerades as justice.

Yes, I am frightened by the terror that has rained upon our country and that continues to haunt us. I want those who commit and who would commit such acts brought to justice. I also know that with so much hatred and fear in the air, we are at risk of losing sight of justice. If you hold your hand in front of your eyes, you can say that it is bigger than the tallest mountain on the far horizon.

In every major conflict our country has faced, the executive branch has curtailed human rights in the name of national security. And every such curtailment has later been found unjustified. The most dramatic example was the forcible relocation of tens of thousands of Japanese-Americans to resettlement camps during World War II, based on false evidence that a few of their number might pose a threat to national security.

There is a dialectic in history. As I wrote in Chapter 1, Heraclitus saw it 2,500 years ago. More to the point, as long as there is injustice, its victims will organize, band together, and struggle against it. We call that the forward march of human history, in the past, now, and in time to be.

Those who advocate bombs and guns and all the rest of the military solution are reliving old mistakes and on the road to making new ones. They are the ones who brought you Vietnam, El Salvador, and Bosnia. Their allies are the ones who right now are seeking to impose a military solution on the Palestinian people. They must take for themselves the words of Herzen, "We are not the doctors. We are the disease."

Fighting terrorism means stripping state-sponsored terrorists of their impunity and bringing them to justice. It means shining a light into the darkest corners of human existence, and bringing a real promise of human rights to all the world's people, so that desperate men and women are not driven to follow leaders whose only real message is vengeance.

When we see that the struggle for human rights in all the world is the surest and best means to prevent and to punish terrorism properly so-called, we then understand what progress we have made, and we will see where we need to go from here.

Appendix

To provide some context for this often nonchronological story, I offer the following brief curriculum vitae.

Born January 18, 1941, Glendale, California; married to Jane B. Tigar; three children (Jon S. Tigar [judge in California], Katherine McQueen, M.D. [on a medical school faculty in Houston], Elizabeth Torrey Tigar [age 18]; three grandchildren [William Stanton Tigar, Adam Avery Tigar, and Mary Elizabeth McQueen]

Education
J.D., 1966, Boalt Hall, University of California, Berkeley
B.A., Political Science, 1962, University of California, Berkeley
Public schools in and near Los Angeles, California

Law school honors and awards
Ranked first in class all three years of law school
Editor-in-chief, *California Law Review*, 1965-66
Order of the Coif

Employment
Professor of Law and Edwin A. Mooers, Sr., Scholar, Washington College of Law, American University, 1998-present
Joseph D. Jamail Centennial Chair in Law, University of Texas, 1987- (member of UT law faculty 1983-98)
Of Counsel, Haddon, Morgan & Foreman, Denver, Colorado, 1/1/96-6/30/98
Visiting Professor, Faculté de Droit et de Sciences Politique de Aix-Marseille, 1994-present

Lecturer, University of the Western Cape, Fort Hare Faculty of Law, and University of Transkei, 1991-92

Member, Tigar & Buffone, P.C., Washington, D.C., 1978-84

Lecturer in Criminal Procedure, State University of New York at Buffalo, 1976-77

Adjunct Professor of Law, Georgetown University Law Center, 1975-76, 1977-78

Attorney, Williams & Connolly, Washington, D.C., 1966-69; 1974-77; partner, January 1, 1976-December 31, 1977

Of Counsel, Kennedy & Rhine, San Francisco, California, 1971-74 (maintained offices for the private practice of international law in Speracèdes, France)

Visiting Fellow, Center for the Study of Democratic Institutions, Santa Barbara, California, 1971

Acting Professor of Law, University of California, Los Angeles, 1969-71

Editor-in-Chief, *Selective Service Law Reporter*, 1968-69

Summer Intern, American Civil Liberties Union of Northern California, 1965

Assistant Editor, *Civil Liberties Docket*, 1963-64

Associate Director of Public Affairs, Pacifica Foundation Radio (KPFK-FM), Los Angeles, 1963

European Correspondent, Pacifica Foundation Radio, 1962-63

Announcer, engineer, reporter, newscaster, Director of Children's Programs, Pacifica Foundation Radio (KPFA-FM), Berkeley, California, 1959-62

Apprentice letterpress printer, 1955-58

Restaurant worker, 1956-57

Day camp teacher, 1955-58

Professional activities and awards (partial list)

Lifetime Achievement Award, National Association of Criminal Defense Lawyers, 1999

Champion of Justice Award, California Attorneys for Criminal Justice, 1998

Frequent speaker, moderator, panelist, bar organizations, law schools, judicial conferences

Frequent appearances on television and radio programs on legal subjects in the U.S., Canada, U.K., France and Switzerland

Argued seven United States Supreme Court cases and more than 100 other appellate cases

Co-director, Intensive Trial Advocacy Program, The University of Texas School of Law, 1984-94

Fellow, American Academy of Appellate Lawyers; member, Board of Directors, 1993-96

Member, Board of Directors, American Judicature Society, 1992-96

Director, The Fourth Amendment Foundation (founded by Hunter S. Thompson), 1991-

Letelier-Moffitt Human Rights Award (Sixteenth Annual), September 21, 1992

Member, ABA Task Force on an International Criminal Court, 1991

Consultant, African National Congress Task Force on TVBC States and constitutional issues, 1991-92

John Minor Wisdom Public Service and Professionalism Award, American Bar Association, Section of Litigation, October 1990

Chair, Section of Litigation, American Bar Association, 1989-90

Member, Board of Directors, Texas Appellate Practice and Educational Resource Center, 1989-94 (Chair, 1989-93)

Reporter, Pattern Jury Instructions, Criminal Cases, Fifth Circuit, 1988-90 (published by West Publishing Co., 1990)

Trial Advocacy Teacher, Black Lawyers Association of South Africa, 1988, 1989, 1990, 1991

Chair-elect, Section of Litigation, American Bar Association, 1988-89

Vice chair, Section of Litigation, American Bar Association, 1987-88

Chair, Section of Litigation, Association of American Law Schools, 1988

Co-chair, Committee on Teaching Litigation, Section of Litigation, ABA, 1984-1987

Member, ABA Litigation Section Task Force on Training the Advocate, 1986-89

Member, Advisory Committee, BNA Civil RICO Report, 1985-89

Chair, Complex Crimes Litigation Committee, Section of Litigation, ABA, 1981-84

Participant (one of 32 lawyers selected from the United States), Smithsonian Institution Folklife Festival, 1986, "Trial Lawyers in America."

Bar memberships—regular

District of Columbia (4/1/67); New York (2/11/93); Supreme Court of the United States; United States Courts of Appeals for the District of Columbia Circuit and the Second (9/12/78), Fourth, Fifth, Sixth (7/6/92), Eighth, Ninth, Tenth, Eleventh, and Federal Circuits; United

States District Court for the Western District of Texas; United States District Court for the Southern District of Texas; United States Tax Court (1980)

Bar memberships—pro hac vice
Supreme Court of the United States (1969)

Several United States Courts of Appeals, a dozen United States District Courts, and state trial and appellate courts in Colorado, Maryland, Florida, California, New York, Texas, and Illinois.

Index

W

Y

Z